CW00833315

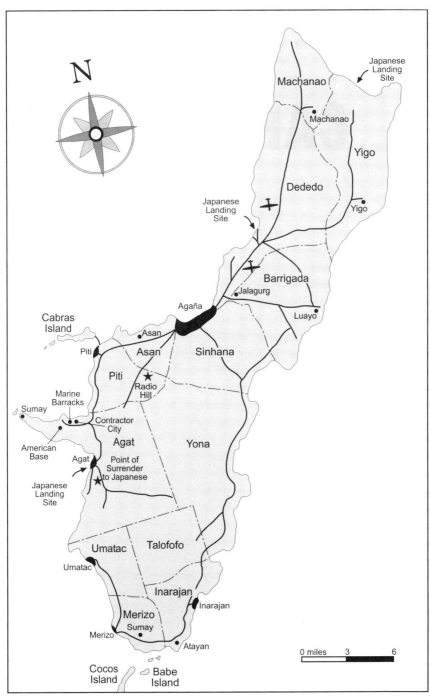

N

Japanese Landing Site

Machanao

Machanao

Yigo

Yigo

Dededo

Japanese Landing Site

Barrigada

Jalagurg

Agaña

Luayo

Cabras Island

Asan

Piti

Asan

Sinhana

Piti

Radio Hill

Marine Barracks

Sumay

Contractor City

Agat

Yona

American Base

Agat

Point of Surrender to Japanese

Japanese Landing Site

Umatac

Talofofo

Umatac

Inarajan

Inarajan

Merizo

Sumay

Merizo

Atayan

0 miles   3   6

Cocos Island

Babe Island

Map by Charles Grear based on original courtesy of the Gregg Collection, Hoover Institution Archive, Stanford University

CAPTURED

The Forgotten Men of Guam

ROGER MANSELL

Edited by Linda Goetz Holmes

Naval Institute Press
Annapolis, Maryland

Naval Institute Press
291 Wood Road
Annapolis, MD 21402

© 2012 by Carolyn M. Mansell
All rights reserved. No part of this book may be reproduced or utilized in any form or by any means, electronic or mechanical, including photocopying and recording, or by any information storage and retrieval
system, without permission in writing from the publisher.

Library of Congress Cataloging-in-Publication Data
Mansell, Roger.
 Captured : the forgotten men of Guam / Roger Mansell ; edited by Linda Goetz Holmes.
  p. cm.
 Includes bibliographical references and index.
 ISBN 978-1-61251-114-6 (hbk. : alk. paper) — ISBN 978-1-61251-123-8 (e-book) 1. World War,
1939–1945—Guam. 2. World War, 1939–1945—Prisoners and prisons, Japanese. 3. Prisoners of
war—Japan. 4. Prisoners of war—United States. 5. Prisoners of war—Guam. 6. United States—Armed
Forces—Guam—Biography. 7. Guam—History—Japanese occupation, 1941–1944. I. Holmes, Linda
Goetz. II. Title. III. Title: Forgotten men of Guam.
 D767.99.G8M46 2012
 940.54'7252—dc23
                                                                                        2012024311

♾ This paper meets the requirements of ANSI/NISO z39.48-1992 (Permanence of Paper).
Printed in the United States of America.

20 19 18 17 16 15 14 13 12   9 8 7 6 5 4 3 2 1
First printing

CONTENTS

PROLOGUE

HISTORY IS ALWAYS WRITTEN WRONG, AND SO ALWAYS NEEDS TO BE
REWRITTEN.

—*George Santayana*

In the confusing first few days after the attack on the U.S. Pacific Fleet at Hawaii's Pearl Harbor, almost 800 people, including 414 American military men and women on Guam, were taken captive by the Japanese. To secure natural resources, labor, and land for its new Greater East Asia Co-Prosperity Sphere, Japan's military swept down from the home islands and across the Pacific. Within weeks Allied forces in Guam, Hong Kong, Singapore, and Wake Island were crushed by the Japanese. Newspaper headlines screamed of the desperate battle for Wake Island and of the gallantry of the men of holding out on Bataan and Corregidor in the Philippines. By the second week of May 1942, the entire western Pacific was controlled by the Japanese. The entire Philippine army and more than 36,000 Americans would eventually be in Japanese military prisoner-of-war camps. The U.S. Asiatic Fleet, stationed in Manila, ceased to exist after almost all of its ships were sunk as they fled south toward Australia. Another 125,000 Australian and British soldiers were prisoners in Malaya and Java.

The loss of the tiny tropical island of Guam, only two days after the attack on Pearl Harbor, barely created a ripple in the flood of war news. The *New York Times*, for instance, gave the capture only a brief mention at the bottom of the front page: "Tokyo Radio declares 'Guam has been occupied and that the Japanese forces were firmly established there.'"[1] In the histories of the Pacific war, the story of Guam's defenders rarely exceeds a sentence, if that—and yet their saga is one of the most heartbreaking and inspiring of the entire war.

All of the American POWs of Guam were transported in the barren holds of the *Argentina Maru* to Japan and then taken directly to the Zentsuji POW camp on the island of Shikoku. In the following months and years, many were sent elsewhere in Japan to slave for Japanese industries—familiar names such as Sumitomo, Kawasaki, Mitsui, Hitachi, and Mitsubishi. Savage brutality, starvation, disease, and beheadings became an everyday experience for the captives.

The Japanese military had seized control of the education system forty years earlier and promoted the belief that the emperor was descended from the sun goddess Amaterasu and, as such, Japan was entitled to rule the known world. The Japanese, being superior, were entitled to treat others—these inferior beings—as brutally as they desired. As the captives soon learned, the exception to this hatred and brutality was as rare as snow in the tropics.

The Guam POWs called themselves the "Zentsujians" and resolved to fight the enemy with every fiber of their being, united in a bond of hatred against the brutality of the prison guards and civilian slave masters, a brutality so unrelentingly savage that each prisoner had to make a conscious decision to survive or he would die.

By August 1945 the war in the Pacific had approached its climax as Allied forces neared Japan. The Japanese War Ministry, determined to sacrifice every Japanese citizen rather than surrender, had already ordered the execution of all prisoners upon invasion.[2] Hatred against the West became a daily, savage brutality against the enslaved men. Equally determined to thwart the Japanese at every turn and tempered with newly developed instincts for survival, the Zentsujians made their plans to survive.

This is their story.

ACKNOWLEDGMENTS

As a young child on Long Island, New York, I watched uncles go off to World War II on Navy ships, followed battles with National Geographic maps, and saw a sky filled with Army Air Force planes headed to a victory flyover of Manhattan. The war was daily news—uniforms, rationing, and fast planes. I watched Civil War, Spanish-American War, and World War I veterans marching in parades. When my sister Mary's husband, John Redmond, gave away the medals he'd earned as a medic with General Patton's forces in Europe, I could not understand.

I studied engineering at Brown University and became an artillery officer in the U.S. Army. While I was posted to Fort Bliss in Texas, a professor at the University of Texas–El Paso introduced me to history. I wish I could remember his name, because he made history come alive for me.

Fast-forward to the day, decades later, when my employee Ken Grimes nearly spat at me when he saw I'd bought a Datsun car. I knew he had been taken prisoner as a child in the Philippines, but until he explained the horrors he and his civilian parents lived through, I had no idea what it was like for "guests" of the emperor and why he hated anything Japanese, even a car.

In 1980 my daughters, Catherine Mansell Carstens and Alice Mansell, introduced me to their newly married high school teacher of French and German, Hildy Jarman Smith. Her husband, Maj. Gen. Ralph Smith, had fought Pancho Villa, led the first U.S. troops into World War I trenches, and taken Makin Island and commanded U.S. Army troops on Saipan in World War II. After the war, he had run CARE programs in Europe with the help of a young assistant named David Rockefeller.

Ralph discovered my interest in history and insisted I join him for weekly lunches at our local American Legion post. He opened my eyes to a new way of looking at history; he'd lived it from the trenches to the highest level of international politics. Through him I started to meet and interview veterans whose stories were being forgotten.

I began to attend gatherings of the American Defenders of Bataan and Corregidor and the Zentsuji survivors' reunions. Soon I was assembling POW camp rosters and death and survivor lists, and I created a website, www.mansell.com, to share this data. As I gathered more stories, I realized no one had written much about the military and civilian personnel captured on Guam in the early days of the Pacific war; this became my mission for the next ten years.

I am in debt to the late John Taylor, chief researcher at the National Archives Modern Military Records in College Park, Maryland, and to the reference room staff there. Researchers such as Dwight Ridder and Wes Injerd (who now maintains my website) have helped me greatly.

I appreciate the willingness to be interviewed, often many times, by former POWs Ralph Baggett, Carroll "Barney" Barnett, Leroy Bowman, Joe "Fingers" Brown, Harris Chuck, Garth Dunn, Robert Epperson, Charlene Hellmers Gloth, Ken Grimes, Robert Hinkle, Herbert Humphrey, Harold Joslin, John Kidd, Stephen Kramerich, Peter Marshall, Dean Morgan, Al Mosher, Frank Nichols, Howard Ross, Edwin Settles, Clinton Seymour, George Shane, Ralph Smith, Yayoe Smythe, James "Jim" Thomas, Charles Todd, and Sterling Warren.

My daughter Catherine, a published writer, insisted I write this book to share all my research; and my daughter Alice, a lawyer, strongly suggested I carefully cite and source all my data (hence the voluminous notes).

Former Farrar, Straus and Giroux editor-in-chief and author John A. Glusman was kind enough to review the draft of this book and make many helpful suggestions, as were Bradford P. Woods and Charlene Hellmers Gloth. I thank them for their perception, expertise, and critique.

My deep gratitude goes to my dear friend and Pacific war historian Linda Goetz Holmes for answering my request to do the final edits of my manuscript, to create a bibliography and index, and to find a publisher for my work.

The most important lesson I learned from former POWs was that in those lethal camps, no one survived without a buddy. My wife Carolyn "Care" M. Mansell has been my buddy since we met in college. Without her love and support, and her willingness to listen to decades of POW horror stories and to encourage me to do all the travel I did for the POWs and their families, I could not have continued to gather their stories.

I have had a charmed life. Never had to carry a gun in anger. Never had my own home or family attacked in a war. I hope through my work to have repaid a small part of the debt I owe to all who paid the price for my freedom, and to have honored them by doing my best to disseminate some of their stories.

—*Roger Mansell*
Palo Alto, California
September 2010

Editor's note: My thanks to Adam Kane, Claire Noble, the production staff at the Naval Institute Press, and copy editor Karin Kaufman, who made this book happen.

—*Linda Goetz Holmes*

Roger Mansell died 25 October 2010.

CAPTURED

CHAPTER 1

Last Days of Paradise

Summer 1941

Sunlight edged over the Oakland hills. Its orange glow spilled over San Francisco, washing the night from its seven undulating hills. An hour earlier, Fisherman's Wharf had bustled with life as fishing boats had cast off in the predawn darkness and headed for deep water, their position lights twinkling as they passed the rough shoals outside the Golden Gate. The blanket of morning fog thinned to a gauzy haze, a finger of fog fading beneath the colorful bridge now bathed in an orange glow. Another beautiful day had begun in California.

A short walk from Fisherman's Wharf, a gleaming white ocean liner, the Matson Line's SS *Mariposa*, held fast to the side of Pier 39. As sailboats skittered across the San Francisco waterfront, the massive ship became a beehive of activity. Limousines and taxis disgorged passengers dressed in elegant finery; stacks of luggage and steamer trunks slowly grew by one of the side hatchways. Stevedores shuffled food, liquors, wines, and freight into the holds. Excitement mounted as the gathering passengers awaited the signal for boarding. Departure for Honolulu, in the distant territory of Hawaii, was posted as 2:00 p.m., 1 July 1941.

A few minutes past noon, a steward walked out of the purser's office, stepped to the top of the gangway, and struck a small, melodious chime. "Passengers may begin to board," he declared. The crowd slowly shriveled as, one by one, they funneled onto the gangplank. With few possessions and a jaunty bounce to his steps, Jim Thomas, a twenty-five-year-old farm boy from Malad, Idaho, and a recent graduate of the University of California in Berkeley, walked past the purser's office for the first leg of his trip to Guam.

A year earlier, as the threat of war with Germany and Japan seemed to grow inevitable, President Franklin Roosevelt had begun a draft of all young men. Japan had savagely attacked China, seizing Manchuria, and had surrounded the Shanghai International Settlement and the British Crown colony of Hong Kong. The bombings, murderous pillage, rapes, and senseless slaughter of civilians in Nanking, China, flashed across movie theaters around the world. German forces had swept across Europe and were now in sight of the onion-shaped domes of Moscow. The conquering armies of Japan and Germany dominated daily news across the United States.

1

Heated debates in Congress from both prowar and antiwar factions drowned out the misery of those still unemployed since the Great Depression. Germany sank American destroyers escorting relief convoys to England. Japan arrested American reporters who dared to write negatively about Japan's "Holy War in China." The fever of war grew as the military announced a new program to train 45,000 new combat pilots and factories across the United States began the conversion to the manufacture of military equipment. A declaration of war was debated without resolution while tension and anger grew. Newspaper headlines rarely mentioned news other than the war in Europe and the threat from Japan.

Jim Thomas, seeking employment pending his induction into the U.S. Army, garnered a short-term job with Pan American Airways along with a six-month draft exemption. With a month's training in meteorology and radio communication on San Francisco Bay's Treasure Island, Thomas received his first assignment—assistant station manager on Guam. For Thomas the lure of tropical islands and the excitement of being part of Pan Am's glamorous Clipper service was irresistible. In the summer of 1941, Guam was the most coveted assignment in the exotic South Seas.

Just four years earlier, the first transpacific passenger seaplane had glided to a smooth water landing in Hong Kong Harbor. Thousands of boats had cleared a wide lane for Pan American's flying boats and with a daylong party, Hong Kong celebrated the arrival. What once took five weeks by ship had been reduced to six days. The world had shrunk dramatically.

Scheduled air service across the Pacific Ocean had become a reality. A mere ten years earlier, Charles Lindbergh's solo crossing of the Atlantic Ocean had enthralled the world.[1] Every advance in aviation was heralded with front-page photographs and extensive radio coverage—live whenever possible—especially the long distance flights of Pan American Airways. The island stops of these flying boats—Hawaii, Midway, Wake, Guam, Manila, and Hong Kong—became synonymous with glamour, excitement, and adventure.[2] America may have been in a depression, but hope for the future was fueled by advances in aviation and communication.

A few minutes past 2:00 p.m., the deep-throated blasts of the ship's horn echoed across San Francisco Bay; the seagulls snapped awake and swirled away from the pier's roof. Confetti fluttered down from the passengers to relatives, friends, and well-wishers blowing kisses from the dock. Tie lines were cast off, and two fire engine–red Moran tugboats pushed the ship back into the bay. Twenty minutes later, as it slipped under the Golden Gate Bridge, the captain rang the engine room for "full ahead." On the bridge above, pedestrians looked down and cheerily waved. Ahead lay five days of calm seas and clear skies.

During the Depression years, transpacific travel for pleasure was considered the domain of the rich and famous, a dream seen only in the movies for most Americans. As a first-class passenger, Thomas donned a tuxedo for dinner, danced the evenings away to a full orchestra, grazed on the elaborate buffets around the clock, swam in the deck pool, enjoyed first-run movies, and slept in his decorator-appointed stateroom. The *Mariposa* was a floating first-class resort hotel. Thomas knew he was a long way from Malad, Idaho.

The morning after he arrived in Hawaii, he boarded the largest plane in the world, Pan American's four-engine Boeing 314 "flying boat." The cabin was spacious, and passengers enjoyed delicious meals and wine served in the dining room of the plane. After a few days of delay on Wake Island for a passing typhoon to clear the way west, Thomas continued to his new home on Guam after another overnight stop on Midway. Seven time zones and 6,382 miles west of the Golden Gate, Jim glanced down to see the straw and tile roofs of Agana slide under the plane. The plane passed at one thousand feet above and parallel to the north shore of Orote Peninsula. In a descending turn, the plane passed back over the fluorescent blue and green waters of Apra Harbor and skimmed to a landing on the buoy-marked channel.[3] The huge Boeing taxied to its landing platform in midharbor, where the passengers, dressed in their Sunday finery, stepped into a launch that carried them to the dock adjoining the hotel. Feeling "as though I had grabbed the brass ring," Jim Thomas set foot on Guam on the late afternoon of 15 July 1941.[4]

Guam, 15 degrees north of the equator, is the southernmost island of the Marianas chain. Twenty miles long and varying from five to twelve miles wide, Guam is shaped like a muddy footprint angling to the northeast and is almost entirely surrounded by coral reefs. The Orote Peninsula juts out as a two-mile appendage just below the midpoint of the island's western coast, sloping from sea level at its base to over 150 feet high at the far end. Less than fifteen and forty-five miles to the north lay the Japanese-owned islands of Rota and Saipan, both believed to be heavily fortified.

Station Manager Charles Gregg, in a crisp blue blazer and tropical white pants, welcomed Thomas and smiled broadly as he shook the hand of each arriving passenger. Urbane, witty, and solicitous, the twenty-six-year-old Gregg supervised the Pan Am passengers' registration for an overnight stay while their luggage was taken directly to flower-laden rooms. Champagne, served in chilled and frosted glass flutes, refreshing drinks, and a sumptuous five-course dinner completed their day on Guam. Navy and Marine officers regularly vied for the attention of the female passengers, inviting them for drinks and dinner at the officers' club or in the governor's mansion.

Thomas' new manager had arrived earlier that month, having already acquired a depth of experience during two years as Pan Am's manager in Noumea, New Caledonia. Promoted to the Guam station, Gregg's main responsibility was to care for the four weekly flights—two westbound to Manila and two returning stateside.[5] The hotel, similar to those on Midway and Wake, was designed for overnight accommodations between each leg of the journey. The station consisted of a single-story hotel with a broad overhang for shade, a screened veranda, and a large dining room featuring white, wicker-style tropical furniture. A large complex of boat sheds, maintenance shops, and offices completed the facility.

As a member of the Pan Am staff, Thomas was provided with clothes, a small house to share with another employee, native servants, superb meals prepared by native chefs, and a workload easily handled in minutes a day. On the days a Clipper was to arrive, an elaborate work ritual began before sunrise. Thomas rose first, readying the weather forecasts for the afternoon arrival. Other staff prepared the guest accommodations and meals and arranged for transportation into Agana or Sumay for the VIPs, guests of military officers, and the governor.

Fishing trips, beach parties, and excursions around the island filled his waking hours. Thomas had ample time to enjoy himself. From the beautiful sunrises to the spectacular sunsets, every day was filled with fun and good friends—snorkeling, fishing, picnics, hiking, and the simple pleasures of sunbathing or reading. For Thomas, "it was paradise."

Directly behind the Pan Am station, a switchback road climbed eighty feet up a steep hillside. Perched on the flat plain above was the Sumay detachment of the U.S. Marine Corps. Overstaffed with 6 officers for the 148 enlisted men, the post had buildings for supplies and maintenance, a radio station, a large two-story barracks for the enlisted men, and a headquarters building clustered in a horseshoe shape around the main parade field. Behind the headquarters building, meandering coral paths crossed broad manicured lawns and led to six private three-bedroom homes for the Marine officers and their families. Sheltered beneath a grove of palm trees, and much larger than the average American home of the time, they were built with concrete, had tile roofs, and featured large overhangs for shade. Every evening officers shared drinks and played cards beneath the soft rustle of palm leaves with the chirping of crickets and cicadas outside the screened verandas.

On the far side of the parade ground, a nine-hole golf course with immaculately groomed fairways meandered through the jungle along flower-laden pathways. The golf and country club at Sumay was open to officers and enlisted men for monthly dues of one dollar. There were no greens fees, but one was expected to pay a caddy twenty-five cents for a round of eighteen holes. Though cars were of limited use on the small island of Guam, the military advised all officers and the higher enlisted ranks that, for a cost of only twenty-five dollars, they could bring their own cars to their new post.

Unless a ceremony was scheduled, duty days ended by noon. For many, the annual thirty-day leave was spent on board the station supply ship, the USS *Gold Star*, nicknamed the "Goldie Maru." The supply ship visited ports in the Philippines, Australia, China, and Japan, allowing ample time for sightseeing tours and shopping. Passage was free, but one had to have one hundred dollars in cash in order to board.

A typhoon had ripped across Guam in November 1940, tearing the top floor from the two-story enlisted men's barracks. With little or no materials available for repairs, the enlisted men lived in rows of squad tents on the parade ground. A second typhoon, in early July 1941, further damaged the partially reconstructed barracks. The power of the second typhoon was such that a piece of corrugated roof cleanly sliced through a two-foot-thick palm tree trunk, leaving the remaining stump with a corrugated top.[6] After the storm the six officers, headed by Lt. Col. William Kirk MacNulty, continued to live in relative splendor in their separate and, by local standards, elegant houses until their families were sent stateside. The only disturbance was the occasional clunk of a falling coconut bouncing off a roof.

Within three weeks of Thomas' arrival, the prospect of war with Japan became a major concern of the U.S. Navy Department and all military dependents were ordered stateside. Until the spring of 1941, the U.S. Navy required that all officers assigned to Guam be married and bring their families to the island. Few objections were ever heard because the accommodations, servants, and social life made Guam one of the best assignments for any military man. However, by early November 1941, the wives and children of the military were no longer allowed to remain, and by mid-November, when the last troop ship departed, all the American men had become "bachelors." Thomas dismissed the subject of a possible war with Japan with youthful disdain. "I had absolutely no doubt that if war broke out with Japan, the U.S. Navy would blast them into oblivion," he recalled. "If necessary, I could simply leave on the next Clipper heading home."

With the tearful departure of the last dependents in November 1941, the remaining officers at Sumay were quartered together, their newly emptied homes used to house the enlisted Marines, who were still living in squad tents on the parade grounds. Colonel MacNulty, commandant of the Sumay Marine detachment, was scheduled to retire and return stateside in January 1942. He considered entertaining civilian guests an important part of his duty. Impeccably dressed in a tropical tan uniform, swagger stick tucked under his arm, he met every Clipper that arrived. The Pan Am staff gave him the derisive nickname "Clipper MacNulty" because he always sought the company of any attractive and willing female passenger.[7] The consensus of the military men on Guam was that MacNulty was simply promoted over the years in order to shift him to lesser assignments, waiting for the day he could retire. Extremely rare was any man who found him admirable.

Typical of the enlisted men was Pfc. Carroll D. "Barney" Barnett, USMC, a twenty-year-old from the town of Waukee, Iowa (population three hundred), who had joined the Marines in February 1941. An experienced truck mechanic, he enlisted in the Marines because it "seemed a better alternative than facing a random draft into the army. I was happier than the dickens to be assigned to Guam since I really wanted to go anywhere in the Pacific: Manila, Guam, or Shanghai. I wanted to see the world and nothing was more different to me than Asia."[8]

Barnett saw his assignment as a joy. "I was an early riser, and after breakfast, I'd get to the motor transport section by 6:00 a.m. My sergeant was John Henry Lyles, a really great guy and easy to work with. I was both a mechanic and driver. One of my first jobs was to work on a staff car that had something wrong in the rear end. It would really 'howl' when driving. I made a few lucky adjustments—mainly aligning gears—and it worked perfectly. After that, I was 'in like Flynn.' Every day was leisurely, and I'd drive wherever they wanted me to go, generally carrying stuff to the various commands. I really got to know my way around the island pretty fast." Like every man on Guam, Barnett spent his off-duty hours on social activities. In a short time, Barnett met every soldier on the island. "I bought a bike," he said, "and spent most afternoons pedaling around the island. I got to know and like all the Marines in the Insular Guard outposts."

For all practical purposes, the Marine detachment was an adjunct for the Navy to provide parades, transport, and music for the administrative staff in Agana. Except for guard duty once every few weeks, no other military details were required. From pre-dawn reveille to the completion of a day's duty around noon, most Marines practiced marching maneuvers or cleaned their antiquated rifles for the weekly parade. Other than an occasional test on the rifle range, no training in combat maneuvers, tactics, or defense were ever conducted on Guam.

In the barracks or private quarters, a full-time houseboy shined a man's shoes and washed and ironed all his bedding, clothes, and uniforms—for two dollars a month. Beer was ten cents, a bottle of premium scotch cost one dollar, and a private's pay was twenty-one dollars a month. It was, as Barnett believed, "truly a paradise." In the barracks, each man had a small closet for his clothes. A lightbulb at the bottom was used to keep the clothes dry and free of the fast-forming tropical mildew.

⁕⁕⁕⁕⁕⁕⁕⁕⁕⁕⁕

Just east of the Pan Am station and a short walk down the hill from Sumay Marine Base lay the tacky town of Sumay, a crowded collection of some seventy steep, straw-roofed cottages and shops. A narrow road of crushed coral threaded down the one-block-long main street while dirt side roads led to the homes of residents, tattoo parlors, shacks with lean-to walls, corrugated metal roofs, and the ubiquitous mongrel dogs. From the small bamboo-fenced backyards came the squawk of chickens and squeals of pigs both of which added a rich supplement to the native diet of fish and rice. Bicycles, dusty, rundown cars used as taxis, and squeaky two-wheel carts drawn by carabao provided the only forms of transportation.[9]

Adjoining the east side of town was the headquarters of the J. H. Pomeroy Construction Company. Pomeroy was part of CPNAB, the specially formed Construction Pacific Naval Air Bases company, created to build harbors, breakwaters, fuel storage tanks, and housing and to dredge shipping channels on Wake, Midway, and Guam. Most of the sixty civilians who worked for Pomeroy lived in Sumay.

Just a short distance off the main street of Sumay was "Ben's" bar, a popular hangout for the Marines, the Pomeroy construction crews, some of the Pan Am staff, and numerous native bar girls. Behind it was a six-foot-high pile of discarded and broken beer bottles. The bar's Japanese owner, Ben Cook, had arrived on the island in the mid-1930s. The military assumed he was a lost fisherman from Saipan because he spoke only Japanese and when asked his name, he replied, "I been cook." The name stuck, and he was allowed to stay, working various jobs as a kitchen helper and handyman. Within a year he had opened his own bar in Sumay, an easy ten-minute walk downhill from the Marine detachment. Ben allowed the men to run up large bar tabs at the end of each month, making his place Sumay's drinking establishment of choice—at least before payday.

A number of Pan Am employees had carelessly extended their credit at Ben's and ignored his pleas for payment. When Gregg arrived as the new manager, Ben immediately sought his help to get his staff to pay the severely overdue bar bills. Admonishing his employees that their conduct reflected poorly on Pan Am's reputation, Gregg saw that the bills were quickly paid. Gregg shrugged off the profuse thanks of Ben Cook.[10]

The road west out of Sumay connected to a single, narrow, crushed-coral road that snaked from a few miles south of the Orote Peninsula and veered northeasterly past Apra Harbor.[11] The oval-shaped harbor was more than three miles wide and four miles deep, flanked on the south by the Orote Peninsula and by a series of islands and reefs along the northern edge. A narrow channel, cut through hundreds of coral reefs just below the surface, provided access for ships and a landing path for the Pan Am Clippers. Tucked into the northeast corner of the harbor was the small naval repair facility, the Piti Navy Yard. From the village of Piti began an endless series of thatched-roof houses stretching northeasterly to Agana.

In the fall of 1941, the Piti Yard was the home of two small Navy ships: the USS *Robert L. Barnes*, an immobilized fuel tanker that also served as a training facility for native mess stewards, and an obsolete minesweeper, the USS *Penguin*.[12] Along with a few yard boats used to transfer men and supplies, the two ships constituted the Piti Yard "fleet."[13] The *Penguin*, with a crew of four officers and fifty enlisted men, patrolled around the entire island every day. Lightly armed with a 3-inch antiaircraft gun and two .50-caliber machine guns, the *Penguin* was a choice assignment for the Navy enlisted ranks.

Typical of the minesweeper's crew was twenty-year-old Eddie Howard,[14] a farm boy from Carlisle, Indiana, assigned as a water tender on board the *Penguin*. His letters home to his mother extolled his new assignment and his life in Guam. "When we go ashore the boat takes us up a narrow half mile long channel to the dock at Piti, which is merely a landing," he recalled, but a seventy-cent taxi ride and three miles northeast lay Agana, where he could while away his free time in "pool halls, a theater, and a dance about once a week."

Howard called his fellow shipmates "a swell bunch of men. It will probably be the easiest tour of duty I will ever have."[15] He added,

There is a crew on here of about 50 men. And what do we do—two things as far as work is concerned—to stand 6 hour watch every 36 hours (fireroom) and overhaul the boiler when it has 1,000 steaming hours on it. Regulations—none. Go ashore in civilian clothes or in swimming trunks. Eat like an officer. Plenty of golden colored butter, etc. Have good bunks and lockers. Nobody ever sweeps down the compartment, though. We have a phonograph . . . and about 30 late records. Can get natives to do our laundry for $4.00 a month. We (in the fireroom) have a native to do all our work for us. He shines bridgework, cleans floor plates, and dries bilges for a dollar apiece each pay [day]. Around $14 dollars a month. Some life, eh? Liberty from 12:30 to midnight, overnight if we want it, but no servicemen are allowed on the streets after 12:30 a.m.[16]

While on routine patrol, the men on board the *Penguin* frequently trailed fishing lines for marlin, dorado, sharks, and yellowtail tuna. Tropical fruits and vegetables to supplement the regular rations were plentiful and inexpensive. Each day, as the minesweeper circled the island, the men never tired of seeing the beautiful vistas. Covering the island were the bright colors of flame trees, bougainvillea, orchids, coconut palms, and breadfruit trees and the tangled stands of banyan trees. Low, rugged mountains with sharp cliffs were cloaked in a deep jungle. The climate was more than tolerable, with warm waters for swimming and showers almost every day to cool the air. Inside a coral reef that surrounded almost the entire island, the crystal clear waters teemed with colorful fish. Seashells lay about in abundance along the palm-fringed beaches.

In mid-October 1941 the *Penguin* changed from daylight to nighttime patrols around the island. Other than observing nightly blackout procedures, the patrols were quiet cruises with the men relaxing on the decks, fishing, and enjoying the starlit sky.

The road from Sumay continued northeastwardly past the Piti Navy Yard another four miles to the island's capital city of Agana, home to almost half of the island's 23,000 residents. The United States had purchased Guam at the conclusion of the Spanish-American War, and by an executive order of President Grover Cleveland in 1898, the U.S. Navy headquarters in Agana was made responsible for the administration and governance of the entire island. Surrounding the central Plaza de España was the government center, which included the Navy administration building (Government House), the Susana U.S. Naval Hospital, the Insular Patrol's barracks, a jail, the governor's mansion,[17] a Catholic cathedral, and a public school, Dorn Hall, where children were required to attend up to the age of twelve.

Social life for the military officers in Agana centered on dinners in the governor's mansion, served with the finest of china and crystal by white-gloved Navy waiters. For physical recreation, there were three tennis courts in the plaza area, numerous basketball courts, and a nine-hole golf course next to the Navy's Officers' Club. Behind the governor's mansion was more than an acre of formal gardens, the pride of the governor's wife.

The center of nonmilitary social life in Agana was the Elks Lodge. Enlisted men were given honorary membership, and the cheap drinks and dance music lured the young women of the island. The enlisted men considered the lodge their personal fiefdom, an alternative to the exclusive Officers' Club.

A daily newspaper, the *Guam Eagle*, with an annual subscription of under three dollars, was avidly read by everyone because it gave summaries of international news along with events on Guam. The transpacific cable provided daily news and direct telephone connections east to the United States and west to Hong Kong and Shanghai. The nearby movie theater had current movies and newsreels flown in by Pan Am. Newsreels, anxiously anticipated because of the war rumors, were shown regularly. Movie viewers witnessed German guns advance to the outskirts of Moscow while British and Australian troops fought a desperate battle to hold Tobruk against Erwin Rommel's elite Panzer divisions in North Africa. Adolf Hitler's forces seemed invincible as Allied armies crumbled before them.

By the fall of 1941, most everyone on Guam understood that Japan was a threat to their island. The vast German possessions in the Pacific were seized by Japan when Germany sought an armistice after World War I,[18] and with little protest, the League of Nations acceded to their total seizure a few years later. Barred from visitations, the Western powers assumed that the Japanese had quickly fortified the many islands and built large military bases on nearby Saipan and Tinian.

A fabricated incident at the Marco Polo Bridge in Peking on 7 July 1937 is acknowledged today as the pretext for Japan's massive attacks against China. Japan's previous seizures of Manchuria had barely caused concern in the world, but the Peking attack ignited the great Pacific War. The following December, the deliberate attack against the American gunboat *Panay* and the bestiality of Japanese atrocities in Nanking flashed across movie screens. America responded with a buildup of its Navy and Army Air Corps while imposing a series of embargoes on steel, iron ore, and scrap metal and, as a result of Japan's troops moving into French Indochina, a total embargo of oil to Japan. In the summer of 1941, the Japanese military finally assumed control of Japan when Prime Minister Fumimaro Konoye resigned and was replaced by the war minister, Hideki Tojo. Seeking to end the embargoes, Japan wanted to negotiate with the United States. A flow of diplomats crossed the Pacific looking for avenues of compromise. None were found as the United States demanded repudiation of Japan's pact with Germany and Italy plus abandonment of its bases in China.

In the fall of 1941, Japanese forces swept across China and surrounded Hong Kong. America withdrew the 4th Marines from Shanghai and Peking for the defense of the Philippines, and graphic images of Japanese atrocities against the Chinese became the staple of the weekly newsreels. Very few men on Guam were unaware that the threat of war with Japan was imminent. Hollywood movies, still featuring western heroes, pirates, and swashbucklers, added the Nazis and Japanese to the list of villains. Typical was the subtle empathy for the British fight against the Nazis with director John Ford's 1941 Academy Award–winning epic of a Welsh mining family in *How Green Was My Valley*. Stories of war heroes appeared again on movie screens, led by Howard Hawk's 1941 production of *Sergeant York*, which told the story of a Kentucky farmer who became a hero of World War I. Movies were the major form of entertainment as fans flocked to see Hollywood's new stars: Humphrey Bogart, Errol Flynn, Clark Gable, Bill Holden, and Jimmy Cagney.

The golden age of comic books had begun three years earlier, in June 1938, with the introduction of the Superman comics. By the fall of 1941, millions of comic books were published every month extolling the adventures of Batman, Captain Marvel, and Captain America. The enemies were not just criminals but also the supporters of Hitler and Tojo. Every young American knew that when trouble arose, Superman or another hero could be called upon to fly to the rescue, save the world, and thwart the villain. The monthly delivery of comics on Guam was eagerly anticipated.

In Agana the largest Navy facility was the U.S. Naval Hospital. Commanded by Capt. William T. Lineberry, it was staffed by ten officers, five nurses, fifty-five enlisted men, and seven Chamorro assistants.[19] Al Mosher, a native of the small town of Richland, Washington,[20] had joined the Navy only the year before rather than face a random draft into the Army. After boot camp in San Diego and further training at the Navy's Hospital Corps School, Mosher was posted as a pharmacist's mate to the Bremerton Naval Hospital near Seattle. In the spring of 1941, Mosher was transferred to Guam.

Mosher was surprised when he first saw the Susana Naval Hospital. It was different from anything he had ever seen. "I was so surprised as I realized it was obviously designed for the tropics, with three separate two-story buildings with the wards on the second floor and offices below. The wards were enclosed in very wide, screened verandas and were frequently used for patient beds." Mosher's assignment, determined by experience and rank, was as a ward attendant, taking care of the many patients. The hospital served the entire island, with one ward to serve the military and the other two wards for the Guamanian men and women. The enlisted men lived in separate quarters while the officers and nurses lived in private homes. Mosher continued:

> Even with the screens, every bed was draped with mosquito netting, both in the hospital and in our quarters.
>
> Frankly, I was quite young and really not that interested in world affairs. I had no sense of danger and few of my friends took war rumors seriously. Most of us felt that we would really not get involved and the diplomats would solve the problems. I remember hearing one admiral boasting that "the Japs would never dare attack the U.S. Navy." We

were told we had the greatest navy in the world and could circle the
Japs and destroy them in a few days. I believed it, too.[21]

Mosher, who wanted to make a career of the Navy, was anxious to make a good
impression.

Agana was also the site of naval communications for this remote area of the
Pacific. Located a few blocks uphill from the plaza, Radio Agana, with its three-hundred-foot antenna, handled all wireless communications for the island—both military
and civilian—and was staffed by twenty-one enlisted men. A second station, the isolated Radio Libugon, was located in the low foothills two miles southeast of Agana.
Staffed by eight enlisted men, the station was built in the mid-1930s and had four
three-hundred-foot radio direction finding (RDF) antennas that were able to track
Japanese communications and shipping across the Pacific. In 1941 the towers were
replaced by sloping V-shaped antennas, which gave better range and were used specifically for the interception of Japanese naval communications.

Typical of the staff was RM2 Harold Joslin, already a four-year veteran of the
Navy at the age of twenty-two. Two years earlier, Joslin had been transferred from
radioman duties on the carrier USS *Lexington* and sent to the Navy's top secret Radio
Intercept School, hidden in a penthouse atop the Navy Building in Washington, D.C.
After successfully completing the course, he married and was then sent to Guam in the
spring of 1940. Joslin recalled, "As an enlisted man, I was not entitled to bring along
my new bride, Marie. Undeterred, she took a freighter to Manila and came to Guam
on the *Gold Star* in July of 1940, where we lived together in a small house, complete
with servants."[22]

Trained in the different version of Morse code used by the Japanese, the radiomen
monitored the flow of coded messages from ships throughout the Pacific. "Within a
short while, we were able to differentiate between Japanese ships, planes, civil traffic,
military traffic, and even the radio operators," said Joslin. With experience, the radiomen could determine the "fist," or transmission rhythm, of each Japanese radioman.
Combined with the direction finder azimuths, individual Japanese ships could be easily tracked, a boon to the American code breakers. This secret mission of the Libugon
station was known only to a handful of men.[23]

* * *

Capt. George McMillin, USN, performed a dual role on Guam, commanding both
the civil and military administration of the island. Guam, however, was not considered
a choice assignment for men aspiring to become admirals. As governor of Guam, the
various commands, for example, the Sumay Marine detachment, the Naval Hospital,
the Piti Yard, the administrative staff, and so on, were under McMillin's supervision,
but he did not serve in direct military command for combat purposes.

As the "chief executive" of Guam, McMillin had the direct responsibility for the Marine Insular Patrol, which served as the island's police. With headquarters next to the governor's mansion, McMillin's personal aide and adjutant, Capt. Charles S. Todd, managed the Insular Patrol with its twelve outpost stations. Each station housed one Marine, with spacious living quarters on the lower floor of a two-story house complete with domestic help. Above him lived a medic detached from the main hospital who acted as the town doctor. With little work to do, the Insular Patrol of Guam was one of the enlisted Marine's most desired assignments—anywhere in the world.

"I was starting my third tour of duty on Guam in 1941," said Sgt. George Shane, who had joined the Marines in 1932 at the age of seventeen. "Every Marine loved Guam," he continued, "and when the Marines offered me the job as assistant chief of the Insular Patrol, I jumped at the opportunity. The patrol was the choicest assignment on Guam—and I was to be the assistant to the head of the patrol, Captain Todd."[24] Shane was given a free hand to run the twenty-eight-man Insular Patrol.

Six-foot-tall Pfc. Ralph Baggett, who joined the Marines in November 1940 to avoid being drafted into the Army, shared Shane's exuberance for Guam and the Insular Patrol. Born on 21 August 1918 in the desert oil town of Hobbs, New Mexico, Baggett was a gifted runner and had garnered an athletic scholarship to the University of Texas in Austin. During his sophomore year in 1940, his hurdles relay team won the Drake Relays. He wore the coveted Drake Relays Championship Watch when his team set a U.S. record two weeks later against Yale University—a record that would stand until 1958.[25]

After the Yale meet, school was out for the year, and Baggett worked in Carlsbad for the summer. Being young and eligible for the draft weighed heavily on his mind, and when he returned to college in the fall, he met up with a friend, "A. J." Robinson,[26] who was a full semester ahead of him. The two young men decided to goof off hunting squirrels with a slingshot. To avoid the draft, they considered hitchhiking to South America, but President Roosevelt had closed the borders to draft-aged men.

With assurances from the school that he could return, Baggett and Robinson left the university and "goofed off," traveling around the area. "It wasn't a total loss," said Baggett, "as I was introduced to this young filly named Sybil Geaslin through her aunt. Oh boy! It was love at first sight and we both knew it." Like others, he opted to join the military rather than wait for a random draft into the Army. "I took a look at the other services and the Marines made quite a pitch for me, so I signed up on the spot." In October 1940 the two men joined the Marine Corps and were shipped to the basic training center in San Diego. A daily letter to his sweetheart Sybil made the training days "zip by in a flash," and for his first assignment, Baggett was posted to Guam. Sybil promised to wait for his return.

On his first day on Guam, Baggett was surprised to learn he was to be posted to the Insular Patrol. "I felt luckier than a wildcatter who's struck oil." With a new promotion to private first class, he drew the station in Agat, a two-story house a few miles south of the Orote Peninsula and the Sumay barracks. Stationed on the second floor was Johnny Ploke,[27] a Navy pharmacist, with his native-born wife and son. His quarters being a short walk from the ocean, Baggett spent untold hours swimming with his Marine buddy Pfc. Hal Burt "or just walking along the beach, gabbing and shooting at birds with our .45-caliber pistols." Twice a month, Baggett went to Agana for supplies and to get paid. Letters from Sybil, if sent airmail, arrived by Pan Am Clipper in a few days. Regular mail often took a month on board the military troop transport or supply ships. Baggett made certain that his letters to Sybil "were always sent air mail."

Twelve patrolmen were placed in various little towns around the island, each outpost having household help and an assigned corpsman. The remaining sixteen members of the Insular Patrol were assigned to the plaza barracks. Together the Marine and Navy corpsmen served as the law and the doctor for the local towns.[28]

⁎⁎⁎⁑⁎⁎⁂⁎⁎⁑⁎⁎⁎⁎

In the last week of November 1941, an eastbound passenger on a Pan Am Clipper was invited to join the Navy officers for the evening. Relating his experiences in China, he stated quite emphatically, "America will be at war with Japan within two weeks."[29] Captain Lineberry, commander of the hospital, took the remarks very seriously. The next day large red crosses were painted on top of the hospital buildings for identification and L-shaped trenches, three feet wide and four feet deep, were dug on the hospital grounds for use in case of a bombing attack.[30]

Throughout the fall of 1941, America's hostility toward Japan's aggression in China accelerated, especially after Japan's naval and army units entered into French Indochina. Japanese diplomats shuttled back and forth to Washington, attempting to alleviate the tensions as President Roosevelt imposed stricter boycotts, more asset seizures, and further embargoes of raw material and oil. In the last week of November, Japanese ambassador Saduro Kurusu, on the way to Washington for one last attempt to resolve the disputes, had to remain on Guam for an additional day because of a passing typhoon.

Governor McMillin ordered that Kurusu and his entourage be restricted to Pan Am's hotel. To guard the Japanese during their overnight stay, Captain Todd selected the tallest Marines stationed on the island. Among them was the lanky Ralph Baggett, who towered over the diminutive Japanese; they barely reached the medals on his chest. Well aware of the pending crisis with Japan, Baggett paid close attention to the movements of the Japanese visitors. Local Japanese were seen meeting with the ambassador and other Japanese officials, frequently exchanging military salutes.

There was no doubt as to the loyalty of many of the local Japanese. Almost every local Japanese official of importance visited the ambassador during his stay at the hotel. The U.S. military assumed they would join the Japanese the instant the island was invaded.[31]

In the last week of November, Lieutenant Colonel MacNulty invited Station Manager Charles Gregg to come up the hill to his office, where he reiterated that war with Japan was imminent. MacNulty told Gregg that the governor had decided that "in case of an attack by the Japanese, the Marine force would be in command of all government personnel and that all civilians and native employees would be sent to their homes." Plans to destroy all sensitive material and to evacuate any Americans in the area who worked for Pan Am and the civilian contractors were made. The Americans were to hide with a week's supply of food five miles southeast of Sumay, on the eastern slopes of Mount Almagosa—long enough, they hoped, to hold out until the U.S. Navy could rescue them.[32]

In the middle of November, the pace of Japanese military activity increased noticeably. The Japanese planes could be heard long before they were seen because the engines had the distinct throbbing sound of unsynchronized motors. Whereas before an occasional Japanese Mitsubishi F1M2 (Pete) observation plane would fly over every week or two, they were now seen every day, frequently circling just high enough over the Orote Peninsula to avoid all rifle fire and then slipping over the southeast coast near Talofofo Bay.

Every sighting was immediately reported by phone to the Insular Patrol. Without planes to defend the island, sighting reports ceased because "there was nothing anyone could do but stare at 'em," said Sergeant Shane. In the first week in December, Japanese planes flew over almost every hour for a twenty- to thirty-minute "look-see." The best the governor could hope for was at least a warning of an attack so that he could flee into the hills. On 1 December he established a secret observation post at the northernmost tip of the island, Ritidian Point. Manned around the clock by four insular patrolmen, it was to report any naval movements coming from nearby Rota Island.[33]

The code interceptors at Libugon, with their powerful RDF antennas, which reached out thousands of miles, noted the disappearance of the Imperial Japanese Navy fleet by the last week of November. The fleet had headed northwest and "was out of their normal operating area." The men at Libugon had no idea where they were.[34]

Early Saturday morning, 6 December, Governor McMillin ordered the destruction of secret and classified documents at all the island facilities.[35] The same day, on the north coast of Guam, the Japanese infiltrated at least three spies in the guise of fishermen.

No change was expected the night of Sunday, 7 December 1941, and shortly after 6:00 p.m., the USS *Penguin* slipped her moorings for another routine patrol. The ship cleared the channel, rounded Orote Point, and turned south. A spectacular sunset of crimson lined the clouds off the starboard side. Within ten minutes of sundown, the deep blackness of night settled over the island and calm sea. A full moon glistened off the ocean and a visible phosphorescent trail streamed behind the ship.

Although under blackout conditions, the crew was relaxed, assured that the U.S. fleet was prepared for any eventuality. A few hours before sailing, they learned

Secretary of War Franklin Knox, in his weekly press release in Washington, D.C., had said, "I am proud to report that the American people may feel fully confident in their Navy. In my opinion [they] . . . are without superior. On any comparable basis, the United States Navy is second to none." The *New York Times* front-page headline read, "Navy is superior to any, says Knox."[36] Left unsaid was that President Roosevelt had already decided that in case of war with Japan, Guam would be sacrificed.

On Sunday morning, 7 December, a mere forty-five miles north of Guam,[37] several transports that had departed the port of Hiroshima a week earlier, dropped anchor at Sosanjaya Bay on Rota Island. The ships were scheduled to wait at anchor for two more days. On board were 5,500 Japanese naval assault troops. In San Francisco and Honolulu, the low clouds in the evening skies reflected the bright city lights as Americans enjoyed another Saturday evening.

On Monday, 8 December, as the blackness of night on Saipan was erased by a misty dawn, bombers and Pete floatplane fighters of Japan's 17th Air Unit lifted off and turned southwest toward Guam.

CHAPTER 2

Japan Attacks

YESTERDAY, DECEMBER 7, 1941—A DATE WHICH WILL LIVE IN INFAMY—THE UNITED STATES OF AMERICA WAS SUDDENLY AND DELIBERATELY ATTACKED BY NAVAL AND AIR FORCES OF THE EMPIRE OF JAPAN.

—President Franklin D. Roosevelt

"For the last two weeks we all knew with a certainty that war was coming," said Pfc. Barney Barnett. "On Friday, we emptied the arsenal and gave out all the ammo. We kept those Springfield rifles from World War I and the small amount of ammunition on our bunks. The worst part was that there weren't enough rifles to go around. Heck, I figured I was dead for sure, but I planned to take a few of those Nips with me. On Saturday morning, two days before the attack at Pearl Harbor, we destroyed all the records and buried all the money from the paymaster's office. Five days before that, we were told there would be no payday as war was about to start and attacks were expected on Guam, Wake, and the Philippines."[1]

At the Pan Am base on Monday, 8 December, at 4:00 a.m., Station Manager Charles Gregg's "Big Ben" alarm clock unwound with a shrill ring. Lights clicked on one after another as the station came to life. The Philippine Clipper, due in that afternoon, would depart from Wake Island within the hour.

Assistant Station Manager Jim Thomas rolled over, groaned, and clicked off the bell of his alarm clock. Slipping on pants, shirt, and shoes, he shook off the last vestige of sleep with a splash of water to his face. The yellow bug light over the headquarters door served as a beacon as Thomas walked to his office, which was filled with weather forecasting equipment. Grabbing his clipboard, he began to read and record data from the meteorological instruments. His twelve-hour weather forecast had to be prepared for the Clipper's arrival in Guam. Barring any weather delay, the plane would arrive before 4:00 p.m., and the crew and passengers would remain overnight in the Guam hotel. Jim knew the station had a "ton of work on arrival days," an exaggeration considering arrival days were the only time the full staff was busy for any length of time. By 4:30 a.m. Thomas had finished his weather forecast and prepared the situation at terminal and release (SATREL) message for Wake Island, releasing PAA Trip 553, the Philippine Clipper.[2] The favorable SATREL was cabled back to Wake Island. Thomas' work for the day was complete, and breakfast was next on his mind. For Thomas, it was the start of just another day in paradise.

Fifty minutes earlier Japanese planes had dropped the first bombs at Pearl Harbor. Already, as Thomas ambled to the dining room, four American battleships had become twisted wrecks, wracked by fire and slowly sinking to the muddy bottom. The ammunition magazine of the USS *Oklahoma* had exploded in a massive ball of flame, the concussion literally tearing the ship apart. The vaunted U.S. Pacific Fleet was obliterated except for a few carriers and cruisers still at sea. Just more than a hundred miles from Guam, excited Japanese pilots on Saipan were finishing their last peacetime breakfast, raising toasts of sake to the glory of the emperor with exuberant shouts of "Banzai!"[3]

At 5:45 a.m. a radio message from Adm. Thomas Hart, the commander in chief, Asiatic Fleet,[4] reached Guam stating that Japan had "commenced hostilities by attacking Pearl Harbor, prior to a declaration of war."[5] Governor George McMillin, roused by a messenger from Radio Agana, read the message with dismay. No longer would he worry about a potential war with Japan. He was painfully aware that Guam was indefensible. He dispatched a clerk to waken his ranking military officer, Navy commander Donald T. Giles: "Pearl Harbor is under attack!"[6]

McMillin's military aide, Capt. Charles S. Todd, USMC, suffering a mild blood infection that caused painful boils, quickly released himself from the hospital and, still in his hospital pajamas, joined the staff officers gathered around McMillin's desk to review the preparations for the defense of the island. Phone lines buzzed as calls were sent to all military commands, Pan Am, and the contractors group, alerting them to the attack. By 7:30 a.m., however, runners had to be used to send messages as all the telephone lines had been cut, an act of preplanned sabotage by a few local Japanese.[7] The native switchboard operators, now useless and fearful for their lives, fled the city.

Governor McMillin ordered the civilian population to begin an evacuation of Agana and told Captain Todd to have his Insular Patrol "round up all Japanese nationals and put them in the jail."[8] All commercial business and church services were immediately banned. Plans to destroy any materials and records that could be valuable to the Japanese were quickly implemented.

At 6:05 a.m. the Pan Am office on Wake Island radioed Charles Gregg that the Clipper had departed for Guam.[9] Five minutes later Lt. Elwood "Pinky" Madson, a member of the governor's administrative staff, phoned Gregg to say the Japanese had attacked Pearl Harbor. Acting quickly, but reluctant to clearly state he knew Pearl Harbor had been attacked, Gregg radioed Wake Island declaring Guam was not SATREL, that is, not in a condition to receive the departed Clipper. He assumed they would take action to recall the departing plane. At Jim Thomas' suggestion, a second message was transmitted specifically asking Wake to recall the Clipper.[10]

At 8:00 a.m. Gregg gathered the administrative staff, mechanics, and hotel staff and told them the news of Pearl Harbor. The staff was stunned into silence and a sense of dread permeated the room. All knew the base would be a prime target for attack. Those not needed were advised to quickly evacuate to the preselected rendezvous area on nearby Mount Almagosa.

During the nightly patrol around Guam, one of the boilers on the aged mine-sweeper USS *Penguin* had developed a leak. Maximum speed was reduced from fifteen knots to five. The morning sun had cleared the hills behind Agana by the time the *Penguin* returned, limping slowly through Apra Bay and up the channel for Piti Navy Yard. She tied up at an outer buoy. Observing radio silence through the night, RM Bob Epperson, USN, had turned the radio on only to listen and monitor for any messages for the last fifteen minutes of every hour. Safely anchored just before 8:00 a.m. and unaware of the attack on Pearl Harbor, the skipper, Lt. James Haviland, released twenty-five men for shore leave or to return to their families.[11]

WT2 Eddie Howard, preparing to go ashore for the day, saw the station boat from Piti Yard pull alongside. A messenger rushed up the gangway and handed the skipper an envelope clearly marked "Confidential."[12] Haviland broke the seal, read the note, calmly turned to his executive officer, Ens. Edwin A. Wood, and said, "War has been declared." Within minutes, Haviland heard the crunch of exploding bombs and, looking into the sun over Agana, spotted three Japanese planes heading directly at his ship. "General Quarters!" Haviland shouted. "All hands prepare to get under-way immediately!" The Klaxon screeched the call to battle stations. The engine room quickly brought the steam back up, and the lines to the buoy and anchor were cut away with an axe. The *Penguin* turned for the open sea.[13]

Recently transferred from a stint on board the heavy cruiser USS *Salt Lake City,* "a miserable, crowded, stinking, non-air-conditioned heavy cruiser," E2 Edward "Ed" Hale was delighted to be assigned to Guam and, especially, the *Penguin.* As the Klaxon blared, men raced for their gear and battle stations. "The sound of airplane engines," Hale wrote, "caused looks of consternation on the faces of the men":

> What planes would be coming at this hour? The Clipper should just be leaving Wake [and] the Dutch planes being ferried through had never flown at night before. Probably some carrier or cruiser was approaching, but it was strange we had no notice. Yes, they looked like cruiser planes, the type adapted to catapulting.
>
> But the marking . . . holy cats! The sun on their wings! Japanese planes. . . . What could they be here for? We had seen occasional glimpses of planes that we had assumed to be Japanese for a long time but they always stayed well off shore. These were coming right at the *Penguin.* The surprise attack was on. This was war![14]

Japanese planes began bombing at 8:27 a.m., striking in turn downtown Agana, the Sumay area, and the *Penguin* in the first attack.[15] Eighteen planes swept over Agana. Splitting into two groups, nine turned to attack the Piti Navy Yard and Radio Hill while the others proceeded toward the Pan Am station and the Marine barracks at Sumay.

The planes attacking Radio Hill and the USS *Barnes* failed to hit anything with their bombs and the *Barnes* withstood the "most inaccurate bombing and machine gunning of modern airmanship."[16]

Three Japanese Petes streaked past Piti and chased westward after the *Penguin*.[17] The bombs splashed next to the *Penguin*, raising geysers of water but failing to damage the hull on the first pass. The strafing caused severe leaking and damaged the lifeboats, leaving only two small rafts. Ens. R. G. White,[18] directing the 3-inch antiaircraft gun, was felled when a bullet ricocheted into the gun mount just before the ship cleared the harbor. One of the Petes disintegrated when hit by a 3-inch shell. At least one more trailed smoke as it flew past the ship.

"He [White] collapsed in my arms," said S1 Edwin J. "Knobby" Settles, "with blood spurting from the wound in his chest, and I could see his heart. He turned his face to mine and said, 'Would you contact my parents?' I nodded yes and he slipped away. He died in less than three minutes." S1 Martin Ratzman's stomach was slashed open by a tumbling piece of ragged shrapnel, and he slumped against the gunwale.

The Japanese fighters wheeled around for what appeared to be a second pass, and suddenly three bombs hit close amidships, opening holes in her side. "I looked down," said Epperson, "and saw water pouring in from a ruptured seam."[19] The Japanese fighters, their bomb racks empty and guns silent, flew back over the harbor toward Agana. Lieutenant Haviland, his arm almost severed by another piece of shrapnel, realized the ship was incapable of continuing in battle and ordered it to be scuttled rather than chance its salvage value to the Japanese. The sea cocks and portholes were opened. In moments, the *Penguin*'s stern began to settle into the water. The ship was more than a mile west of the Orote Peninsula. One man lay dead and almost every man had been wounded in the short battle. The gun crew eased the body of Ensign White on to a raft. The severely wounded crewmen were moved to the remaining rafts and the rest of the crew stripped to their shorts and began to swim ashore.[20]

Ensign Wood made a final sweep of the ship and discovered the boiler crew still at their posts. They had not heard the call to abandon ship. Scrambling topside, the firemen arrived on deck to see the last of their shipmates swimming away. Jumping into the shark-infested water just as the *Penguin* slipped below the surface, the battered crewmen swam for up to three hours, finally crawling onto the rocks and jagged coral below the cliffs along the west end of Orote Peninsula. Without shoes, the jagged coral ripped at their legs and feet, adding to the misery of the morning. The two ship's mascot dogs, Gertie and Jiggs, survived to join the men on shore. The dogs' survival was the only bright spot of the morning.

The battle and loss of the *Penguin* was plainly visible from the top of the Orote cliffs. Marines rushed to the shoreline to help the crew climb the sharp, volcanic cliffs. The two most seriously injured men, Seaman Ratzman and EM3 Rex Wilson, were sent ahead to the hospital in Agana by taxi; the rest of the men were carried into Agana on a Marine quartermaster's truck.[21]

More than a dozen of the *Penguin* survivors decided to form a patrol for the coming night. In the late afternoon, they approached Government House at the governor's mansion and asked for food and clothing—particularly shoes and pants. In their struggle to survive after their ship sank, almost all had lost their shoes and most of their clothing in the three-mile swim to shore. For some inexplicable reason, the officer in charge[22] refused to open the warehouse, insisting that since records were lost, no clothes could be issued because there was no way they could charge their accounts.[23] The crew of the *Penguin*, except for seven now in the hospital and two men helping at the island's power plant, realized they were defenseless. A few volunteered for the Insular Patrol, but most scattered into the boonies.[24]

✦✦✦✦✦✦✦✦✦✦

Shortly after dawn, Capt. William T. Lineberry called for silence among the men and women assembled in one of the barracks halls at the U.S. Naval Hospital in Agana. All gasped as Lineberry announced that Japan had just attacked Pearl Harbor and stated, "We are at war." Twenty-year-old PhM3 Al Mosher recalled, "It was really the first day I was aware of a pending invasion. Coming from the small farm town of Richland, Washington, I had not been interested in current affairs, nor in learning much about Guam or its military role. Obviously, a few hours later, when the Jap planes began to strafe and bomb us, we were certainly at war."[25]

The men of the twelve Insular Patrol outposts had been ordered by Captain Todd[26] to stay at their posts in case of attack. The men in Agana immediately rounded up all the Japanese nationals who were known to be supportive of Japan and placed them in the local jail, a concrete structure near the Plaza de España. Following the governor's orders, the civilians in Agana, Agat, and other small hamlets evacuated the towns.

On the planes' first pass over Agana, a bomb dropped next to the jail, "scaring the devil out of the Japs inside," Captain Todd recalled. When they loudly complained they were in danger, Captain Todd suppressed a smile as he said, "They're your own people. There's nothing I can do about that!"[27] The raucous wail of the air-raid alarm high on the power house smokestack added to the cacophonous sound of roaring engines, exploding bombs, and rifle and machine-gun fire.

The first Japanese bombers carefully targeted the Libugon radio station, the Pan Am radio, the Pacific cable station, and the radio shed at the Sumay Marine barracks. The stations were abandoned and, except for the shed at Sumay, were not effectively hit by the bombs. However, to the outside world, Guam fell silent. Other than a quick message of "signing off" the following evening by the Pan Am radio, no word of the men would be obtained for another six weeks.[28]

Without air cover, the island lay vulnerable to the Japanese attack. From the top of the old Spanish fort overlooking the plaza, Pfc. Knute Hanson, USMC, fired a .50-caliber machine gun at passing planes. Not finding the pin to mount it on a tripod, he braced it on the ledge using his chest. The recoil so bruised his chest that he was black and blue for months afterward. Hanson is certain he shot at least one plane out of the sky.[29]

The obvious targets for the Japanese were the radio station towers and the main administration buildings. Every bomb missed and the strafing proved entirely ineffective. The Marine barracks, contractor supply office, and storage areas were bombed without opposition. The light antiaircraft guns on the *Barnes* and the one machine gun fired in Agana by Private Hanson, forced some of the Japanese planes up to five thousand feet, but the bombing continued.[30]

Many men lived or worked outside the towns of Agana and Sumay. Most were totally surprised when the planes attacked. In Agat Navy Corpsman Johnny Ploke (a member of the Insular Patrol and Baggett's assigned medic) had just returned from mass with Father Ferdinand. As Father Ferdinand and the Ploke family settled down for breakfast, the phone rang. It was his wife's father, Antanacio Taitana "Tata" Perez, calling to say Japan had declared war and that he was sending his car to pick them up. Avoiding the strafing planes, the family safely fled to the Dueñas Ranch in Barrigada, approximately five miles northeast of Agana. With his family now in relative safety, Pharmacist's Mate Ploke hid in the nearby jungle as Japanese planes continued to attack.[31]

At the Sumay Marine detachment, that day began like many others, each man proceeding about his normal duties. For the previous month, a few "recon" exercises—actually nothing much more than a march to potential bivouac areas—and limited practice at the firing range were the only indications that preparations for war were under way. Early reveille, breakfast in the galley, and a leisurely stroll to a duty station signified another normal day. Sgt. Tom Honan[32] opened the Base Exchange, Private Barnett walked toward the motor pool, and Pfc. Stan Kozlowski,[33] cotton stuffed in his ears to protect himself from the noise, mounted the seat of the lawn mower tractor and began mowing the fairways on the adjacent golf course. A few off-duty men settled back on their bunks, reading the latest issues of comic books, a popular pastime at Sumay.

"On 8 December I had just left the galley for the motor pool and I was walking toward the Marine Radio Station when the first bombing raid started," said Barnett. "A bomb hit next to the radio station and killed a guy inside.[34] We started to run across the field when the first bomb exploded. 'Babbs' got hit and was thrown to the ground, his leg torn to shreds.[35] From the first attack on, the Marines at Sumay couldn't do a damn thing. Our weapons were useless relics. I was assigned to a transport section, given a truck, and told to wait at a particular point away from the base. Many of us were unarmed and Lieutenant Colonel MacNulty was absolutely useless. No one had much respect for him. He was simply sent to Guam to finish out his years until he could retire."[36] As the senior line officer, MacNulty should have assumed command over any and all administrative or medical officers.

The Japanese planes, swooping past the Pan Am station, dropped more fragmentation bombs on the Marine reservation. Most of the Marines were in barracks or on their normal duties throughout the post. About fifty more were scattered about the island on various patrol duties. Several were injured as they ran across the golf course, rushing for cover in the surrounding thickets.[37] Amid all the chaos, a Marine was heard to shout at the top of his lungs, "Where's Superman when you need him?"

The sounds of exploding bombs, ricocheting bullets, and exploding gas tanks and the black smoke of fires did not deter Kozlowski as he continued to mow the fairways. Fellow Marines shouted and waved to get his attention but to no avail. Kozlowski suddenly looked about and realized what was happening. Shifting to fast gear, he raced toward the jungle edging the course. The tractor jammed against a tree, its drive wheel losing contact with the ground. Kozlowski jumped off and fled into the jungle. The wheel spun for hours until the gas ran out.

Below the golf course and down the hill from the Sumay detachment, the first wave of six planes struck the Pan Am facilities. The first bomb hit open ground by the flagpole and another ignited the fuel tank. A bomb blew apart the kitchen, and another hit the water just below the main office.[38]

Toward the end of the first air raid, Charles Gregg and the assistant station manager, Jim Thomas, returned to the Pan Am headquarters. Thomas had been given the duty to empty the safe of secret codes, money, and other records that should not fall into possession of the Japanese. "Bombs were falling and the Japs were strafing everywhere—or so it seemed. When I entered the office with Charlie Gregg, a bomb hit at the end of the slip and water gushed through the broken windows. I got soaked but wasn't injured. I was shaking so much I couldn't open the safe. I had to grab my right hand with my left to steady myself, finally opening the safe after the fourth try."

The contents of the safe were dumped into a sack, the safe door slammed shut and the two men ran for their lives. "Just clearing the door," continued Thomas, "I saw a bomb coming and dove flat onto the gravel. When it exploded, I was covered with dirt and gravel. I lay still for quite a while but decided I should make a run for a safer place. I ran along the side of the hangar to Sumay and through the town, trying to locate the Marine commander, MacNulty."

When the raid ended, Thomas and Gregg picked up the two badly injured Pan Am men and arranged to transport them to the hospital.[39] The Pan Am buildings were rendered useless by the bombs; all the windows, most of the walls, and the roofs were torn away. At the radio transmitter tower, Gregg and Thomas finally found Colonel MacNulty and informed him that the Pan Am radio was still operative. "I found him cowering under a tree," said Thomas, "a disgrace to the uniform.[40] However, with his approval, I decided to burn the money. I proceeded to burn over twenty-five thousand dollars. How I wish we had kept the money as we could have really used it as POWs. It probably would have been confiscated by the Japs but still, it would have been very handy to have a few years later."[41]

By 11:00 a.m. the last of the Japanese planes had flown off toward Rota, leaving much of the island a smoking ruin. Around one o'clock in the afternoon, at least fifteen planes returned to bomb and strafe with particular attention to destroying the radio towers. Again, the bombs missed the towers. Small-arms fire and the machine guns of the Marines drove the planes to a higher altitude, effectively minimizing their damage. One bomb skimmed over the administration building and exploded on the rented house of RM1 George Ray Tweed, scattering personal property for blocks. A garbage truck nearby was tumbled on its side. For the next two hours, the planes roared over the island, strafing roads and targets of opportunity without hindrance. A few minutes past three o'clock, the Japanese planes assembled high over Agana and flew back toward Rota.

The local Chamorros from Agat and Agana sought refuge on the mountain slopes of Tenjo, Almagosa, and Lamlam. Thousands fled south along the one-lane road that turned to dirt after passing Sumay. Chamorros clogged the road, loaded with everything they could carry on overloaded bicycles, wheelbarrows, and carabao pulling carts. When Japanese planes began to strafe the long columns, the natives fled in panic into the jungles. Water was scarce, the heat oppressive, and the mosquitoes voracious in their appetites, all of which added to the misery and fear of the people. By nightfall Agana and every hamlet on Guam was deserted.

By the end of the first day, the town of Agana was relatively unscathed, but the USS *Penguin* had been sunk and the military and Pan Am facilities at Sumay had been destroyed. In a cooperative effort, the Marines, contractors, and Pan Am employees hauled most of the remaining foodstuff and cans to the top of Mount Almagosa, where they were dumped and camouflaged. Halfway up the mountain, the Pan Am employees hid their cars in the brush and fled into the jungle. The road up Almagosa ended in a cleared bluff, surrounded by a deep jungle that provided some shelter from aerial visibility.

In Agana, Governor McMillin ordered the Insular Guard (natives) to their downtown Agana barracks, a building with thick, concrete walls. The senior line officer, the Navy's Cdr. Donald T. Giles, then instructed Captain Todd to recall the Guam Insular Force, the Insular Guard, and, to the displeasure of Todd, the Marine Insular Patrol into Agana. Todd and Sgt. George Shane drove a staff car to all the outposts but instructed only the native forces to come into Agana. Todd deliberately left the Insular Patrol's Marines in the villages. Left alone in the villages, the Marines would be subject to the mercies of Japanese soldiers. Shane felt they had a better chance for survival in the plaza, but at Todd's behest, half the Marines of the Insular Patrol would remain in the outposts. As events unfolded, Todd's decision probably saved all of their lives.

Expecting an invasion at any time, McMillin declared all military stores and provisions as surplus. Base exchanges and most private stores were thrown open to all who wanted any supplies. Knowing of the savagery Japanese troops exhibited in their conquests of China, exemplified by the Rape of Nanking, all military personnel expected the worst. All military and civilian bars were thrown open with free drinks for all. As one Marine said, "It was a clear case of 'Drink hardy for tomorrow you may die'—and we certainly did."

Blackout conditions were imposed upon the entire island. As night descended on Mount Almagosa, the eerie glow of burning wreckage and fuel tanks could be seen at the Pan Am station, the Marine barracks, and the Piti Navy Yard. Fear of imminent invasion and the swarming mosquitoes kept the exhausted and fearful refugees in a tense condition throughout the night. Discussions about the sudden war dominated every conversation. Speculations of when and where the Japanese would land kept most people awake through the night. Numerous rain showers during the night added to the misery of those encamped on the mountain. Those who slept did so only in short naps.

The following morning, Tuesday, 9 December 1941, Gregg and his fellow Pan Am men awoke from a restless sleep at 5:00 a.m. Joined by the men of the Pomeroy Construction Company, they began to divide the food and organized a crew to feed the many refugees. From the top of Mount Almagosa during the morning, all could see the Japanese planes return and continue to bomb Sumay, Piti, Agana, and the Pan Am station.

The second and smaller flight of planes arrived about 2:30 p.m. Incendiaries destroyed the balance of the Pan Am site. The final raid did little more than bomb already demolished buildings and perform random strafings of crossroads. Small groups of planes attacked Barrigada, Dededo, and the schoolhouse in Tumon and the numerous naval recreation facilities around the island.

Gathering his fellow employees together, Gregg informed them that for all practical purposes, Pan Am no longer existed, but if they stayed together, their chances for survival would probably increase. Each man was given twenty dollars with a reminder that the company might require repayment when the war was over. Gregg carefully destroyed all records so the Japanese had no way to trace the distribution of the money.

Jim Thomas noted,

> Twisted vines tore our clothes, piercing thorns lacerated our faces, and tangled undergrowth tripped our feet. The smell of rotting vegetation stung our nostrils. Scorpions, centipedes, tarantulas, giant cockroaches, and what seemed like fifty million mosquitoes per cubic inch bade us a foreboding welcome. This was our first taste of what hellish conditions awaited us.
>
> That night turned into a dripping nightmare. Intermittent showers soaked us to the skin. We slept uncovered on beds of soggy leaves and slippery mud. My arms flailed in vain at the hordes of voracious mosquitoes chewing on my face, hands, and ankles. They crawled through my hair, pierced my scalp and sucked blood through my wet clothing. Their high-pitched whine sounded like a screeching violin stuck on high C. Like hyenas on a downed gazelle, they were eating me alive. Slapping to kill the swarming pests, my hands became red

with my own blood. The next morning, debilitated and nearly deliri-
ous, I could hardly open my swollen eyes. My face felt like a festering
piece of raw meat. At sunup, squinting through distended eyelids, I
shared a can of our cold soup with Max [Brodofsky]. Someone, thank
God, had brought a can opener. Having no utensils, we used flat
sticks as spoons. We wolfed down the soup and licked the can lids. We
looked like escapees from Devil's Island—muddy, unshaven, hungry,
wet, scared and miserable.

Panic-stricken, we crawled and staggered through the underbrush,
trying to hide from an enemy we didn't know and couldn't see. Max
carried the case of soup on his broad shoulders, harboring it like a box
of precious diamonds. After an hour, we lay on the ground, exhausted.
Eventually, reason returned and we took stock of our situation. We
needed blankets, shoes, food, clothing, and, most of all, mosquito
repellent. A call was made for volunteers to return to our barracks
after dark to scrounge supplies and send a final message to the states.[42]

In the fading light a number of the Pan Am employees decided to return to the station, hoping to salvage clothes and possessions. Max Brodofsky loaded six of his fellow employees in his car, and drove down the mountain into Sumay and the Pan Am
station.

"Without lights for security purposes," Thomas remembered,

we drove down the mountain in a cloak of semidarkness. In the misty
moonlight [Tuesday night, 9 December 1941] and the flickering glow
of burning buildings, Sumay was empty and silent, occupied only by
ghosts, shadows and two lonely dogs. Our hotel was smoldering but
the dependable diesel engine still hummed in the distance. The Pacific
cable station on the hill was empty and burning. By some miracle,
our cottage was intact and my flashlight was still on the wooden apple
box that had served as a night stand. We worked quickly and silently.
I stuffed a pair of pants, a shirt, shoes, shorts, and a pith helmet into
a pillow case. Blankets were in the closet. I paused a moment to pick
up a silver dollar and Band-Aids from the dresser. While Gregg kept a
lookout at the car, Bob and I rummaged through the other cottages,
some of which were burning and giving off an eerie glow. All the garments and blankets we could find were stashed in the car. There was
no mosquito repellent and no food—the commissary had been blown
up with the hit on the hotel kitchen.

Dick Arvidson had fired up the generator at the radio station and
sent the last message from Guam to Pan Am, San Francisco, reading "GUAM UNDER ATTACK STOP SO FAR NO COMPANY CASUALTIES

STOP LANDING IMMINENT STOP GOOD-BYE." Then he smashed the equipment.

Thomas whispered to his companions, "I think we'd better get out of here. I feel queasy about this place. I smell Japs." What Thomas did not know was that the Japanese would shortly land less than a mile away.

Loading up more clothes and, from the ruins of the Marine barracks, two boxes of desperately needed mosquito nets, the men fled again to the mountain refuge. Later that evening, Gregg carried messages down to Colonel MacNulty, apprising him of the refugees' conditions. By moonlight, Gregg refueled his car and took a long-needed shower. Thoroughly exhausted, he lay down near the back of the Marine firing range at 2:30 a.m., and fell into a deep sleep.

At first light on Tuesday morning, Navy personnel continued to repair the sabotaged telephone lines, restoring communication among the major concentrations of survivors. The native telephone operators had fled for the boonies, and Navy men filled their posts on the switchboards. Expecting an invasion at any time, the Pomeroy contractors waited on the bluffs of the Orote Peninsula, ready to drive their large trucks over the cliff. Included were some of the largest trucks in the world, the ten-cubic-yard Euclid General Motors dump trucks being used to build the breakwater. Dynamite was planted next to the oil tanks on Cabras Island. By nightfall, most of the Insular Guard were housed, along with most of the Guam Insular Force, in the Agana Armory and Dorn Hall.[43]

The second day ended like the first. As night fell under a heavy overcast with intermittent showers, a menacing darkness descended upon Guam. For two days, the raids had continued, with attacks on every military Libugon station, but to no avail. More than one man remarked, "The safest place to be was where they were aiming!"[44] Numerous Japanese transports and warships could be seen offshore near Agat and Agana. On the eastern coast, more transports could be seen near Pago and Talofofo Bays.

CHAPTER 3

The Japanese Invasion

By failing to prepare, you are preparing to fail.

—*Benjamin Franklin*

The Insular Patrol, under the Marine's Sgt. George Shane, prepared positions behind sandbag barricades, ditches, and overturned benches in the Plaza de España in front of Government House. On the far side of the kiosk and across the plaza, the native Insular Guard placed their three machine guns in sandbagged foxholes. The entire defense of Guam lay in the hands of some eighty members of the Guam Insular Force and eleven members of the Insular Patrol under Shane's command.[1] The Marines at Sumay, under the command of Lt. Col. William K. MacNulty, would never mount a defense against the attack, most heeding Maj. Donald Spicer's admonition to flee into the jungle surrounding their camp.

At 2:30 a.m., 10 December 1941, four hundred men of the elite Imperial Japanese Army's naval assault force from Saipan landed on Agat Beach, two miles south of Sumay. Under the command of Captain Hiromu Hayashi,[2] the force pushed immediately toward the Sumay barracks. Duped by poor intelligence that 1,500 Marines and heavy artillery were on Guam, the assault troops were to serve as a diversion while the main force of five thousand waded ashore at Tumon Bay, just north of Agana. Designated as the Imperial Japanese Army's South Seas Detachment, the entire invasion force of 5,500 men was under the command of Major General Tomitaro Horii.[3] Simultaneously, small companies of soldiers landed at Merizo in the south and in the Talofofo Bay area on the east coast.

Less than thirty minutes later, an open platform jitney carrying seventeen natives departed Agana fleeing northward for Yigo on the upper part of the island. At Tumon, the jitney intersected the main Japanese landing force. The Japanese fired mass volleys into the exposed seats, and the soldiers ripped into the passengers with bayonets. Thirteen civilians were killed and three seriously wounded. One man, hanging onto the rear of the jitney, jumped off at the first shot and escaped straight up the hill beside the road.[4]

Forging inland from the landing area at Tumon Bay (Tamuning Beach), the main Japanese landing force seized two sailors passing by on the way to see their girlfriends, earning them the dubious distinction of becoming the first Americans captured on Guam and the first Americans captured in *combat* by the Japanese.[5]

Facing the Japanese force of more than five thousand soldiers, Governor George McMillin earlier decided a defensive position, however futile, was to be taken at the plaza. This decision enabled the entire island's military to effect a surrender as a single entity rather than to have smaller units fight and, most likely, be slaughtered. Planning to surrender proved a wise course of action, as it kept losses to a minimum. McMillin instructed the power plant manager to blow the steam whistle three times to signal a surrender when the time seemed right, but the Japanese invaders swept by the plant, isolating it from contact.

Selected to defend the plaza were twelve men of the Marine's Insular Patrol, a few Marines from Sumay, a few men from the Navy administrative offices, some survivors of the *Penguin*, and some eighty men of the Guam Insular Force. Equipped with a total of three machine guns, half a dozen pistols, and fewer than fifty of the island's obsolete bolt-action Springfield 03 rifles (stamped "not to be fired"), fewer than one hundred men prepared to fight the 5,500 invaders.

RM2c Bob Epperson,[6] a survivor of the *Penguin* and assigned to patrol in the San Antonio district between the plaza and the beach, found himself restless and unable to sleep. Epperson reported for duty an hour early. As he departed for his patrol area about 2:30 a.m., BMC Robert Bruce Lane told him that, despite an earlier report of heavy gunfire in the district by Tumon Beach, the area was safe—it was probably "some of your drunken *Penguin* sailors shooting at the moon." Unknown at the time, six sailors from the USS *Penguin* defending Recreation Beach had already surrendered after a short firefight, only to be wired together and bayoneted to death on Tumon Bay.[7]

About three o'clock Radioman Epperson stopped a pickup driven by a retired Navy chief who reported the large Japanese landing force. The Japs had raked his pickup with gunfire and bayoneted two of his family before he broke free. Epperson immediately broke down the door of a grocery store and used the telephone to call his command post—only to be told to "stand by." He now saw the approaching Japanese, sweeping the streets in front of them with machine-gun fire. Epperson, headed toward the plaza, stopped at the power plant to again call and alert Chief Lane. Again told to "stand by," Epperson replied, "Stand by, bullshit! We're getting out of here!" Taking FN Bill Reed, USN, with him, he ran for the plaza. Reporting to Chief Lane, Epperson was again told to stand by. At that exact moment, the Japanese entered the plaza.

On the plaza the Insular Guard and the remaining Insular Patrol waited for the attack. "On a scale of one to ten," said Sergeant Shane, "our pucker factor at that instant was fifteen." Among the patrolmen was Pfc. Harris Chuck, USMC,[8] a 1936 graduate of Sullivan High School on the north side of Chicago. Trained by the Ford Motor Company as a mechanic in the depths of the Depression, he landed an assignment with Litzinger Motor Company in downtown Chicago, the largest auto dealer in the Midwest. A few months later, the siren lure of better pay and closeness to home brought Chuck to a north side dealer, but within a few months, that dealership closed and his paycheck bounced. After a temporary job with the U.S. Post Office and a stint with the CCC (Civilian Conservation Corps), Chuck joined the Marines on 6 November 1940.

After boot camp, Chuck was assigned to Guam, eventually joining the Insular Patrol in the late spring and garnering his private first class stripe in August 1941. From the poverty of the Depression to a life of luxury and no cares on Guam, Chuck felt he "was standing in high cotton."

"As the invasion began," said Chuck,

> Captain Todd ordered me to take some men uphill to the motor pool and armory—we were to destroy everything. I commandeered one of the vans and along with Bill Bomar and Hal Burt we headed up the hill.[9] As we entered the motor pool, we grabbed a few sledgehammers and began to smash the engines, cracked the blocks, and made certain the trucks and cars were unusable. At the armory I realized I didn't have the key. Without a second thought, I unholstered my .45 pistol and shot the lock off. We then soaked the place with gasoline and lit it off. We climbed back into the van and headed back to the plaza. We all knew we had no chance of survival. I guess it was at this time that Bomar and Burt decided to flee to the boondocks and jumped out of the van. They were to be caught a short distance away from the plaza by a Jap patrol.[10]

In the predawn darkness the Japanese started to infiltrate into the downtown streets of Agana, approaching the Plaza de España from the north and northwest.[11] The Japanese advanced shoulder to shoulder in the narrow streets, sharpened bayonets pointing at the defenders. The sound of the Insular Guard's three machine guns broke the fearful silence as the guns raked the Japanese front and took a fearful toll.[12] The Japanese advance was halted twice. On the third wave of the attack, the flashes from the guard's machine guns were answered by a fusillade of rifle fire from the advancing Japanese. The machine guns fell silent. The surviving men of the Insular Guard began to withdraw toward the kiosk on the west side of the plaza as the Japanese brought up their machine guns and mobile artillery to begin the final assault.[13] The slow-firing Japanese machine gun raked the plaza, its distinctively slow *burp-burp-burp* sound echoing back from the cathedral walls. A pack howitzer was wheeled into place across from the administration building as the sound of gunfire reached a crescendo. The Japanese began to flank the defenders from the south side of the plaza.

The Navy's Lt. Graham P. Bright attempted to join the defenders in the plaza but was caught by a platoon of Japanese soldiers as he drove his car down the hill from the

Officers' Club.[14] Wounded by gunfire, he was dragged from the car and bayoneted to death. From the back of Government House, CMM Malvern Smoot and a civilian, John Klugel, attempted to join the others on the plaza side. Running into heavy rifle fire, Smoot returned fire with his .45 and hit a few Japanese soldiers. Both men were cut down in a hail of bullets. A Japanese officer stepped forward and beheaded Smoot's crumpled body while others tore Klugel's body apart with bayonets.[15]

Joseph Blaha and Lyle Eads made the same attempt and were shot and left for dead by the Japanese.[16] It was standard policy for the Japanese soldiers to bayonet all bodies lying on the battlefield, to make certain that all enemy soldiers were dead. After the surrender, Eads, who had feigned death, rose and raised his hands in surrender just as a Japanese soldier began to bayonet Blaha. The two men were later sent by the Japanese to the hospital for treatment.

As the furious battle raged in the plaza, the defenders moved behind hedges and trees and fired back. "Firing my .45 automatic blindly at gun flashes," said Epperson, "my twenty-two rounds were soon gone. We were ordered to retreat into the Insular barracks building. As we rose and ran toward the barracks, one of our men, 'Gwinnie,'[17] was machine gunned through the ankles. Two other men grabbed him by the elbows and dragged him to safety. Inside, I field stripped my .45 and threw it out the window."

Epperson and Pfc. Bob Hinkle[18] tried to escape out the back door. At the same time, they saw two men come out of a small store across the alley, apparently with the same idea. A machine gun opened up, killing them both. Epperson and Hinkle ducked back inside.[19] Suddenly a car horn sounded three long blasts.[20] Within seconds there was silence. The Japanese assumed that it was a signal to cease fire or that the Americans wished to surrender. The gunfire quickly ebbed, and the silence seemed to last an eternity. The sound of the horn was taken by the defenders as a signal to retreat. On orders of Captain Todd, most of the natives had fled into the Insular Guard barracks to seek protection behind the barracks' solid concrete walls.

Inside the barracks the men pressed against the walls in an eerie silence. No sound of gunfire could be heard. With images of the Japanese rage, brutalities, and savagery visited upon the people of Nanking on their minds, every man assumed his own death was imminent. A minute later, the Japanese spotted a few men attempting to flee and again opened fire. Within a few minutes, all firing stopped. Again there was silence in the predawn darkness.

Standing next to a Japanese officer, an interpreter lifted a bullhorn and called across the plaza, "You are surrounded. You must surrender. Captain! Come forward!" In the short battle for Guam, seventeen American military men and Chamorran insular guardsmen lay dead, along with an estimated fifty to eighty civilians. Estimates of Japanese losses were two hundred men and at least two planes. In Governor McMillin's postwar report,[21] he summarized the action:

> About 0400 on Wednesday, 10 December, I was informed by the
> watch that flares had been seen in the vicinity of the beach to the

eastward of Agana (Recreation Beach, Dungca's Beach), and it was thought landing operations were in progress. There were no defenses at this point, or at any other point on the island. Orders were immediately sent to all stations to carry out the mission assigned. About 0445, shooting was heard in the San Antonio district (east of the Plaza), and fires were observed. The Insular Force Guard took up defense positions in the Plaza, with no equipment except a few .30-caliber machine guns and rifles. The Japanese approached rapidly through the San Antonio district, and approached the Plaza on the narrow street alongside the Naval Hospital and the cathedral. The Insular Force Guard stood their ground, and opened up a fire with machine guns and rifles hot enough to halt the invading force for a short time. The situation was simply hopeless, resistance had been carried to the limit.

Confirming the sequence of events, McMillin then states the car horn blasts were not a prearranged signal, but all seemed to interpret the signal as a cease-fire order. Commander Giles, sensing that the power plant horn was destroyed, wisely used a car horn to indicate the prearranged surrender.

"A few seconds later," continued Giles, "firing again commenced behind the Government House but quickly subsided.[22] The Japanese shouted across the Plaza from the Cathedral, 'Send over your captain.'[23] Commander Donald T. Giles, the aide for civil affairs to the Governor, and Chief Boatswain's Mate Robert Bruce Lane, U.S. Navy, stepped out. They were marched through the San Antonio district, and made contact with the Commander of the Naval landing force, returning about a half hour later to the Plaza with the Commander."[24]

In the predawn darkness, the plaza defenders laid down their weapons. The shadowy figures of the few remaining Americans on the plaza slowly rose, one by one, with their arms reaching upward. Those inside, including some of the Marines of the Insular Patrol, were ordered to come out into the plaza. From the darkness, the Japanese soldiers stood tall. Raising their rifles to high port, bayonets fixed and screaming, "Banzai! Banzai! Banzai!" the Japanese soldiers charged across the plaza to surround the new prisoners.

Epperson recalled that "the Japanese Commander ordered us to throw down our weapons and to come out with our hands in the air. As we came out, it was just half light. We could see and hear the Japanese approaching. In full camouflage and split-toed shoes, completely covered with netting and foliage, the Japanese appeared nonhuman, alien like—their screaming increasing as they came toward us. If they were trying to frighten us, they were very successful."

Desperately wanting to live but fearing a painful injury more than death, they awaited their fate. Whispering "Good luck!" to each other from throats dry with terror, the young Americans were thankful the darkness hid their fear. Commands shouted in Japanese were incomprehensible to them, and the men were jabbed with bayonet points, shoved, punched, and savagely beaten as they were pushed to the grassy area to the left front of Government House.

"I had no idea what would happen," said Harris Chuck. "I thought they were going to kill us all. They corralled us into three ranks, shoving and pushing and poking bayonets at everyone. For some reason, a Jap soldier ripped his bayonet into Private Kauffman. He was in a rank right in front of me. He dropped to the ground—dead. Much later, when we were marched away, they let him lie there with his insides hanging out."[25] Epperson, standing in the small area in front of the Insular Guard barracks, observed, "They made gestures with hands and bayonets to disrobe. If a man was slow, they would flick their bayonet and cut off the buttons. A Marine, Private Kauffman, standing next to me on my right, apparently was too slow so a Japanese slashed him in the stomach with his bayonet. I heard a gasp then saw his intestines go flying by as he fell face forward."

Not every man in the Agana plaza area was aware of the surrender. "The day of the invasion, Dick Ballinger[26] and I were guarding the back gate of the palace [Governor's House]," said Pfc. Garth Dunn of the Insular Patrol. "We didn't get the word about the surrender, but it was obvious when the firing stopped. As we headed towards the front of the palace, I helped another Navy yeoman strip his pistol and threw the parts into the fish pond. With a round stuck in the chamber, he could have started the shooting again. We ran into a group of Japs, threw our arms in the air, and were hustled out toward the plaza. Dick was slashed in the back with a bayonet. I was still in pretty clean Khakis with my sun helmet on, so they threw me in with a group of officers. A Jap soldier charged toward me, bayonet fixed and aimed at my head. I thought he was going to kill me but he just nicked my ear as he knocked the sun helmet off my head. Scared the hell out of me."

"After we were undressed," said Epperson, "we left all our clothing on the walkway and were herded through a break in the hedge to the center of the plaza. The person in front of me was a little slow so a Jap Marine stuck him in the buttocks with his bayonet. That speeded me up, then I heard the man behind me gasp as he received the same treatment. We were made to sit down on the wet grass in a circle—naked as jaybirds—and wait. It was still not full light. We had long since decided that we were about to die, or as we said, 'Our soul belonged to God but the Emperor owned our ass.'"

Controversy surrounds the death of Bomar and Burt on the plaza. Epperson stated he witnessed the decapitation of both men, but no corroboration or confirming witness to either death has been found. Pfc. Paul Meletis from the Sumay Marine barracks,[27] in an affidavit taken upon his release at the end of the war, stated Bomar was decapitated, but he does not say he was a witness. All interviewed men agree Bomar was decapitated, but none could confirm the location. Meletis stated the decapitation was by Lieutenant Nayama. Sergeant Shane and others recalled that after they were in the cathedral for a few days, "the Japs brought us outside to watch two natives being beheaded. This was after warning us not to try to escape. Tried to impress us again . . . and they did!" The extreme emotional stress experienced by the men could explain the unresolved controversy regarding Bomar and Burt.[28]

At the naval hospital, Captain Lineberry informed the assembled personnel that the island had surrendered. Under Japanese orders, Lineberry moved all the patients to Ward Two, clearing the remainder of the hospital for Japanese. Twenty hospital corps-men were retained by the Japanese to service the hospital. Ten worked in the galley, six in the laundry, and four in the wards. All twenty men were to remain in the hospital until the evening before departure to Japan.[29] The balance of the staff were marched directly to the cathedral. "A number of men were retained at the hospital," said Al Mosher, "as the Japs deemed them necessary to treat the wounded and tend to anyone that was really sick. Two days later, the remaining bodies of the Americans killed in the invasion were gathered up and placed in a shed behind the main hospital." The following day, the American dead were buried together near the beach.[30]

By the morning of the invasion, most of the Marines at the Sumay barracks had scattered to the jungle, a few had fled to Agana, and the remainder had stayed in the wreckage of the camp. Contrary to the official postwar action report by Captain McMillin, none of the Marines had joined Lieutenant Colonel MacNulty in the rifle butts. MacNulty had waved men away during the bombing, shouting that "they would draw fire from the strafing planes."[31] On the second day of the bombing, 9 December, the Marines were informed by Major Spicer that the island would not be defended. MacNulty countermanded the order and directed Spicer to set up a small defense force at the road junction leading into the Marine base. As this order was being implemented, MacNulty was directly informed by the governor's office not to resist but to prepare to surrender.

As dawn broke the remaining Marines were assembled, and the bugler, Dewey C. Danielson, sounded retreat.[32] The men, with tears welling in their eyes, lowered and buried the American flag. Major Spicer told the men to quietly await the Japanese. Within minutes soldiers of the Japanese naval assault units streamed into camp from the Sumay road. Still expecting a slaughter, the men evacuated the barracks, hands raised above their heads. Like the captives at the plaza, they were immediately stripped naked and forced to sit in a circle on the adjoining golf course. About one hour later, the few officers were permitted to return to their quarters to retrieve a few personal items. All were transported by truck to Agana, where the officers were taken to the Sick Officers Quarters (SOQ) at the U.S. Naval Hospital. Here, they met all the other officers captured by the Japanese, except for McMillin and Giles, who were to remain in their offices until 8:30 that evening. The enlisted men were placed in the cathedral.[33]

For some of the Marines who evaded capture at Sumay, their period of freedom would last only a few hours. Others would evade capture for days. Typical of the exploits was that of Private Barnett.[34] As the men gathered to surrender in front of the barracks, Barnett moved off into the underbrush, planning to hold out until rescued by the American fleet. "The morning of the first aerial attack," he said, "was pure chaos and confusion. After the attack, MacNulty told me to take his truck—a twelve foot, stake body, International K7—and wait near the gravel pit, about three miles south-east of Sumay. Major Spicer advised me to 'stay out of the way.' The only person I saw for two days was the bugler, Dewey Danielson, who checked up on me and brought me a couple of sandwiches."

On the morning of the invasion, Barnett was in his truck when he was told by a passing Marine that the island had surrendered and that he was to go to the barracks to surrender. As some thirty-five to forty men began to assemble, Barnett recalled, "I decided to simply hide out until rescued. I felt certain the Japs were going to kill all of us." In midafternoon, with four other Marines joining him, Barnett drove the truck toward Mount Almagosa, intent on hiding out until the American fleet arrived. As they headed uphill, about fifty Japanese soldiers suddenly stood up on both sides of the road and aimed their rifles at them. "This was one ambush we were not going to get out of, so I stopped and we raised our hands."

Nineteen-year-old Barnett, his truck now overflowing with Japanese soldiers, was forced to drive back toward the Sumay barracks. The other four men walked.[35] Two guards were in the front seat with him and two others hung from the running boards on each side. "With the back crammed with Jap soldiers," said Barnett, "I started to think that, since I was soon to die, I'd kill as many of these Japs as possible. About a mile ahead lay a curve and I would drive over the cliff. As I started to shift gears, the Jap guard next to me stopped my hand, indicating I was not to shift out of first gear. I could never get up speed to kill the bastards, so we arrived in camp some twenty minutes later."

The five men were placed in front of the Marine barracks, stripped of their clothes, watches, wallets, rings, pens, and anything of value. The earlier captives had already departed for Agana. "We sat outside, stark naked on the grass, while they continued looting the barracks. Under the burning sun, we simply sat in a circle, praying for something to happen to end the tension. The total lack of water simply added to the terror. Just before dusk, we were given some clothes, taken inside and spent the night in what had been the pool room."

The following morning, 11 December 1941, the men with Barnett were taken across the golf course and lined up against the fence near the Pan Am station. In front of them were two machine guns and a firing squad. The officer in charge shouted a sequence of orders, and the Japanese raised their rifles and cleared a round into each machine gun. At the final command, the soldiers charged toward them, bayonets fixed and screaming "Banzai!" at the top of their lungs. "Just as they came within a few feet," said Barnett, "they turned their rifles sideways and struck each of us in the chest. We were sent sprawling against the fence and onto the ground." The sadistic ritual was repeated three times.

When the Japanese prepared for the fourth time, a new set of orders was shouted by the officer. The soldiers removed clips of ammunition from small leather boxes on their belts and loaded their rifles. "Now we knew the end was coming," said Barnett. At that instant, a Japanese soldier came running across the field, spoke briefly with the officer, and an order was given to stand down. The officer departed with the runner. Twenty minutes later, the officer returned and addressed the prisoners in almost perfect English.

"'We have decided not to kill you if you will be slaves. If you agree, your lives will be spared. If you do not agree, you will die now.' We all nodded our agreement. The officer continued, 'If you are ever unhappy, we will gladly complete at any time.'" Barnett and the four others were taken to the small city jail (not the main jail), convinced they were the sole survivors of the invasion.

Next to the jail was the island's only cold storage unit, now being systematically looted of all the contents. When the Japanese discovered some canned peaches, the prisoners were told to "sample a half peach" to see if it was poisoned. When Barnett and his fellow Marines did not die, the rest of the cans were removed by the Japanese. All that remained were twenty-one cases of butter—eighteen-inch cubes weighing about fifty pounds each. The Japanese hauled them into the cell and stacked them along the wall. A tropical jail cell is not a refrigerator, and within hours melting butter covered the floor, seeping into every crevice and saturating the men's clothes. The cell floor had a gentle slope to the center, and the oily ooze made sleep nearly impossible as the floor became a slippery slope that seemed vertical. The butter was all they were to eat until the night before they left Guam.

A few weeks later the Japanese publicly announced that they were taking all the prisoners to Japan. They made it clear that any Americans left on the island would be killed on sight. On 6 January, Sgt. John Henry Lyles and Pfc. John Henry "Little" Jones[36] surrendered and were shoved into Private Barnett's cell. "It was the first indication we had that others had survived," said Barnett.

Two days later, on the afternoon of the eighth, the seven men were taken to the cathedral. Weakened by starvation, Barnett had to be carried inside. For Barnett and his friends, it was "exhilarating to discover that all these men were alive!" Barnett's buddies had been certain they were the sole survivors. That evening, Barnett was given a tiny potato, his first food in almost thirty days.

On the day of the invasion, *Penguin* survivor S1 Edwin J. Settles hid in the boonies north of Agana with his Navy buddy, S1 Walter "Maggie" Magelssen.[37] When the

Japanese planes flew over, they fired their .45 pistol and .30-caliber Springfield at them. The planes chased the men, strafing the road until they disappeared into the jungle. That night, a local Chamorro, a Mr. White, volunteered to hide Settles and Magelssen. Other natives made similar offers to many other men. Hiding out seemed a logical idea. Settles assumed it would take only fourteen days for the great American fleet to retake the island.

The lightning fast attack at Agana had given the Japanese complete control before dawn. Quickly raising their flag in the plaza, the Japanese surrounded the armory with field cannon and machine guns. A number of Japanese surrounded the large American flag now lying on the plaza, lighting it with their flashlights. It was a signal to the planes flying overhead that the fighting had ceased. The planes returned to Saipan without further incident. Shortly before 7:00 a.m. at the plaza, Governor McMillin signed a document surrendering Guam. Within the hour, captured officers and non-commissioned officers (NCOs) were dispatched to all known sites where the civilians and military had withdrawn, including the Sumay barracks and Piti Navy Yard.

At the plaza the Japanese did a thorough search of all the clothing. When Epperson was allowed to put his clothes back on, he discovered that his can of fifty cigarettes had not been stolen. "I passed them around to friends," he said, "and realizing my addiction could trouble me in captivity, I smoked my last cigarette that morning." With little water and a boiling sun, it was a long, uncomfortable day. In the late afternoon, the men were finally sent back into the Insular Guard barracks.

As word of the surrender spread, sailors and Marines returned to Agana, surrendered, and were placed with those already captured. In a reaction to the quiescent fear, the Marines started a lighthearted banter among themselves, laughing often at the appearance of the "bandy legged Japs" who carried rifles that were taller than they were. A Japanese officer continued to demand to know where the rest of the "1,500 Marines and the big guns" were located. The Japanese still firmly believed there was a much larger defensive garrison, which would have justified the massive size of the invasion force relative to the small number of Americans.[38] By evening, the truth became obvious.

In Barrigada on the eastern coast of the island opposite Agana, Johnny Ploke continued to hide out with his wife's relatives. Japanese soldiers forced Beatrice Perez Ploke to call out for her husband. Fearing for her life, Ploke walked out of the jungle with his hands raised over his head. After being stripped and searched, he was taken directly to the cathedral.[39]

At dawn on invasion day, Wednesday, 10 December, Pan Am station manager Charles Gregg awoke to learn the Japanese had landed and were nearby. Dispatched by Colonel MacNulty to carry a message to the men on Almagosa, he joined with cable station employees Sidney MacMichael and Patrick O'Connor and departed for Mount Almagosa. He passed the Marines as they started to blow up their ammunition dump. On the road Gregg saw hundreds of Chamorros pulling overladen carts, a few military personnel, and numerous contractor's men heading into the boondocks. The contractor's men said Agana had fallen, but they did not have confirmation. From the top of the mountain, groups of men carrying boxes of food headed into the jungles, dispersing as quickly as possible.

By 11:30 a.m. Lt. Dean Morgan had passed the word to both the Marines at Sumay and the civilians on Almagosa that the governor had surrendered the island. All Americans were ordered to report for immediate surrender to the Japanese.[40] Clark Eldridge, manager of the Pomeroy Construction Company, ordered the company's huge dump trucks driven over the cliff on Orote, the fuel on Cobras Island set afire, and disposal of all weapons.

About 10:00 a.m. on the morning of the invasion, Jim Thomas, the twenty-five-year-old assistant manager for Pan Am's Guam station, saw a car coming up the mountain bearing a white flag, its horn constantly honking. The car stopped where groups of natives had gathered and met up with the Pan Am group at the two-thousand-foot level. "A young Marine sergeant climbed out and said, 'I am Sergeant [unknown] of the U.S. Marine Corps,'" Thomas recalled. He and the others listened intently. "We are here on behalf of the Japanese commander. I've been instructed to tell you to surrender now and you will be safe." Reading from a written note, he continued, "You will be able to return home on a POW exchange. Cooperate with us now and surrender, or you will be shot on sight."

The Marine sergeant told them to go down to the golf course in Agana. The men briefly discussed the possibility of hiding out until they were rescued or sailing to another island. "Bob Vaughn," said Thomas, "one of our best mechanics, was an ex-sailor with a very 'down to earth' attitude. He suggested that it was a choice ' . . . between the Japs and their guns and the mosquitoes. We'll never kill the mosquitoes. I'd rather take my chances with the Japs.' We voted to surrender."

The men climbed into two sedans and proceeded down the mountain toward Agat.[41] They passed large numbers of natives along the road, all crying. As they approached the Harmon Road intersection to head toward Agana, they came upon a squad of Japanese soldiers marching in the same direction. "Max honked the horn and the startled Japs 'jumped' and swiftly surrounded the cars," said Thomas. "I remember my first impression that they were so damn short. Their guns were bigger than they were."[42]

The Japanese Marines, still wet from having waded through the surf in the invasion, had dilated eyes, noted Charles Gregg, and appeared to be under the influence of drugs. The eleven men were taken from the cars and lined up at the ditch on the edge of the road facing a Japanese machine gun. A car, speeding from Agana and billowing dust behind, came to a stop amid the crowd of Japanese and prisoners. Gregg was surprised to realize he knew one of the Japanese officers. Out of the car stepped two Japanese officers in white Navy uniforms with epaulets on their shoulders and wearing Navy swords. A third officer got out without as much brass, but he was still well decorated. It was "Ben Cook," the owner of the very popular bar and Marine hangout in Sumay. Having once befriended Cook, Gregg and the others, although surprised, were relieved to see him. After much discussion among the officers, the local commander gave the order to stand down, and the Japanese stepped back. Cook told the men to get back into their car and follow his truck. In the back of the truck was a mounted machine gun.

The men were taken to the Pomeroy Construction building adjacent to the Marine barracks. Despite the damage there, the utilities were functioning, and the men were allowed to take showers. Again, they were lined up, counted, and searched, and rosters of names and occupations were recorded by the Japanese. For the rest of the afternoon, they were kept on the lawn facing the barracks. Fed a ball of rice for dinner, the men were dispatched into the partially destroyed Marine recreation hall and spent the night on the cement floor.

The following morning all were fed a cup of rice and a small piece of fish. At 11:00 a.m. the men, now totaling fifty-three, were quickly hauled outside, counted, loaded on trucks, and taken to the main jail in Agana. While overcrowded (forty beds), the jail had ample sanitary facilities, and the food was deemed adequate for the interned civilians. On Sunday morning, 14 December, the Japanese moved the civilians from the jail to the cathedral, where they joined the Marine and Navy personnel. Next door was the armory, housing the native enlisted men. One toilet now served more than five hundred men. On Monday, Commander Giles received permission to move all the officers and ten of the civilians to the second floor of the Catholic recreation hall. Believing the request was made by MacNulty rather than Giles, Gregg said, "MacNulty had to argue like hell to get us permission to stay as [the] Japanese could not understand how high-ranking military people could be friendly with civilians!"

Checking the assorted rosters, Gregg determined that two Pan Am men had died (Jesus C. Cruz and Ignacio Mendiola) and two had been wounded.[43] Comparing notes with Lt. Dean Morgan and Dr. Jim Eppley of the U.S. Naval Hospital, they estimated fifteen Americans and an undetermined number of natives had died. Rumors were rife, but no factual reports of massacres were known at this time.[44]

About 3:00 p.m. on the day of invasion, the last large group of seven men marched into Agana led by Lt. Cdr. Oliver Gaines, commanding officer of the Piti Navy Yard. Most of the men of the yard remained hidden in the hills. Most of the contractors and Pan Am employees had already gathered on the Agana golf course. By evening, all the captured military personnel in Agana were jammed into the Insular Guard barracks, and the smell inside was fetid. Each group took roll calls of their members to determine who was dead, injured, or in hiding.

Other than the short fight in the plaza, the only resistance to the entire Japanese invasion was by the six *Penguin* sailors on Dungca's Beach. For Guam, the fighting was over. Guam had surrendered. More than a dozen men remained hidden out in the boondocks, fervently awaiting rescue by the U.S. Navy.

CHAPTER 4

The Japanese Occupy Guam

The surrendered men uniformly noted an almost complete failure of military command by the officers after the surrender. George McMillin was not considered an officer in the actual military command, and as the governor he reasonably expected to receive diplomatic privilege and immunity. The ranking military officer, Lt. Col. William K. MacNulty of the Sumay Marine detachment, refused to accept command when he arrived in Agana after the surrender. To many of his subordinates, this was not a surprise because he was considered a "coward, a rake and a disgrace to the Marine Corps."[1] His perceived cowardice, particularly during the initial bombings and the subsequent invasion, was apparently well known to every Marine. Cdr. Donald T. Giles therefore became the senior ranking officer.

The intentions of the Japanese as to the disposition of the prisoners was extremely confusing. "As it got lighter," said RM Bob Epperson, "there was a lot of activity with the Japanese troops. They would line us up facing a firing squad—then sit us down again. Always with machine guns and angry-looking gunners sighting in on us. Then they would line us up again. We just knew it would be the end. Again, they would send us back to our circle."

One of the men on the plaza, BMC Robert O'Brien,[2] was fluent in Japanese and his wife was Japanese. He had overheard much of the Japanese conversations and later told everyone that the landing force commander wanted to "execute us because we had killed about two hundred of his troops." However, the fleet commander said they were to be taken as prisoners. "We were pleased the latter won the discussion," said Epperson.[3]

The day prior to the invasion, the staff at the Libugon station took the emergency radio equipment up onto Mount Tenyo.[4] They remained well hidden in a canyon on the far side of the island away from Agana during the invasion. The radio maintenance man from the station in Agana, RM1 George Tweed was assigned to ensure that the emergency radios were working. He came up to the hidden cave but stated he had to go back for extra parts, and took the only walkie talkie with him. "We never saw him again, and we never got the radio on the air," said RM2 Harold Joslin.[5]

On the day of the invasion, the Japanese swarmed over the mountains hunting for all the Americans. The Japanese were scouring the ridge above the cave when the men decided "it was time to surrender." RM2 Merkle Smith tied his skivvy shirt to a stick, and with raised hands, the men walked into the open. The Japanese quickly surrounded them and, with bayonet prods and the usual shouts, made it clear they were to go to the top of the ridge, where they were stripped naked. The Japanese commander wanted to know if there were others hiding in the same area, but the men merely shook their heads no. It was obvious he thought the men were lying. The Japanese lobbed mortar shells and mass fired their rifles down toward the hiding place. A few moment later, the Japanese soldiers climbed down to the cave area, retrieved the stored food, and allowed the prisoners to eat.[6]

━━━━━━━━━━━━

For two days the captured men (including the detained Guamanian civilians and Insular Guard) remained in Dorn Hall, the Insular Guard barracks, the small jail, and the Catholic cathedral—relatively well fed except for the men in the jail and the Insular Guard barracks. The Japanese persisted in counting the men, day and night, over and over again. Regular sleep became a luxury, but little brutality was exhibited. What was not known by the defenders of the plaza was that a number of men were missing—and were presumed by the Japanese to be hiding out on the island. Most of those hiding out on the island assumed they were the only survivors.

The guards from the elite Japanese navy assault force were replaced on the morning of the eleventh by ordinary army ranks, and abuse became standard fare. During the nights, the men were now required to stand at attention anytime a Japanese soldier entered the hall, regardless of his rank. On the third day, Friday, 12 December, almost all the surrendered American military personnel were moved to the Catholic church and the adjoining parochial hall, and the food ration was dramatically reduced. During the next three weeks, weight losses of thirty pounds a man were common. Some of the "old-timers," with native girlfriends or extensive local contacts, had food smuggled in for their consumption. The willingness to share became unknown, and inexorably, it became "each man for himself."

Within three days the Japanese began a determined effort to find the missing Americans. Natives were told, "If we find that you have aided them in any way, we will kill your entire family." Despite the threats, the Chamorros continued to hide the men, although they would rather have had them leave. Patrols of hundreds of Japanese soldiers scoured the hills and jungles seeking to find the missing soldiers.

"We understood the danger," said S1 Ed Settles, who remained hidden north of Agana with his buddy Maggie Magelssen. Fearing retribution upon their friends, on the first night of occupation, friendly Chamorros had reluctantly guided them to the road, and the two men walked into Agana: "We walked right past some guards and entered the office of the Jap commander. He was surprised as hell that we managed to even get into his office. It was obvious he was quite upset with his staff and appeared to 'chew them out.' They questioned us and threatened to cut off our heads if we lied. I lied anyway since I was never going to tell them I shot at two of their planes. One of the Japs reared back and swung his sword right at my neck. As it swished by I thought,

'Wow, that sword was sharp! He cut off my head and I didn't feel it!'" After a few hours of questioning, the two men were taken to the cathedral.[7]

On 13 December, three days after the surrender, the War Department in Washington acknowledged the loss of communication with Guam, listing the Marines and all naval personnel as "missing in action."[8]

Under the protection of the naval assault troops for the first two days of occupation, the prisoners received two to three meals each day, although the portions were far smaller than normal. As none were performing manual labor, the rations were considered adequate and nutritious. However, the high humidity and heat, extreme body odors, and ever-present swarms of mosquitoes made life extremely uncomfortable for most men. In a florid accounting of the misery, EM2 Ed Hale described the mosquitoes as "microscopic" and in swarms of "skillions," particularly during the nights. Often called "no-see-ems," the tiny mosquitoes hovered around eyes and ears of the men during the day.

On Tuesday, 16 December, the Japanese gave permission for a number of officers to return to their homes for supplies. All found their homes looted and most with Japanese living inside. A few managed to collect extra uniforms, but none selected any winter gear, an oversight that would later be regretted.

As with almost every group of men, there were mixed acts of generosity, selfishness, greed, stupidity, and arrogance. Most Navy officers and chiefs did little to create an atmosphere of cooperation, seeking personal comfort over the needs of their ranks. The exceptions were far and few between. A number of men, particularly the men of the *Penguin*, were without sufficient clothing or the necessary sundries of daily life. When the Japanese brought in three hundred hammocks from the naval stores in Agana, BMC Robert Bruce Lane merely had them dumped into a pile and said, "Help yourself." Many men, already with adequate bedding, grabbed extra hammocks, while others were unable to secure any at all. One civilian had five quilts and a hammock while the man next to him slept on the bare concrete floor. The majority of civilian contractors refused to acknowledge they were in the "same boat" as the military personnel and insisted they deserved special consideration, asserting it was "not their war."[9]

The differences in lifestyle among enlisted men of lower ranks, noncommissioned officers, and commissioned officers was enormous, each jealously guarding their perquisites. This behavior was considered normal in the prewar years. From the beginning of captivity, the senior ranking enlisted man, Chief Lane, insisted on a separate room for himself and selected friends. He was immediately perceived by the lower ranks as having failed to evenly distribute the small rations of food. For the captives, Lane's inability to treat all ranks fairly within the prison environment was quickly seen as tyrannical and made Lane a scorned and thoroughly disliked man by almost all of the lower ranks.

Despite their captivity, few men thought the war would last more than a few months. Confidence remained very high that American forces would quickly retaliate and that they all would be freed within a few weeks—if not a few days. That sense of certainty began to slowly diminish when the men were moved into the crowded Catholic church, and the food rations were severely reduced, causing rapid weight loss. Within days, conversations about food became paramount, and the talk of family and female friends receded to the background.

The Japanese military, determined to live off the land, seized more than half of the existing food on the island, creating an instant and severe shortage for the civilians. By Christmas, the last of the invasion troops had been replaced by an occupation force from Saipan. The Japanese replacement soldiers from Saipan were far more strident and abusive than the invasion troops, frequently entering homes and seizing prepared meals.

Despite the Japanese predations, the Chamorros continued to bring food and supplies to their friends and relatives in the cathedral and the Knights of Columbus hall. For a short period, the enlisted men had more food than both the officers and senior civilians because of the food supplied by their girlfriends. It was a condition that would not prevail.

On Thursday, 18 December, all prisoners were marched up to Agana Heights (Tutujan Hill), a bluff overlooking the town and bay. To celebrate their continued victories, the Japanese prepared a demonstration of their military prowess in the use of artillery and small-arms fire. Artillery shells missed buoy targets in the harbor by wide margins. A Japanese flamethrower demonstration went awry when the lighted fuel failed to propel to a nearby target and the burning fluid dripped on the foot of the soldier. No one dared to laugh, and the prisoners were quickly marched back to the plaza.

At the side of the plaza, the prisoners were stood in ranks at attention as Major General Tomitaro Horii, astride his white horse, reviewed a parade of about two thousand Japanese troops—along with trucks, tanks, and horses. At the conclusion a Japanese officer mounted the stand and gave a long lecture to the men, declaring that Japan had established a new order, the Greater East Asia Co-Prosperity Sphere, and that as prisoners of war, they were to be obedient. With more than six thousand Japanese troops now on the island, few men now felt rescue was imminent.

On Sunday, 21 December, the Japanese delivered canvas cots for the POW officers and the ten senior civilians, segregated from the other civilians and lower military ranks and now assigned to the upper floor of the church hall. On the same day, the Japanese also allowed the cathedral's Capuchin monks and natives to observe a Catholic mass. Until this day, all the men had been confined and fed a constant ration of a weak vegetable stew and boiled potatoes. For the officers and senior civilians, Gregg noted that for breakfast, the monotony was broken this day with cocoa and scrambled eggs, a treat that was surpassed only by spaghetti served the next day. For the ordinary ranks, the same dull rations continued.

The men endured long days of boredom and tedium, and conversations diminished as each man began to contemplate his own survival. The murmurs of conversation slipped into silence each night, long before lights were turned off. Assignment of regular work parties began the next day, when the first group of 120 prisoners was taken to Agat and the Piti Navy Yard for labor details. More than enough men quickly volunteered because anything was welcomed to break the monotony. Taken by truck to Piti, the men passed by numerous stores and homes that had been looted. At regular intervals machine-gun emplacements had been constructed for security and as a possible defense against an American invasion. In the harbor the only American vessel that remained was the scuttled barge *Robert L. Barnes*, settled on the bottom but still usable.

On the Piti pier, one detail unloaded Japanese barges full of rice and canned food while another detail worked to clear the bomb damage. Working alongside the local Chamorros, the Americans learned that severe rationing had been imposed, but they were pleased to hear that the Japanese were still treating the natives fairly. A former native mess steward reported that two Japanese soldiers were beheaded by the Japanese commander for raping a local woman. The work party was returned to Agana for lunch, and very light work was performed for the rest of the afternoon. While unloading the ships, the Americans stole a fair amount of food, a prelude to the constant scavenging for food that was to last until the day of liberation.

The work details were given an extra ration of food for their evening meal before returning to camp. Chief Lane, learning of this "gift," demanded that the extra food be turned over to him for use by all. Amid much arguing, the men complied. Thereafter, the men consumed their extra rations before returning. To the men on work details, the hard labor required extra food, and the animus between Lane and the men, particularly the Marines, deepened.

The tension and despair felt by the men continued to worsen. By Christmas Eve, the overcrowding and efforts to adapt to the crowded quarters was reflected in the lack of chatter and a discernible sullenness. For the Christmas observance, the Japanese permitted only one Catholic mass to be observed—on Christmas Eve. Almost everyone attended, but most sat in isolation, reflecting on their own family, trying to recapture the happiness of Christmases past. Typically, men wondered what their families were doing at that very moment, hoping all were safe and not worried.[10]

"Our first Christmas in captivity," said Ed Hale, "was a bit melancholy. Many of the fellows received gifts of food from native friends or relatives, but for most of us Christmas meant only a very thin breakfast, no lunch, and a light supper. With official permission, we had services and songs led by a chaplain. If any of us had known there would be three more (and far worse) Christmases before we had a better one, I don't doubt that a lot of men would have been starting to swim."[11]

In celebration of their conquests of Hong Kong, Singapore, Wake Island, and Manila, the Japanese made the internees watch a succession of "victory parades." Despite the obvious Japanese victories, the prisoners could not bring themselves to disbelieve the false prewar assurance that America was more powerful than any nation on earth.

For more than a decade, the American policy of seeking peace by treaty and negotiation took precedence over maintaining a viable military. Clinging to the false premise that one could negotiate with evil, the pacifist mantra that "Peace is preferable to war" swayed the political will of the country. Aided by the inevitable preference of the State Department to rationalize and accept the status quo rather than advise the need for military strength, the country wallowed in its ignorance. The United States had allowed its military to decline to a state of unreadiness that made it impossible to mount a reasonable force in the Pacific for almost another nineteen months.[12]

Days dragged by inexorably, and the only exercise was a daily run around the plaza, scrupulously avoided by the starving lower ranks, who wanted to save energy. The lack of food caused a general lethargy, and time continued to weigh heavily on the men. New Year's Day passed as another gloomy and rainy day. Scuttlebutt abounded that the American fleet was steaming to Guam or that everyone would be exchanged in a few days. The same rumors persisted until the day of departure from Guam. The reality of imprisonment became apparent as dysentery, athlete's foot, ringworm, and heat blisters took a toll. The first effects of malnutrition had begun. For many, the simple act of standing became a painful experience because of the early effects of beriberi.[13]

Two or three days after Christmas a young Guamanian, Alfred Flores, was caught smuggling a message to an American employee of Pomeroy Construction. Flores wanted to know what to do with the dynamite stored in the harbor area. Another young man, Won Pat, was caught taking supplies from a Pomeroy warehouse after receiving approval from the Americans. To the Japanese this was considered theft of the emperor's property—a capital offense.

On the morning of 6 January, a small group of Agana residents were ordered to the Pigo Cemetery to witness an execution. Won Pat and Alfred Flores were blindfolded, forced to kneel in front of a grave, and executed by a firing squad. The citizens of Guam, with stunning clarity, learned how brutal the new conquerors would be.[14] Word of the execution spread with lightning speed. By noon, everyone knew that any trouble would mean death at the hands of the Japanese.

Japanese control was now total. Guam, renamed Omiya Jima,[15] was now part of Japan. By decree, all property and all the people belonged to the emperor. Every cattle ranch had been seized "in the name of the emperor," and the owners were to slaughter their cattle, whenever required, for the benefit of the Japanese army. The new "natives" of Japan learned what it meant to be part of the Greater East Asia Co-Prosperity Sphere.

On 6 January 1942 the prisoners were told to prepare to move to the Piti Navy Yard, where they would be again moved to a permanent POW camp. Speculation centered on a POW camp at the Sumay barracks; some thought they were to be taken somewhere on a ship. Endless speculation as to their destination abounded, but the Japanese remained silent. Going to Tokyo or Honolulu for some sort of exchange was the most popular assumption. Over the next two days, all but six of the men in hiding came out and surrendered as word passed through the "jungle telegraph" that the POWs were to be moved. One of the contractors, Larry Neass, walked up to the church with his hands in the air, only to be turned away by the Japanese guards. Frustrated, he later managed to sneak in the back door of Dorn Hall before the Japanese finally accepted his surrender.[16]

By the evening before departure for Japan, it had been confirmed that the missing six American military men had fled into the hills in a desperate attempt to survive until the Americans could return.[17]

CHAPTER 5

Voyage into Prison

A fter the war a small diary was discovered on the body of a Japanese soldier found in the jungles of a South Pacific island. Takamura Jiro wrote of more peaceful days on Guam:

> Coconut trees, and other trees I do not recognize, grow in wild profusion. South Seas cities are indeed very beautiful and romantic. There is such a romantic atmosphere about sitting on a stool on a wide balcony of a native hut, built on high stilts painted a pure white and in the midst of a coconut grove. Flowers of wild and gaudy colours do not seem so disagreeable here in this southern land. This village [Agana] is peaceful and a wonderful place in which to live. It is not very large, but the largest on the island. It does not seem possible that enemy troops were here only a few days before.[1]

Although the Allied military was in retreat, few men thought their time as prisoners would last very long. Ignorance of the actual preparedness and strength of American forces in the Pacific theater was widespread. Such optimism was expressed in a 7 January 1942 letter home written by an Army officer on Corregidor. Although U.S. forces had retreated to the Bataan Peninsula, most soldiers believed ample help was on the way, and American soldiers would roll over the Japanese like a steamroller: "When she does roll, watch out! It might take a few months to mop up on the yellow boys and everyone will be really packed aboard another tin pot and we will grunt and roll across the wet Pacific again. Some people figure that we should be in the Fourth of July parade up Market Street. It sounds right to me. I hope to see you then."[2]

At midmorning on 9 January 1942, the sick and wounded on Guam were transferred from the hospital to the church hall. Suddenly, Capt. George McMillin and his aide, Capt. Charles S. Todd, were taken away with their luggage to an unknown destination. The rumors of movement appeared to be valid. Men with native families were allowed to say good-bye, and two sailors who were still in hiding turned themselves in to the Japanese guards. By evening, an air of excitement and expectation electrified the prisoners. None knew exactly where they were going, but they believed anything would be better than the isolation and boredom of the plaza.

At 4:30 a.m. on Saturday, 10 January 1942, the prisoners were woken by the Japanese and told to eat their breakfast quickly (a slice of bread, a small slice of ham, and a weak cup of broth), gather up all their belongings, and be ready to move. At 6:30 a.m. the men were assembled on the plaza and counted multiple times. At this time McMillin and Todd were returned to the plaza by the Japanese, but no announcement was made regarding their whereabouts for the past day. Based mostly on statements made by the guards, rumors swept through the ranks that Japan was to be their destination. The few trucks available were loaded with baggage, the six women, the monks, a few men (such as Pfc. Barney Barnett) who were unable to walk, some of the senior civilian men, and about thirty Marines. At 7:30 a.m., with the heat of the day starting to bear down, the prisoners were marched around the plaza for review by the Japanese commander. Formed according to rank, the column of four abreast wrapped around the plaza. The column, led by Captain McMillin, Capt. William T. Lineberry, Cdr. Albert H. Checa, USN, and Colonel MacNulty, started a four-hour, eight-mile, grueling walk under a broiling sun to the Piti Navy Yard.[3] EM2 Ed Hale would later write,

> The unforgettable picture that will never fade from my memory of that miserable march was the expressions on the faces of the hapless Chamorros. I could see hope itself turned into a torturing memory on the faces we passed along the street. . . . Many of the natives knew . . . that sooner or later the overwhelming superiority of the American, British, and Russian resources would crush the Axis. But now, as the Chamorro natives watched a miserable column of starved prisoners being taken from the island, they must have experienced that helpless, hopeless feeling with which a man might watch his home burning. But whenever they felt safe from the eyes of the Japanese guards, they smiled and waved at the Americans.[4]

In Apra Harbor numerous small landing craft scurried about amid a collection of decrepit and rusted ships. Two destroyers were visible on the horizon outside the harbor. On the dock the prisoners were placed in ranks and counted and recounted, again and again. After an hour's delay, the men and their meager baggage were loaded on board small landing barges. Passing through the crowded array of combat ships and merchant-style rust buckets, the men were surprised to see a large luxury liner anchored directly in their path. It was the *Argentina Maru,* flagship of the Japanese OSK Line and noted for its elegance and speed, having recently set a transpacific speed record from Tokyo to San Francisco.[5] En route to Japan, after having served as a troop transport for the Japanese invasion of Wake Island, the ship was diverted to pick up the prisoners of Guam. Laboring up the gangway, the weakened prisoners climbed onto the deck. All realized that rescue was now out of the question; they had stepped onto Japanese territory.

Because deck space was limited, the military men were assembled separately from the civilians. Captain McMillin, as the senior military officer, rose and called for order. Dressed in neat civilian garb, he began to explain to the men the reason he had surrendered. He made it clear that there was no shame in surrendering since the island was absolutely indefensible. Any further fighting would have caused needless deaths, especially of the nurses and civilians. As he started to say the men had fought honorably, the Japanese commander strode directly in front of McMillin and viciously slapped him a number of times across the face. Pushing McMillin aside, the Japanese officer shouted, in English, "You were in charge here, but not anymore! You and your men are all cowards for surrendering, and we will treat you accordingly. We will give you all the punishment that the human body can withstand!"[6]

For another hour and a half, the prisoners suffered through a series of interminable counts. All the luggage was hoisted on board and stowed in a separate hold. Amid the now usual shouting and shoving and slappings, the men were lined up a last time and, in single file, walked through the elegant ballroom, across a deep red carpet, and into a series of hallways. Descending a series of stairs, corridors, and more stairs, they finally arrived in the two forward steerage compartments. Officers were given a small, slightly more comfortable compartment.

"As we entered the ballroom, I looked around at the elegant furnishings and thought at last we would live in style," Lt. Dean Morgan recalled. He said to himself, "'I can handle this!' Unfortunately, we passed through this room and down stairs to another series of comfortable cabins. Again, I thought, 'OK. Not as elegant but I can handle this.' By the time we reached the steerage holds, all I could think was, 'I hope we can survive this!'"[7]

Loaded on board the *Argentina Maru* were all the military prisoners, the civilian contractors, the five Navy nurses, the Capuchin monks, the American Pan Am employees, and a scattering of Guamanian civilians. Officers and civilians were treated more graciously than the rest, although all were uncomfortably crammed into small compartments. The five American nurses from the U.S. Naval Hospital[8] and military dependent Ruby Hellmers with her newborn daughter Charlene[9] were assigned a separate cabin on the second deck. Expectations still remained high that the war would not last very long. In the many wagers as to the date of Japanese surrender, none were more than three months in the future.

In the stern of the ship were two large steerage holds, four levels below the main deck. The ranking military men were crowded into the forward of these two steerage areas of very small compartments. In the poorly ventilated aft hold, the enlisted men were placed in an area fitted out to transport large numbers of troops. Six tiers of shelves lined the hold, each tier about two feet apart. Each man was allocated a space twenty inches in width in which to sleep or rest. With inadequate room in the open area, it was impossible to have more than half of the men out of their shelf-bunks at any time. During daylight hours the men were taken to the deck for fresh air and individual exercise, a break all looked forward to because boredom and inactivity weighed heavily.

Despite the crowded conditions, the only major concern was the real fear that American submarines might torpedo the ship. Doubting the Japanese version of the Pearl Harbor disaster, the capture of Hong Kong, and the fall of Manila, few men believed the Allied fleet would take more than another month to assemble and blast the Japanese into oblivion.[10]

The civilians, slightly less crowded, were also crammed into the aft steerage. Again, ranking civilians were given separate but crowded compartments.[11] The Japanese certainly recognized the distinction in classes of command or power. All civilian prisoners had bunks and blankets and, although crowded, were able to spread out into the hallways. All of them were allowed on the promenade deck twice daily. Washing and sanitary facilities were extremely limited; water was available for only one hour daily in the two washrooms. Each washroom had six sinks but no showers. The general stuffiness and heat was not conducive to pleasant living. None of the men had bathed in days, and by the second day, the locker room stench of unwashed and sweaty men was prevalent below decks and the two half-hour breaks on the promenade deck offered the only relief from the pungent odors.[12]

At 3:30 p.m. on 10 January 1942, the engines of the *Argentina Maru* rumbled to life. Weighing anchor at 4:00 p.m., it slowly got under way and steamed off in a northerly direction. The five-day voyage to Japan began with the distribution of rice with a sauce of ground green beans and a cup of ersatz coffee. The ship's china and trays added a sense of opulence as this was the largest meal the POWs had eaten since the capitulation. The daily routine became established: early call at 5:00 a.m., wash facilities available from 6:00 to 7:00 a.m., POWs permitted on deck from 9:00 to 9:30 a.m., breakfast at 10:00 a.m., POWs allowed on deck again from 2:30 to 3:00 p.m., dinner at 3:30 p.m., and all the men back in their bunks by 7:00 p.m.

With American prisoners clearly appearing to outnumber the armed Japanese guards, numerous officers and Navy chiefs discussed plans to seize the ship and attempt to sail toward U.S.-controlled areas. Captain McMillin rightly advised that there was no way to preclude the guards sending a distress call from the *Argentina Maru,* nor could they avoid Japanese warships that would clearly take up a pursuit. Further, McMillin realized that the ship would undoubtedly be low on fuel and would be unable to even reach U.S.-controlled areas of the Philippines. The frustrated men settled back to await their fate.

By the third day, the weather began to rapidly cool as the tropics receded, and the frigid winter weather of the seas off Japan became noticeable. The ventilation, while poor, was adequate, and a decided drop in temperature was noted on Tuesday, 13 January. The Japanese dumped most of the heavy winter clothes they had looted from the Agana storerooms and Marine barracks into the hold where the civilians were kept. Almost everyone in this hold managed to obtain warm clothes, including heavy

Navy peacoats, woolen uniforms, and hats. In the other cargo hold, the military men remained dressed in the remnants of summer uniforms.

On Tuesday, 13 January 1942, Charles Gregg of the Pan Am group noted in his diary:

> Third night aboard and we are still going northward. It's getting colder now. Fortunately we have some heavy clothing. I drew a pair of Marine pants, Marine overcoat, sailor middy and stocking cap—[and] have also fallen heir to 2 wool business suits (sans vests) and my own smoking jacket! Big loss these days is news. What are the States doing? Where is the fleet? What battles are being fought? We will not know until after it's all over! Time now seems to pass fairly fast however, so things are not too bad. We are always tired by evening although there is not a great deal to look forward to [except] sleep. Did some washing this evening and hung it on the upper bunk rail by the air duct. They are piping us heated fresh air today, so clothes will dry fast.

Gregg's diary continues on Wednesday, 14 January:

> Rumor in the air this morning—supposed to have early breakfast and arrive perhaps at Kobe sometime today. Lots of changes in speed last night and at 11:00 a.m. we stopped for a while, supposedly while passing across a bar near the head of the peninsula. They now say we may be at Kobe around 8:00 p.m. and may or may not have to sleep aboard this evening. We are supposed to be taken to a prison camp off the main island and across from Kobe. I, for one, will welcome some place less crowded than this hold. Foul air is nothing to enjoy! Four days and nights are enough for any one. . . . We arrived off Kobe (so they told us at 6:00 this evening) but did not stop. At 7:00 [p.m.] we dropped anchor, had dinner and [were] told we would stay there all night. . . . They have cut off the hot air, so it's cold now.

By breakfast of the fifth day, the *Argentina Maru* had arrived a few miles north of Tadotsu, a small port on the northern coast of Shikoku. The throb of the engines slowed and finally ceased. The eerie silence made each man suddenly realize the import of the moment. The trip to Japan was over. They had arrived. With the engines shut down, the heating system ceased to operate and a cold chill seeped into the steerage. Soon the prisoners were directed up to the freezing topside decks where they were to remain for a major part of the day. Poorly draped in tropical clothes, the prisoners' hands, feet, and faces turned numb in the frigid air. A light snow blew intermittently across the assembled men. By sunset all were anxious to get to the POW camp in hopes of getting warm again. On 15 January Gregg wrote,

Boy, was it cold last night! We slept with all our clothes on but still almost froze. Up at 5:00, washed, packed, and had breakfast at 7:15. Then commenced the waiting. They opened up the hatch above us and some snowflakes drifted down. At 9:00 we were allowed up on deck and saw Japan for the first time. We were anchored some place in the Inland Sea, with sharp mountain peaks on all sides of us. It was a beautiful sight, but plenty [cold] for us only 4 days out of Guam [with its] average temperature of 80 degrees Fahrenheit. There were small settlements or towns on all sides of the bay . . . but little sign of activity . . . [or] signs of other ships. We took all our baggage to the lower deck, ready to transfer it to a launch, and were then taken down into the hold again. At 11:30 we were again taken out, lined up, and inspected by our new army guard. We stood in the cold at attention from 11:45 to 12:15 then [were] told to go below. Then commenced the worst part of our prisoner fate to date. We waited in almost freezing temperatures from then until 6:45 p.m. for them to move us. Our bags were all packed and unavailable. We barely had room to move. We were hungry and had nothing to eat. They told us we would be taken ashore first at 3:00 then 5:00 then 6:00. At 6:45 a launch bumped against the ship and we were herded out onto the dark, wind-swept, freezing deck. . . . 510+ were crowded aboard.[13]

The harbor of Tadotsu, too shallow for ships as large as the *Argentina Maru*, was more than adequate for smaller merchant steamers, cargo ships, and smaller navy vessels. At 6:45 p.m.[14] a small, open-hold cargo vessel approached and was made fast alongside the *Argentina Maru*.[15]

As day passed into night, the lights of the small cargo ship were turned on, and the prisoners began to clamber down the Jacob's ladders from the *Argentina Maru*. Trying to avoid the frigid wind and swirling snow, the prisoners huddled to one side of the open hold. The weight of the men caused the freighter to slowly heel over, its boom clanging against the port side of the *Argentina Maru*. Had the mast not struck the *Argentina Maru*, the steamer would have capsized. With unintelligible screams and shouts, the men were forced, at the point of bayonets, to shift to the opposite side as the loading continued. The women and a few men managed to find relief from the bitter wind by gathering in the wheelhouse. The steamer, now fully loaded, waited another thirty minutes before casting off lines. About 8:00 p.m., its engine came to life, and it turned toward the docks, gunwales barely clearing three feet above the choppy water. The sea spray cast a frozen mist over the shivering prisoners.

CHAPTER 6

Those Left Behind

The Chamorros and Military in Hiding

FACTS DO NOT CEASE TO EXIST BECAUSE THEY ARE IGNORED.

—Aldous Huxley

For the 23,000 Guamanian natives, the quick seizure of their island by the Japanese came as a shock. The vaunted power of the United States, even though represented by only a token military presence, was expected to crush the "dwarfs of Nippon." In less than four hours, the Imperial Japanese Army had eliminated all opposition. Any rifle company, no matter how well trained, is incapable of holding off or defeating a full Japanese division.

The undamaged U.S. Naval Hospital continued to be used by the Japanese, although with a greatly reduced staff. During the invasion, Capt. William T. Lineberry had carefully ensured that none of his medical staff had engaged in actual combat. This action allowed the Japanese to "save face" in their treatment of the wounded. It was one of the few instances in which the Japanese fully complied with the Geneva Convention and treated medical staff as noncombatants.

Two Americans, CY Joseph Blaha and civilian Frank Perry, were severely wounded during the invasion and remained in the hospital after the other prisoners were transferred to Japan.[1] Lineberry had insisted that their wounds, being quite severe, prohibited their being moved. The Japanese commander agreed to Lineberry's request and the men remained. Both were accorded medical treatment, recovered, and, nine months later, were transferred to Japan.[2]

Major General Tomitaro Horii, commander of the Japanese invasion force, issued a proclamation within hours of the island's surrender: Guam, "liberated from the oppressive heel of the Americans," was now to become part of Japan and its Greater East Asia Co-Prosperity Sphere:

> We proclaim herewith that our Japanese Army has occupied this island of Guam by the order of the Great Emperor of Japan. It is for the purpose of restoring liberty and rescuing the whole Asiatic people and creating the permanent peace in Asia. Thus our intention is to establish the New Order of the World.
>
> You all good citizens need not worry anything under the regulations of our Japanese authorities and my [*sic*] enjoy your daily life as

we guarantee your lives and never distress nor plunder your property. In case, however, when use demand you [*sic*] accommodations necessary for our quarters and lodgings, you shall meet promptly with our requirements. In that case our Army shall not fail to pay you in our currency.

Those who conduct any defiance and who act spy [*sic*] against our enterprise, shall be court-marshalled [*sic*] and the Army shall take strict care to execute said criminals by shooting!

Dated this 10th day of December 2601 in Japanese calendar or by this 10th day of December, 1941.

By order of the Japanese Commander-in-Chief[3]

For the natives, the act of surrender was met with a great deal of confusion and deep fear. Still, for the average Chamorro, it was done in a docile and accepting manner. The internment of the Catholic priests created an immediate fear for the deeply religious Chamorros. Physically, Guam was intact, with all its roads and bridges passable. On the island, ample fuel stocks remained, and rice, sweet potatoes, and cattle were more than adequate to feed the population.

The false calm changed quickly, however. Within two hours, the Japanese began to demand property and possessions, particularly cattle, from the non-Japanese inhabitants of the island.[4] Every vehicle was seized in the name of the emperor. Released from jail, the local Japanese immediately collaborated with the Japanese forces and were rewarded with vehicles and property owned by the American military and other civilians. Numerous natives were summarily ordered out of their homes—some while eating dinner—and forced to seek refuge with friends or survive in the open.

Late in the morning on the day of invasion, all residents of Guam were instructed to come to the Leary School on the plaza for registration and identification tags. Waiting in long lines to be interviewed and registered, the Guamanians also suffered under the broiling sun. Crowded with Japanese soldiers, horses, and tons of equipment, the plaza was a frightening scene. While the humiliated and seminaked American soldiers sat on the grass, Japanese soldiers could be seen looting and destroying property everywhere. The bodies of soldiers, Japanese and American, lay where they had fallen. The smells of war—cordite, rotting bodies, and wafting smoke from fires—hung like a gauzy shroud over the plaza.

Passing Japanese soldiers routinely subjected many natives to brutal beatings as they stood in line. Saipanese nationals were used as interpreters at the registration tables. The Japanese singled out and arrested local Guam leaders, Insular Force members, and retired military men. These men were placed in the already crowded Insular Guard headquarters.

Japanese officers declared that "from this day forth, you are all natives of Japan" and that all would, henceforth, be required to face north each day, bowing three times to the emperor. Within the first hours of the occupation, the Japanese began to interrogate and beat countless members of the Insular Guard and local landowners, demanding to know the whereabouts of additional weapons, radios, generators, and foodstuffs. Typical was the use of a horse whip on Juan San Nicholas and Pete Diaz Perez, who were accused of hiding an electric power condenser. Forced to their hands and knees, they were whipped until they collapsed, then repeatedly pulled up and whipped again.[5]

For the next three months, the Japanese continued to bring additional troops to the island. Guam became an assembly point for future conquests; mock landings and field maneuvers were commonplace. To house more than 14,000 soldiers, the Japanese appropriated hundreds of buildings and homes. Military control was omnipresent; all natives required passes to move about, even within the small town of Agana. Sentries and machine-gun emplacements stood at every intersection. Japanese celebrated their victories over Singapore, Bataan, and Corregidor with parades and exhibits. Every day Agana's residents were forcibly gathered in the plaza to hear speeches—laden with propaganda—extolling the glories of the new order and the future one hundred years of "Glorious Nipponese" rule.

By early April final conquests of New Guinea and the Solomon Islands depleted the occupation forces. All but five hundred Japanese soldiers had departed to continue their triumphal march across the South Pacific and Burma. Sixty "comfort women" (including fifteen enslaved natives) were now servicing the sexual needs of the remaining military.[6]

By the fall of 1942, the remaining Japanese had settled into a quiescent occupation. Schools had reopened under Japanese teachers, with lessons taught for the most part in Japanese. However, children with even the smallest part of Japanese heritage were considered superior and educated separately.[7] Every morning at school, the children would bow to the emperor, salute their new flag, and sing their new national anthem.[8]

Prior to the war most American servicemen and civilians had looked down upon the native Chamorros as somewhat beneath them in both status and morality. Navy governors had issued orders banning the marriage of whites with non-Caucasians. With an active political movement to restrict Asian, particularly Japanese, immigration the United States likewise exhibited a widespread disdain of most Asian peoples.[9]

When a member of the Guam military desired to marry a local woman on Guam, permission was required from his commanding officer *and* the governor. To marry a native woman was a daunting task. BMC Robert O'Brien fought for two years before being granted "the right" to marry a local Nisei, Maria Santos Inouye, in 1939. The governor, hoping to prevent the marriage, delayed permission until a few hours before O'Brien was to depart for the Philippines on a month's leave. O'Brien, with the assistance of friends, arranged to be married in the cathedral just before the ship left the harbor.[10] Knowing of these discriminatory rules, the average Guamanian understandably harbored a moderate dislike for many in the U.S. military.

A clear exception to anti-American bias was PhM1 Johnny Ploke's father-in-law, Tata Perez.[11] He was a trusted member of the governor's staff, fluent in numerous languages, and a confidant of numerous American servicemen. At the time of the invasion, he was retired and almost sixty-five years of age. He skillfully managed to deceive the Japanese regarding his loyalties.

Chamorros were not permitted to join the regular Navy except as mess stewards, and rarely would they be promoted above the lowest possible ranks. The establishment of the Insular Guard in early 1941 had begun a dramatic change. BMC Robert Lane, a dedicated taskmaster, drilled the men constantly on marching maneuvers and rifle drills, instilling a great pride in their unit. Membership in the Insular Guard became a position of status within the Chamorro community. Still, although they appeared competent, the Insular Guard was never trained in military tactics or weaponry.

The Chamorros quickly recognized that their new Japanese rulers were not only oppressive but brutal beyond any expectations. By the end of the first day of occupation, the Chamorros had begun to yearn for the Americans' return. For those who believed the war would end in a few months, the continued presence of the Japanese became a maddening frustration.

From Japanese-owned Saipan the military brought to Guam an additional fifty Japanese investigators and interpreters to assist in the control of the local population. Primarily to enforce Japanese rule, classes were begun to train the former Insular Guard in the discipline of the Japanese, including mastery of the infamous "goose step" and the proper way to bow to every Japanese soldier, official, or institution. Included among these officials were a limited number of Guamanians of Japanese parentage or origin who chose to support the new order.

Bowing, considered a sign of respect by the Japanese, was completely alien to the natives of Guam. When walking by a Japanese municipal office, it was now a requirement to stop and bow in the direction of the door. Failure to properly do so would often result in a severe beating. Normally a fifteen-degree bow was sufficient, but to a picture or likeness of the emperor, a slow bow of ninety degrees was required—and rigidly enforced. Omiya Jima, the newly renamed island of Guam, became a small and, unfortunately, distrusted part of Nippon. Anyone over the age of twelve, male or female, now had to labor for the emperor, raising food or cattle or building new airfields.

Rumors circulated of clandestine radios and of six Americans who had not surrendered. Six men had indeed fled: from the Radio Communication Center in Agana, RM1 Al Tyson, RM1 George Tweed, Y1 Adolphe Yablonsky, and CAerM Luther Wilbur Jones, and from the USS *Penguin*, CMM Michael L. Krump and MM1 Clarence Bruce Johnston. Throughout the war, the Japanese relentlessly conducted daily efforts to locate the radios and the missing American sailors. With each passing day, their determination grew and their hatred against possible collaborators multiplied. Anyone suspected of aiding the missing Americans was taken to the jail and severely beaten with whips or baseball bat–sized staves. Hundreds of natives, including a few individuals and shopkeepers of Japanese heritage, helped the Americans by providing food, medicine, and clothing. Within three weeks the six men had split into smaller groups because it was difficult to travel together and not leave tracks for the Japanese to follow. For months the Japanese received no information regarding the missing men.

Manuel Aguon, one of the first men to help the escaped sailors, was arrested and severely beaten when a piece of khaki clothing was found on his ranch. Radiomen Tweed and Tyson met with Manuel's brother, Vincente, and suggested they were considering the possibility of surrender. Vincente shook his head quickly. With a fearful and frightened look in his eyes, he expressed deep reservations as he responded to the suggestion.

"I talked by paper and pencil to a Jap Army officer," Vincente said. "Eight years ago, the University of Tokyo taught him to speak and write English. He doesn't remember how to pronounce words, but he can still write them down. He told me that the Americans who surrendered when Guam was first captured had been taken to Japan. I asked him, 'What about the others?' and he put down, 'Any American captured in the bush *will be killed.*' I wrote, 'If they come in and give themselves up, won't they be taken to Japan as prisoners?' He didn't answer. He just made a black line under the words that said, '*will be killed.*'"[12]

On 11 September 1942, Adolfo Sgambelluri, a loyal supporter of the Americans yet working as a somewhat trusted policeman for the Japanese, was summoned to the police headquarters to serve as an interpreter for the Japanese. After midnight, he was forced to accompany the Japanese and two Guamanian guides into the area by Togcha and Manengon, about nine and a half miles northeast of Agana. Here, the two guides, Francisco Aguon and Felix Aguero, led the Japanese to where the Americans were hiding. Jones, Yablonsky, and Krump were caught by surprise just before dawn and surrendered without a fight. It was clear to the Americans that they had been betrayed by Francisco Aguon. Sgambelluri later observed that the two guides and their families were obvious victims of extremely brutal torture by the Japanese Kempeitai.[13]

The three Americans were severely beaten by the Japanese soldiers then forced to dig their own graves. Krump was beheaded, and Yablonsky and Jones were bayoneted to death. The guides were forced to bury the men even as they could still hear their moans of pain. At the completion of the burial, Kimura, the Japanese officer in charge, inexplicably saluted the victims with his sword.[14]

Only three American soldiers now remained on the island. The Japanese intensified the interrogations, beatings, and torture in the relentless effort to find them. Tyson and Johnston paired up, seeking to avoid capture, while Tweed decided to survive alone. All were given constant support by the local populace, although no more than five natives ever knew their whereabouts. Relocating frequently from place to place, the fugitives continued to hide. Japanese patrols of ten to twenty men continued to search every day for the Americans. Anyone suspected of giving aid to the Americans was beaten until near death, allowed to recover, then beaten again. Some of the worst beatings were given to Joaquin Limtiaco, who was brutally beaten on eight separate occasions. He knew the exact whereabouts of the Americans every time but never betrayed the men.

In the early morning of 22 October 1942, Japanese soldiers entered the ranch of Tommy Torres in Machanao.[15] Enduring threats of the immediate death of his wife and children, Torres was forced to lead them to two of the Americans, Radiomen Tyson and Johnston. The Japanese obviously had been informed that the Americans were on the Torres ranch. Who was responsible for the betrayal was never ascertained. In the dark, the Japanese soldiers stealthily formed a semicircle around the sleeping men. Both men woke at the first sound but were killed in an exchange of gunfire. Surrender was not an option offered. They were simply to be killed.

Now only Radioman Tweed remained, the sole military representative of America's presence for the last forty-four years. He was to move numerous times and, during his last eighteen months on the island, was successfully hidden in Urunau by Antonio Artero.[16] Using a purloined radio, Tweed produced a single-sheet newspaper called the *Guam Eagle* in which he factually reported news of the war, good and bad, based upon broadcasts from the powerful KGEI radio station in San Francisco. A single copy of the paper was passed hand to hand, and by the jungle grapevine, news of the war spread across the island.

Tata Perez also maintained a secret radio. With family members acting as lookouts, he would press his ear to the radio and listen for news. In complete secrecy, he would pass the information along to his trusted friend Adolfo Sgambelluri, who passed the news along as "rumors." By now, possession of a radio meant a death sentence from the conquerors.

As the search for Tweed intensified, the viciousness of the Japanese accelerated. Even Tata Perez was dragged into the Governor's House and questioned in the usual manner of the "Sons of Nippon." His was the simple "crime" of playing poker, an *American* card game. His family maintained a vigil of weeping and wailing women outside the house until he was released. Described as a typical Guamanian "dramatic gig," the effect exacerbated by the palpable fear that Tata may be beheaded, wails of "Aye, joos" (Oh Jesus) and "Aye, a day, Tata" echoed across the plaza. A day or so later, none the worse for wear, Tata walked out into the arms of his family.

✦ ✦ ✦ ✦ ✦ ✦ ✦ ✦ ✦ ✦

As the Japanese war machine crushed the Allied resistance in Southeast Asia, the island of Guam renewed its role in 1943 as a staging area and its new use as a fixed "aircraft carrier" with the construction of two major airfields. On the Orote Peninsula, the town of Apla became the site of a new airstrip.[17] Construction on a second and much larger strip began on the northern part of the island near Jalaguac. The construction of a third strip was begun at Finaguagoc. With limited equipment, the Japanese impressed thousands of men, women, and children to construct the fields. Coral was mined, crushed, and laboriously hauled to the airstrips. Battalions of workers scraped, leveled, and tamped the surface in endless days of slavery. By the time Guam was recaptured in 1945, two fields had been completed.[18]

Opposition in any form met with the omnipresent and severe Japanese system of justice. The dreaded Kempeitai routinely administered beatings and torture to those they arrested. A trial, if conducted at all, would consist of a Japanese judge, a Japanese prosecutor, and, if available, an interpreter. No records exist of any findings of innocence, and the standard penalty was always death. The accused would frequently be threatened by the sword-bearing prosecutor if any objections were proffered. The Japanese justice system proved very effective in the suppression of the native Chamorros.

Most of the food grown by the natives was seized and transported away from the island by the Japanese. Grubbing in the fields for camotes and green vegetables became a daily ritual for survival. By the end of 1943, starvation was rampant, and its attendant consequences became a part of everyday life for the Chamorros. The heavy yoke of their new oppressors belied their "joyous" inclusion in the Greater East Asia Co-Prosperity Sphere.

CHAPTER 7

Zentsuji

The First Months

SOMETIMES I THINK WAR IS GOD'S WAY OF TEACHING US GEOGRAPHY.

—*Paul Rodriguez*

A s snow swirled in the dark, the barge bumped against the dock in Tadotsu. A foot-wide plank was hastily laid from the dock and made fast. Urged forward by the guttural commands of the guards, the men and women stepped warily across the wobbly, narrow board onto the soil of Japan. Beneath their feet lay the fabled land of Shoguns, Madame Butterfly, and, on this night, the most powerful military in Asia. Pictures of the hated enemy prisoners' arrival would soon be splashed in triumphant glory in newspapers across Japan.

Shivering uncontrollably in the frigid and gusty wind, the men stood, wrapped in blankets, spare clothing, and makeshift hats, while they were again counted—and recounted. Camera floodlights swept the ranks as sporadic bursts of light from flashbulbs blinded the men and added to their despair. As their names were read, the prisoners were again separated into groups: women, officers, NCOs, civilians, and, finally, enlisted men. Gathered into groups of forty, most were forced to wait again in the bitter cold. A small group of very reluctant prisoners was drafted by the Japanese, placed back on the barge, and returned to the *Argentina Maru*, where they removed the remaining luggage.

The five nurses, military dependent Ruby Hellmers and her baby Charlene, the stretcher-borne wounded, and those—such as Marine Barney Barnett—too weak to stand were immediately hustled into unheated ambulances and buses. Within minutes, the vehicles headed off into the night toward Zentsuji. The remaining military personnel and civilians crowded together for warmth.[1]

Charles Gregg, the Pan Am manager, wrote in his diary, "[We] civilians were then separated from the military and marched into a small store and out of the wind. Following a 20 minute wait in a cold room, they passed out chunks of bread to each of us. It was a sight I'll never forget—some 120 civilians, improperly clothed, dirty, unshaven, some with tropical sun helmets, others with white priest robes, all half starved and on the verge of freezing—tearing off huge chunks of bread and stuffing it into their mouths faster than they could chew and swallow. It made a lump come into your throat to see the great change that had been forced upon these people in so short a time."[2] For the military prisoners, a small bowl of hot, watery soup was served as they huddled in a shed near the Tadotsu docks. Other than a small rice ball distributed before dawn, this was the only food served the entire day.

Gregg was surprised at the reaction of the civilians who witnessed their arrival:

> We were marched about four blocks to a train station, passing down dark streets and followed on all sides by Japanese clattering along in wooden shoes, staring at the American prisoners. A large crowd of people and small children were there to stare at us—but they were friendly and would smile back at you and return waves. All of us [civilians and military] were loaded into four trolleys and taken [about] four miles inland to our new camp.[3] Snow and frost were . . . on all sides. [From the trolleys] we were marched [approximately one mile along a] snow-covered road to the prison, a military camp with barbed wire and guards.[4] [We were] placed in a large barracks building, 32 to a room. Grass mats [tatamis] covered a layer of straw on both sides of the room, [and] along the walls. [In] neat piles at the edge of the mat were 5 blankets, a rice husk or sand pillow block, two aluminum bowls and a fork. They brought in a bucket of hot soup for each room and boy, did our spirits rise. We made bed rolls with the blankets and turned in dead tired at 11:40 p.m.[5]

Seven-foot walls, made of wood planks, surrounded the camp.[6] Having been accustomed to the "blackout conditions of Guam," the prisoners were surprised to see the many camp lights—although at low intensity—as they passed under the opened gate. A large two-story barracks building loomed to their left, and with the now customary shouting, most of the men and women were pushed into the first building. Assigned upstairs were the Marines and civilians, while the Navy personnel were placed on the first floor. Transported earlier and now occupying part of the first floor were the wounded patients, the five nurses, the Hellmerses, and a few men who had arrived earlier.

Nine other men were already in the barracks when the first Guam prisoners arrived. One American, seven New Zealand Coast Watchers, and a British administrator from Butaritari[7] had arrived only five hours earlier.[8] The Coast Watchers and the British administrator, after their initial capture and interrogation in the Makin Islands, arrived 7 January 1942 on Yokohama, where the men were subjected to additional interrogation. Initially housed in the Yokohama home that had belonged to a Mr. Dennison of the Standard Oil Company, they were photographed in the luxurious surroundings for propaganda purposes.

On 10 January the eight men were joined by RM1 Arthur Griffiths, USN, an American who had been left behind in early December when the Marines and diplomats were evacuated from the consulate in Tsingtao, China. Griffiths, now claiming diplomatic status, had remained behind in order to keep radio contact and, at the last moment, destroy all the equipment. On the fourteenth, the nine men were transferred to Zentsuji; they arrived on the fifteenth, only hours before the Americans from Guam.

USS *Penguin* crewman EM2 Ed Hale described the barracks as

> hardly elaborate. [It was] a two-story building approximately fifty by two hundred feet, divided into ten rooms about twenty by fifty feet, like slices of bread with doors through the center to connect them. [The] nine-foot ceilings, all made of thin floor and ceiling lumber, were full of cracks. Exterior walls were cement and plaster; inner partitions were of plasterboard, with two large windows for each room at each end. Each room, holding twenty-eight men, contained a small charcoal heater, straw mats placed over loose straw for sleeping, blankets, Japanese pillows,[9] a table, and two small benches. No bunks; straw was spread along each side of each room. Later, we built sleeping platforms about fifteen inches high and placed cabinets at each end for the mess gear. A shelf built over the sleeping area served for personal gear.[10]

A wide degree of variety existed in the accommodations for the prisoners. For some, particularly the officers, a coal-fired potbellied stove, sleeping platforms, and mats were already in place. Most, however, slept on discarded straw. Within days, the stoves were removed and replaced by small hibachis. By the next winter, all forms of heat were removed permanently from the barracks. Again, some officers and civilians did have tatami mats for sleeping, but the majority used the thin blankets to form a cocoon for warmth.[11]

———————

The Japanese could not understand the deference and courtesy extended to the nurses by the Americans. Upon entering Zentsuji, the Japanese had insisted that the Hellmerses and the five Navy nurses be placed in the same room as the men. Although Cdr. Donald T. Giles and Colonel McNulty were unable to convince the camp commander of the need for separate quarters,[12] the nurses were finally accorded a separate room by a Japanese lieutenant in order to get the prisoners settled in their barracks.[13] The Japanese guards attempted to treat the nurses in the same manner as male prisoners by suddenly walking in and inspecting their quarters. Every attempt by the women to achieve privacy, particularly as they started to undress, was thwarted by guards who would suddenly walk into the room.

"When a few Jap guards entered her area," said Pfc. Garth Dunn, USMC, "Chief Navy Nurse Olds[14] began screaming at the top of her lungs, 'Get out of here! Get out of here, you perverted sons of bitches!' as she threw her shoes and anything she could grab at the guards' head. They stumbled back and couldn't get out of there fast enough! In no uncertain terms, she made it clear that her nurses were going to have their privacy respected."[15] To protect their privacy, a "watch" was established at the nurses' quarters, the Guam men taking turns to warn of approaching Japanese guards. Just after dawn on the following morning, Nurse Olds was seen by all, "stomping into the comman-dant's office and shouting at the top of her lungs," demanding privacy for her charges. Cloth was found to cover the windows and the problem of privacy was resolved.

Exhausted and severely chilled, the prisoners dropped their few possessions to the floor of their new quarters. The civilians, many of them elderly, needed assistance to prepare their beds and stow their gear. The spirit of cooperation lasted another hour until the prisoners, huddled together to share their body warmth, dropped into an exhausted sleep. Straw or tatamis and thin blankets were all that separated the prisoners from the severe cold. Water in the buckets, used for firefighting, had frozen solid. For Ralph Baggett, the "pain from the cold made this the most miserable night of my entire life."

"As dawn broke over Japan the next morning after arrival," said Jim Thomas, "we were awakened by banging gongs, whistles, and brutish shouts. Rifle butts and baseball bats, slamming the floor, punctuated the wake-up call. It was sad to see the tired and disheveled inmates, scratching and mumbling, as they stirred to life. Little was said. In our despair we'd almost forgotten how to talk."[16]

The harsh and frigid introduction to Japan at Zentsuji was a prelude of the future for the men of Guam. The entire night had been a series of movements, count-ing of men, yelling, and enduring the frigid temperatures. The war would continue without them; their fight became a battle for survival. Each would struggle in his own way to keep body and spirit together. The shadows of fear, despair, pain, and endless hunger would haunt them for more than three and a half years.[17]

In one of the coldest years on record for Japan, the effort to keep warm was fore-most in the memories of every survivor. Arriving in mid-January, the sudden change to winter conditions adversely affected every man. Having served only in the tropical warmth of Guam, the men lacked heavy clothing and were completely unprepared for a winter in Japan. No one was exempt from the "Zentsuji chill." As each day passed, the effects of the cold weather were magnified by the progressive weakening from malnutrition. Those fortunate enough to be assigned to the cooking sheds gained some warmth every day, but the brutal cold would rule the nights. The daily struggle was focused on ways to ward off the deep-seated chill, which former POWs describe as being centered in the lower back. The constant shivering—hands and feet blue from the cold—was exacerbated by the lack of food. Paradoxically, the overcrowding of men in the barracks was a hidden blessing, as they were forced to huddle together, sharing multiple layers of thin blankets. The body warmth of one's buddy helped to alleviate—but never eliminate—the penetrating cold.

For the next few weeks, most prisoners remained in pain and deeply chilled. A small, unvented charcoal hibachi, approximately ten inches square, provided the only heat allowed in each barrack room. With thin walls, no insulation, drafty windows and doors, little difference in temperature could be discerned between inside and outside the buildings. Even the small hibachi, not allowed for use after 7:00 p.m., would be permanently removed the following winter.

―――――――――――

As the POWs formed into ranks in the bitter cold, *tenkos* were called over and over until the Japanese commander was satisfied with the final count.[18] An hour later, from large barrels, the prisoners were given hot and watery rice soup, a cold piece of fish, and a small, hard biscuit. The food was sufficient for the moment, and few could imagine the future days of starvation in Japan.[19]

After breakfast the Japanese distributed light overcoats to the POWs. Because of the coats' wood-shaving and fiber filling, they were extremely lightweight yet surprisingly warm compared to a standard Navy jacket. Parkas made of the same material were issued, but their usage was limited because the Japanese insisted the prisoners' heads and faces be visible at all times. As a supplement to the blankets, the parkas became treasured possessions. A pair of grass slippers was issued to every prisoner, and for more than a dozen who had no shoes at all, the slippers were a welcomed solution to their desperate need. Each prisoner was assigned a number, and all baggage was ordered to be opened for a "customs inspection." Dumping possessions on tables, the Japanese searched everything, seizing most of the remaining money, watches, and pens.

Tony Iannarelli, remembering his seabag contained his cigars, six pounds of coffee, and six cartons of cigarettes, quickly opened his bag, retrieved a few packages of cigarettes and stuffed them into his pockets. Determined to avoid inspection, he lifted his bag to his shoulder and headed back to the barracks. A Japanese soldier confronted him with an order to halt. With his free hand, he quickly withdrew a pack of cigarettes from his pocket and handed them to the guard. "These are for you," he stated in Japanese. The guard stepped aside as Iannarelli, not looking back, ducked into the barracks.[20] It would not be the last time Iannarelli's fluency in Japanese would serve him well.

For the nurses the next order of business was to provide heat for their quarters since the small hibachi was far too inadequate. Pleas by Commander Giles for a pot-bellied stove in the nurses' area were immediately rejected by the Japanese commander, and Giles was bashed for his insolence in asking. Giles repeated his requests each day and was always met with bashings and vicious slaps to his head. Five days later the Japanese made a formal presentation of a stove. After four days' delay, the camp commandant could save face, presenting the stove as a gesture of kindness and generosity rather than as a response to an American request. Slowly the men started to realize how important it was that their new "benefactors" be given opportunity to save face.

On the afternoon of the first day in Zentsuji, Governor McMillin addressed all the prisoners with Captain Lineberry, Commander Giles, and BMC Robert Lane by his side. McMillin, having demanded diplomatic immunity as the governor of Guam, formally relinquished command. Lt. Col. William MacNulty had earlier refused to accept any position of authority, preferring to simply "sit out the war." The ranking military officer was thus Captain Lineberry. However, as a medical officer, he deferred to the Navy line officer, Commander Giles, who assumed command of the prisoners. Giles proceeded to create an internal command structure for the administration of the camp, with himself as head and Lane as the senior enlisted man and camp administrator. Without considering any Marine NCOs, Giles simply placed Navy men at every level of command.[21] The command of food, sanitation, and camp discipline would rest with the Navy men only. Giles considered his work complete and removed himself from everyday contact with the ordinary ranks. Further isolating himself, Giles never participated in the Saturday morning lectures conducted by the officers to maintain morale. According to the prisoners interviewed, Lineberry reexerted actual command after a few days and retained actual command until Col. Marion D. Unruh arrived from the Philippines on 16 January 1943. The camp command structure put in place by Giles, however, was retained.

At 2:00 p.m. of the first day, all the prisoners were again gathered in ranks, counted numerous times, and ordered to remain at attention. In a few minutes, in one of his very rare appearances in the camp, Major General Mizuhara, commandant of prisons, mounted a platform and addressed the prisoners. Reminding all that they were prisoners of the emperor, he commanded them to rid themselves of feelings of superiority over the Japanese. A copy of his speech was handed to each prisoner (see the addendum to this book). After Japan's series of lightning victories over the Allies, Mizuhara had every reason to feel superior and magnanimous during his speech.

At 5:00 p.m. a second meal of the day was served, much the same as that served for breakfast. Watery soup and a slab of bread did little to assuage the prisoners' gnawing hunger. At 9:00 p.m. on Friday, 16 January, lights were turned out, and the men began their second night in Japan.

On Saturday and Sunday the men were completely segregated, civilians from servicemen. As no one had taken a bath since the surrender of Guam, the smell of the men in their confined quarters now became unbearable. The news that they would be allowed to take baths the coming Sunday was greeted with a feeling of profound joy and relief. Adjoining the galley was a small room, approximately eighteen by thirty feet, containing two large, rectangular concrete tubs, each measuring eight by twelve feet and about four feet in depth.[22] An ancient coal-fired boiler outside the room was used to heat the water.

On Sunday the bathing ritual began with the Japanese commandant bathing first, followed by the guards according to their rank. The first prisoners to enter were the nurses, followed by the officers, the civilians, and, finally, the enlisted ranks—always in groups of ten. In the unheated room, each prisoner stood on the low concrete coping surrounding the tubs, washed with a scrap of soap, then rinsed off with water scooped from the tub. Properly washed, the men were allowed to soak in the water for an additional ten minutes. Regrettably, not many men prewashed adequately before entering the tub, and by the time the last group entered, the tub had a thick layer of crud floating on top.

By the end of the second hour, the water was barely lukewarm but for the first time the Zentsuji chill was eased. Each man was handed a clean *fundoshi* (loincloth), which would serve as underwear for the next few years.[23] When all had bathed, the prisoners were told to use the same water for washing clothes. Within hours of their baths, the Zentsuji chill returned, and until spring, the prisoners rarely felt warm. Bitter cold with temperatures well below freezing were common until late March.

In a blatant propaganda ploy, a Japanese camera crew recorded some of the now-washed men passing a table where they were given more soap, cigarettes, hard candies, wool socks, and cookies. The selected fifty men were surprised and rather joyful at their bounty. The laughter and wide grins of appreciation were carefully recorded by the Japanese. For these men, Christmas had finally arrived. Determined to share their bounty with fellow prisoners, the chuckling men turned the corner heading back to the barracks. All were quickly brought to a halt by carefully placed guards, not visible to the rest of the camp. Here, all the gifts were seized by the guards, and a token ten cigarettes and a small bar of soap were given to every third man.[24]

Resentment for this perfidious act immediately increased the morale of the Americans as despair changed to hatred.[25] A compromised settlement to the war was no longer considered; only the utter defeat of this treacherous nation would satisfy the prisoners. Honorable respect toward the enemy was discarded, and efforts were begun to thwart the Japanese on every occasion. An ingrained and moral revulsion against thievery would be translated into an honorable effort to destroy or steal anything of value, particularly if it could provide sustenance for the hungry men.[26]

On Monday, 19 January, all were issued a small bar of soap, one toothbrush, and tooth powder. On Tuesday a tangerine, laundry soap, and more cigarettes were given to all prisoners. Restrictive as the diet and amenities appeared compared to the American standards on Guam, it was no different from what the average Japanese endured. By the end of the fifth day in Zentsuji, most had settled into a routine and accepted their incarceration with equanimity, but each man had developed a strong hatred of their captors. The food supply at this time actually was more than adequate, and a number of men regained the weight lost over the first month.

Every man looked forward to the warmth of the bedding but feared the voracious appetite of the bedbugs and lice. Weary from exhaustion and a shortage of food, the men learned quickly that nothing could stop the blood-sucking bedbugs gorging on their bodies. Over the next two weeks, Dr. H. J. Van Peenen,[27] by sheer force of personality, managed to get the cooperation of everyone in an attempt to rid the buildings of the dreaded bedbugs. Boiling every article of clothing and bedding finally brought the infestation under control. Lice tended to hide in the seams of clothing, earning them the sobriquet "seam squirrels." Although the lice and flies were numerous, they were far less annoying than the bedbugs, which were never eliminated. Nothing appeared to be very effective against them. Not until January 1943, with the arrival of the first prisoners from the Philippines, were lice again a matter of concern.

Of all the Japanese prison camps during the war, Zentsuji maintained the reputation as the best for treatment of its military POWs.[28] Until the final year, although close to starvation levels, food was generally available, along with reasonable medical care compared to other camps. Van Peenen's last-minute packing of medical supplies before leaving Guam provided a modicum of medicine for many afflictions. His ability to "bribe and squeeze" the guards ensured a reasonable supply of medicines into the camp.

Eventually most enlisted men would be sent to other prison camps in Japan. Zentsuji became a camp limited mostly to 900 officers of the Allied nations—the civilians and enlisted ranks generally passing in transit. Approximately 150 enlisted men were always retained as orderlies or as slave laborers for the nearby port facilities, factories, and rail yards.

One week after the prisoners arrived in Zentsuji, the Japanese announced that the civilians would be moved the next day to a new camp in Kobe. Along with the two military dependents,[29] the civilians made their farewells to the nurses and military men.[30] The civilians, while anxious, exuded a festive anticipation because all were supremely confident the move was a prelude to a prisoner exchange. As noncombatants, none considered their current status to be more than a few months of inconvenience.

Friday, 23 January 1942, was spent packing meager belongings, preparing accurate lists of prisoners to take home to their loved ones, meeting with friends for the last time, and arranging to carry letters stateside for relatives of the military prisoners. Assembled again in the bitter cold at 4:45 p.m., the civilians were given a farewell address by Major General Mizuhara. Fifteen minutes later, the civilians boarded a train back to the arrival port of Tadotsu.

For the military personnel remaining at Zentsuji, life settled into a dull routine. Compared to those captured and interned elsewhere in Asia, for example, the Philippines, Hong Kong, and Singapore, the men at Zentsuji were initially treated extremely well. The Japanese had selected this camp for the internment of officers, honoring to a very limited degree the Geneva Convention that required accommodations according to rank. The Japanese retained a limited number of enlisted men for use as cooks, stewards, and orderlies for the officers. A larger block of enlisted men was retained to prepare a nearby hillside for the cultivation of crops and as slave laborers on the docks of Takamatsu and the rail yards in Sakaide. For the first few months the men received supplies of clothing, hand soap, toothpaste, pencils, and notebooks. In prison camps established elsewhere for lower ranks, the possession of pencils and notebooks could easily result in brutal punishment, including beheading.

Sgt. George Shane, still believing it would be a short war, was initially reluctant to learn the Japanese language. "The Japs began a school right away to teach us their language," he said. "I learned fairly quickly, but the best was probably [Captain] Todd. Because of his ability, he always managed to get a bit more food or anything we desperately needed. For the first six months, it was tilling the soil all day and going to school at night to learn Japanese. Those who learned survived more easily than those who refused to learn. I quickly realized that being obstinate about learning their language could make your life miserable."[31]

Petty annoyances were a common attribute of the Japanese staff in Zentsuji. If you broke a dish, you were required to write a letter of apology to the camp commander, explaining in full detail how you broke the property of the emperor and including a "prayer" that your apology was acceptable to the Japanese camp commander, the representative of the emperor.[32] Before getting a replacement dish, the prisoner was made to stand outside the commandant's office, holding the broken pieces at arm's length for hours. Inclement or freezing weather would not stop this harassment. The Japanese obviously enjoyed humiliating the prisoners whenever possible.[33]

Private Baggett, a talented athlete in civilian life before enlisting as a Marine, said, "I suspect that the Japs enjoyed the chance to humiliate us, but we looked upon it as simply a pain in the butt. At first we all thought the camp commandant was a Jap General, hence we always began our letter, 'Dear General.' Within a short time, whenever a man dropped his cup, shattering it on the floor, a chorus of prisoners would turn to the hapless fellow, loudly laugh, then shout at the top of their lungs, 'Dear General!'"[34]

Of immediate concern to the prisoners was the supply of cigarettes. Smoking at this time was socially acceptable and almost universal in all social classes. Little thought was given to addiction. When regular issues began after three weeks, cigarettes immediate acquired a currency value, frequently in excess of their real costs. Initially, the ration of food was marginally adequate, and cigarettes were used mostly to barter for services and clothing. Those who did not smoke could sell their rations for money, goods, or services. As currency, cigarettes rose and fell in value in predictable patterns. When extra rations were issued, a bowl of rice would cost two or three cigarettes. A week later the same bowl could cost twenty cigarettes.

Typical was the use of cigarettes for services such as washing and mending clothes or haircuts. More than one man provided the much-needed barbering service for the camp in exchange for cigarettes. Tailoring and shoe repair were soon added to the list of services that could be obtained for cigarettes. Within a month the Japanese guards of Zentsuji began to avail themselves of these prisoner-provided services. Rationed at all times, cigarettes would ultimately represent the difference between life and death. Years later, in the death throes of final starvation, some prisoners would still trade their meager ration of rice for a cigarette. In all cases cigarettes' true value eventually centered on the ability to exchange them for food. To the very last days of the war, cigarettes or some form of tobacco were supplied to the prisoners and Japanese soldiers.[35]

Ample supplies of books,[36] playing cards, and English versions of the Japanese newspapers[37] provided a respite from the boredom and lassitude in the camp. Language classes, history lessons, and instruction in writing and accounting were provided by fellow internees. When 2nd Lt. Clinton C. Seymour arrived at Zentsuji from the Philippines almost a year later, he considered Zentsuji to be a paradise compared to his prior camps of Cabanatuan and Bilibid: "I was amazed that there were classes conducted on nearly every subject. If you desired, you could take classes in languages—even personal, one on one, instruction!"[38]

Navy medic Adolph W. Meyers noted in his diary that the officers "organized classes on myriad subjects: hygiene, bookkeeping, math, salesmanship, the characteristics of motor oil, travel experiences in Central America, and many others. 'Sing Songs' by loosely formed choral groups and talent shows became quite popular."[39] Barney Barnett fondly remembers the music, saying, "Some of the singing groups, particularly later in the war, were equal to any chorus in the world. A rendition of '[The Song of] the Volga Boatmen' by almost one hundred voices stunned not just the prisoners but the Japs. The quality of the singing was simply unbelievable."[40]

The Japanese newspapers provided a one-sided view but a fairly accurate portrayal of major war developments. For the first six months, the constant reports of Japanese victories were essentially true. The details were exaggerated—in claims of Allied ships sunk, planes and bombers destroyed, and troops annihilated—and none of the prisoners believed the claims of minimal losses on the part of the Japanese. By reading between the lines, one could easily see the change in Japanese military fortunes. Reports of dozens of American carriers being sunk and Japanese pilots downing American fighters by throwing rice balls, and the guards' taunts about capturing San Francisco, were met with yawns.

Although gambling in any form was forbidden by the Japanese, every night would see men gambling with cards or dice—the currency often being cigarettes, scarce matches, or future servings of rice. No Japanese regulation was about to stop the prisoners from gambling, even the overt hostility of Lane to such activities. Ace-Deuce (pronounced ace-ee-doo-see) and poker were the games of choice in the officers' quarters, while poker and craps reigned in the enlisted barracks. Clinton Seymour noted that "five or six officers, mostly captains and majors, engaged in a continual poker game. There was always someone waiting. If someone left, another would simply step in."[41]

The Japanese, under provisions of the Geneva Convention, paid the officers and enlisted in yen. With the constant bargaining for food and necessities, large sums of yen were exchanged, much of it accumulating in the constant card games. By the war's end, pots of thousands of yen were frequent. The Japanese insisted, however, under the pain of severe punishment, that the prisoners should never steal, lie, or gamble. For the POWs, this was simply accepted as a challenge, and "challenging the Nips is what we did at all times," said Pfc. Frank Nichols. Nichols made a set of dice by shaping two cubes out of wood, and burning spots in them with a piece of red-hot wire. The men now could easily "shoot craps" for yen—or cigarettes, the real currency of the camp.[42]

In short order the internees confirmed the loss of Hong Kong, Manila, and Singapore. On 29 January 1942, four days after the departure of the civilians, thirteen men captured on Wake Island arrived in Zentsuji. With instant celebrity status, they were able to relate the heroic battle waged by the military and civilians on Wake Island but sadly confirmed news of defeats in Hong Kong and the surrender of Manila City. On 28 February 1942, four more Wake Island survivors arrived, including one additional officer.[43]

Being held prisoners in Japan slowly caused a widespread depression during the first few months of captivity. The constant drumbeat of the Japanese extolling the power and success of their military efforts weighed heavily on morale. The loss of Wake Island and Guam were not unexpected, but the news that the mainstay of the British fleet in Asia was destroyed within days of Pearl Harbor was devastating, particularly to the Navy officers.[44] By 1 March 1942, the last of the U.S. Asiatic Fleet had disappeared beneath the Java Sea when Admiral Hart's heavy cruiser, the USS *Houston,* was sunk near the Sunda Strait.[45]

Movies were shown that featured newsreels of Japanese attacks at Pearl Harbor, the Philippines, China, and Malaya. Other newsreels during the next six months confirmed the continuing success of the Japanese onslaught. Many slowly began to realize the war might last many years. The battles in the Coral Sea, in the Sunda Strait, and at Midway were reported rather accurately in late May, and for those who understood their significance, it was clear from later reports that the Japanese advance had been stopped. Fortunately, until the very last day of the war, and despite extreme shortages of paper, the English version of the daily Osaka newspaper, the *Mainichi,* was published and exhibited an unusually high degree of accuracy.[46]

What few copies of the *Mainichi* were available were sequestered in the officers' quarters. From newspapers smuggled into the camp, one could later trace the progress of the Allied advance from Makin Island and Guadalcanal to the final assaults on Okinawa and Iwo Jima by noting the locations where the "Imperial Japanese Army has repositioned in preparation for the massive attack on the enemy." Interest in the progress of the war became second only to the matter of securing adequate food.

All cooking was done in a separate building where a dozen large hemispherical cooking pots were placed over coal-fired brick stoves. Each stove had its own chimney, and coal or wood was burned on grates below the pots. All rice, soups, and the occasional fish or meat were cooked in these oversized woks. In each room of prisoners, a monitor was selected to go to the kitchen and oversee the proportioning of the food. The monitors carried the food in wooden buckets back to their rooms, where it was then divided and served. In the first few weeks, constant bickering over size of portions led to numerous fights. Most of these disputes diminished when the Japanese issued china bowls of uniform size, but tension remained as the men began to become malnourished. Typical of military units the world over, the cooks remained well fed despite starvation rations. Navy cooks from the Agana administrative staff were assigned to manage the kitchen and galley, and the charges of favoritism began to mount immediately.

Pfc. Garth Dunn noticed that "when they [Navy cooks] carried the food into the building, the Navy men definitely had larger portions. After lights out [Private] Orr[47] and I snuck over to the galley, gathered all the burnt rice scrapings, and brought them back for everyone to share. After a few days, the Navy men caught on and tried to set a trap for us. In the dark, a Navy man tried to grab me and I gave him a real whack across the head with a pot. The next day, I noticed Chief O'Brien with a big lump on his head."[48]

With little variation, the meals were the same: For breakfast, the men would normally be served hot green tea and *lugao,* a bowl of rice gruel that was 90 percent water. Few cooks cared enough to learn how to steam rice, preferring the ease of preparing *lugao.* Other meals would often consist of a small portion of rice, seaweed, daikon (turnip-sized radish cut into very small pieces), rare pieces of meat, and, again, hot green tea. Occasionally, a watery *benjo* soup would be served.[49] Aptly nicknamed, it was always bland in taste and would contain almost anything, including rotted fish heads. The officers remained ignorant of the cooking procedures and rigidly believed the men responsible for cooking were scrupulous about serving a fair portion to everyone.[50]

The Japanese, preferring the polished long grain white rice, frequently gave the prisoners the "brown" or unpolished rice. Fortunately, brown rice retained most of the rice shell and, to the advantage of the prisoners, was of a higher nutritional value. The Japanese made no effort to keep the prisoner's rice in proper storage, and it was frequently mixed with dirt, small pebbles, straw, insects, rat droppings, and other impurities associated with floor sweepings. Little could be done to clean the rice, and the prisoners simply learned to be careful not to bite too hard lest they break a tooth on a small stone. In January 1943, prisoners from the Philippines arrived, some with mining experience; they devised a simple miner's sluice to wash the rice. Debris, such as straw and small pieces of wood, floated to the top and was thrown away. The heavier pebbles and rat droppings settled to the bottom and were caught in the ridges. This simple yet elegant solution solved the problem of grossly contaminated rice for the duration of captivity.

The Japanese allocated rice rations by the weight of the rice bag markings. If the bag marking read "sixty kilos" but weighed only fifty kilos, it was credited as sixty.

Theft by Japanese personnel of prisoner rations was therefore of no consequence to the Japanese. When any meat or vegetables were supplied, it was cut into extremely small pieces and either added to a soup or mixed into the vats of rice prior to serving. Rarely was any man able to see more than a few specks of vegetable or meat in his portion. The meat and bones, when available, were usually scraps left after the Japanese staff and guards had removed the better cuts. What little extra existed was distributed by rotation among the messes.

For the cooks, any bones or pieces of meat were valuable as a nutritional additive to the benjo. Ralph Baggett recalled his shock when he realized that any food was important. "I was in the camp kitchen one afternoon when I peered into a large cauldron of soup. Boiling in the water was the complete head of a horse—hide, hair, and all—with its eyes staring back at me. After that, I never wanted to know."[51]

With a diet extremely low on vitamins and almost completely lacking in protein, the effects of malnutrition quickly became apparent. Within two weeks after their arrival in Japan, the wrists, ankles, and elbows of the prisoners started to painfully swell. The first major effect of malnutrition was caused by the lack of vitamin A and proteins.[52] The first sign of lack of vitamins (avitaminosis) was a chafing and redness in the area of the scrotum. Severely irritating, the painful condition was uniformly known as "rice balls." From the lack of vitamin A, the loss of night vision was pandemic.[53] The lack of vitamins (especially thiamine, or vitamin B1) caused one of two kinds of beriberi. Wet beriberi caused painful and debilitating swelling of the body, particularly the abdomen, legs, and testicles. When extreme, it would literally drown the heart and kill a man. Dry beriberi, often called "dancing feet," was characterized by extreme pain, similar to electrical shocks, on the bottom of the victim's feet. Appetites diminished, and starvation-induced depression was the norm. Some men actually avoided eating for days as a direct result of this listlessness. For those not suffering from diarrhea, bowel movements rapidly decreased to no more than one or two each week. For some, the intervals stretched to three weeks.

Ed Hale vividly remembered that "getting enough food was a challenging problem. Generally we had soup at every meal, with bread one meal (about six ounces) and rice two meals. On holidays and Mondays there was no bread; we ate rice for three meals. Sometimes the diet would be varied with a bit of fish, fried or stewed into the soup, and after a couple of months, an egg about once a week. Rare indeed was fruit; even rarer was sugar, which, when it did come, was approximately equal to two lumps per man, never more than once a week."[54]

Regardless of rank, a number of men began to look out solely for themselves. A man who did not smoke would begin swapping cigarettes for food, regardless of the consequences to his fellow prisoner. The officers, separated from the enlisted men, were initially accorded noticeably better rations. While his delegation of authority decision was logical, McMillin made no effort to explain to the entire group of prisoners why he had assigned Navy men to all positions of control. What appeared to be a presumptive "grab" of leadership by Lane was resented by most enlisted men—particularly the Marines, who chafed under Navy command. The lower ranks no longer saw themselves as subordinates in the classic military sense but "equals as prisoners." Lane, along with other Navy chiefs, lived in a conspicuously better style than lower ranks. Compounding the problem, the Japanese, in a deliberate insult to the officers, accorded privileges to the noncommissioned ranks equal to those of the officers and directed that all communications be through Lane.

The prewar animus between enlisted and officer ranks was now transformed into a deeper resentment between the lower ranks and the Navy noncommissioned officers. Lane and his fellow Navy chiefs would become objects of deep scorn, if not outright hatred. When McMillin was transferred to Formosa (Taiwan) on 24 August 1942,[55] Commander Giles continued as head of the Prisoner Committee, retaining Lane as camp administrator. However, despite many differences, Lane's basic honesty would never be questioned. In that regard, all ranks held him in equal esteem while disdaining him for his imperious manner and favoritism to his fellow chiefs.

To his credit Lane instituted rigid control of the distribution of rice and other rations, the foremost concern for all ranks. The servers were rotated each day to prevent favoritism and a "heavy hand" in serving of the rice. At first eating utensils were a mixed collection of discarded cans, broken spoons, bent forks, mess kit cups, and sheet metal fabricated into plates. No two men had the same utensils, and portions of food appeared dissimilar when served on the various containers. When the Japanese issued uniform rice bowls to the prisoners Lane was provided a foolproof means for giving equal shares of the rice. Each man would mark the bottom of his bowl with his initials, and before meals the bowls would be placed on a table, neatly lined up and with no way to know who owned each bowl. The food servers would enter the barracks carrying buckets of rice. A portion of rice would be placed in each bowl, the servers scrupulously attempting to have all portions exactly equal. A small can, with both ends removed, was adapted as a measuring device. A plunger, made from a discarded can lid, pushed the rice from the can into the bowls. When the apportionment was complete, a server would lift each bowl in turn, calling out the man's initials. This procedure was to be the standard throughout the war for all the men in Zentsuji and for those who were later transferred to Osaka and subsequent camps. Any extra rice not served was served as "seconds" or "extra" in a strict order according to a roster rotation.[56]

Although Lane's Navy cooks worked long and hard hours, the cooks and Lane were able to maintain their weight and health. Few men trusted the cooks to take a share of food equal to their own. A common complaint in the later years was that the Navy chiefs and Lane's friends tended to have overflowing buckets of rice and soup brought to their mess. More than a few men I interviewed made note of the appearances of favoritism on part of the Navy personnel. Very few Marines served as cooks in the Zentsuji camp.[57]

As an example of disparity that bred resentment, the Japanese-provided ration of cigarettes was ten per day for officers and chiefs, twenty every three days for petty officers and sergeants, and ten every three days for corporals and ranks below.[58] Not a single officer or NCO considered pooling the cigarettes and sharing them equally among the fellow prisoners. The concept of officers and higher ranks caring for the welfare of subordinates was noted more for its absence. Lane, along with a few other Navy chiefs, exhibited a distinct lack of concern for the general welfare of his subordinates. Postwar reports by McMillin and Giles acknowledged the disconnect between the ranks. Giles remarked, in a classic statement of naïveté, "Unfortunately, some of the enlisted men felt that he [Lane] catered to the Japanese and tended to wave his authority about the camp. For one reason or another that I could never sort out, many of those who were critical of Lane had also disliked him on Guam."[59]

The enforced idleness, beginning on the day of capture, served to breed not only a sense of despondency but also a general refusal to accept discipline. The leadership of the officer corps was, with rare exceptions, conspicuous in its absence. Colonel MacNulty's abhorrent behavior, refusal to accept command, and perceived cowardice clearly furthered the breakdown of military discipline. Instead of acting as a united military unit serving to protect one another, the men simply began to look out only for themselves. Some formed groups, but rarely of more than four men. Officers, rather than looking out for their men, looked out for their own comfort. As a direct result, when the officers were placed on half rations, rare was the enlisted man who would share stolen food with his superiors until the effects of starvation became too severe to ignore. The prewar gulf between enlisted men and officers deepened to a distrust and, between the enlisted Marines and Chief Lane, a palpable hatred.

Garth Dunn, typical of most enlisted men, resented the continued ritual saluting of all officers in the POW camp. Enlisted men, united in captivity with the officers, considered themselves not bound by the rigors of ritual saluting since they assumed, as prisoners, they were all equals. One particular British officer insisted on sharp salutes and would constantly berate the Americans. Despite arguments to the contrary, he persisted. The Americans arranged to walk past him constantly, at a five-foot separation, each man saluting in turn. After fifteen minutes, he got the message and saluting became optional—and it eventually disappeared altogether in the camp.[60]

British officers maintained a system whereby an officer was entitled to a "batman," an enlisted man assigned to him as his personal "butler." With no other British ranks in the camp, Americans were asked to volunteer for extra income. A British officer, upset with the performance of his American batman, struck him across the face during a reprimand. The American instantly struck back, knocking the British officer to the ground. In a rage, the officer demanded that the enlisted man be severely punished. Major Spicer, his eyes burning with anger, stood within inches of the officer's face and said, "If you ever strike another one of our Americans, I'll personally kick your teeth down your throat." The British never crossed the Americans again. The enlisted ranks gladly participated in assisting officers—for pay—after that incident.[61]

Resentment further grew as all ranks began to understand they had never been equipped or trained to fight a war. Many of the men from Guam concluded that they were merely "toy soldiers," used as bait to bring Japan into a war against the United States. Their experience was no different from that of other men in the Pacific as no military service was given funds to train effectively. Other than occasional rifle practice or, if ammunition was made available for the rare firing of a machine gun, no Marine on Guam received any additional training in weapons or combat tactics. The virulent pacifism and determination to remain neutral by America's political leadership had left the military completely unprepared. The prisoners of war resented being the pawns for such political arrogance.

CHAPTER 8

Civilians in Kobe

A fter departing Zentsuji by train on Friday, 23 January 1942, the civilians arrived about an hour later at the port of Tadotsu. Transferred to a ferry boat,[1] most merely lay on the floor, garnering a few hours of needed sleep. Space was found inside the pilot house, away from the cold, blustery wind, for Ruby and Charlene Hellmers, wife and baby daughter of the Navy enlisted man John Hellmers.

Before departing Tadotsu a Japanese general addressed the civilians, saying, "You were brave men. You served your country well. Now you are guests of the emperor!" The captives were placed on a small boat and ferried overnight to a Kobe wharf. At dawn the following morning, the shipload of civilians lay off a pier in Kobe. A small Japanese breakfast of rice and tea was served, and by 7:00 a.m. all were disembarked to another flurry of photographers' flashbulbs. There, the men were separated into two groups. Those in the M group were all over the age of fifty-five, and those in the S group were under fifty-five. The M group was then sent to the large Butterfield mansion,[2] while the S group was sent to the local seamen's mission.[3] Both places had quite good accommodations. The seamen's mission was located in the warehouse district close to the waterfront. The men were crowded but comfortable. Both accommodations had regular china, silverware, closets for suitcases, beds, and blankets. The men were to stay in these locations for another year.[4]

The older civilians walked a few blocks to the large private residence owned by Butterfield and Swire, a steamship company that ran ships along the China coast and south to Singapore. For the older internees this would be a blessing because the home was quite comfortable and well heated. Few expected to be there very long. Rumors abounded that a prisoner exchange would occur in a few days or weeks. With comfortable surroundings, morale soared and optimism prevailed. Ruby Hellmers and her daughter Charlene were moved immediately to the Eastern Lodge Hotel. Hellmers joined other local women, mostly missionaries and teachers, awaiting the anticipated prisoner exchange.

With the Imperial Japanese Army sweeping away the Americans and other colonial powers, a great deal of public attention was focused on this first large group of internees. With the press in attendance, excellent meals were served for the first few days, catered by expensive local restaurants and hotels. The chores of setting household rules, allotting space, distributing foods, liaising with the Red Cross, and preparing for an exchange were viewed as temporary inconveniences. Although remaining optimistic regarding an exchange, many prisoners suffered a loss of morale from boredom, crowded conditions, and the capricious regulations of the Japanese. All continued to believe they would be sailing home in an exchange of diplomats and nonmilitary personnel.

Set amid the waterfront warehouses at 109 Ito-Machi, the seamen's mission was designed to accommodate twenty-five people but now held seventy-four internees. The largest room, a dormitory on the second floor, contained twenty men, with bunks set one foot apart. Men were assigned living space according to their age group, but the Capuchin priests were given a separate room. On the third day, the elegant catered meals came to an abrupt end and were replaced by low-grade rice, occasional fish heads, rotten meat, and weak tea. The stench of rotten meat frequently drove the internees from the dining rooms. The photographic images of contented internees continued to circulate in Japanese propaganda.[5]

The internees continued to hope for repatriation, each week bringing new rumors of progress in the negotiations. A number of additional foreign nationals, many prominent in the local community, were soon added to the men from Guam. Referred to as "the locals," most retained contact with their companies or families living nearby. With funds from families of the locals and the Swiss consul, the necessary supplies, clothing, and services were readily available. Numerous books were purchased for camp use. On 30 April Charles Gregg noted that he had secured 115 yen from the Swiss consul to purchase a variety of books on subjects such as "civil and electrical engineering, all branches of math, metallurgy" and bilingual language grammars in French, Japanese, and German. On the same shopping venture, all were treated to ice cream. Similar shopping trips in Kobe and Osaka were conducted for food, sporting gear, medical and dental care, and needed supplies. The news that the Swedish ship MS *Gripsholm* had been chartered for a diplomatic exchange in Mozambique continued to keep hope alive that the prisoners' confinement would soon end.

In the middle of May, the Japanese temporarily cut off all outside funds. Most internees believed it was an action taken in anticipation of a quick departure for a prisoner exchange. On 18 May 1942, all hopes appeared to be dashed, however, when the Japanese announced none of the internees would be exchanged "for the present." The Swiss consul, a Mr. Gutknecht, continued to express hopes that the Japanese would relent and continued to process the necessary paperwork, including Swiss passports for everyone. Rumors would continue regarding dates set for repatriation, many fostered by the Japanese guards and the local police. On Saturday, 13 June, the Swiss consul arrived to state that none of the men would be repatriated for now but "perhaps on the next boat."[6]

Earlier, on 12 March 1942, Chief Nurse Marion B. Olds and her four charges, Wilma Leona Jackson, Doris Yetter, Lorraine Christiansen, and Virginia J. Fogarty, had been transferred to Kobe for a pending exchange of prisoners. The evening before departure from Zentsuji was marked with many of the men gathering to sing a fond farewell to the ladies, ending with "Auld Lang Syne." "As long as I live," wrote Leona

Jackson, "I shall remember standing at the door—tears in my eyes, a lump in my throat, and the voices of the men, singing their goodbye." Before leaving, the nurses wrote down messages from anyone who wanted to send letters home.[7] Dressed in their cleanest white uniforms, silk stockings, and white shoes, the nurses did their best to appear elegant. With tearful good-byes the five nurses and the Hellmerses were loaded on a truck. Permeating the entire camp was a mixed sense of joy for the departure of the women and sadness for their own future safety. For many it was clear there might not be another contact with the home front until the war was over. The next day the nurses arrived at the Eastern Lodge Hotel in Kobe, described by one nurse as a "fifth-rate" Westernized hotel where the food and accommodations were barely satisfactory (some of the women found the hotel so dirty, they thought it was yet another prison camp). Still, the internees retained a hope for repatriation. On Tuesday, 16 June, Gregg scribbled, "150+ Americans left Kobe today for Yokohama as [the] first step in their repatriation. Approximately 100 of them were . . . marched past us on their way to the [train] station. We waved and shouted words of cheer. . . . It gave us a queer feeling to see them leave us behind. Well, perhaps the next boat."[8]

After many delays the Navy nurses, the Hellmerses, and selected internees and diplomats, gathered from various cities across Japan and China, boarded the *Asama Maru* in Yokohama. On board the *Asama Maru* were almost five hundred people, including Radioman Griffiths, the Marine captured at the American embassy in Shanghai and recently interned at Zentsuji. The exchange ship was to rendezvous in Mozambique with the *Gripsholm*, coming from New York.

Shortly after midnight on 25 June 1942, the *Asama Maru* weighed anchor in Yokohama Harbor, bound for Lourenço Marques in Mozambique with stops in Hong Kong, Haiphong, and Singapore. During this passage, Navy nurse Virginia Fogarty met a U.S. foreign service officer named Mann, and by the time the ship arrived in Mozambique, both had fallen deeply in love. In a blizzard of communications, Fogarty obtained permission to marry her young man, obtain a discharge, and departed the ship in port.[9] Together they left for his new assignment in Brazzaville.

At Lourenço Marques the prisoners joyfully left the *Asama Maru* and boarded the *Gripsholm*, now bound for America. Of all those who passed through Zentsuji, these were the only internees to ever be exchanged. All other American prisoners taken from Guam, military or civilian, would remain in Japan for the duration of the war. The *Gripsholm* reached the New York area on 25 August.

+ + + + + + + + +

Kobe, like Osaka, was continually bathed in smog. On Sunday, 28 June 1942, a number of the internees were allowed to hike to the Nunobiki Waterfalls in the hills north of Kobe. Looking down on Kobe, the men saw a heavy smoke haze covering the harbor.

Life in Kobe for the internees settled down to a diet of fish heads, rotten vegetables, and rice. Continued blackouts required the windows to be closed, trapping the voracious mosquitoes inside, along with the high humidity and heat, during the sum-mer months. Internal strife among the internees slowly grew, and petty regulations by the guards increased. The grievances against restrictions imposed by the guards and the Kencho (Japanese police) were exacerbated by the crowded conditions and bad food.[10] Hopes for repatriation soared when a few British citizens departed in mid-July for a separate exchange of British personnel on board the *Tatsuda Maru*.[11] By summer's end the Swiss consul was again able to provide money to the internees on behalf of their governments.[12] A few noncombatant Americans living in Japan at the start of the war were permitted to leave for an exchange in September 1943. At that time the consul informed men from Guam that *under no circumstances* would any of them be allowed to participate in *any* exchange until after the war ended.

Businessmen who had lived in Japan many years were among the numerous local alien internees. Those with Japanese wives remained in contact with their fami-lies, relying upon them for extra supplies of food and necessities. A few were ardent supporters of the Japanese military, arguing endlessly in support of Japan's conquest of Asia. Of note was a "Mr. Toms," who was "avowedly pro-Japanese . . . friendly and . . . intimate with the police. Because of this, he was considered an informer (which he undoubtedly was) and particularly disliked by most of the local internees." His release from confinement on 15 April 1944 was greeted by a sigh of relief.[13]

On 9 October 1942, prisoner survivors of the *Lisbon Maru* disaster were scheduled to arrive in Kobe.[14] The Japanese, having decided to use the internee quarters for the new prisoners, announced that the young internees would immediately move from the seamen's mission to the Marks House and the monks would be moved to the Canadian Academy. Because the Marks House was too small, the group was again divided and the Pan Am men were added to the academy roster. Conditions imme-diately improved when food was prepared by household staff rather than the nearby restaurant. The internees were now in three locations: the Butterfield mansion, the Marks House, and the Canadian Academy.

Basic necessities would remain in short supply, the shortages worsening as the months passed. The first Red Cross packages and supplies, sent on board the *Gripsholm*, were finally made available to the internees on 30 November 1942. Regular distribu-tion of Red Cross packages would continue for a few months. Later deliveries were sporadic at best, and all deliveries were stopped in the spring of 1944.

As 1943 progressed the Allies began to roll back the Japanese across the Pacific. The 1942 summer offensive on Guadalcanal was finished in January 1943. Gen. Douglas MacArthur was striking across New Guinea, German defenses had collapsed at Stalingrad, and the Allies were roaring across North Africa in pursuit of the vaunted

Afrika Corps. By November 1943 the Americans would begin slicing across the mid-Pacific as the Gilbert Islands were invaded by American forces.[15] By February 1944 the Marshall Islands would be secured, the Carolines would be under attack, and the Marianas would be laid bare to carrier attacks. The POW camps, as well as civilians within Kobe, experienced a dramatic shift in living standards. Severe rationing, long lines for basic foodstuffs and goods, limited hours for electricity, minuscule supplies of charcoal, and shortages of clothing affected all of Japan. By December 1944 conditions for local civilians were reversed markedly from the heady days of 1942.

On Christmas Day 1943, the Guam internees gathered the coffee and cocoa from their Red Cross kits and generously shared the scarce "ambrosia" with the local families of fellow internees. In contrast to the harsh treatment of the military POWs from Guam, the civilians enjoyed a moderate Christmas celebration complete with small amounts of roast beef. New Year's Eve would likewise be celebrated with wine and whisky. The only difficulty was the lack of heat from the inadequate wood-burning furnaces.[16]

Hunger and cold stalked the lives of the internees. The never-ending cold, shortage of food, and inadequate clothing began taking a toll on the health of the elderly internees in Kobe. Their extremities would become swollen, red, and itchy as a direct result of malnutrition. Soon, their skin would burst, and pus would seep from the cracks. Without heat and adequate treatment, the men became disabled and unable to attend to basic housekeeping chores. By February 1944 food shortages in Japan reached a crisis level. News had filtered into camp that the American government was charging Japan with deliberately starving POWs to death.

The food shortage in Japan had become so acute that even the civilian population was restricted to two buns per person per day, one-quarter pound (approximately) of meat per month, and fish twice a month. Vegetables were likewise scarce and rationed. Canned goods of any type became a great luxury. For the internees, the effects of starvation, coupled with the freezing temperature, made the gathering of wood a nightmarish chore. Cutting logs, splitting wood for cooking, heat, and the occasional bath, required more energy than could be replaced by the reduced rations. Japanese officials, fearing expected bombing attacks and retaliatory attacks by angered Japanese civilians against the prisoners, advised the prisoners to stockpile wood and avoid contact with any civilians. The fierce winter weather caused most to remain indoors for weeks on end, further adding to the isolation and misery. The first death from malnutrition occurred on 20 March 1944; the victim was Martin P. Gahley, age forty, one of the contractors from Guam.

Disagreements, fights, acts of pure selfishness, and theft began to haunt the desperately hungry internees. In late March 1944, Gregg noted that he and three others surreptitiously purchased two roosters and secretly prepared and ate the "feast" alone: "Last night, four of us had a real 'big' and 'filling' meal. For once in 2 1/2 years, I went to bed filled to a point that I did not care for another bite of food. . . . The necessity of having this banquet on the Q.T. detracted from the joy of the feast, but such is [the] way of life in an internment camp. Then, too, four more of the PAA fellows are having the same experience." Bribery of the guards and a thriving black market were all that supplied the prisoners with enough food to stave off certain death by starvation.

The cohesiveness of the men broke completely as food became even more of an obsession. The twenty-seven men in the Marks House could not find a way to cooperate amid claims of partiality and the unfair division of scavenged food. Small groups of two to five men simply began to look out only for themselves.

On 9 May 1944, the internees were informed they would be moved three to five miles outside of Kobe, safely away from the coming raids by American bombers. Two and a half years of "junk and stuff" had to be packed, and on 23 May 1944, the internees from the Marks House, Butterfield mansion, and the Canadian Academy began a laborious eight-day move to a former boys' school in Hyogo-Ken (prefecture), five miles north of Kobe in the low-lying Futatabi mountain range. Among the internees, the camp was simply called Futatabi.

Food had to be hauled by cart from Kobe every day, a round trip of six miles. Details of up to nine men would haul the six-hundred-pound cart uphill to the camp. In their weakened condition, many avoided this detail because the only reward was an additional four ounces of bread. Over the next few months, additional men would arrive from other locations throughout Japan to add to the crowding of the barracks. Again the men were separated by age. Those over fifty-five and all the men from Nagasaki were placed in one building, with the balance in the larger barracks.

Japanese newspapers continued to report on the progress of the war, as usual distorting the nature of Japan's losses and continuing the exaggerations of American losses. The Great Marianas Turkey Shoot was reported by Japanese papers as an American defeat, categorically stating the Americans lost five aircraft carriers and two battleships.[17] Discounting the propaganda, the internees could plot the Allied military advance into the Marianas.

In July 1944 the war cabinet of Hideki Tojo resigned, and upon the American invasion of Guam on 21 July, the police cut off newspaper service for the camp "due to present unsettled political situation."[18] It would be more than a week before another newspaper would be available.

Within weeks of arrival in Futatabi, a secret radio had begun to be assembled in the ceiling of the room housing six Pan Am men: Dick Arvidson, Jim Thomas, Fred Oppenborn, Ev Penning, Hal Brinkerhoff, and Grant Wells. The radio was built by Dick Arvidson from parts purloined by Fred Oppenborn from a Japanese storage shed. On 14 October 1944, Arvidson, with a huge smile, announced the radio was finally working. "That crude, bastardized electronic gadget with cheap, ill-fitting earphones could pick up Tokyo, Moscow, Berlin, London, New York and dear old San Francisco," said Jim Thomas. "It brought a world we had almost forgotten into our measly, stinking room and changed our miserable lives for the duration."[19] Oppenborn quickly learned the broadcast schedules and passed on important news, the first scoop being the invasion of the Philippines on 23 October 1944. No one outside the room was ever informed of the radio's presence for fear of retribution by the Japanese. A vow was made never to reveal its existence because there were many who would instantly inform the Japanese for a favor. Thomas faithfully kept the secret even from his two close friends, Bob Vaughn and George Conklin. Subsequently, no attempt was ever made to dispel false rumors.

CHAPTER 9

Life in Zentsuji

A MAN MUST MAKE HIS OPPORTUNITY, AS OFT AS FIND IT.

—*Francis Bacon*

The words of Governor George McMillin clattered from the teletype machines: "I want to tell President Roosevelt [that] we, of the American forces, fought valiantly and defended our posts until the last." On 17 January 1942 the Japanese news agency, Domei, released to the world press an interview with McMillin.[1] Prior to the actual invasion, the radio stations at the Marine barracks, Libugon, and the Pan Am station were abandoned, ending radio communications with the outside world. For America, all calls to Guam were met with a deathly silence. For six weeks, nothing was known about the men and women stationed on Guam.

The governor further stated that he had been transported to Japan and his treatment had been "satisfactory." McMillin's words were the first official acknowledgment that any of the military personnel who were on Guam were still alive. A Red Cross report received by the U.S. State Department on 24 January contained an accurate list of the captives.

As part of a continuous propaganda program, the Japanese recorded statements by a number of the POWs, broadcasting them via shortwave to United States.[2] Numerous Ham radio operators monitored these broadcasts, making recordings or transcriptions for prisoners' families. On 4 February and again on 18 April 1942, as was typical at the time, a shortwave broadcast by Commander Giles was intercepted by Mrs. Adam Welker of San Francisco. Welker transcribed the broadcast and sent a copy to Giles' family.[3] Like a number of other Americans, she listened for these broadcasts, hoping to bring comfort to the families of the captives. Some families were called by phone, but all were contacted by mail. Hundreds of Americans performed this service at their own expense.

On 23 April 1942 the POWs in Zentsuji received their first visit by Dr. Frederick Paravicini, the Swiss Red Cross official stationed in Japan. Prisoners were queried regarding their conditions; every single man stated that the food and heat were extremely inadequate. The shouts of "We are being starved to death" were simply ignored. Not one word of these conditions was noted in Paravicini's report. His report, received in Washington in June 1942, contained a complete list of prisoners, a list of the dead, and a statement of camp conditions—a statement far removed from the truth considering the severe shortage of clothing, heat, and food. All relatives of the living were notified by the Department of State, and the Army was tasked to notify families of the deceased.

During the first seven months of the war, when large numbers of military personnel and civilians fell under the control of Japan, confusion, duplication of efforts, and misinformation plagued the military and State Department's efforts to inform relatives of the POWs. At the behest of Secretary of State Cordell Hull and Army Chief of Staff George C. Marshall, the War Department and Navy Department jointly announced the creation of a new department, Special War Problems, within the Office of the Provost Marshal to coordinate all information regarding military prisoners, civilian internees, and foreign aliens. A central clearing point was finally established that would keep track of all prisoners and internees. For the relatives, the new department was to be the only source of valid information. However, when information was available, the State Department often usurped the military by mailing notices to families before giving the information to the provost marshal. The internecine department battles in Washington and miscommunication continued unabated throughout the war.

The Japanese had little interest in providing information about the POWs. Considering prisoners of war as dishonored soldiers, the Japanese also cared little about their living conditions. Until the prisoners were sequestered in a formal POW camp, that is, a camp in Japan proper, the Japanese rarely acknowledged their presence. Prisoners held on the Philippines, Malaya, Java, Borneo, and other islands in the South Pacific were considered as being held in temporary confinement. Until transported to the prisons in Japan, no accounting of prisoner's names or whereabouts was deemed necessary. Further, because these lands were considered liberated rather than conquered, no Red Cross officials would be permitted to visit the military prison camps in these areas. This convoluted thinking made the Japanese consider the captives from Guam, now in Japan, enemy soldiers taken in the conquest of territory rather than from a liberated area.

With Japan's liberation of the Philippines, the Japanese determined that U.S. diplomatic interests were null and void in the archipelago. The Swiss, and the Swiss Red Cross, acting as a neutral power, could represent the United States only in Japan—not in the liberated countries.[4] The Philippine Red Cross was permitted to supply a limited number of items, such as clothing, to internees and some military prisoners, but they could not represent the diplomatic interests of the United States. Until a neutral nation upon which both sides agreed could be found, no diplomatic concerns could be addressed. The process would be further complicated as the Japanese heavily propagandized the internment of Japanese nationals in North and South America, an internment that effectively ended Japanese espionage and sabotage in the Americas.[5] Convoluted as this reasoning appears, a Red Cross contact was initially permitted in Japan yet denied in other areas conquered by the Japanese, except for Mukden, Manchuria. The result of this diplomatic maneuvering meant the men and women from Guam would remain at the mercy of their captors, particularly the military.

With the initial introduction of work details at Zentsuji to clear land for growing food, the Japanese did honor part of the Geneva Convention. No objections could be voiced to these labors because no war material was being handled by the men. The clearing of land, dike building, and planting were fully authorized by the Geneva Convention. This adherence to the Geneva Convention would last less than a month.

Since their capture on Guam, except for stevedore and a war-damage cleanup details, few men had exerted any energy on labor for more than six weeks. In early February, however, the Japanese announced the beginning of regular work details.[6] Using fewer than half of the enlisted men, the first two work details were created. One detail worked within the camp, creating a tile drainage system, while the second created terraced paddies on a nearby mountainside. Those who worked would be paid the rate of ten to twenty-five sen per day, depending upon rank. Officers were paid the equivalent of eight to twenty-five yen per month, even though they refused to work. The Navy chiefs were chosen to supervise when the officers refused to do any work.[7]

For the enlisted men, being sent on labor details was a mixed blessing. Those sent to work were given extra rations of food and, more important, were placed in positions where they could steal additional food and supplies. Theft and sabotage, despite the risks, continued on a daily basis. Being caught was the only crime.

BMC Robert Lane, with five other Navy chiefs, led the first detail of 150 men to nearby Osa Yama (Mount Osa, elevation: five hundred meters) to create terraced paddies on the steep slopes.[8] After walking approximately four miles to the work site, the detail began a climb of one thousand feet to the work area. Using only pry bars and chunkels,[9] the land was to be cleared of rocks and roots and terraced along the steep slopes. With a short break for lunch, the men worked eight hours each day. This project, with work details of varying sizes, would continue for more than a year.

As night fell on the first day of labor, the men returned to the Zentsuji camp, where Lane formed the weary men in ranks and began berating them for "dogging the work" during the day. A single Bronx cheer rose from the back rank. Lane, racing toward where the sound emanated, said, "Who did that?" Another cheer rose from the opposite end of the ranks. Within seconds, Lane had lost control of the men to a chorus of jeers.[10] His threat to turn men over to the Japanese for discipline was not taken lightly by the men. Lane's action removed the last ounce of respect the men had for him as a work party leader. However, the Japanese and American officers still treated him with a modicum of respect because he was considered the *ichi ban*—the number one soldier of the camp—and the prisoners learned not to create trouble when Chief Lane was around.

Navy PBY Catalina crewman S2 Joseph R. Brown, captured when his plane was shot down near Kiska, Alaska, wrote, "Sometimes we dug over so small an area in a day that the Japanese decided to set stakes each morning to show how far we were to dig before quitting time. When nobody was looking (they couldn't watch everyone at once) we moved the stakes back down, a little at a time so they wouldn't notice. Each man was allotted a strip about four feet wide, where we were expected to dig twenty-five feet or more up the slope, but we often got by with only five or six. We were able to do this shirking because the guards were usually off somewhere sleeping. We would obligingly awaken them at mealtimes or if we saw an officer coming—no use in ruining a good thing."[11]

The labor detail building terraces on Osa Yama continued until late in the summer of 1943. The work was boring and often difficult. Following the contours of the hill, paddy dikes were created every fifteen inches of elevation. The dikes enclosed a terrace that varied in width depending upon the slope. All rocks, tree stumps, and roots had to be pried out with the inefficient tools. Each terrace was then planted with vegetables. Labor details would continue to tend the terraced vegetable gardens throughout the war.

Dirt was moved in two small baskets attached to the ends of a pole. The yo-yo pole was a simple six-foot bamboo pole with rope at each end to which were tied two hanging baskets or flat, woven trays. With woven baskets barely clearing the ground, the prisoners lifted the load by merely flexing their legs. The dirt would become part of the dike. The prisoners thought this was an inefficient procedure compared to the use of a simple wheelbarrow. However, carrying the yo-yo pole was relatively easy work because one could rest a few minutes between loads.

The Japanese exchanged dollars for yen on a basis of one for one. As such, little money existed other than the wages paid to officers or to the men working on labor details. With scarce opportunity to purchase goods outside the prison, the wages paid were of little use. Men not on work details often served as batmen for the officers, thereby securing funds for purchasing or trading for rice, cigarettes, or a rare piece of soap from the civilians and guards.

With the minuscule payment on their first payday, and in a typical American reaction to such absurdity, many jocularly said they would save up to buy a ranch, a car, a house, or some other item when the war was over. When a few refused to collect their pay, the Japanese commandant demanded the men step forth and receive the money. Considering the refusal to accept pay as an insult, the Japanese became determined that all accept their pay. Chief Lane again was called to gather the miscreants, and under the threat of punishment by him, all signed for their pay. In short order, card games used the yen for betting purposes, and some men wallowed in their extensive winnings.

Like a restoration of the "divine right of kings," the three divisions of ranks lived in isolated ignorance of one another. The separation was most extreme in the Navy. The average Navy man would further look down upon the Marines as mere guards and toy soldiers for their amusement. Most of the Navy leadership tenaciously clung to the belief that the battleships—with the possible addition of aircraft carriers—would be the first line of defense and attack in any war. Lane's authoritarian behavior, often repeated, was a typical example of the separation from and disdain for the non-commissioned officers and lower ranks.

An even wider gulf existed between the officer corps and all enlisted men during the prewar years. The prewar style of imperious leadership by most officers, particularly the retention of perquisites, continued to fester and poison the relationships between the prisoners. From the entire cadre of men from Guam, only three groups were to create a sustained bond of mutual support during captivity. First were the medics under the direction and leadership of Lt. Cdr. H. J. Van Peenen, and second, the work gangs of enlisted men. Under the leadership of Maj. Donald Spicer of the Sumay Marines and Capt. Mortimer Marks, another unique bond of mutual support and camaraderie was established between the Marine officers of Guam and their enlisted ranks.

By the end of February, the daily routine was well established. Lt. Cdr. Samuel L. Newman, after a ceremony of facing the sun and bowing to the emperor, conducted daily calisthenics for fifteen minutes.[12] The Americans had already converted the beginning bow to the emperor into a morale boosting ritual by softly saying as they bowed, "Good morning, Mr. Roosevelt." Warmed by the exercise, the men would be served a sparse breakfast in the barracks followed by the sick call and the muster of work details. The mountain detail received an extra ration of food while those on sick call were cut to half a ration. The evening meal would not be served until after the mountain work party returned to camp.

For those remaining in camp, occasional marches through the town of Zentsuji and the countryside were conducted by the Japanese guards. Exiting the camp, the men turned left, passing Gokuku, a Shinto shrine where they were required to stop, face the shrine, and bow. Whenever possible, they stole the food left as offerings. The forced bow to the shrine grated upon the men until one wag noted that, as they bowed, their rear ends faced north toward Tokyo, the home of Emperor Hirohito. Deep bows, accompanied with wide grins, thereafter were looked upon as a silent means of insulting Hirohito. "As the men passed through populated areas," said Sergeant Shane, "we would often sing and march in unison as a way to show the locals that we might be prisoners but we weren't beaten. Sometimes we would do intricate marching routines, despite the shouts by the guards to stop. It was our way of regaining some control over our lives."[13]

For most these walks were the first exposure to Japanese customs and conditions. Few had ever seen the wood-burning cars and trucks or the gauze masks that covered many faces. The women of Zentsuji were dressed in brightly colored kimonos, the clatter of their wooden shoes echoing through the very crowded streets. Japanese men were dressed uniformly in a lightweight gray overshirt or, in colder weather, brown coats.[14] The few who made detailed observations were struck with the natural beauty of the area. From the hillsides, the rice paddies created a quiltlike pastiche of green and brown across the countryside, which flowed downhill to the Inland Sea. Seasonal color changes served only to enhance the beauty of the scenery. Strange to the men was the simplicity of the Japanese homes, with their sliding doors, opaque paper serving as windows, and paucity of furniture, all of which reflected a minimalist lifestyle.

In the winter the prisoners were mystified to see trees girdled with straw stalks—only to learn the Japanese rationale—the straw served to trap bugs that would infest the trees. As spring approached the straw would be removed and burned. To those with farm experience in America, little credence would be given to the effectiveness of the straw wrappings.

Additional work details of forty men each were formed within another week. One detail worked as stevedores in the port of Takamatsu and the second detail working at the rail yards in Sakaide. Takamatsu, a small port on the northern coast of Shikoku, was approximately eight miles northeast on one rail line while the rail yards of Sakaide were ten miles via another rail line that ran northwest then turned eastwardly. Over the ensuing years, labor details were sent to other rail yards but rarely for more than a few days.

Separate trains would carry the prisoners because the destinations were in opposite directions from the camp. Each day, shortly after dawn, the details would be placed on local trains for the one-hour trip, the men mixing in with local Japanese traveling to work. The prisoners were to work six days a week handling nonwar material. Boxcars or ships—the work was the same. Cargo was to be loaded or unloaded by hand with few mechanical devices.

At the docks the men worked alongside Korean stevedores who had been pressed into labor by the benevolent masters of Nippon. A typical railway freight car would be loaded with two-hundred-pound burlap sacks of rice, flour, beans, or another commodity. Each man was required to carry a single sack, lifted by two other men onto his shoulder. At first the Japanese took great delight in humiliating the weakened men as they struggled to stand erect under the crushing loads. Each man, determined not to give the Jap guards any satisfaction, called upon his inner reserves of strength to carry the load, and each man quickly learned how to balance the weight and move slowly to the next destination. It was grueling, hard, exhausting labor, and the men were given only a short break to eat around midday. Within two weeks, having developed a technique and sufficient strength to handle these bags, the men started to concentrate on looting food. The same grueling work was performed in the rail yards as trains were unloaded and reloaded.

Crowded into trains with ordinary Japanese as they traveled to and from work, the men began a systematic pattern of theft. By the end of the first week, the prisoners had developed techniques to jostle the civilians and successfully pick their pockets. They began stealing any material not nailed down. Many became very proficient as pickpockets, stealing wallets, purses, and food—or anything they felt could be traded for food. Pencils, pens, writing paper, newspapers, and cloth became objects for theft.[15] Those who opposed the theft on a moral basis were soon won over when convinced that theft and sabotage were just another way to wage war against the enemy.

The prisoners soon found unique ways in which to practice their new craft of thievery. Pieces of wire were formed for picking locks in order to enter cabins on board the ships in Takamatsu. Sergeant Shane recalled, "Some men became so proficient they could pick the lock of a shipboard storeroom, let other men enter, and then lock them in to gorge on any food. The guards, as they passed by, would check the door locks and continue on their rounds. The locks would again be picked and our men would change places with other men. One could say we 'stole in shifts.'"[16]

Another simple tool was the "looting tube" or "rice whistle," a hollow bamboo rod that was approximately half an inch in diameter, six inches long, and sliced diagonally to a point on one end. Carefully avoiding the gaze of the Japanese guards, a prisoner would jab the stick into a burlap bag of sugar, extracting the sugar into his pocket, a sock, or other container that would be sewn inside his clothing.

When bags of rice arrived at the rail yards, the bamboo rod proved inefficient. The rice would jam in the slender tube, and little rice could be stolen. Larger pieces of bamboo were tried until it was found that a one-inch circumference prevented clogging. Because the bags were tightly packed, only a small amount could be stolen from a bag without causing a noticeable difference. The men became expert at hiding the loot bags and frequently returned to camp with five to thirty pounds of looted rice in one day.

Fearing that too many men trying to steal would lead to recklessness and a possible cessation of the work parties, a few men on each detail were designated as the primary thieves. This did not preclude the crimes of opportunity that would often come to men working in semi-isolation from the guards. When food was located that could not be hidden, for example, bulky canned items, word quickly spread to the other prisoners of its location. Frequently, a disturbance would be created to distract the attention of the guards. One or more men would slip away to gorge on the items. The thefts had to be accomplished quickly since any slowdown in work was met with suspicion and beatings. Theft of food was considered a major offense by the Japanese because all food was property of the emperor. Getting caught was a risk that most would accept in order to alleviate the "hairball of hunger."

When caught stealing or resting at an unauthorized time—or if a sadistic guard simply wanted to punish the men—brutal beatings with sticks were administered. The sticks, two inches wide and three to four feet long, were always swung at maximum speed against the men. Favorite targets were the head, elbows, knees, groin, and shinbones. Guards, armed with rifles, would stab the men with bayonets or, at full force, bash the butt of their rifle into the head or back. Frequently, multiple numbers of guards would attack a man, kicking, whipping, punching, and slashing in a frenzied orgy of hatred. If a prisoner protested or sought to deflect the blows, the bashing escalated. If the POW fell to the ground, vicious kicking continued until the prisoner rose or the guard became tired. Few Japanese could resist going a day without bashing the hated Westerners. No matter how one bowed to the Japanese or observed an obedient behavior, almost every encounter was met with a hard slap or punch to the face. The punches were in the style often described as "a John Wayne,"[17] a powerful assault aimed at the eye, nose, or ear. Always delivered with force, such punishment became part of everyday life.

Prisoners referred to this technique as "slapping." In a typical slap, the guard would fold his fingers down at the first knuckle, rather than folding the fingers into a fist. With a sweeping motion, the guard would slap the prisoners with this semi-opened hand. The effect was equal to any direct punch in the face and caused ear damage to most prisoners.

The Japanese, seeking order and uniformity in their procedures, selected the same men to work the same details each day. Rarely was a man moved to another detail. If selected to work the railroad yards, the prisoner would rarely, if ever, work on the Takamatsu docks or Osa Yama details. Once assigned to any of the three details, a prisoner expected to be sent on the same detail every day. Pfc. Barney Barnett recalled, "I never worked on the hill. With the exception of two or three days at the Sakaide rail yard, I always worked at Takamatsu. By going on the same detail, we learned how to 'work the system' in order to steal or avoid heavy work."[18]

As a result the larger "tribe" of prisoners became a collection of "subtribes" who worked, ate, and lived together. Rare was the man who knew many men outside his small subtribe, and details able to steal or bargain for extra food shared the "booty" only within the subtribe. The division of men in every camp was similar, and the resulting jealousies caused many fights.

＊＞＋＞＋＜＞＜＋＞＜＋＞＜＋＞＜＋＞＜＋

In Zentsuji a well-functioning drainage system was constructed in a few weeks. Gardens were planted and frequently tended by officers seeking relief from boredom. Dr. Van Peenen had few drugs, bandages, and instruments to minister to the medical needs of the camp. Sergeant Shane said, "To everyone in camp, he was a real hero in the way he took care of the sick. Arguing to keep sick men off the work details and constantly demanding drugs, raising the ire of the Japanese. He was subject to frequent and violent slaps for what the Japs considered impertinence.[19] Always at his side, and equally favored by the men, was the medic Pharmacist's Mate Keck, doing all the dirty work."[20]

Many years later Van Peenen reflected on the ability of Keck to steal extra food for the sick: "Keck, as an enlisted man, was able to bring in extra food, secreted in his trouser cuffs and shoes. He had to move carefully or he rained rice."[21] What Van Peenen did not acknowledge was that the Japanese guards and civilians operated a black market. Monies paid to the men for work were often used to purchase medicines. In a postwar letter to the Red Cross, Van Peenen noted that ample amounts of novocaine were available from Red Cross issues but the Japanese doctor (Saito, aka Doctor Sade) refused to allow its use. Saito, on rare occasions, would issue small amounts of spinal novocaine for extensive surgeries.[22] "We even had one man who required insulin to stay alive," said Lt. Dean Morgan, USMC, "and Van Peenen always managed to get enough and the man survived."[23] A Marine from Wake Island, Pfc. Warren D. "Bull" Conner, earned the moniker Black Market King for his uncanny ability to bribe guards and civilians to obtain the necessary medical supplies.[24]

Punishment by the Japanese for any offense normally involved not only bashing but also being thrown into the camp prison. The camp brig, a small, two-room shed, was located adjacent to the fence of the camp and fifty feet directly opposite the space between the two barracks buildings. The filthy, bug-ridden shack was surrounded by a separate wooden fence that created a two-foot space between the brig fence and the outer fence of the camp. The only source of air or light was from the one door, which, when closed in the summer, caused the cell to become a stifling oven. Men thrown into the brig were stripped of clothing, regardless of the weather. In one incident, a number of officers were placed naked in the mosquito- and bug-infested brig during the summer heat. The stated offense was that they were "suspected" of stealing sugar from the Japanese army's warehouse. After three days, bitten by mosquitoes, bedbugs, and lice, and without food or water, their survival became tenuous. The enlisted men devised a plan to sneak water in to the prisoners using bladders from two footballs. Carefully ensuring the guards were distracted, the men, S1 Don Binns and S1 Joe Brown,[25] rushed from the chicken coop behind the brig, clamored over the brig fence, and ran around to the brig door, lobbing the bladder of water to the men. On subsequent trips the empty bladder was retrieved. The officers, much to the surprise of the Japanese, survived the deliberate and sadistic suffering imposed by a lack of water.

* * * * * * *

Morale continued to erode as the heady exuberance of every Japanese victory was trumpeted with formal announcements, newspaper headlines, and boastful braggadocio by the guards. On 12 May 1942 work details were suspended as the Japanese conducted a two-day series of endurance and physical tests of the prisoners. In their malnourished condition, the prisoners were not anxious to excel.

Typical was a test to see how far an American could throw a grenade. In usual fashion, most prisoners deliberately underperformed, but the bragging of the guards did frustrate at least one man. PhM1 Abner P. Rowe,[26] a superb athlete and still in good physical shape, reached down, picked up a simulated grenade, and threw it over the barracks building. Looking back at the startled Japanese, he said, "Someday, one of these things is going to land right in your lap when you're seated in the bomb shelter."[27] The Japanese guards stood in slack-jawed amazement.

Determined to demoralize the prisoners, the Japanese decided to test their well-conditioned guards in a series of footraces against the prisoners. A section of the main yard was selected for the races. The prisoners, in groups of three to five, were instructed to run a specified distance as fast as possible. Recording the times, the guards continued to smile at the now-proven inadequacy of the American competitive spirit. Selecting their best men, the Japanese asked for an American volunteer to engage in a relay footrace. Again all shrunk back in reluctance. Taunting the Americans for their competitive weakness, the Japanese began to offer money bets, even giving odds that their man would embarrass the Americans.

Bantering back and forth, the Japanese smilingly offered even larger wagers as the Americans exercised the crafty art of a pool hall hustler. With an exaggerated prodding by fellow Marines, Pfc. Ralph Baggett and three other men were proffered as the designated competitors. Now underweight by more than fifty pounds, Baggett looked like a six-foot scarecrow. The wagering dramatically increased as the Japanese smugly assessed the skinny American standing aside the healthy Japanese soldiers.

Having slowly jogged to the starting point, the competitors turned, and to the shout of "Aru!" the Japanese soldier leapt into the lead. By the end of the third leg, the Japanese were leading by at least twenty-five yards. Baggett, preparing to run the anchor leg, was extremely wary of the Japanese propensity to beat up anyone who may embarrass them. But with a shrug and a sense of determination, he said to himself, "Oh hell! I'm going for it." Bursting past the Japanese soldier, Baggett crossed the finish line twenty yards in the lead. With hands held high, the prisoners jumped for joy, lustily cheering the lanky Texan who had so easily defeated the best Japan had to offer.[28]

"Let me tell you," said Pfc. Garth Dunn, "we felt as if we had just won the war! Until then, our morale was heading to rock bottom. After that race our morale simply turned around and we never felt that dejected again." With much grumbling, the Japanese guards honored their wagers, but discipline and punishment notably increased in the next few days.

CHAPTER 10

Labor at Zentsuji

A DESIRE TO RESIST OPPRESSION IS IMPLANTED IN THE NATURE OF MAN.

—*Tacitus*

The use of prisoners as laborers has a long history in Japan. Convicts were used as cheap labor in the government-owned mines for hundreds of years. Simply put, it was an easy way to lessen the costs to keep convicts. In the late nineteenth century, when various companies owned the ports and mines, the tradition carried over into the commercial market. By 1900, almost 75 percent of mine laborers were convicts, a satisfactory arrangement for the cash-strapped government and the many mining companies, such as Mitsui, Mitsubishi, and Aso. The government contracted for the use of convicts at half the rate of regular laborers. The use of POWs appears to have been contracted for at one-fourth the normal rate. Health and safety considerations were rarely part of the company concerns.

In the small port of Takamatsu, no cranes were available for unloading ships. Instead, a rickety structure of bamboo and planks was erected for this purpose. Plank walkways were stepped back and forth and rose to the ship deck. Similar walkways were constructed to enter the holds, and a second major series of walkways rose back to the deck and down to the pier. Working like coolies, the men carried baskets of ore suspended from shoulder poles, emptying the ship with small loads of less than a hundred pounds like "an endless stream of worker ants. By the end of a day, the men were totally exhausted."[1]

One of the worst cargoes to unload was bauxite ore, a claylike substance mixed with small rocks and boulders. Used in the manufacture of aluminum, the ore was extremely difficult to shovel when dry, but worse, if it was wet, it would stick to shovels, doubling their weight. The absolute worst cargo was sulfur. The dust would get into the nose and lungs, causing uncontrolled coughing. Sulfur dust, mixed with sweat, caused extreme itchiness and rashes in the prisoners' armpits, on their backs, and on their genitals. The POWs suffered the aftereffects for days.[2]

Whether bauxite, sulfur, or coal, the drudgery never varied or ceased. The food rations, adequate for a sedentary lifestyle, were far from adequate to fuel intensive labor. The miserly rations began to physically show within a few short weeks. Clothes began to hang loosely as waistlines shrank. The early signs of severe malnutrition, beriberi and pellagra, rapidly appeared. The Zentsuji camp Navy cooks and chiefs, however, remained healthy despite the "universally" reduced rations. Because their work was not as physically demanding, their loss of weight from the Japanese diet was substantially slower that those on labor details. While the Navy chiefs may have shared the same ration—few believe they did—their imperious attitude toward lower ranks worsened the tide of resentment.

In real need of more food, the men turned to thievery and smuggling. Desperate to relieve the "hairball of hunger," the POWs would walk into crew areas on board ships, storage areas, dockside sheds, anywhere—seeking food. If a man was seen, he quickly hunched over as if in distress and simply brazened his way out by asking, "Benjo?" More often than not, the guards laughed at the man's agony as they pointed in the direction of the facility. Those who could, picked locks, but most simply smashed past locks and doors to find food.

The older and more experienced soldiers quickly realized that the Japanese were no different from most people around the world. They could be easily bribed for simple amenities and favors. Some of the worst guards would "turn away" when observing a theft as long as they knew they would get their share. Some of the most brutal and feared guards became active participants. Still, every man knew that with little provocation—or if the guard felt threatened—he would turn on a man with unbridled anger, beating him senseless.

The Japanese were aware that the food rations were inadequate. The men were weighed regularly, and if weight gains were noted, rations were reduced. One of the shortest men in the Marines was young Pfc. Larry "Bud" Budzynski, barely standing over five feet.[3] Eating the same rations as men over six feet, his weight remained almost constant. The Japanese were perplexed. "They had two men follow me for days," said Budzynski, "even into the *benjo*. They recorded everything I ate and they actually weighed my excrement!" After two weeks the surveillance was ended, continued Budzynski, "but except for the last year when I also starved, they never stopped checking me over—trying to figure out why I didn't lose much weight."

By the end of April, conditions in the camp became more tolerable as the Japanese dropped the hated morning exercises, reduced the number of inspections, and conducted the *tenkos* only twice each day. The spring weather erased the hardships of the bitterly cold winter and survival seemed assured.

On 20 May 1942 the camp was surprised when RM1 Arthur Griffiths, USN, captured in Shanghai's consulate, departed to Tokyo for repatriation.[4] Griffiths was the prisoners' last chance to let their families at home know of their condition, and he departed with a satchel of messages. Two weeks later the Battle of Midway bloodied the Japanese fleet, but news did not reach the camp. The only change noted was that the *Osaka Mainichi* (the English version newspaper) was not delivered, and for the first time, a typewritten report was posted stating a major naval battle was fought to an indecisive conclusion. The Imperial Japanese Navy hid the defeat from the War Ministry for more than two months and from the people for the entire war.[5]

＋＞＋＋　＋＞　＋＞　＋＞＜＋

As in all other camps, the behavior of the guards was never predictable. At the beginning of internment, any civilian who even touched a prisoner could expect a severe beating by the military guards. By the end of 1942, military guards began to look the other way when civilian supervisors assaulted the prisoners. Punishment by civilians varied from mere shouts to beatings that would cause permanent damage to the men. In one of these beatings, just as a guard punched Pfc. Herb Humphrey in the throat, another guard bashed his head forward with the butt of a rifle. He was never again to speak above a soft whisper.

"Sometime in late February 1943," said Pfc. Ralph Baggett, "I was working in the rail yards in Sakaide. A civilian guard with no authority over us had been slapping a number of the men for the past few days . . . just a vicious jerk."[6] While working Baggett noticed a few slices of dried sweet potato scattered on the ground. As he scooped them up, his glance caught the same guard approaching. Baggett knew the guard was intent on punching him for stealing from the emperor. "I noticed there were no other guards around as he came at me," Baggett recalled. "As he swung, I deflected his blow and struck back, slightly pulling my punch. At that exact moment, two other guards came around the corner and saw him reel back from the blow. They grabbed me, kicked me about, and took me back to camp."

Back at the camp, Major Hosotani directed the Japanese supply officer, known as "Smiling Jack,"[7] to administer punishment to Baggett. Smiling Jack was exceptionally tall for a Japanese man and often described by the prisoners as handsome. In general his treatment of the prisoners was benign. "That evening, Smiling Jack slapped my head with the palm of his hand but with the fingers tucked into the palm," Baggett said. "He hit me as hard as possible, about ten times on each side of the face, knocking my head from side to side. With my face and head swollen and every inch covered with bruises, they dumped me in the brig and said I would remain there for ten days. With no heat, I darn near froze to death. The next morning, Smiling Jack came by and indicated he was sorry for the beating but that he had no choice. I told him I understood his predicament."

Normally a beating or placement in the camp brig was considered sufficient punishment. However, striking a Japanese civilian was considered equal to hitting a soldier. "On the ninth day, they released me," said Baggett:

> I hung around the camp for a few weeks until the Japs held some form of military trial. I never understood a word. I remember an interpreter asking me why I "hit the man so hard." I said, "If I wanted to hurt him, I would not have pulled my punch!" I was sentenced

to four months in a Japanese penitentiary. I was put in a buggy with two guards, flaps hanging down on all sides, and taken to the train station. In Takamatsu I was taken to the city prison. I was placed in isolation, the only American in the jail. I managed to make contact with the trustee bringing me food and with sign language, managed to convince him I needed more food as I was so much larger than the Japanese.

In a letter to Capt. Mortimer Marks, Baggett described his time in the penitentiary:[8]

[Upon arrival] the handcuffs were removed and I was fingerprinted. All my prisoner of war clothes were taken from me and I was given a "G" string for my underwear, a well-worn, dingy, red kimono, a red quilted vest, and a pair of straw sandals. Since I was over six feet tall all the clothes were small. I was then taken by two guards to another building. I was led into a long hall on each side of which were twelve doors. Near the center of the hall they stopped, unlocked one of the doors, which was about six inches thick, and motioned for me to enter.

My cell was six feet square. In one corner was a small hole in the floor. In the hole was a wooden box eight inches deep. This was my toilet. The box was removed and emptied every two days through a small door to the outside of the building. I could see outside into the courtyard through the bars of a small window above which had a heavy black curtain that could be rolled down during bad weather and air-raid blackouts. The floor was covered with a straw mat. A single low wattage electric light bulb hanging from the center of the ceiling remained lit all night. On one wall hung a Japanese calendar depicting a small map of Japan and the Pacific islands. In the massive door was a small glass slot. I could see the eyes of a guard observing me through the slot. I think every guard in the penitentiary must have come by to stare at me.

This cell was my home from the twenty-eighth of March to the twenty-eighth of July [1943]. Twice a day a Japanese convict passed in food through a six-inch-square hole in the wall. He was a "trustee" and had the freedom of the hall. The food consisted of rice and some-times a vegetable served in a tin bowl. I ate with used chopsticks—well enough to pick up a grain of rice. I often wondered how many Japanese criminals had eaten with those same chopsticks.

Once a day a guard entered and inspected the cell. Once a week I was shaved with a straight razor by the trustee in the hall. Every second week the trustee clipped my hair as close as possible. Every Sunday I was taken outside to another building for a bath. I arrived just in time to see the other convicts, all Japanese, finishing their baths. Baths were taken in three iron cook pots similar to the old fashioned, black iron wash pots used on early American farms. The water had been heated over a wood fire. When my turn came to take a bath, after all the convicts had finished, there was scum about one inch on top of the water in each pot. No soap was available. I still looked forward to my "dirty bath" each week.

Each time I was taken outside my cell, a cone-shaped straw hat was put on my head. It came down over my face and ears and rested on my shoulders. I could see through the loosely woven straw. The first time it was put on me I tilted it back so that I could see better but the guard made me lower it. I deduced that the purpose of the hat was to allow me to "save face" since I was supposed to be ashamed. What a ridiculous sight I must have been—in my small dirty kimono and tiny sandals with the straw dunce hat covering my entire head—guided by a little guard who did not reach my shoulders.

Once, when the trustee was shaving me, we had an opportunity to talk while the guard was at the opposite end of the hall. We spoke only in Japanese and sign language. He told me he was serving a life sentence for killing his wife. After this conversation I looked forward somewhat apprehensively to my weekly shaves.

The loneliness of four months of solitary confinement was the hardest to endure. There was nothing to distinguish one day from another except for the haircut and the weekly shave and bath. I sang and talked to myself under my breath. I recalled almost everything that had happened in my life. I remembered Harold Burt and Bill Bomar—two of my closest friends who had been killed by the Japanese in the brief battle on Guam—and wondered if they had not been luckier than I.

I received absolutely no news of any kind. I wondered how the war was going and if I would ever get out of Japan alive. I was afraid that the POW camp might be moved and that I would be separated from my friends. Worse still, what if the war ended and I was forgotten and left in Japan?

The slightest thing that happened was of interest to me. I listened to the sparrows outside my cell. I soon detected the difference in the sounds they made such as their cry of alarm when a cat was stalking them. In watching cockroaches in my cell I discovered one pure albino cockroach. We stared at each other for hours at a time.[9]

On the twenty-eighth of July 1943, I was taken to the warden's office where my clothing was returned. A soldier from camp was waiting to take me to Zentsuji, where, upon arrival, I was given a royal welcome from all the POWs.

Major Hosotani was also there to meet Baggett, and in a raspy, deliberately cold voice he said, "If you ever lay a hand upon another Japanese, you will be shot." Baggett recalled, "I can't describe the happiness I felt to be back with my friends and to the 'security' of a prisoner of war camp."

+·+·+·+·+·+·+·+·+·+·+

Not every day was without humor. The detail sent to the docks at Takamatsu was often transported in the baggage car of the local train. Allowed to smoke, one prisoner casually flipped his cigarette butt out the window. However, his aim was off and the smoldering butt dropped between the window and the car wall. In short order, smoke began to rise from the opening. "Without a fire extinguisher," said Pfc. Howard "Seagull" Ross, USMC, "we had no way to put out the fire. Sure as hell, the Japs would make our life a living hell if the car burned up. One of the guys came up with a very simple solution. One after the other, we lined up and urinated into the opening. The fire was soon out and we had given Japan a urine soaked train."[10]

On another occasion S2 Joe "Fingers" Brown almost lost his head to a Japanese sword. Brown, a gangling young man with very large hands and feet, rarely joined in the chatter as the trains carried them to and from Takamatsu. With remarkably deepset eyes, bushy eyebrows, and a pensive glare, he began staring at a Japanese soldier who was, in turn, staring at Brown. It became obvious to all that Seaman Brown's actions were grating to the Japanese soldier, particularly as other Japanese soldiers also noted the exchange of glares. To be stared at, particularly by a prisoner, was considered a loss of face. "Fortunately," said Pfc. Barney Barnett, "Brown got the message as the Jap's buddies restrained him from attacking Brown with his sword." Brown, with an impish smile, said, "It was not the brightest thing to do and I never did it again."

The Sakaide rail yard was bordered by small Japanese farms. Less than one hundred yards away a milk goat was staked. Before the end of every workday, the farmer's wife would retrieve the goat and take it to her home for milking. One afternoon, the men noticed that the lady had left the area. The prisoners quickly stole the goat, milked her dry, and returned it to the stake. That evening, when the woman attempted to milk the goat and failed, she rose and shouted—what most assumed were epithets—in their direction. The goat was never visible again.[11]

No effort was ever spared in the prisoners' attempts to perpetrate sabotage. Boxcars were loaded in such a manner as to make unloading almost impossible. Boxes and cartons were slit so contents would pour out upon movement. Castings, parts, and equipment were broken whenever the guards relaxed their vigilance. Barrels of oil, with the fill hole cap loosened, would be loaded upside down. Sabotage was the one instance in which cooperation was always given by fellow prisoners.

On one occasion at Sakaide, Seaman Brown and others punched holes in a large number of oil drums as they finished loading a freight car. The oil immediately began flowing out the sides of the car, clearly visible if any of the Japanese stevedores looked in their direction. The prisoners scrambled to push the car out into the yards so the stevedores wouldn't see the oil pouring out the bottom of the car. Two men, Sgt. Robert "Red" Newton and Pfc. Howard Ross, used brooms to frantically sweep— "rocks, dirt, anything"—over the oil that trailed along the tracks.[12]

At Takamatsu a civilian guard nicknamed "Pee Wee" was responsible for loading and dispatching the cars. Unknown to the Japanese, a number of the men could read Japanese and secretly switched the destination tags on the sides of the boxcars. Located six years after the war by Pfc. Artis "Big Jones" Jones, Pee Wee was shocked to learn of the prisoners' shenanigans. "I told him what we did," said Jones, "and that really caused his eyes to open up! After the empty freight cars had been brought alongside the dock and loaded up, sealed, and tagged for their destination, they were shunted by a switch engine to parallel tracks. I told him that Brown could read the labels. While a bunch of us stood guard, he [Brown] would go out there, pick up as many as ten of those tags and reroute the cars to other places."

Jones concluded, "When I got through telling that to Pee Wee, he sighed, 'Ah so! It is now no wonder we kept getting those complaints from all over Japan about freight that was never ordered, and other things they ordered never did come!' When he got through explaining it to the rest of them, they all [the local Japanese] expressed genuine surprise that we were that smart."[13]

CHAPTER 11

Transfer to Osaka

During the last week of May 1942, the Japanese called for "volunteers" to go to Osaka for a period of three months. Recognizing that stevedore work enabled the men to frequently steal food, more than a hundred men quickly volunteered. Late in the afternoon of Monday, 8 June 1942,[1] a total of 150 men were selected, assembled, and marched for three hours to the port of Tadotsu, their arrival point almost six months earlier.

The eight-mile daylight walk to Tadotsu, hidden from view the night of their arrival, now revealed close-up views of Japanese homes, small villages, and the remarkably beautiful scenery. Were they not prisoners of war, most would have been delighted to visit the area. Shortly after 10 p.m., having waited at dockside more than two hours and with no room to lie down, the men were crammed into the hold of an inter-island steamer,[2] departing at midnight for the port of Osaka. At midmorning, the steamer tied up to the pier at the foot of Osanhashi Street. A one-mile march brought the men to the Osaka stadium.

The prison, bearing the Japanese designation Minato-Ku (in Minato District), was built under the stands of the stadium.[3] The spectator stands lay along one side of a large soccer field, encircled by a racetrack. On the south end of the field was an empty swimming pool, unnoticed by most prisoners. The prisoners' living quarters, or barracks, was a shed beneath the stadium seats. The room, about 20 feet wide and approximately 165 feet long, tapered from a height of almost 25 feet down to 3 feet. Two rows of sleeping platforms ran the entire length with a three-foot aisle down the center. Unfortunately, tables were in the aisles and, with only one entry at the center, movement within the barracks was quite awkward. "Those of us who lived on the low side were horribly cramped," wrote EM2 Ed Hale. "On the other side, with high ceilings and windows, it was fairly comfortable."[4]

Labor details began the following day. The prisoners were marched one mile to the waterfront and placed into smaller details of five to twenty men for stevedore work on ships or railroad freight cars along the piers. A separate Japanese boss (*honcho*) would take charge of a work detail and march the men to a job site. Arriving at the pier, the very first detail was met by a Japanese foreman. Attempting to courteously greet the men, he slowly said, "O-hi-o," the Japanese equivalent of, "Good Morning." Standing in the front rank was Pfc. Charles Seymour. A native of Louisiana, Seymour spoke constantly of the day when he would go home again and open a restaurant called Seymour's Seafood by the Seashore. With youthful insouciance and southern wit, Seymour looked the honcho in the eye, pointed at his chest, and said, "O-hi-o? Nai. Nai! Me . . . o-kla-ho-ma!"[5] Laughter was choked back but the tone of the day had been set. The Japanese may have been in charge, but the American POWs were not to be deterred in their attempts to loot food, sabotage equipment, and create havoc whenever humanly possible. Horrendous as captivity in Osaka would prove, morale for the men from Guam always remained high.

From prior experience in Takamatsu, the men knew that balancing 220-pound sacks on weakened backs was considered normal.[6] A detail of six men would daily be required to load or unload up to ten freight cars filled with any form of commodity from rice to canned goods or mixed freight. The work in Osaka was identical to that in Takamatsu, except for the availability of dockside cranes. An endless stream of ore and coal ships gave no relief to the daily drudgery. In the summer heat, the effects of malnutrition and reduced rations were multiplied. Unless additional food could be obtained, death by starvation would become inevitable.

The stadium camp would serve as the POWs' home while a new camp was built to house the increasing numbers of prisoners. During this interim period, the medical needs of the Guam men in Osaka were met by Lt. (jg) Henry Williams, and later by Lt. (jg) James Eppley.[7] Itchioka barracks would later serve as one of two prisoner hospitals in Osaka. The stadium would eventually be the main medical facility for the thousands of prisoners working in the Kobe-Osaka area.

In early August the prisoners were moved to the new barracks, designated Osaka Camp #1, also known as Chikko or Headquarters Camp, built nearer the waterfront. Located along the southern shoreline, south of the main city and directly west of the modern-day Sumiyoshi Shrine, the new camp was considerably larger and comprised eight barracks that could hold about six hundred prisoners when crowded. One block away was the headquarters building for the Osaka POW area commander, Colonel Sotaro Murata. Each barrack building, holding approximately seventy-five men, was eighteen feet wide and thirty-three feet long and had two rows of bunks, three levels high.[8] The nearness of the camp to the docks reduced the long walk to and from the piers, a convenience particularly appreciated at the end of a grueling workday. Each barrack was quickly organized into squads, messes were established, and duties were assigned for maintenance of health and safety.

"At Osaka," said Sgt. George Shane, describing the endless work, "we loaded and unloaded ships in the harbor . . . tons of looted material from the newly conquered areas arriving constantly. The Japs were still the masters of the war and the ships were lined up for unloading."[9] Al Mosher noted, "We continued doing the same back-breaking labor, unloading ships, barges, rail cars, and working in a warehouse. . . . The Japanese guards would take us to a work detail where we would be turned over to civilian supervisors."[10] The civilian stevedoring contractors were paid to supervise and maximize the efforts of the prisoners. The contracting companies were required to provide food for the prisoners while at work. It was not long before the contracting companies realized that skimping on the noon *bento* was no way to inspire the prisoners to work. The small amounts of food proffered were still inadequate for the prisoners, and other means had to be found for sustenance.

The theft of *bentos* from civilians and the looting of rice bags, beans, and anything edible continued unabated. Ten to fifty pounds of rice were drained from every grain shipment using the POWs' rice whistles. Concurrently, efforts continued to sabotage and disrupt the Japanese war efforts. Typical was the deliberate breaking of shipboard winches by a number of the prisoners. Booms would be overloaded, straining the gears of winches already sabotaged by dirt, wood, and metal chips poured into the crankcases. Loads of material would be "accidentally" dropped over the sides into the water or onto the deck. More often than not, the Japanese accepted the results as proof that the Americans were incompetent and inferior. Oil barrels' bungholes were loosened and barrels placed upside down within the holds, vehicles were sabotaged, wires were cut, and lit candles were set as fuses in hidden piles of flammable material. No effort was considered too small a chance to sabotage the Japanese.

RM Bob Epperson recalled,

> Our efforts to sabotage the Japanese war effort began in earnest after a few weeks in Osaka. Oddly, we were given a fair amount of freedom as most of the guards were civilians and we worked for civilian supervisors. The civilians were not yet permitted to abuse us. We were often allowed to stop and buy food and other items in the stores along the way back from the piers. We could buy cigarettes, some food, soap, and other sundries for most of the first six months. Still, there was an ever-present hunger and, during the winter months, a bitter cold that left us always chilled to the bone.
>
> Most of our labor details were small. Generally, I always worked with [RM2 M. A.] Windham,[11] [RM1 Merkle] Smith, and [S1 Ernest] Molnar. On the docks, it took a while to learn how to handle the heavy loads of lumber, one-hundred-pound rice sacks, and the laborious shoveling of ore, coal, and bauxite. Aside from our constant search for food, we tried to create as much damage as possible by sabotaging shipments.
>
> Near the Osaka docks, we found a warehouse full of high-vacuum transmitting tubes. Over a two- to three-week period, we managed to render useless every tube we could reach by twisting the connections and breaking the vacuum. I would love to have seen the looks on the radio repairmen when they used these "replacements."

Another ship arrived with a full load of bulk sugar. As we shoveled the sugar, we ate as much as we could yet large amounts remained in the corners and crevasses. We were forced to reload the same ship with all sorts of Army trucks, tanks, and other combat vehicles. Sugar was poured into every tank, ignition wires cut and spark plugs destroyed by fellow prisoners. I doubt one single vehicle could have been driven off without extensive repairs.

One of our best instances of sabotage was while loading tons of barbed wire. The Japanese rolled the wire into extremely tight coils, bound with a few loops of thin wire. When placed in the field, the bindings would be cut and the coils would spring out to three or four times in size. As we placed them into the hold, we carefully cut the bindings on every third roll. The unloading process must have been a nightmare to the front-line Japanese troops.[12]

Work injuries plagued the men. By the middle of July, ten seriously injured men were sent back to Zentsuji, including Pfc. Ralph Baggett, Pfc. Gayle Neal, and Cpl. Martin Boyle. "I was hurt unloading soybeans off a ship," said Baggett:

The beans were in huge, heavy, burlap type bags—stacked four to five high. When a stack began to fall over, my foot was caught between two bags and I could not escape. My knee was severely twisted and the pain was indescribable. I lay there, unable to move, writhing in pain.

They carried me topside and I was laid out on the deck for the rest of the day. When the shift ended, the Jap guards began to walk us the five miles back to the stadium camp. I could not walk. Two other POWs stayed behind to help me. I put my arms over their shoulders, hopping on my good leg. I have no recollection who they were, but I do know I could not have made it back without their help. By the time I got back, I literally fell unconscious into the barracks.

Accidents were not always the fault of the prisoners. Every prisoner was aware that numerous guards and civilians considered it acceptable to harass, taunt, or deliberately injure the *horios*, the slaves they considered as subhuman. S1 Ed Settles recalled a winch operator's deliberate attempt to kill him. "One day, I was working on a ship unloading some bulk bauxite," said Settles, "and the Jap working a clam shell scoop deliberately tried to drop it on me. I caught a glimpse as it came down and dove to the side. It still caught me in the shoulder and broke my clavicle bone. He came at me again trying to grab me but I scrunched down next to the raised hatch cover. After a few more attempts, he finally gave up. There was no question he considered it a sport to try to kill me."[13] A broken shoulder was not considered an injury that precluded working. Settles was unable to take any time off to recover.

Deliberate injuries, caused by Japanese civilian supervisors and employees, plagued the men until the end of the war. Likewise, the starved and weakened men suffered severe loss of vision and reflexes, causing needless accidents and death. Regardless of injuries, heavy labor details continued. Not all details were brutal. Al Mosher remembers, "Most times, I always worked with the same small group of six to eight men. We all tried to keep a low profile to avoid any punishment from the Japs. As a result we could often bargain with the civilian supervisors for extra food and, if we finished early, we could hide out and take the rest of the day for rest."

Unloading coal and ore ships remained onerous and backbreaking, each day ending in complete exhaustion. Ore buckets, up to six feet in diameter, almost five feet high, and holding more than three tons each, were lowered into the hold to be hand loaded by men—every shovelful having to be lifted up and over the top. The work was complicated by the nature of the ore, pieces varying in size from small fists to chunks weighing up to 150 pounds. When the center of the hold was emptied, the men had to shovel the remaining coal into the center, where it was reloaded into open buckets or, if available, grabbed by clamshell scoops. If no scoops or buckets were available, the ore or coal was shoveled onto wire mesh nets for transfer onto the docks.

"The buckets," said PhM1 Tony Iannarelli, "were due every thirty minutes, which meant that we had to work like hell to get a moment's break." For those handling coal, fine black dust would add to their misery. "[Except for a short break at midday to eat] this monotonous, excruciatingly physical routine, continued nonstop all day long," Iannarelli noted.[14] Covered with dust from the various ores, one could not tell an Allied prisoner from the Korean slaves who worked in the same holds.

As mentioned earlier, most feared were the cargos of bauxite, particularly if the hatches had been left open to the rain. The ore became as thick as heavy clay, sticking to the shovels like glue. The weight of the waterlogged ore, combined with the constant need to scrape the shovels, made the backbreaking work almost unbearable, yet the demand for speed never diminished and the punishing assaults multiplied.

In their own world, unfettered by time and space, the POWs repeated the endless days of hunger, exhausting slave labor, random beatings, filth, and illness. Recurring malarial attacks and the malnutrition diseases of pellagra, scurvy, beriberi, diarrhea, dysentery, boils, scabies, and scaling skin simply added to the general misery. None but a few were immune. Feeling like forgotten men, their only surcease was to know that someday this too would pass. All that was needed was a will to live, an epiphany that welled up from within crying, "I shall live! I shall make it home!" No Allied soldier believed that Japan could win the war, and all believed that sooner rather than later the Allies would destroy Japan. "There was never any doubt," said Pfc. Harris

Chuck, "not even for an instant, that someday we Americans would beat these bastards and we'd be set free. Not a single man lost that belief."

The last week of August 1942 brought the first mail from home, letters that
arrived via the prisoner exchange ship *Asama Maru*. The mail was deliberately delayed,
pending the "censoring" by Dejima, the American-born interpreter. Nicknamed
"Buttons," Dejima had developed a hatred for the Americans and refused to release
the mail until the end of October.[15]

CHAPTER 12

The Doolittle Raid

THERE ARE SMALL VICTORIES THAT CAN BE GREATER THAN THE
WORST DEFEAT.

—*Unknown*

A fter Chief Nurse Marion B. Olds and her four charges left for Kobe, a sense
of melancholy and lethargy settled over Zentsuji.[1] The Red Cross representative, obviously hostile to the prisoners and overtly friendly to the Japanese,
had pointedly ignored their shouted pleas for food and heat. Without the support
of the Red Cross or the willing cooperation of the Japanese, there was no way to get
another report of their actual living or physical conditions back to the states. The
freezing winter had passed, but the constant overcast and lashing spring rains further
demoralized the prisoners.

The Japanese firmly believed theirs was a sacred land protected by the sun goddess Amaterasu and her direct descendant, Emperor Hirohito. The prime minister,
Hideki Tojo, bragged that no harm could ever befall the sun goddess's blessed children
and that their sacred homeland was inviolate. Hirohito was *God,* and damage to his
land simply could not happen. The military, samurai of the Sun God, would never
permit such a sacrilege.

Unfortunately for Japan, no one told Col. James H. Doolittle that his attack could
not happen. Thirty-seven days after the nurses departed, the trauma of Doolittle's raid
would shake Japan to its core and permanently change the morale of the prisoners.

Eight hundred miles east of Tokyo, at midmorning on Saturday, 18 April 1942, sixteen B-25 Mitchell bombers from the 17th Bomb Group struggled off the heaving,
wave-swept deck of the USS *Hornet.* Each carried three 500-pound high-explosive
bombs and one 500-pound incendiary bomb. Each plane had a specific target assigned
in either Tokyo, Yokohama, Nagoya, Osaka, or Kobe. Plans to launch within four
hundred miles of the coast were dashed when the carrier spotted a Japanese picket
boat shortly after dawn. Capt. Marc A. Mitscher, commanding officer of the *Hornet,*
urged Doolittle to immediately launch his planes. The last bomber lifted off at 10:00
a.m., and the long string of planes cruised a few feet over the waves at a reduced speed
to achieve maximum fuel conservation. Less than three hours later, under a cloudless

sky, the Doolittle raiders crossed Japan's coastline well north of Tokyo. Turning south, the planes skimmed over small towns and endless rice paddies as they raced to their targets. Once over land, the planes cruised at five hundred feet or below to avoid detection, climbing only when the target was in sight.

Outside the American embassy in Tokyo, Robert A. Fearey, private secretary to American ambassador Joseph C. Grew, heard the sound of large planes and exploding bombs. Startled, he looked up and saw an American bomber flying low over the Japanese Diet.[2] Black puffs of antiaircraft fire formed harmlessly above and behind the plane. Rushing back to the embassy residence, he encountered Grew bidding good-bye to Swiss minister Gorgé. All had seen and heard the attacking planes. The three men saw "fires burning in different directions, with lots of smoke. Sirens and gunfire could still be heard as we stood there," but the planes had disappeared from view.[3]

Tokyo received a scattering of bombs along the waterfront and at a steel mill. The planes swept on, unimpeded, to the next targets. Each city's target would receive a precise number of bombs, and no deviation would be made for targets of opportunity. Each plane spotted its target, climbed to 1,500 feet to avoid the blast, and dropped its bombs. The mission was simple: Hit the targets and escape to China.

Pfc. Garth Dunn was on the Osa Yama detail clearing another terrace. "In midafternoon," he said, "air-raid sirens began to wail—their undulating sounds drifting up from Zentsuji and all the small hamlets bordering the coastline." The sirens had never been sounded before in unison. "Even the guards appeared nervous, as if a calamity was approaching. We had an eerie sense of foreboding and the men slowed the pace of work, almost to a halt." Speculation rippled through the work details, but after fifteen minutes—"which seemed like hours to us"—the guards forced the prisoners back to work.[4]

In Kobe the Guam civilians were equally surprised by the Doolittle raid. Navy nurse Leona Jackson was sitting with some friends in the garden of their Kobe hotel. She heard the sound of plane engines, looked up, and saw "a formation of planes" coming over: "They were proceeding at a leisurely pace and they were flying low. We hadn't seen any planes overhead for some time so we gave them a good look. Suddenly, in a voice of surprised excitement, my companion said quietly, 'Those are not Japanese planes.' 'No,' I answered. 'They're American! I don't know if they're Army or Navy, but I know some fellows in both just nervy enough to fly that low around here.'" A few seconds later Jackson heard the dull thunder of bombs from the Kobe waterfront, a mile away.[5]

Charles Gregg, the Pan Am station manager, was at the Kobe Athletic and Racquet Club park across the street from the Canadian Academy. A mile north of the waterfront, he was startled to first hear, then see, a twin-tailed bomber "fly almost directly over us at an altitude of approximately two thousand feet." Seconds later the plane dropped its bombs on the waterfront and dove down to skim the water. Antiaircraft fire bursts again blossomed above and behind the fleeing planes that headed toward the southern end of the harbor. As heavy black smoke rose from the docks, hell broke loose. "Sirens wailed," Gregg recalled. "The Japanese people around us began to run for cover, their faces white with fear."

The guards rounded up the internees and ran them back to the Canadian Academy. In the chaos that followed, the Japanese covered all the windows with black cloth and turned off all the lights. "The police brought in large sake barrels of sand and water and bamboo poles [and on] the end of each was attached a two-foot-by-two-foot square matting for the purpose of beating out fires," Gregg stated. "We later learned these same measures were taken [all over] Japan. To say our guards and all the Japanese people were frightened is an understatement. They were nearly petrified."[6]

Jim Thomas, like fellow civilian internee Charles Gregg, had been permitted to meander in the park. The local Japanese had bragged that Babu Luthu (Babe Ruth), on a tour of Japan in 1934, had played on its baseball field and hammered a home run 450 feet over the distant fence. Baseball fans had placed a small monument where the ball landed. As Thomas and his friends discussed the chances of being exchanged for Japanese prisoners held in America, his conversation was interrupted by the sound of an approaching plane. Looking north toward the hills, he saw a low-flying bomber coming directly toward them.

Thomas was "shocked to realize the plane was American," clearly identifiable by the red circle in a white star on the wings. He watched as the plane dove toward the warehouse area by the docks, saw the bombs drop, and heard the muffled report of the explosions. "In one blazing, exhilarating moment, 2:40 p.m., 18 April 1942," Thomas said, "the Doolittle raid on Kobe had happened. The attack had lasted less than ten seconds. As the plane disappeared, pandemonium broke loose. Every siren in Kobe whined into action. But too late. Frightened, everyone ran for safety, sometimes in circles. Police whistles filled the air. Mystified about the planes' launching point and whether more bombers were coming, officials sustained the alert for several hours. Zero fighters took to the skies only to find disinterested birds and puffy clouds."[7]

The following morning the Zentsuji prisoners were certain something unusual had happened. Besides the sound of massed air-raid sirens and reports of antiaircraft fire, a sudden change in the guards' behavior was obvious. "When we went up the hill on Sunday to work," said Ed Hale, "many of the Japanese had seemed less stoical."[8] Something had obviously shaken the Japanese guards, if not the nation. At midafternoon on Sunday, 19 April 1942, official news of the Doolittle raid reached Zentsuji. A single typewritten page was placed on the bulletin board stating that "American planes had bombed Tokyo, Nagoya, and Kobe."[9]

"Hearing the news that day," said Al Mosher, "we were quite pleased. We never thought the war would last even *this* long!"[10] Morale soared on news of this first Allied strike at Japan. The news was savored as a massive victory.

The psychological impact of the raid shocked the entire nation. Nihon Nippon, the sacred Land of the Rising Sun, had been bombed. How could this have happened?

The physical damage was minor, but the reality of war affecting their homeland shattered the faith of an entire nation. It had been impossible to imagine six months earlier. The people's blind trust in the military was shaken for the first time. A violent tornado of fear and doubt swept across Japan, destroying the illusory safety of the home islands.

The raid deeply embarrassed Admiral Yamamoto, head of the Japanese navy. Alerted by the early warning from a Japanese trawler at dawn, he had sortied his fast fleet under Admiral Nagumo *before* the Doolittle flyers left the *Hornet*. At flank speed, the fleet of fast cruisers and battleships steamed east toward the *Hornet*. Convinced the Americans had escaped, Nagumo turned back shortly after midnight, less than two hours before he would have intercepted the fleeing *Hornet*.[11] Little known even to this day, one of the Doolittle raiders dropped a bomb on a carrier at Yokosuka Naval Base in Tokyo, effectively destroying the elevator to lift planes to its deck and leaving the Japanese one carrier short for its retaliation attack against Midway.[12]

The Zentsuji prisoners carefully restrained their joy to avoid the wrath of the Japanese guards. Speculation as to where the bombers came from was secondary to the pleasure of knowing Tokyo, Yokohama, Nagoya, and Kobe had been attacked by American bombers. Compounding Japanese fears, air-raid sirens would sound again every day for another week, although no planes were seen.

The Japanese news media immediately denied any substantive damage, claiming only schools, hospitals, and civilians were the targets of the bombers. The hated Americans, Japan's newspapers charged, "had machine gunned many children on the ground as they completed their dastardly mission," an amazing accomplishment because all the guns had been removed to reduce the planes' weight. Banner headlines in the *Osaka Mainichi* screamed, "USA Airmen Machine-Gun Children" while a subhead proclaimed, "They killed non-combatants even after clearly recognizing the objective as a primary school and seeing many children at play in the schoolyard with the sudden thought of, 'Let's give the Japs hell,' diving and machine-gunning deliberately and indiscriminately."[13] The planes, the military declared, had been shot down and their crews captured.

In fact, only eight men were captured—when betrayed by a Chinese soldier. Pictures of six airmen, some with blindfolds covering their eyes, were displayed on the front page of every newspaper. The government clearly implied that *all* the crews had been captured and executed: "The members of the *crews* of the United States airplanes that raided the mainland of Nippon on April 18 were duly caught by the military authorities and *have been dealt with* in accordance with Military Law" (emphasis added). The commander of the General Headquarters for Home Defense, on the same front page, issued the following proclamation: "If members of the crew of enemy aircraft, who raid the territory of Nippon and come within the reaches of our authority, are found to have committed a cruel and inhuman act, the same shall be tried before a military court and punished with death or severe penalty."[14]

By Monday, 20 April 1942, the *Osaka Mainichi* was carrying the headline "Severe Punishment Is Meted Out to Barbarous American Aviators—Death Penalty Decreed in Proclamation by Commander for Enemy Flyers Guilty of Barbarous Acts." The gauntlet had been thrown down by Japan. If a plane bombs Japan, its crew will die if captured. In the case of the Doolittle raiders, only one crew was captured, but future aviators would perish by the hundreds.[15]

The nature of the Japanese claims about the raid convinced many prisoners that all the planes had been shot down and all the crewmen executed. The prisoners' jubilation at the success of the mission was tempered by the shock of the crewmen's execution— men who were acting under military orders. Buried in the paper was a small article saying that the date of the exchange of diplomats and internees would be postponed at least another forty-five days.

Japan's invasion plans for northern Australia and the balance of New Guinea were temporarily postponed in order to seize Midway. Admiral Yamamoto immediately authorized a plan to take Midway Island and annihilate Admiral Nimitz's fleet in the process. The Japanese naval leadership firmly believed a victory at Midway could be the long-sought defining battle, a Japanese victory that would force the United States to seek an armistice. The Japanese had assumed the carriers and the planes used by the Doolittle raiders came from Midway. Once Midway was captured, Japan could seize Pearl Harbor at its leisure.[16]

As an unintended consequence, the Doolittle raid would precipitate the Imperial Navy's disaster at Midway. On 7 June four Japanese carriers and the cream of Japanese naval aviators sank to the bottom of the Pacific Ocean near Midway. The invasion was turned back, and Midway was never again threatened. A short two months later, Guadalcanal was invaded by the Americans, and never again would Japan have the initiative. The tide had turned.

The Doolittle raid created a seismic shift in the relations between the Japanese and the Allied prisoners. None doubted the savagery of the Japanese. The world had condemned their slaughter of millions in China during the 1930s. Now, severe beatings and punishments of Allied prisoners became the norm throughout the Japanese Empire. From Java, Burma, and Malaya to Formosa, the Philippines, and Japan, gross mistreatment was at the direct instigation of Japan's military leadership.

Civilian companies, such as Mitsui, Mitsubishi, Sumitomo, Hitachi, Aso, and NKK, issued a cascade of requests demanding prisoners for slave labor. Prisoners were shipped to islands throughout the conquered territories for the construction of airfields, docks, mining operations, and railroads. Starting in May 1942, thousands of prisoners were shipped from Indonesia and Singapore into Burma for construction of the Burma-Thailand Railway, later known as the Death Railway. In September 1942 the first major shipment of 500 men arrived from Manila in Japan on board the *Toko Maru*. Thus began a flood of over 100,000 Allied prisoner-slaves to the homeland.

On 1 August 1944 the War Ministry confirmed the longstanding directive to "kill all the prisoners" wherever and whenever Japanese forces were threatened.[17] If the homeland was invaded, all prisoners and internees—everywhere—were to be killed as rapidly as possible by any and all means. Guards were quick to inform the prisoners of their impending doom.

Aviators became "special actions" as Japanese fighter planes strafed and killed men dangling from parachutes. Others were ripped apart with the planes' propeller blades. If a plane was shot down in or near Japanese-held territory, a failed rescue effort meant almost certain torture and death. Japan's animus toward Allied airmen was horrific. In retaliation against the Chinese province where many assisted the Doolittle fliers, more than 300,000 men, women, and children were slain, fields were burned, animals were slaughtered, and every water well was poisoned.

CHAPTER 13

Hirohata #1

Home for the Eighty Eightballs

DISOBEDIENCE IS THE TRUE FOUNDATION OF LIBERTY. THE OBEDIENT
MUST BE SLAVES.

—*Henry David Thoreau*

After a period of time the effects of sabotage in Osaka became obvious, even
to the Japanese civilians. Tighter security and surveillance proved inadequate.
Something would have to change if the Japanese were to effectively utilize
their prisoners. With plans to bring up thousands of Allied prisoners from Hong
Kong, the Philippines, Malaya, and the Netherlands East Indies, more rigid controls
had to be exerted by the captors to find and punish the culprits.

Before any men were moved from the stadium to Chikko, the main Osaka POW
camp,[1] the Japanese had clearly identified the Guam men they suspected of sabotage
and theft. By the second week of August, a list of what appeared to be the eighty worst
offenders was posted, and a plan was made to move the men on the list from Osaka
to another "rest camp." Those not selected thought the process was random, but all
eighty assumed otherwise.

The incident that triggered the search for the offending prisoners took place on
a Japanese hospital ship when the POWs were told to load ammunition and weaponry
on board the ship, which was destined for the South Seas. Standing in the hold, forty
men refused to continue working and sat down. Despite threats of gunfire from the
guards, the men continued to sit, refusing to work, because loading war matériel was
labor forbidden by the Geneva Convention. In a few minutes, a group of almost one
hundred wounded Japanese veterans were gathered up, armed with clubs and sticks,
and sent into the hold. Nearly every man was beaten into unconsciousness as ribs,
noses, and arms were broken. The shattered men completed the loading but were
barely able to walk back to the stadium compound.

On 19 October 1942, the Japanese assembled the eighty men, conducted at least
five *tenkos,* and loaded their baggage and two crippled men on trucks. PhM1 Tony
Iannarelli and others noted that the ranking American, BMC Philip Earl Saunders,
fearing retribution, was glad to see the eighty men depart. The remaining sixty-six
men watched as the "Eighty Eightballs" left for the main rail station in Osaka. "By the
time we left Osaka," said Sgt. George Shane, "large numbers of prisoners from Hong

Kong, Singapore, Java, and the Philippines had started to arrive. These men were in real poor health and with every disease imaginable. Until they acquired better sanitary practices, they died like flies."

At the Osaka railroad station, Colonel Murata, commandant of the Osaka prisons, decided to humiliate the prisoners in front of a crowd of more than a thousand civilians. Standing across the street, civilians giggled and laughed as the colonel bragged of how he "was treating these evil Americans as cruelly as possible." The men were formed into four ranks, facing across the street toward the officer. At Murata's command the guards forced each rank, in turn, to run across street and bow to him.

"We deliberately gummed things up, infuriating the colonel even more," said Pfc. Garth Dunn, despite being forced to repeat this routine. For the moment, annoying the colonel became the newest American sport. With the civilians and Japanese guards laughing, the men were forced to repeat this ceremony, over and over, until Murata tired of the "game." Finally, after being allowed to sit and rest for only a few minutes, the men were marched up a ramp at about 2:00 p.m. and jammed into two passenger cars on the waiting train. Before the train left, Colonel Murata issued the following instruction to the guards: "Treat them as cruelly as possible, but remain with the limits of humanity."[2]

From the four-story-high elevated tracks, the prisoners took one last look at Osaka. "We could see clearly in three directions," wrote EM2 Ed Hale, "but all we could see was an ocean of two- or three-story paper and bamboo shacks lining little narrow streets where two bicycles could hardly pass. Although many were covered with straw thatch roofs, most were roofed with heavy tiles. I could imagine what hell could be loosed by a few heavy bombers. . . . If the narrow streets were being blocked by debris, fire would rapidly rage out of control." In minutes, the train departed for Hirohata, a special hell specifically designed to punish problem prisoners. For now, few could ever envision the hell that would visit Osaka on 10 March 1945.[3]

Passing through Kobe, the train headed west, forty miles to the small city of Himeji. Before arrival, all noted the lights of the huge steel mills, stretching for miles along the shoreline. The men were marched eight kilometers to a new camp: Hirohata #1. Luggage and the two crippled men were again trucked ahead.[4]

"There was such a cool, fresh smell to the air," wrote Hale,

> that I thought we must have come high up in the mountains. The little town (150,000 people, we learned later) had many small sawmills. The clean odor of pine sawdust surrounded us. I wondered if we would work in the sawmills.
>
> A truck took our baggage, and the few [sick men]. We were mighty glad not to carry our baggage any further, because the skies were darkening rapidly and the air was growing cold. The guards said eight miles. As we walked briskly along a railroad track, the very train

we had left passed us. Then we followed the river and soon crossed it over a long narrow bridge. We passed rice paddies by the mile—all small [and] hand-worked. Occasionally [we saw] a tiny garden: carrots, corn, cowpeas, the inevitable daikons, and a few stalks of sugar cane. The shops looked impoverished. A few seemed to have some sort of cigarettes we did not recognize. People stared at us but made no moves [and] said nothing.

The world looked black when we stopped in front of a new-looking building with a new bamboo-shaped fence. We were cold, hungry, tired, and almost bereft of hope. After counting us, the guards opened the gates and we marched into our house of hell. There was a race for "spots" on the mats. I missed the corner I wanted; got close to it, however. We were given five blankets each, the stiff but soft-finished staple fiber Army blankets like the two we had at Zentsuji. We each got our own bundles from the pile (the truck had arrived ahead of us) and then looked over our new "home."

The small camp was a single, three-story house set in the middle of endless rice paddies. A fence surrounded the house with a guard shack barring the entrance. A single room on the first floor was to be the prisoners' home for a full year. A few weeks after arriving, SM1 Reginald "Reg" Reed wrote,

80 [of us are] jammed together in a building, 30 feet by 80 feet. It's so crowded that a cigarette paper cannot be forced between sleeping men. We sleep on thin mats, nailed directly to the boards of the raised platform. In order to get any room at all, we must take off our shoes and lie on the mats. Though the temperature is forty degrees Fahrenheit, there is no heat whatever and the poor grade concrete floor in the center is dirty, cold, damp, and at ground level.

The grounds and building are six feet below the level of the road, and a ten foot high board fence topped with pointed bamboo spikes encloses the compound, which is nowhere more than 20 feet [away] from the building! The fence is the most ludicrous of all because if we wanted to, we could easily get over the fence and spikes. On one side of the camp is a stinking rice paddy. The other three sides are comparatively dry.[5]

During heavy rains the floor flooded with one to six inches of water. Mildew and mold covered any objects not sufficiently protected. Efforts to keep the quarters clean never ceased, but the sour smell of mildew, mixed with the ever-present stench of the latrines, permeated the site. "It was like living in a cesspool," said Garth Dunn.

On the fifth day after arrival, the men were marched four miles to the huge Seitetsu Steel Mills (Nisshin Seitetsu is part of Nippon Steel). Offices, huge gas tanks, piers, rolling mills, blast furnaces, coke mills, cement plants, conveyors, sheet metal shops, blacksmith shops, wood shops, and railroad tracks spread for more than five miles along the shoreline and one mile inland. The men were simply shown the size of the plant while the various stevedoring and labor companies assessed them as potential slaves. From the many piers, the island of Awaji was clearly visible across the Inland Sea to the south. The prisoners toured the plant but did not do any work on this day. Returned to camp, the men were not assigned any labor details for another ten days. It was to be their last rest for many months.

On the morning of Wednesday, 21 October 1942, seventy men were sent to work at the mill while ten men remained in the camp as cooks. At the mill, like slaves at auction, the men were selected by representatives of two stevedoring companies. Two Japanese subcontractor companies, Kamagumi (handled iron ore) and Tomashima (handled coal), were responsible for unloading all arriving ships.[6] Other small subcontractors, including Tabata and Okawa,[7] handled the various yard details at the mill. The Kamagumi Company consistently received preference in the selection of prisoners for work details, always selecting the fittest men for the exhausting labor of emptying the ore ships.

"Work began in earnest," said PhM Leroy Bowman, USN, "and the Japs made it clear the camp was for punishment and they intended to work us to death. Working in the nearby steel mill and railroad yards, the labor was generally backbreaking. We moved heavy bricks, iron and lead ingots, shoveled coal, coke, and bauxite from holds of ships. At times we labored for up to three months without a single day of rest."[8]

In the usual manner of American soldiers, a certain insouciance developed among the men, particularly Pfc. Harris Chuck. In his disdain for the Japanese guards and *honchos*, he accorded nicknames for each of them. Colorful and descriptive, the nicknames stuck like stink to manure. Most of the Japanese were civilians or former military men given semimilitary positions of importance. Over fifty years later, most former prisoners still recall the nicknames:

Sailor: Shinichi Motoyashiki, one of the meaner guards
Kodomo ("baby"): Always at the side of Sailor and had a very youthful appearance
Squeaky: Masaji Yamamoto (per Leininger), the guard whose leg brace squeaked
Gimpy: Walked with a limp
The Cigar Store Indian: Civilian guard who looked like an American Indian
Whisky: Guard who looked like an Irish bartender
The Texas Cowboy: A very large guard

Fish Face: Always pursed his lips

Green Hornet: Senior member of the guard group who rode a bicycle
    to the docks and announced his arrival with a siren-type noise

Ota San: A good guard who let men off with minimal punishment
    ("Don't do that again!")

Frog: Akira Nishio, replaced Tsujino as Jap medical corpsman (was just
    as mean and enjoyed beating Captain Seid)[9]

Bull: Kaoru Fujita, frequently acting camp commander and the mean-
    est of all guards (even guards feared him)

Spider: Guard on board ship who constantly spied on the POWs, was
    generally mean and vicious, but looked the other way at thefts
    if he was given a share

Dippy Dog and Mickey Mouse: Military guards who appeared shell-
    shocked (Iannarelli called them a "Jap version of Laurel and
    Hardy")

Texas Slim: A reasonably decent guard anxious to master English

Singapore: A particularly vicious civilian boss[10]

Within a few days of arrival at Hirohata #1, it was obvious that the food rations had been reduced. The effects were immediate. Sick calls increased, and the food rations were again cut in half. The men, desperate for food, began raiding storerooms and kitchens on the ore and coal ships. In any group of men, one or two would sneak away, hunting for food on board the ships. As it was normal for many prisoners to be moving about at any one instant, the men would brazenly walk in and out of a ship's passageways, racing away if they thought they would be detected. "Often," said RM1 Bob Epperson, "the crew of the Chinese and Korean ships would either help us steal or leave us food, hidden from the Jap guards."

"I think the best thief we had was [PhM3 Richard] Salisbury,[11] said Dunn. "He even survived a bout with meningitis while in camp. Strong as an ox, he could break open locks in the ship storerooms with his bare hands. Pfc. Harris Chuck and Sergeant Shane had the reputations as the best lock pickers within the camp, rarely taking more than a few seconds to bypass the best Japanese locks." Men would gorge on any food located and attempt to bring extra food back to their buddies. "If there was a lot of food," said Shane, "we'd send guys into the storeroom, one or two at a time to eat what they could. We would lock them in so the Japs would think the room was secure. They would signal when ready to leave, and we'd again pick the lock and let them out. Sometimes, up to ten or more men could loot a room before it became noticeable."

Harris Chuck had quickly learned Japanese and was frequently used as a camp interpreter by the Japanese. With his lock-picking skills refined to an art, he could bypass any lock within seconds and inevitably carried loot somewhere on his person. By the summer of 1942, Chuck had the reputation as a "master thief" among his fellow inmates. One afternoon, upon return to the camp, the guard at the gate insisted that Chuck translate his lecture to the prisoners on the evils of stealing or lying and that punishment was assured for those who did.

"Only [PhM1] Tony Iannarelli and I could speak any Japanese," said Chuck, "and there wasn't any interpreter assigned to the camp. I started putting on a pretty good show as usual, shouting, waving my arms, and all that jazz. I really made it look good. Well, the guys out there could hardly keep a straight face; the biggest crook of all was out there in front, all loaded up himself [with stolen loot], telling them all that stuff. I thought some of them were going to crack up and bust out laughing. I couldn't have blamed them a bit—how much more ridiculous could things ever get?"[12]

When the Japanese caught a prisoner stealing, they did not simply confiscate the pilfered food. The man—and most often the entire camp—was punished. A fairly standard punishment was for all the men to be formed into two ranks with hands stretched out before them. Two Japanese soldiers would stand in back of each man and two more in front. "The men in back hit us with their rifles," wrote WT1 Jack Leininger, "and the men in front beat us with their belts. . . . They hit us thirty to forty times. Even if they [did] not have anything on us, we were all beaten. The whole camp of eighty prisoners would suffer every time someone was caught, an almost daily experience."[13]

Ship after ship was to be unloaded and reloaded as the people of Japan luxuriated in their conquests and Japan's invincible navy. The navy continued to publicize its invincibility, assuring the nation it sought to defeat the cowardly American fleet in a "defining battle." Unfortunately, while the Imperial Japanese fleet sought a defining battle with the Americans, convoys of merchant ships would rarely be accorded protection from submarine attack. Patrol and convoy protection was deemed beneath the dignity of Japanese naval officers. The seeds of destruction were sown in the ego of the samurai-influenced staff. Desperate to avoid any admission of defeat, the Imperial Japanese Navy hid even the disasters of Midway and Guadalcanal from the Japanese nation. In fact, the navy hid the disaster at Midway from War Minister Tojo's office for more than four months.

"We shoveled endless tons of coal, iron ore, and bauxite," said Shane, "and all the equipment in the plant was stamped 'Made by Bethlehem Steel.' Since we were on starvation rations, the eighty of us from Guam banded together to steal food and anything we could trade to the guards for food. Second to getting food was to do damage. The men working the winches constantly managed to sabotage the operations, often badly enough that we could get hours of desperately needed rest."[14]

Men were forced into the holds carrying short-handled shovels. From the corners, men would bend over, endlessly shoveling ore to the center for loading on nets or into buckets. In the bitter cold or the blistering heat of summer, detail after detail of four or more men loaded the nets and buckets like worker ants, scurrying back and forth into the dark corners of the holds. Four to five nets or buckets would dangle into each hold. Every thirty minutes, a full load was lifted out. Woe unto those men whose nets were not full. *Honchos* always stood ready with their *kendo* sticks to beat any men who appeared to be too slow in filling their quota. As the load was lifted out of the hold, one could hear the audible sighs as the detail of men sagged to the ground for a few moments of rest.

Under the watchful eyes of civilian supervisors, the prisoners still managed to steal with abandon. One particular civilian, known as "the Spider," had the habit of surreptitiously peering down into the hold to check on the men. "It wasn't long, perhaps a day or two," said Harris Chuck, "before we knew that as long as he got his share of the loot, the theft was ignored!"[15]

In the steel mill, details of men shoveled coal into furnaces, moved never-ending tons of hot slag, operated milling machines, wound electric motors, and performed a hundred tasks required to manufacture steel. Although some details required less physical effort, working the ships gave the prisoners direct access to shipboard storerooms, cabins, and holds where food could be found. Yelling "Benjo!" to a guard was the magic word to begin a hunt for food. While his fellow mates labored to pick up the slack, the prisoner would go topside and head for the latrine hanging off the deck. Out of the sight of the guards, he would sneak into the passageways in a hunt for food or trading material. Ducking into cabins, he would quickly search clothing and cabinets for cigarettes and money. Any food spotted was quickly devoured or slipped beneath his shirt or *fundoshi*—the extra food to be shared with the others on his detail.

In a postwar claim to the War Reparations Board, SM1 Reg Reed said,

> In our weakened condition we were often made to run to [and] from work. This was usually done if any of us straggled due to fatigue. Then, before we were allowed to go into the camp, we were drilled up and down the road, right and left faced, marched, etc. With our shoes so heavy and our bodies swollen with beriberi, it was agony. Sometimes, if someone had done something wrong, the whole working party would be required to sit on their heels. That's all. . . . Just sit on their heels for an hour or more without moving. Try it! Before going to work in the morning, all the guards would look us over and rap anyone across the arms, legs, and head if his hands weren't absolutely flat against his sides or if he moved in the slightest. During the worst winter of 1943–1944, every morning one or two men would collapse in ranks. Beriberi would get them and after a beating, the man would be dragged into the camp by our own troops.[16]

Within the steel mill, a small shack was set aside in which the prisoners were to store their *bentos* and clothes. The men had to stoop over to enter through the small door. Small stoves permitted the men to prepare their tea and, when provided or stolen, extra rations of rice, fish, or vegetables. Among the "Eighty Eightballs," most food was shared but only within the smaller subsets who worked together.

Garth Dunn recalled stealing a two-hundred-pound bag of rice from a ship at dockside, secreting the life-giving loot in the underground area of a nearby conveyor system. Concurrently, his confederate stole two five-gallon cans of butter. The butter was brazenly hidden in the *honcho*'s cabinet inside the blacksmith's shop. "At each meal, Dunn said, "we would add extra rice to our rations and mix in a large tab of butter for each man. Unfortunately, another POW spotted us when we took the rice from our hideout. He was later seen appropriating some of our rice and a fight ensued, the rice spilling out of his pants leg onto the floor. The Japs quickly rounded up those involved, slapped them around, and recorded the names. Fortunately, I was sick and unable to work that day."

That evening, Pfc. Frank Nichols observed, "three Jap soldiers, one with a large hawser type rope, another with a length of hose, and the third with a wood stick, proceeded to lash the men across their bare buttocks. Within a few minutes, their rumps looked like hamburger meat." After ten minutes, the men could no longer feel the pain of the lashes. "The Japs stopped the beatings," continued Nichols, "and made the men sit in the concrete tubs of water scattered about the camp. These were supposedly for fighting fires started in air raids but were really useless. However, the Japs assumed this would restore feeling to the buttocks of the men so they were made to sit for a few minutes in the freezing water. Again, they were hauled out, stood into one rank and the beating continued. After an hour, the men were dismissed and returned to the barracks."

Such beatings were common for men caught stealing food. An unwritten code developed among the men: If caught stealing, avoid implicating others and take your own punishment. One man who refused to abide by this code was shunned by all. No one spoke to him again until the war ended, and even then, they spoke only when required.

Defiance of the Japanese took a remarkable turn on 11 November 1942. As the eleventh hour of the eleventh day of the eleventh month drew near, the entire detail of prisoners gathered for a moment of silence. The work stoppage, to honor Armistice Day, surprised the Japanese guards. One guard, called the "Mouse," shouted, "Sanyo!" (Work!) The men continued to ignore him, and as he approached, PhM1 Tony Iannarelli lifted his shovel as if to hit him. The Mouse backed away, but it would be another six weeks before the prisoners had another day of rest.[17]

Allied efforts to thwart Japanese shipping started to achieve results. The number of ships arriving from the conquered territories had noticeably declined by the end of 1942. With fewer supply ships arriving, the coal and ore ships afforded scant food susceptible to theft. Another source of food had to be found. In concert, the men decided to refuse to work unless the Tomashima Company added more food to the meager rice given to them at camp. The following day, the Japanese company augmented the prisoner's rations with *bentos*. The extra *bento* was now given to all laborers, including the enslaved Koreans.

Within the same month, two incidents served to remind the men that their keepers had not become soft at heart—nor could they always rely on fellow prisoners. In the course of looting a ship, one man purloined a satchel, which upon investigation was found to contain the ship's payroll. Certain of a shakedown inspection, the prisoner tossed the bag overboard. When the payroll was discovered missing, the entire camp was savagely beaten. With the Japanese military still in charge of the work details, no one would admit to the identity of the man, for it meant his certain death.

Within a few days, another prisoner was caught by the mess hall personnel stealing bread from the camp storeroom. Incredibly, he was turned over to the Japanese for punishment by fellow prisoners. Stripped naked in the snow, he was beaten with bats, sticks, and a two-inch-thick wet rope. His screams of pain, between pleas to be shot, could be heard in every corner of the camp. The punishment left scars for life and further deepened the distrust between factions of prisoners.

One particular faction of six men determined that only they could raid the ship's storerooms. The hidden loot was not detected for months, but tension increased when some of the loot was discovered by Pharmacist's Mate Iannarelli. When confronted in the act of eating the food, Iannarelli said, "Get lost!" and, in a quick fight, knocked the man to the ground. Back at barracks, the clique leader said, "Out the door, Dago." With his own buddies assisting, the two groups fought to a draw, but the faction was dissolved. The two camp leaders, Sgt. Earl B. Ercanbrack and Chief Radioman Barnum, gave Tony a nod of appreciation.[18]

As the effects of malnutrition became apparent, physical infirmities became noticeable. Bob Epperson observed, "Many men's eyesight was affected to such an extent they could not read at all. No one could think clearly or quickly. Reflexes [became] so slow that for some men it was impossible to avoid danger. Men were hurt in the coal and ore ships because their reactions were dulled." When hurt or sick, the prisoners relied upon PhM Joseph S. Arnold, but the Japanese gave Arnold no authority to classify men as unfit for duty.

By 17 November 1942, the effects of starvation and physical abuse were pandemic. The sick list now included eighteen men who were unable to work. Disabilities ranged from severely injured backs, gunshot wounds, and sprained ankles to fevers, severe diarrhea, vomiting, and severe cramps from beriberi. "We thought the days would never end!" said Seaman Reed. With morale at a low ebb, the men were finishing their evening meal when a truck backed into the compound, accompanied by the frenetic shouting of the guards. Rushing from the barracks, the men discovered that Red Cross packages were being delivered, and each man was to receive a separate box weighing almost five pounds. "Christmas comes but once a year, 'tis true," said Reed:

This night was but the seventeenth of November, but to us it was Christmas—one of the very best any of us could ever remember. I [cannot] recall any time in my life when I was so excited—so clumsy and slow as I was trying to open that Red Cross package. Other men managed to open their packages quite handily, but there I sat like [a] bear cub with boxing gloves, some fifteen minutes trying desperately to open the gift. Finally, I slipped off the strong steel band and gazed [with] amazement at the wonders within.

[The first items I saw were] two large bars of chocolate, two packs of cigarettes, and a package of tobacco. How fragrant the tobacco was! I was in no hurry now so I sniffed the aroma of the good burley rough cut, and almost came to tears as I thought of bountiful America looking after its sons.

All around me, my comrades laughed hysterically as they planned how best to tackle their box of food. Inside each box was one tall can of evaporated milk, a small box of hard tack, cocoa, oleomargarine, instant coffee, dried soup, some sugar, pipe tobacco, cigarettes, orange extract, cheese, sardines, and prunes.

Then I looked up—an enemy soldier was pressing his face against the frosted window pane, admiring the good things which had befallen us. Suddenly, I felt ashamed. There [he] stood, like a hungry dog, the results of 2,600 years of [his] civilization, yet in all his history, not one item of this parcel could be matched! I [knew] that he fought for his concept of life and I, for mine. But before his eyes and mine lay the ordinary things of my way of life—the luxuries he'd never know in [his]![19]

Two days later the Japanese reduced the prisoners' rice ration from thirty kilograms per meal to twenty kilograms for the eighty men, approximately nine ounces per man. By the end of the month, control of the prisoners was transferred directly to the Seitetsu Company, and the rice ration was further reduced to fifteen kilograms per meal (6.6 ounces per man, or about two hundred calories per meal) for the entire camp because, as the commandant said, "too many men sick and [too many] unable to work. No work, no food." George Shane remembers the desperation of severe hunger. "I learned to eat silk worms and fish heads so rotten they smelled of ammonia. It was food so I cooked them and ate them."

On Christmas Eve one Canadian Red Cross box was distributed for every five prisoners. The men held Christmas services with WT2 Eddie Howard reading passages from his Bible. The extra food, primitive decorations on a "gnarled, crooked pine," and the singing of hymns brought a measure of comfort to the men. Religious services were again held on New Year's Eve. However, as they had been on Christmas

Day, the prisoners were forced to work at the mill and piers. For these two days, the rice ration was increased to twenty-seven kilograms per meal, but it was reduced again the following day.

By the end of January 1943, the ration had been reduced to twelve kilograms of rice per meal and the abuse worsened as the civilians took control of the prisoners. Typical was the abuse forced upon the men even on their day for rest. On Sunday, 17 January 1943, the civilian *honcho*, Shinichi Motoyashiki, took the men for a walk to a nearby park. Upon arrival, "we were ordered to take off our coats," said Seaman Reed. The temperature was below freezing and a dusting of snow covered the ground." Reed continued: "It was so cold that everyone objected vociferously, whereupon the *honcho* became exceedingly wroth and raised a bit of hell. More than half the men took off their coats, and those who had only a thin shirt underneath, refused. Among the latter was George Shane. The *honcho* swung a hefty right to Shane's jaw. Shane blocked [as EM3 Rex] Wilson rushed in and shoved the Jap. The Jap seized a rifle from one of the guards and swung at Wilson. Wilson danced nimbly out reach again and again. The Jap leveled the rifle, but it wasn't loaded." After the excitement died down, the men returned to camp, whereupon Wilson was brought to the office and beaten severely.[20]

Such provocation would result in similar beatings. "One afternoon," said S1 Ed Settles,

> when we were off loading a ship, Sergeant Shane managed to engage the Jap guard in a humorous contest. Shane, picking up a six-foot length of bamboo, motioned to the guard that perhaps he would like to take him on with the guard's *kendo* stick. Playfully, the guard made a pass at Shane who neatly deflected the guard to the side. A few civilians, watching the action, could now be heard laughing.
>
> The Jap guard became a lot more serious and came at Shane again. Just as quickly, Shane deflected him to the side, causing the guard to stumble. The Jap, gathering his wits, came at Shane with the intent to kill. Shane knocked him aside to the laughter of everyone, all of whom were now watching. Shane, the best bayonet instructor in the Marines, smiled. For that moment, we won another battle with the Nips. However, the Jap guard called Shane to attention. "Kiotsuki!" he shouted. Shane stood rigidly at attention while the guard proceeded to lash him with the stick, finally knocking him into semiconsciousness.

Stealing became an art form for the prisoners. Nothing Japanese was sacred, and everything not nailed down was potential loot. Stealing in large quantities was relatively easy, as with Garth Dunn's theft of a two-hundred-pound bag of rice, but getting it past the guards, searches, and shakedowns into the camp was almost impossible.

"In the winter of 1943–44, a ship came in from Formosa carrying tons of roasted nuts, something like beer nuts, that we unloaded for three days," said Ed Settles. "As we shoveled the nuts onto mats, everyone was trying to figure a way to carry some back to the barracks. I knew we would be searched and anyone carrying the nuts would be beaten badly. By midafternoon of the first day, I figured out a solution to smuggling the nuts back to camp. It was chilly that day so I wore my long-sleeved overcoat. Spotting some binding twine, I tied a slip knot over the sleeve, just above my elbow. I poured the nuts down into my sleeve from inside the shirt. Close to the shoulder, I tied another string over the sleeve with a slip knot, sealing in the nuts."[21] Leaving the ship, the men were lined up and counted. Searches were made of all pockets while another guard patted each man down for hidden loot bags. Like all prisoners, Seaman Settles kept his arms raised during the search. "They [the nuts] were delicious," said Settles.

The Japanese never stopped trying to catch the men in the act of stealing. However, few Japanese made any effort to learn a man's identity other than by a number affixed to his cap. "We were working an ore ship one afternoon," said PhM3 Leroy Bowman, "when [F1] Art Dahlstedt[22] had obviously been roaming the ship hunting for something to steal. Suddenly, we saw him up in the superstructure, being chased by a sword-waving Jap. Dahlstedt ran toward our hold and, attempting to grab the ladder, lost his grip and fell some twenty feet. He landed flat on his back atop the propeller screw shaft and bounced upright to land on his feet. He was shaken but scurried back into the shadows. The Japs, knowing all occidentals looked alike, gave up the search. We all knew that if you ever got caught, they would beat the hell out of you."[23]

The beatings and abuse of prisoners became so expected that by 20 April 1943, Seaman Reed, in his diary, described a day of sadistic abuse as being normal and commonplace:

> Singapore informed us in the morning that there would be no *bentos* for noon and for the men to take food with them. Most of us obeyed, but about ten men didn't. There was an inspection of mess gear at noon, and the disobedient were caught short.
>
> Many men [made it a practice to eat] their breakfast and lunch for breakfast, then making out on the job by stealing, trading, or bumming anything they could for their noon meal. All hands were ravenously hungry all the time. No ordinary common sense rules of civilization apply. It was dog eat dog or drop in one's tracks of starvation and exhaustion.
>
> When we returned to camp that evening, the guilty men were lined up and thoroughly caned with a bamboo pole [with] such force that [the bamboo canes] splintered. No tears or laments lost over [the beatings]. We all know the penalty for the infraction of rules here.
>
> At evening muster some of the men failed to have either a coat or jumper on, or had no number sewn on, or a button undone. Summary slappings took place.

Reed then added a special notation to his diary that explained his failure to record the Japanese brutalities every day:

> [I note] the gradual tone of indifference over events that normally shock the senses. [These] incidents, though grave—since at least a dozen men were struck and beaten over minor matters—created practically no stir other than my reference to it.
>
> Daily slappings [have become so] frequent, and at the slightest pretext, until [it has become] a foregone conclusion that nearly everyone in the camp would receive a punishment of some kind in a matter of 48 hours.

Apparently following the edicts of Colonel Murata, any pretext was used to harass or inflict punishment upon the men. At the end of a normal workday, the men would assemble at the shack at 5:00 p.m. to wait for other details to return from the far reaches of the steel mill. On a bitterly cold winter's day in 1944, ten men, including Sgt. George Shane and WT1 Jack Leininger, arrived at the shack, cold and dirty from shoveling coal. The guard permitted them to return to the camp immediately without waiting for the other men. Another guard stated it was permissible to begin their bath upon returning. The ten men washed and began soaking in the tub. The camp guard, Masaji Yamamoto (aka Squeaky), imperiously decided they were too early. All were dragged out of the tub and lined up at attention, naked in the snow. Seizing Leininger for special retribution, Squeaky made him stand at attention while a second guard swung a baseball bat at full force across the back of his bare legs. Near midnight, the ten frozen men were allowed to soak in the lukewarm water for ten minutes but were denied food for the night. "Somehow," said Shane, "you had to find something humorous every day. If you didn't think that way, you would give up and die. Some did. In some ways, the Japanese were absolutely childish and stupid. On that particular day, we almost died as we were almost frozen to death but we laughed at the pettiness of the Japs."[24]

On another occasion an understanding of the language and culture of the Japanese paved the way for Tony Iannarelli's crew to successfully steal from the Japanese transport ship, the *Heinie Neilson Maru*. Used for transporting troops into the South Pacific, the ship was being loaded with supplies on 18 February 1943. A storeroom was located and the locks broken. Two or three men at a time hid in the room, gorging on the food. As the men left the ship at 5:30 p.m., a Japanese sailor spotted Seaman First Class Magelssen leaving with a coat stuffed with stolen food. All the men were lined up and searched, whereupon two more men were found with stolen food.

The looted storeroom stood as mute testimony that more men had to be involved. One of the cans was streaked with blood, obviously from one of the thieves. Thinking quickly, Iannarelli asked a local laborer, "Didn't you see that man cut his hand working in the hold?" The man nodded agreement.

Turning to the guard nicknamed the "Weasel," Iannarelli said, "None of us could have robbed anything because you were in charge of us, and I know well enough that you would not let anything like this happen!" Weasel had to agree to save face and marched the men back to camp. Weasel separated the three men and, together with the entire camp staff, "beat the hell out of them for a solid hour." It was the first group beating by the entire camp staff. Later that evening, as the men recovered in the barracks, one was heard to say, "I wonder if we can get aboard that same ship tomorrow."[25]

The very next day Iannarelli was caught red-handed eating stolen food on the same ship. As the *honcho* reached for him, Iannarelli reflexively punched the man. The civilian *honcho*, along with other civilians and the Weasel, proceeded to beat Iannarelli senseless. He was taken topside, again beaten severely, and tied to the forward lifeline. PM3 Leroy Bowman, working with a deck gang, saw the incident escalate. "The Japs tied him to the life lines up on the bow," said Bowman, "and beat the living hell out of him. Sticks, rifle butts, punches—they threw everything at him. It was freezing cold and they doused him with water then kept him there until late in the day. He was as tough as nails and never gave an inch."[26]

Stabbed by the Weasel's bayonet, Iannarelli felt death was certain and shouted at him, "You are the poorest soldier I have ever seen! You do not abide by the Bushido Code." Weasel quietly backed away, but four hours later, he untied Iannarelli, gave him food, and allowed him to rest an hour before going back to work. That evening, the camp commander, Kaoru Fujita, known as the "Bull," berated the guards for permitting civilians to hit a POW.

The Swiss Red Cross official, Max Pestalozzi, visited on 10 March and again on 12 April 1943, and his report to Washington stated all the men were alive, well fed, and happy. Nothing could have been further from the truth.[27] A bonanza of twenty-five-pound Red Cross packages arrived on 18 April 1943 containing dried pears, sugar, cereal, salt, and soup mix. Also delivered were twenty individual boxes containing wonders such as corned beef and, to the joy of many prisoners, eighty pairs of U.S. Army field shoes to replace the tattered remnants of shoes and sandals. Amid much grumbling, Sergeant Ercanbrack distributed the dried pears but retained the balance of the food to add to the meager rations over the next four days. What few knew was that Ercanbrack was continually smuggling food to the sick since their rations were cut in half. "No work, no food" was the Japanese mantra.[28]

CHAPTER 14

The First Christmas in Japan

A s the holiday approached, the prisoners attempted to create a festive atmosphere, hoping to counter the depression of internment. Scraps of paper were turned into hand-drawn Christmas cards with clever cartoons, pictures of camp scenes, and images of holly, bells, and Santa Claus. A few days before Christmas, all the prisoners were given a subpoena to appear in Room 29 on Christmas afternoon. On Christmas Day, the Japanese allowed the men a day of rest. To the surprise of all, extra food was served at every meal.

Capt. Mortimer Marks wrote in his journal, "The Japanese went the extra mile . . . when a sumptuous meal was served this Christmas morn—corned beef in the bean soup, sardines, and rice. For lunch we had the balance of the sardines, rabbit burgers, two sweet potatoes, and a slice of bread—a special treat." For men facing continual hunger, the meals were a feast beyond imagining. Answering the subpoena, each man was announced as he entered the room and handed a number for a door prize.

Marks continued:

> The transformation of the plain, somber room into an atmosphere of festivity was breathtaking. In the center of the room was a table covered with a blanket upon which was a Christmas tree and a plate of candy crumbs. . . .
>
> On one side of the room were more blanket-covered tables set end to end. [On top] were a number of teapots wrapped in blankets. A phonograph was playing but the music was drowned by the din of voices of a jam-packed room of POWs drinking tea—really hot water.
>
> Strung across one side of the room were cut-out block letters, alternately red and green, that read "Merry Christmas." Surrounding a light bulb hanging from the ceiling was a box which had been cut out in letters that also read "Merry Christmas." Pine branches decorated the windows, walls, and uprights. The appearance of Christmas filled every nook and corner of the room.
>
> Peter Kenny[1] of the RAF, the master of ceremonies, gained our attention by banging on a tin plate. Windy Winslow, an aviator from the USS *Houston*, recited an amusing poem. Limericks satirizing several of the senior officers were read by members of the host room. In a beautiful tenor voice, Ned Gallagher, survivor of the USS

Houston, sang the Ave Maria. Wood, Bateman, Hoffman, Vandergrift, Gallagher, Loft, Page, and Hilton introduced as the "Bathless Gang" (they rehearsed in the bath house), rendered a number of popular songs in foot-tapping, syncopated rhythm. It was so refreshing to hear stateside music with a good beat.[2]

Not mentioned by Captain Marks, a second singing group, known as the Hungry Harmonics, joined in entertaining the prisoners. For dinner, the men dressed in their best attire. An elaborate meal of corned beef stew with onions and dehydrated potatoes, saved from the earlier Red Cross packages, was added to by the Japanese with an extra ration of rice and three tangerines per man. The evening concluded with songs, prayers, and toasts for fellow soldiers, and the singing of the prisoners' national anthems.

Late that evening, Marks reflected on the events of his second Christmas in captivity:

It is paradoxical, this merry display of celebrating Christmas in the forlorn and dismal surroundings of a Japanese prison camp and at a time when the whole world is in the throes of suffering. In spite of all this misery, we POWs, in our isolated little world, made the best of it by producing, through our own ingenuity and hope, an atmosphere of merriment and brotherhood—the real spirit of Christmas.

None of us have any earthly possessions but the clothes on our back and a Red Cross food parcel. All of us—Englishmen, Australians, Canadians, Dutch, and Americans—found ourselves not only allied in war but also sharing the same spiritual truth. Yesterday we sang Christmas carols heralding in the Christ. This afternoon at the party we drank tepid tea to each other's good health. It was a stirring spectacle to see all of us from different countries standing in unity to pay homage to our respective nations and to our one God.

There was simplicity and purity in our childlike joy as we cut out paper stars and ornaments for our Christmas tree, made Christmas cards, and composed greetings to wish others well. A good, happy feeling exuded from everyone. There was neither liquor, gifts, nor any material incentive to arouse this feeling. It was spontaneous and uncontrived. It was a Christmas I shall never forget.

In mid-November each of the eighty men at Hirohata #1 had received a ten-pound box of food from the Red Cross. To the starving men, it was as if manna had dropped from the heavens. Christmas had arrived early. Tears of joy choked many into silence, except for the occasional soft murmurs—"Oh, my God," "Oh jeez," "Ain't this swell," and "Thank God"—as the men sat along the rows of bedrolls and tatami mats and slowly opened their boxes. Every man offered Doc Seid a portion of the dried milk (KLIM, or milk spelled backward) and other items for the sick men under his care. Tins of butter, meat, and chocolate were squirreled away to savor on hungrier days.

Christmas Day was just another miserable day working for the Japanese. Late that evening, the men gathered to quietly sing Christmas carols, read a few prayers, exchange handwritten greeting cards, and eat a generous portion of the Red Cross package saved for the day. The next day, the deadly routine of slavery continued.

The new Chikko Camp (Osaka Hoincho) received the men from the Ichioka Hospital a few days after the "Eighty Eightballs" were sent to Hirohata. BMC Phillip E. Saunders, USN, remained in control even as hundreds of additional American, British, and Dutch troops arrived. Slaving for Japan Transport Company (Nippon Tsuun), many of the men were able to steal enough food to prevent the ravages of starvation. For those men who had recently arrived from the tropics, the winter months were to prove very deadly; one or more succumbed almost every day to dysentery, pneumonia, or acute colitis. As usual, Japanese wisdom dictated that rations for the sick be reduced by half, and no medicine was given to the camp doctors.

The men of Guam continued to band together, albeit in small groups, to share in efforts to steal food. Food was always on their mind—how to get it, steal it, cook it, and eat it. Like the men of Hirohata, they had received food packages, but one box was to be shared by up to six men. The Japanese simply looted the balance after forcing the prisoner camp commander to sign a receipt for the full shipment.

Like the men of Hirohata, Christmas for the men at Chikko was simply another workday. However, after the standard dinner, the men gathered to sing Christmas carols in a multiplicity of languages and styles. Handmade cards, menus for mystical meals, and paper decorations festooned many of the barracks. Men's thoughts of home brought the tears of loneliness, yet each prayed this would be their last Christmas spent among these "evil bastards."

CHAPTER 15

The Men of Bataan and Corregidor Arrive

The men of Corregidor and Bataan had endured a captivity that was unknown to the men of Guam. Under constant attack, they had fought a delaying action against the Japanese forces. Bataan had held off surrender until the first week of April, and Corregidor capitulated the following month. By the time of their capture, the men had endured severely reduced rations for months, stricken with debility and illnesses—dysentery, severe malnutrition, beriberi, pellagra, and malaria—and deprived of any hope for rescue.

Some 25,000 American military men were employed in the defense of the Philippine Islands, joined by more than another 50,000 Filipino soldiers. Of the latter, except for the Philippine Scouts, the vast majority were untrained and poorly equipped. From the Pearl Harbor attack on 8 December,[1] the loss of the Philippines was inevitable. The best the United States could hope for was a few weeks of delay before final defeat.

In the War Department's Operational Plans Department, Gen. George Marshall confirmed the decision made at the Arcadia Conference that the war must first be fought to conclusion in Europe before attempting to push back the Japanese juggernaut. No formal written approval was ever made to sacrifice the Philippines, but no supplies were to be sent. All that could be expected was that it could be held until the end of February. Any defense would be at a line across Java, Sumatra, Malaya, and Ceylon (present-day Sri Lanka). Except for minimal resupply by submarine, no consideration was given to sending additional planes or supplies. Unfortunately, this fateful decision was withheld from Gen. Douglas MacArthur. As late as 3 January, General Marshall repeatedly and deceptively offered encouragement, stating that streams of bombers and "armadas" of fast ships laden with fighter planes were headed toward MacArthur's theater.[2]

Shortly before Christmas, MacArthur withdrew his Luzon army into the Bataan Peninsula, a brilliant tactical move in the face of a mobile Japanese army. From the north, troops streamed south and from Manila to the southern reaches of Luzon; more streamed north along the eastern edge of Manila Bay and hooked west into Bataan. More than 12,000 troops had successfully withdrawn into the peninsula flanking the north side of Manila Bay. Thousands of civilians also fled into the area seeking the protection of the army. Regrettably, insufficient food was available to sustain everyone. Large elements of the U.S. Army, particularly Air Corps units, remained on Corregidor, Mindanao, and Cebu.

Japanese general Masaharu Homma called the retreat into Bataan the most brilliant maneuver in the history of war, for it solidified the front and prevented the Japanese conquest for another five months. The lack of air cover, food, medicine, and mobility forced the defensive lines across Bataan to slowly fall back from the first week of January. Rations had been reduced to one-third of normal, which had a deleterious effect on morale and physical stamina.

A defensive line was initially set up along a rough line from Abucay on the eastern coast across the mountains to Mauban on the west side. Slowly the American defensive line withdrew south, with the final line drawn from Orion in the east to Bagac on the west. Shortages of food and oppressive heat sapped the strength of the men. Every animal found was eventually slaughtered to provide meat for the troops. Carabao, horses, mules, monkeys, snakes, and lizards supplemented the meager diets. Daily strafing by Japanese planes, endless artillery barrages, and constant attacks by the Japanese degraded the defensive lines. Still, the men held on, long after they were expected to capitulate.

The weeks wore on, and the American public, desperate for any good news, saw the defenders of Bataan as the first heroes of the war. Wake, Guam, Malaya, the Netherlands East Indies, and Singapore had fallen. Still, the suffering men endured, denying the Japanese access to the great port of Manila. On the home front, General MacArthur had become the symbol of the United States' tenacity and courage—a genuine national hero. The defenders of Bataan created sensational headlines that inspired a nation when defeat was everywhere.

Japanese premier Hideki Tojo openly bragged that when they captured General MacArthur, he would be taken to Japan and hanged in front of the Imperial Palace.[3] Politically, General Marshall and President Roosevelt clearly saw this as a threat to their war efforts. MacArthur was ordered on 22 February to leave the Philippines, but he refused to leave, stating he would remain with his gallant men until the bitter end. Realizing the capture of MacArthur would reflect badly on himself, FDR resolved the issue two weeks later by giving MacArthur a "direct order as your Commander-in-Chief" to depart immediately. MacArthur, a soldier dedicated to the chain of command, reluctantly agreed. With his small family and senior staff, he departed on 11 March by PT boats, which linked up to planes for evacuation to Australia.

A final Japanese attack began on 3 April, and by the eighth it had smashed through the last defensive lines. Bataan finally fell on the ninth when Gen. Edward King asked for surrender terms. The starving, sick men of Bataan streamed out of the bamboo jungles, bunkers, and foxholes to gather along shoreline roads. Confused, scared, hungry, and thirsty, the men stacked their weapons and endured endless searches by souvenir-seeking Japanese soldiers. For those carrying any Japanese money or obvious Japanese military items, summary executions were the order of the day. Hundreds of men fled by rafts or *bancas* or simply swam out to the fortress island of Corregidor, still held defiantly by Gen. Jonathan M. "Skinny" Wainwright.

To excuse the massive abuse heaped on the prisoners, revisionist historians choose to say that the Japanese were unprepared for such a huge number of POWs. The simple reality is that the Japanese society had become extremely racist and considered all other human beings as inferior. For almost seven decades, they had been indoctrinated in the belief that the emperor was a god, a fiction created by the feudal shoguns in order to retain their control over the peasants. This was the mythology deliberately created in the Meiji Restoration of 1868. Japan's heinous behavior in the conquest of China was essentially ignored by the world, further emboldening Japanese hostility toward others.[4]

Formed into groups of one hundred to five hundred, the men struggled to walk nearly sixty miles to a rail station in San Fernando in an infamous drive that was later called the Bataan Death March. Food was rarely made available and water even less so as the men struggled night and day to move north. Extreme thirst drove men to drink from fouled water sources; if seen, they were frequently shot or murdered by bayonet. Some men, attempting to defecate by the side of the road, were bayoneted to death in the squatting position. Passing Japanese troop trucks would deliberately run over prisoners, or Japanese soldiers would attempt to bash the prisoners—some even slashing at the men with swords. Inattention could cost a man his life. Stragglers were shot, bayoneted, or beheaded. Along this march some seven hundred Americans and thousands more proud Filipino soldiers perished because of the savage brutality of the Japanese. The leaders of the vaunted Philippine Scouts were gathered up, hands tied behind their backs, forced into a canyon, and murdered.

In San Fernando the prisoners were packed into freight cars and sent to Capas. Again the dead littered the freight car floors after the prisoners were offloaded and marched another eight miles to their camp. The final destination, Camp O'Donnell, proved to be a hellhole worse than any American could conceive. In thirty days another twelve hundred men perished from the effects of forced starvation and abuse; the death toll once exceeded two hundred in a single day.

The distance of the march varied from sixty to one hundred kilometers depending on where a man began the march. However, a few were not placed on the march but were sent northward in trucks and delivered directly to Camp O'Donnell. The severely wounded were allowed to remain, unmolested, at the Bataan field hospitals, and some five hundred were retained to work clearing the battlefields. O'Donnell, a partially completed training camp for the Philippine army, had inadequate sanitation, severe water shortages, minuscule amounts of food, and no medicine. At the end of April, the Japanese began to move the Americans to a new camp called Cabanatuan.

Meanwhile the thousands of men on Corregidor endured ceaseless shelling and bombing. Compared to the men of Bataan, they had greater access to protective shelters and ample food and medicines. On the morning of 6 May, after the Japanese had successfully landed two tanks along with thousands of troops, General Wainwright ordered the surrender of his men.

Contrary to many erroneous versions by noted historians such as William Manchester, the men of Corregidor were not taken to Bataan, nor were they on any death march. They were simply gathered in the open area of the 92nd Garage facility. With almost no water or food, they were held here as hostages to secure the surrender of all other troops in the Philippines. Eventually, most were taken by barge to Manila, marched past the civilians to show Japanese superiority, and placed into Bilibid Prison. The next day, most were sent by train to Capas and then marched to the Cabanatuan POW camp. As always, Japanese brutality reigned, and deliberate efforts were made to starve and weaken the prisoners.

In the ensuing months the health of all continued to decline, and the horrendous death rate weeded out the weakest. Death was as common as the flies that covered every surface. Months would pass until a day of "no deaths" was noted. The daily struggle to survive consumed every waking thought. Men were sent to work on farms and on details to build bridges, expand runways, and work as stevedores at the Manila docks—sending back to Japan a steady flow of produce, scrap metal, and loot. If anything of value was found, the Japanese seized it and shipped it back to Japan. Barrels of silver coin, jewelry, and gold flowed in a steady stream to the coffers of the emperor.

Japanese industrialists, in need of labor, made requests that "white" prisoners be transported for use in their factories and mines.[5] In the summer of 1942, a few thousand men were transported to Taiwan to work as farmers and in the mines. In early October the Japanese began sending massive numbers of Allied prisoners north to Japan and Manchuria to become slaves for Japanese companies such as Mitsui, Mitsubishi, Kawasaki, and Hitachi. For those unlucky enough to be sent up in the fall, the sudden change of weather exacerbated the death rate. For example, in the first three months of 1943 at the Mukden POW camp in Manchuria, nearly three hundred men perished as a direct result of malnutrition and inadequate housing. The ground was so frozen that the dead could not be buried. The bodies were stacked like cordwood as they waited for the spring thaw.

In the fall of 1943, the Japanese freighter *Taga Maru* eased out of Manila Harbor carrying some 850 malnourished American prisoners bound for the Kyushu Island port of Moji on the Shimonoseki Straits. Below decks, the men were so crowded that they had to stand in shifts so others could sit and rest. Fed less than a cup of water per day and only a rice ball the size of a tennis ball, the men endured a harsh fifteen-day voyage, rarely being allowed on deck. With so many suffering severe dysentery, the heat and odors were overpowering. Men started to die on the first day, and by the time the ship reached Japan, seventy men had died, their bodies simply thrown overboard by the Japanese guards. One survivor noted, "It is almost impossible to recall that among us were those who hoped our misery would end quickly by a torpedo that might mercifully explode into us with a flood of cooling, cleansing water, washing away the terror and the incredible filth and the noise of our teeming mass. It was chilling as it may seem now, true, and I can hardly expect anyone who was not there to understand or really believe it."[6]

Dressed in the shabby remnants of tropical clothing, the men stepped on to the ice-covered docks of Moji on 5 October.

Pan Am Clipper in Agana Harbor, Guam, 1941. *Pan Am Collection, Guam Museum*

Four of the five U.S. Navy nurses captured on Guam: Lt. (jg) Doris Yetter; Lt. (jg) Wilma Leona Jackson; Lt. (jg) Lorraine Christiansen; Chief Nurse Marion Olds. Not pictured: Lt. (jg) Virginia Fogarty.

Collection of Charlene Hellmers Gloth

Ruby, Charlene, and CCStd John Hellmers, USN, with interpreter Mr. Yoshida at Zentsuji, January 1942.
Collection of Charlene Hellmers Gloth

Guam officers photographed by the Japanese after capture: Capt. Hubert Schurtz, USA; Maj. David Satterwhite, USA; Maj. Arnold Boettcher, USA; 1st Lt. Nelson Russell, USA; Lt. Cdr. Orel Pierson, USNR; Cdr. Donald Giles, USN.

Collection of Mortimer Marks

Three POWs photographed by the Japanese at Zentsuji after their capture: Pfc. George Summers, USMC; Sgt. Cloyd C. McMurry, USMC; Pfc. Birdyne Boyd, USMC. *Collection of Joseph R. Brown*

POW officers in quarters at Zentsuji, March 1942: left foreground, Ens. Frank Wolfsheimer, USN; right rear, Lt. (jg) Jack Schwartz, USNR; right front, Lt. Cdr. Tilden Moe, USN. *Collection of Mortimer Marks*

Photo taken by Japanese of POW S2c Joseph R. Brown, USN, showing his POW number around his neck.

Collection of Joseph R. Brown

Zentsuji P.O.W. Camp

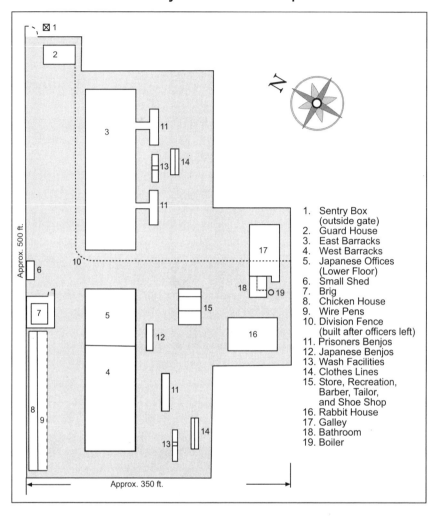

1. Sentry Box
   (outside gate)
2. Guard House
3. East Barracks
4. West Barracks
5. Japanese Offices
   (Lower Floor)
6. Small Shed
7. Brig
8. Chicken House
9. Wire Pens
10. Division Fence
    (built after officers left)
11. Prisoners Benjos
12. Japanese Benjos
13. Wash Facilities
14. Clothes Lines
15. Store, Recreation,
    Barber, Tailor,
    and Shoe Shop
16. Rabbit House
17. Galley
18. Bathroom
19. Boiler

Adaptation by Charles Grear based on sketch of Zentsuji camp (first published in Joseph R. Brown's book, *We Stole to Live*). *Collection of Joseph R. Brown*

Morning exercises at Zentsuji, 1942. *Collection of Kenneth Menzies*

Louise Hellmers greets Ruby Hellmers and baby Charlene at Port Newark, New Jersey, 25 August 1942. *Collection of Charlene Hellmers Gloth*

POW Pfc. Ralph Baggett, USMC, champion runner.
Collection of Joseph R. Brown

Guam POW barracks, Futatabi *Guam Museum Collection*

(NY16—MARCH 25)—'PAID AGRICULTURISTS," GERMANS AVER—THESE ARE
AMERICANS ON SHIKOKU, ACCORDING TO THE CAPTION APPEARING WITH
THIS PHOTO IN THE BERLINER ILLUSTRIERTE ZEITUNG, WHO "CAN VOLUNTARILY
TAKE PART IN PAID AGRICULTURAL WORK." JAPANESE SOLDIERS LEAD THE
PRISONERS "TO THEIR PLACE OF WORK," THE CAPTION ADDS. (EDS: SEE ALSO
NY14 AND 15)(APWIREPHOTO)(FES71230BIE) 1944

Japanese photo titled "Paid Agriculturists" printed in German magazine *Berliner Illustrierte Zeitung,*
showing POW work party being led out of camp in Shihoku, 1944: left foreground, Pvt. John LaGrone,
USMC; left rear, Pvt. Herbert Humphrey, USMC; right rear, Pfc. John M. Smith, USMC; right center,
Pfc. Alfred Schlegel, USMC; right front, Pfc. Max Martin, USMC. *Collection of John LaGrone*

Newly liberated POWs raising American and British flags at Hirohata, 2 September 1945. Holding flag rope, 1st Sgt. Earl B. Ercanbrack, USMC; holding American flag, Cpl. James S. Ward, USMC. *Collection of Steven Kramerich*

Liberated POW survivors at Zentsuji, August 1945. The survivors hired a Japanese photographer to take this photo. Ex-POWs are from Guam, Wake Island, Australia, and New Zealand. Seated, front row: E. W. Dunsmoor; Frank W. Stone; (behind) R. A. Schiffbauer; A. S. Johnston; Alfred L. Donila; Jay S. Combs; H. D. Ross; A. J. Carillo; G. E. Olson; William Reed; G. C. Golich; John LaGrone; Earl Rotzmon; Rex Wilson; Wylie Slomon; William Pogue; Paul R. Ritthaler; J. J. LaCasse; C. E. Heinson; Joseph Hansek; F. K. Linn; Frederick C. Guith. Leaning: D. U. Albertozzi; E. C. DuPins; J. A. Jones. Second row: George Wells; John E. Wickham; Glen Gardiner; C. D. Barnett; Max Martin; L. S. King; A. W. Jones; John C. Odom; C. R. Kuonen; Louis Bell; A. R. Wilkinson; Woodrow Bagwell; A. A. Schlegel; John H. Smalling; F. E. Baker; Jacob Taylor; Marvin McLeod; M. P. M. Guinn; J. W. Sprague; David Shively; E. S. Perkins; William H. Sager; K. F. Whittaker; C. E. Foshay; L. E. Rathbun; Abner P. Rowe; A. R. Miller; Jack Menzies; Paul Weaver; Willard R. Dunlap; Marvin Rozlansky; John Sawyer; P. A. Law; Warren D. Conner. Rear: Joseph R. Brown; Elwood Smith; H. C. Goetz; James A. Drolette; Truman Keck; Irvine Frontis; Olin S. Lake; Donald Binns; T. K. Honan; J. M. Jones; Jack Walsh; J. F. Hellmers; Michael Menzies; Knute Hansen; Vincent Jones. *Collection of Joseph R. Brown*

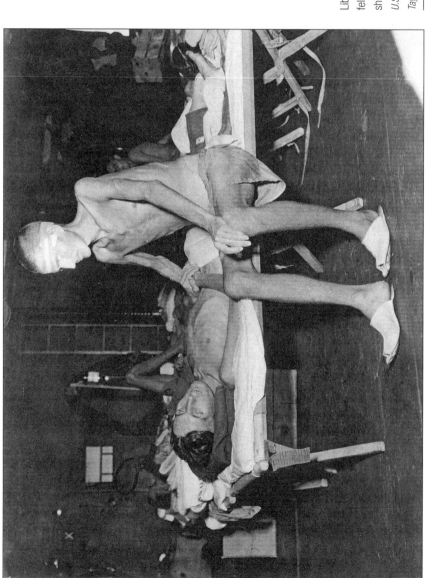

Liberated POW comforts comatose fellow survivor on board U.S. hospital ship *Block Island*, 5 September 1945.

U.S. Navy Photo, collection of Lt. Henry Taylor, USN

CHAPTER 16

Hirohata #2

A New Camp and POWs from the Philippines

I n September 1943 the camp commander at Hirohata #1, Kohkichi Asakawa,[1] took Sgt. Earl B. Ercanbrack and PhM1 Tony Iannarelli to preview a new prison, about one mile closer to the mills. A few days later, on Wednesday, 15 September 1943, the eighty prisoners were moved to their new camp, Hirohata #2, officially designated by the Japanese as Osaka Camp 12-B, Hirohata, Hyogo Prefecture.[2] The newly constructed camp was eight kilometers west of Himeji, three kilometers from the shore, and located amid numerous rice paddies. The stench of the rice paddies was to remain part of the prisoners' lives.

The small compound, surrounded by a ten-foot wooden wall, consisted of two large two-story wooden barracks, a wash rack, two latrines, Japanese officers' quarters, a guard house, and a series of smaller buildings that contained the kitchen, bath, sick bay, storeroom, brig, and cobbler and tailor shops. The eighty prisoners were placed inside one of the two barracks, originally designed to hold one hundred men. The entire camp area was less than half an acre, with more than half that space covered by the buildings.

Less than a month later, on 6 October 1943, 406 men from the Philippines would arrive in camp, having survived a fifteen-day trip on board a hellship from Manila, the *Taga Maru*.[3] All were Army veterans except for ten Marines. With the new men crammed into the two barracks, space was now at a premium. Each man had the equivalent of 1.9 square meters of living space.

The new men, although appearing physically fit, were suffering the effects of severe malnutrition. Dysentery was rampant, beriberi afflicted more than half the men, and most had colds verging on pneumonia. The new arrivals, familiar only with the sparse facilities of POW camps in the Philippines, marveled to see running water for washing clothes and the tub used for bathing. Compared to their experiences on Bataan and Corregidor, Hirohata #2 appeared heavenly.

Sgt. George Shane noted the new arrivals had little understanding of proper sanitation. "As Marines, we were trained in survival in the tropics," said Shane. "Two of the most important things we learned was that all water had to be boiled and, because human excrement was used as fertilizer (night soil), all food had to be carefully washed. You simply could never eat an unwashed vegetable. When the POWs arrived from the Philippines, they were all suffering from dysentery. These men would not wait for food to be washed nor water boiled. As a result they would grab stuff, cram it in their mouths, and continue to die like flies. It took a long time for them to acquire sanitation discipline."

"We were happy to see the men from the Philippines," said RM1 Bob Epperson, "since now the work—*and punishments*—were spread around to more people. They certainly made life easier for us."[4] With the arrival of the men from the Philippines, the Japanese guards introduced their new clubs, euphemistically called "reform bats," for beating prisoners. The civilian guards, especially Matsumoto, Shimitsu, and Numata,[5] were consistently savage in their use of these clubs. Any excuse was used, from a button undone to a shoe unlaced or a missing button—or simply because the guards just wanted to beat a white man.

Immediate tension developed in the camp. With no "unit cohesion" like that among the men from Guam, a deeper sense of conflict arose between the two groups. The newly arrived Army soldiers were all from different units and instantly suspicious of the command structure imposed by the Navy and Marine leaders already present. The Guam men had well-established routines and cliques, particularly regarding the methods of stealing and negotiating with the Japanese. The new arrivals instantly resented the fact that the Guam men would not share the proceeds of their thievery. In addition the new arrivals brought a major infestation of lice into the camp and were reluctant to take the steps necessary to stop the spread. Fortunately Ercanbrack recognized the tension and, after separating the men, began rigidly enforcing a semblance of military discipline. The men were separated into seven squads of approximately eighty men each. Ercanbrack's overbearing command, while necessary, was reluctantly accepted by all as a matter of survival. United only in their hatred of the Japanese, dissension was never adequately quelled.

With the extra men on the work details, the Guam men slacked off even more. The Japanese *honchos* quickly noted that the original eighty men were derelict in their work and so divided them among the other squads. Their unit cohesion remained however, as the Guam men continued to meet at night. Despite the tensions between the groups of men, most continued to find ways to sabotage the Japanese war effort. "All of us sought to sabotage the Japanese," said Epperson. "When we were forced to load antiaircraft shells, a bunch of the men up from the Philippines, having extensive experience with similar weaponry, simply removed and destroyed the fuses."

Being caught stealing continued to have dire consequences. Pfc. Harris Chuck's work detail suffered one of the worst beatings ever administered. "It was sometime during February of 1944," said Chuck:

> By then most of the men were sick and suffering from swollen legs caused by beriberi. They caught two Marines on the ship with food but knew others had to be involved since so much was missing. As the weather was freezing, the Japs had us all down on our knees and the

Bataan guys were really suffering, so I passed the word to my men that I was going to stand up and admit the theft and I expected them to do the same. The four men of my detail rose from the ground. Everyone was sent to the barracks except the five of us, the two Marines they had seized earlier, plus the overall camp NCO at the time, Marine Sgt. Howard Moore. Then, supervised by that sadistic bastard "The Bull," the guards proceeded to beat us with baseball bats. I was black and blue for almost a month. It was the worst beating I ever got, and I had quite a few over the years.[6]

In a letter home to his mother after the war's end, EM2 Ed Hale reflected on the harsh winter of 1943–44: "The corruption and rotten politics that developed among the Americans was even more disgusting to me on occasion than the conduct of the Japanese. There was stealing, kowtowing to the Japanese foremen or guards, cliques, and chiseling among ourselves. I often wondered that we did not half die during that winter of 1943–44."

As 1943 came to a close, the production from the mill lessened each day. The submarine attacks, coupled with wide-ranging carrier attacks, reduced the flow of materials to a trickle. Small, one-hundred-ton barges became the primary method to move coal and ore from the conquered areas of Manchuria, China, Korea, and Formosa. To survive the perilous journey, the ships came up the eastern coast of China by hugging the shore lines and hiding during the nights, then making a final dash across the Sea of Japan into the inland sea. Cargo cranes along the piers, because of a lack of shipping, would remain idle for months at a time. The mill continued to operate, but real production was almost negligible for the rest of the war.

In bitter cold, snow, or rain, the work details continued and the abuse worsened every day. The first of many deaths at Hirohata #2 was recorded at 12:45 p.m. on 17 December 1943, when a Bataan Death March survivor, Cpl. Arthur A. Haley, USA, 7th Chemical Company, died as a result of starvation, beriberi, pneumonia, and dysentery. SM1 Reed called Haley's death "murder," and no prisoner would disagree with that assessment. The first, and only, man from Guam to die at Hirohata was Pfc. Lawrence R. Bustamente, USMC, who died 17 March 1944 from a combination of pneumonia, starvation, and an infection from massive boils.[7] Unfortunately, fellow prisoners noted a sense of "give-up-itis" among those who died, without understanding that such depression is a classic symptom of starvation and beriberi.

Control of the kitchen was rigidly enforced by Ercanbrack. To maintain discipline and serve as camp leader, he insisted that his own overall health must be maintained. At all times he was to be given a full ration, regardless of shortages. His weight, while reduced, never diminished to the skeletal form of others. However, many of those on sick call noted Ercanbrack surreptitiously fed much of his own food to those on the verge of death by starvation.

Rice was apportioned to each of the established messes and served on unfinished tables in the barrack passageways. Ercanbrack, describing the mess system, said that "everyone [shared] every grain of rice *absolutely equally* without respect for personal desires. I honestly believe that we ate better, had better morale, and fewer deaths than any camp in Japan."[8]

A major effect of starvation, aside from beriberi, pellagra, and scurvy, is dementia and depression. Cpl. Thomas M. Hammel of the 7th Material Squadron (Philippines) had developed severe "wet" beriberi and appeared to lose his mind, staring into space and being unresponsive to any conversations. He began carrying a small box, calling it his "tool box." Ignoring all admonitions, he wandered in and out of barracks and into the quarters of the Japanese. To the Japanese, he was now considered insane.

In the superstitious Japanese society of the time, people considered insane were looked upon as spirits of ancestors and were, as in Hammel's case, to be given freedom to wander and allowed to sleep in a separate area of the Japanese guard house. Fed by the Japanese, he regained his health, but his mind appeared to remain hopelessly lost. His fellow prisoners, while feeling empathy, feared even more that such dementia would happen to them.[9]

Other men would suffer mental distress as a result of work they were forced to perform. "Early on at Hirohata," said S1 Ed Settles, "the Japs caught Eddie Howard with a Bible. Normally they would seize it and beat the hell out of you. In this case they decided that Eddie was to read a eulogy for the men who died, just before each man was to be cremated. The Japs would take the dead man—generally very skinny from starvation—and break his body to force the remains into small wooden kegs that once contained the pickled daikons. Eddie would have to read the eulogy as they shoved the keg into the furnace. It completely broke his spirit and mind. He was never again the same ebullient young man we all knew."

The callousness of the Japanese guards cannot be encapsulated in a few stories. To the prisoners, their actions rarely seemed rational and calculated. One afternoon, while pushing a freight car along a pier, S3 Fred "Fox" Wells[10] sensed the approach of another car and, at the very last moment, jumped clear as the cars smashed together, receiving a glancing blow that knocked him to the ground. As he started to rise, a Japanese guard known as "Fish Face" began pummeling Wells. Wells struck back, shouting, "You son of a bitch. I'll knock you into the water!" Fortunately, the Japanese guard backed away. Turning to Tony Iannarelli, Wells said, "Tony, what the hell is this? I almost got killed and here this son of a bitch wants to beat me up!"[11]

"The Japs liked to punish Fox Wells," said PhM3 Leroy Bowman, "with a unique water torture in the winter. Fox was a fairly tall guy and, compared to most, in fairly good physical shape. Around the camp we had a number of concrete basins sunk in the ground to store water. These were to be used in case of fire as every building was very flammable. The Japs would strip Wells and, using sticks or ropes, whip his backside raw. The Japs, after breaking the ice on the basins, would make him sit in them until he passed out. Then they would rouse him and beat him again. He never once complained."[12]

"For some reason," said George Shane, "the Japs took a particular hatred towards anyone who was tall, especially if they were blonde or red haired. They would stand up on chairs just so they could punch you in the face and bash your head."

To prevent looting, the guards would often affix seals on the doors to ship's storerooms. The prisoners, hating their captors, nevertheless realized that in many ways, the Japanese guards were as gullible as children and conditioned by a deep-seated fear of losing face. The prisoners took advantage of them at every chance. They simply broke through the inside walls from the hold side and continued to loot. On one occasion, the guards discovered six men were missing from a work detail inside one of the holds. Certain the prisoners were stealing elsewhere on the ship, the Japanese began a methodical search of the ship. The six men easily sneaked back into the hold and, after almost an hour, the Japanese recounted the men. With all now present, it took very little to convince the Japanese that they must have made a mistake in the original count for there was no way for the men to have gotten back without being seen by "one of your alert guards."

Many men, keenly aware of the consequences, took great pride in their ability to steal in large quantities while right under the noses of the Japanese. Two such prisoners were Pvt. Russ Dalrymple and Pfc. John Rucker.[13] Dalrymple once grabbed a box of soap and, spotted by a guard, was chased around a ship. The other prisoners surrounded him, but the guards backed away rather than admit they lost face in not capturing the thief. On another occasion, Dalrymple brazenly walked off a ship carrying a large stalk of bananas. Rucker continually raided the ship's galleys to steal burnt rice and any food laying about. Both men were rarely caught.

Similar thefts were noted by EM2 Ed Hale: "A rice ship, the *Indus Maru*, had just come up from Burma with a deck cargo of bananas. Watching the ship, I verified what I had suspected of the people who live and work on the barges that abound among Japan's hundreds of canals. We could see them swinging their barges alongside the ship. Getting a sack of bananas, and then visiting other barge people. The black market had been well organized long before we ever went to war with Japan."[14]

Pranks and overt behavior designed to humiliate the Japanese became another routine of daily existence. Even if guards gave a man a break from punishment, they would insist the man continue to work hard. The frequent reply from the prisoner was a loud "Fuck you!" When the guard Matsumoto asked Tony Iannarelli what the term meant, he replied, "It is a compliment. It means your are the best guy on two feet."

A few months later, when the camp was inspected by Colonel Murata, he was accompanied by a Japanese interpreter who spoke perfect English. With a gloating grin, the interpreter informed Sergeant Ercanbrack and Chief Radioman Barnum that he told the guards exactly what "Fuck you" meant. At the next formation, Ercanbrack informed the men of the bad news and warned them to watch out as the "Japs will want revenge." Paradoxically, the Japanese did not increase the usual punishments, for to admit they had been so naïve would have meant a loss of face. Taking every opportunity to thwart the Japanese or increase morale became the mission of every man.

Some of the prisoners fully understood the social structure of Japanese society. Perhaps the most cognizant of the Japanese sense of pride, fear of retribution, and fear of losing face was Tony Iannarelli. On one occasion, when the guard known as "Frog" started to beat up Iannarelli for stealing food, Tony warned him that he knew Frog was stealing food from the prisoners. "I warned him," said Tony, "that if you ever hit me again, I would tell Bull." Frog never beat Tony again.

Unfortunately, few prisoners ever fully understood they had the ability to terrorize the guards and *honchos* by threatening to report them to superior officers. For example, when the prisoners learned of a Japanese defeat, they could have threatened a guard by saying, "If you hit me again, I will tell the commandant that *you* told me that Japan was losing the war." Any guard or civilian *honcho* would know that such a statement could cost him his life. Few prisoners ever realized this power over their keepers.

Every prisoner remembers specific instances of brutality. That the instances seem repetitious is only because the Japanese inflicted mass punishments, over and over again, regardless of their futility. Sadistic mass punishments were so common that few men bothered to record the instances in their secret journals. The hatred and contempt for the prisoners was abundantly evident, day in and day out. "I think the worst thing I saw in camp," said Pfc. Frank Nichols, "was one very bitterly cold day in late February 1944. During a shakedown inspection, about eight to ten men were found with food. The Japs stripped them naked and lined them up, standing barefoot in the snow. There they stood for hours with their arms at their sides, literally turning blue. As they entered the barracks, they all smiled and said, 'We'll do it again tomorrow, only not get caught this time!' In a perverse way, this sense of humor kept us all going."

Another prisoner, Ed Settles, remembered similar mass punishments while at Hirohata: "During the winter of 1943–44, the Japs discovered one day that we had stolen food from the camp storeroom and demanded someone confess. They soon realized no one would ever admit to that. With snow on the ground, they lined us up in the bitter cold. We were forced to strip to the waist and remain at attention. If you made *any* movement, they would beat you senseless with their clubs. They kept us there at least two hours but no one would cooperate."

The Japanese continued to insist, under the pain of such punishment, that the prisoners should never lie, steal, or gamble. "For the POWs," said Private Nichols, "this was not a threat but a challenge—and challenging the Nips is what we did at all times."[15] The prisoners would shoot craps for cigarettes, the currency of the camp.

Fear of injury while working remained foremost in the mind of every prisoner. With deteriorating health, the reduced rations given while they were sick created additional stress on the men's weakened bodies. Every detail had elements of danger, whether one handled molten slag, fed coal into furnaces, repaired rail track, unloaded ships, emptied rail cars, operated drill presses, or filled ore buckets in cargo holds. Beatings, while common, were expected and rarely caused permanent injury. However, numerous Japanese guards, and in particular, many civilian supervisors, deliberately sought to injure, if not outright kill, the prisoners.

Bob Epperson vividly remembered how the Japanese continually tried to injure him. Like other tall men, he suffered even more at the hands of the short Japanese. "I was injured three times while a prisoner," said Epperson, "all at Hirohata":

> The first two times, a Jap crane operator dumped a load of ore on me and the second time, a load of slag. My buddies dug me out but I darn near died each time. The third time was a sequence of deliberate acts by the Japs to kill me, just as they tried to kill other prisoners . . . perhaps seeking revenge for the loss of a family member in the war.
>
> We were unloading an ore car on a train trestle. Normally we carefully let the side down in a series of moves to prevent any accident. A Jap civilian deliberately opened a J hook holding the side wall, suddenly dropping the side over the trestle. I tumbled out and down the slope, coming to rest beneath a descending ore bucket. [S1] Ernie Molnar immediately scrambled feet first down the ore pile and pulled me out of the way. It still caught me and fractured my back—but I was alive. I spent the rest of the day lying in a wheelbarrow before they were able to carry me back to camp. As a direct result, I lost an inch and a half of my height.

The medical facilities and supplies were far less than adequate. For the first year at Hirohata, the only medical services were performed by fellow Navy pharmacists. When the men arrived from the Philippines, an Army medical officer, Major Seid, was among the prisoners.

"Doctor Seid was a real saint of a man," said Epperson, and the opinion was shared by all prisoners. Epperson continued:

> One particular man, suffering from a broken back, failed to properly bow to a guard. In a furious rage, the guard knocked him to the ground and began beating him with his kendo stick. Seeing this brutality, Doctor Seid demanded the guard stop. When he did not stop, Seid placed himself over the prostrate body of the soldier for protection but the guard simply struck at Seid with all his fury. Lee "Cowboy" Garner ran out of the barrack and decked the guard.
>
> The head guard, Ishida (aka "The Bull") arrived and Doctor Seid began to explain what happened. Fortunately Doctor Seid also treated

the Japanese soldiers and "The Bull" dismissed all with the admonition, "Nobody is to ever hit this doctor, Oisha-san—Mister Doctor." In disbelief, Garner and Seid returned to the barracks, free from the expected beating.

Seid and his assistants were the epitome of compassion, but little could be done to stem the deaths from dysentery and starvation because the Japanese provided few, if any, medical supplies. It was starvation and the side effects of boils that had earlier caused the death of Private Bustamente. Despite valiant efforts, including a blood transfusion from Harris Chuck and Sergeant Ercanbrack, "Busti" could not muster the strength to survive.

Dysentery and starvation were the primary cause of all medical problems. The most dreaded result of malnutrition was beriberi. Describing the effects, Settles said, "There were two types you could get, wet and dry. If you got wet beriberi, you will swell up from water retention. In some cases, we had to puncture the men with bamboo rods to drain out the water or the pressure would cause death by heart failure. With dry beriberi, open sores like carbuncles would form and cause extreme pain. Using sharpened edges of spoons, we would lance ourselves to drain them. Kruger [from the Philippines] had three huge sores on his forehead that started to distort his whole face. I lanced them as a few other guys held him down. Dr. Seid used all sorts of substitute tools. In one case, he even used a razor, screw driver, and hammer to work on one man."

By spring of 1944 prisoner deaths became more frequent, with eight dying in March and April alone. The prisoners could never accept death easily, and with each death, they resolved to survive to see justice done to the guards.

"Sometimes death was sudden," wrote Ed Hale,

striking quickly at someone we supposed to be comparatively strong. But usually it was a slow, agonizing, horrible death, with constricted muscles, moaning or even screaming, semiconsciousness, and the victim begging for merciful death. Once the violent form of this disease took hold, it seemed that food was useless. Men could not eat, could not even assimilate what was forced down them. We tried to allot extra food from the meager rations of the working men to those who seemed in direst need, but it was impossible to know who was weakest.

Then came the dysentery. Men loosened, passing a "jelly like" liquid. Even rice was not digested, but passed uselessly through our gaunt bodies. We tried everything imaginable to check this horrible, killing diarrhea and dysentery. Some men had to run to a toilet as often as every hour, night and day. It is impossible to describe the utter agony of such a disease in the cold of winter, making rest impossible, deeply draining the tiny reserve of strength we [had] left.

I had this horror for nearly a year. Sometimes fourteen or six-teen times per day I would pass water and grains of rice. My weight dropped to 120 pounds. I became so weak I could hardly rise from a chair, even with the use of my arms for help. The Japanese routine still insisted on early morning exercises, which became an ordeal compa-rable to torture. Our body temperature at this time averaged two or three degrees below normal, due to the lack of fuel for our systems and the almost complete absence of fat and sugar in our diets. We were slowly and surely dying en masse.

I discovered that I could digest bread far more efficiently than rice. So I traded all my rice for bread, with good results, though I still had loose bowels and did not gain any weight or strength. I found that I did not gain by eating the weeds that were stewed and served to us for greens. They only aggravated my diarrhea. One horrible day in April I discovered the deadly blood spots and mucous that signified dysentery. I tried to get off work. A few days' rest would have helped, but the Japanese corpsman would not allow it. There must have been a hundred of us enduring the same ordeal—too sick and weak to do more than plod feebly around, hoping in the face of hopeless despair that something might break. For me, it did—in April of 1945. The Japanese released a quantity of sulfathiazole to our doctor. It worked miracles. After two days of treatment my dysentery cleared. The agony within my belly disappeared, and I passed the first solid stool in over fourteen months. Immediately I felt stronger, and it seemed that I had turned the corner enough to look toward home, that almost forgotten fantastic land where people ate when they got hungry, and had faucets that ran hot water, and had stoves to heat their homes.[16]

Under the most primitive of facilities, without anesthesia or proper medi-cal instruments, Dr. Seid ministered to the men with effectiveness beyond measure. George Shane recalled that "one of our men, Pfc. Robert M. Hinkle, was operated upon for appendicitis, without any anesthesia nor medicine of any form. It was a miracle he managed to survive. We held him down as he went in and out of uncon-sciousness due to the pain. Seid constantly fought the Japs to get us more medicine. Every time he would ask, they would beat him senseless, but he never gave up asking."

"The regular Army guards," recalled Shane, "were relatively decent compared to the reserve guards. One guard, Sergeant Mitsunaga [not listed on Japanese prepared staff list], was really quite helpful. In fact, he would steal food and medicine for us. He would turn his back while we stole. Another was a real SOB, who bragged, 'If hungry enough, you will eat seaweed.' We did and were glad to get the seaweed."

The severity of starvation is indicated in postwar reports of men gaining as much as forty-five pounds in two weeks. For many, it was six months before their bodies were again conditioned to process proteins and their intestinal tracts were clear of parasites. Unfortunately, few photographs remain to show the men in their actual condition before rescue. Dachau and Auschwitz victims were identical in appearance to the prisoners of the Japanese. One photo of liberated POWs on board the hospital ship USS *Block Island* was taken by a U.S. Navy photographer when POWs were liberated from a mine camp on Taiwan on 2 September 1945.[17] As a U.S. sailor carried one of the weakened POWs in his arms to board the *Block Island,* he whispered, "God! What did they do to you?"

CHAPTER 17

Tanagawa

IF YOU HAVE NOT PASSED THE BITTERNESS OF STARVATION, YOU
KNOW NOT THE BLESSINGS OF ABUNDANCE.

—*Chinese proverb*

O
n 12 January 1943 and again on 16 March 1943, a total of 160 men were
sent in two details from Zentsuji to Osaka. As usual the Japanese assured
the prisoners that the work would be similar to their work at Takamatsu
but easier. The men assumed life would continue much as they had experienced it in
Zentsuji and that they could survive by a continued theft of food. After being ferried
across the Inland Sea to Osaka, the prisoners were carried by trucks and buses south-
ward along the shoreline for just over two hours, arriving at Tanagawa Bunsho, eighty
kilometers south of Osaka in Wakayama.[1]

In the frigid midafternoon of Saturday, 16 January 1943, 150 officers, veterans
of Bataan and Corregidor, and at least 30 men from Tanagawa staggered though the
Zentsuji gates. From the barracks windows, the prisoners stared in shocked disbelief
at the filth-covered, emaciated bodies of fellow soldiers. Arrayed in the main yard, the
prisoners were counted, searched, and counted again—and again. The harassment
seemed interminable to the men staring from the windows. Finally, with the counting
complete, the Japanese released them into the care of their fellow prisoners.

The men, filthy beyond description, were wearing tattered rags for clothing,
much of that clothing covered with excrement. Long hair and beards, matted with
mud and dirt, open sores, boils, swollen legs and feet from beriberi, scabrous faces
from pellagra, and tongues swollen from scurvy hid the youthful but boney skins of
the emaciated men.[2] "My God," said 2nd Lt. Ned Gallagher, "how could any person
do this to another human being? I just stood there and actually cried. One man, almost
naked, had even wrapped a mosquito net around his stomach trying to keep warm."

Swarming out of the barracks, the prisoners carefully removed the rags that
passed as clothes, covered the shivering men with blankets, and carried them to the
bathhouse. Here, the new arrivals were gently washed, rinsed, and placed into the tubs
to thaw out their frozen limbs. "These men were so weak," said Lt. Dean Morgan,
"that they couldn't climb over the lip of the bath tub. They all were so thin that I was
able to reach in, lift one of them up, and carry him singlehandedly into the barracks."
Others quickly arranged space and extra blankets to begin the process of restoring the

health of the new arrivals. Tears of gratitude trickled from their dark, sunken eyes as their quivering hands reached out from under the blankets, seeking to touch and thank the men who ministered to their comfort. Rank held no meaning in the level of care because every man knew that, except by the grace of God, he might be one of them.

Desperate to have the men regain their health, every man, regardless of rank, contributed part of his rations to the new arrivals for the next thirty days. The incredible horrors of the Bataan Death March and the defense of Corregidor, unknown until that time, became the substance of all conversation. These new men were the courageous defenders of Bataan and Corregidor. They had already endured those long battles, the deprivations of O'Donnell and Cabanatuan, and the nightmare of a hellship voyage to Japan.

* * * * * * * *

The conditions at Zentsuji would pale in comparison to the brutality of Tanagawa. Until the end of the war, no one at Zentsuji would learn that the 160 men who had recently departed had been sent as replacements for those who had just arrived. The mind-numbing labor of tearing down a mountain to create a dry dock and submarine base at Tanagawa would rank as one of the most brutal prisoner details in all of Japan. No man would survive the entire war at Tanagawa. Constant replacements flowed in every three to four months as the men either died or became too weak to work. For the owners of Sumitomo Metal, the prisoners' deaths meant nothing, for there were more than ample supplies of "white POWs" to be gathered from Malaya, Hong Kong, the Netherlands East Indies, and the Philippines.

The first prisoners at Tanagawa, the survivors of Bataan and Corregidor, arrived on 23 November 1943 after a perilous seventeen-day voyage from Manila on board the *Nagato Maru*. The severely malnourished prisoners from Cabanatuan began work the next day to tear down a mountain and haul the dirt to the waterfront to make a primitive dry dock.[3] The Japanese camp commander ignored all requests for medical help or extra food and made the officers slave alongside the enlisted ranks. To the Japanese commander, it made no difference whether or not you were an officer; the brutal treatment was the same.

"At Tanagawa there was nothing," said six-foot-tall Pfc. Herb Humphrey of the Insular Patrol on Guam. "This was the worst time of my POW existence. We were using picks and shovels to tear down a mountain for a Jap submarine base. We would load small ore cars with rock and dirt, push the cars out over the water, and dump them. Rain, snow, it didn't matter—it was back and forth, hour after hour, day after day, month after month, and with damn little to eat. Within the first few days, we were all sick with dysentery, but that never stopped the Japs from forcing us to work. Constant and savage beatings were normal, everyday happenings."

Within a week the lack of food and exhausting labor began to take a toll on the men. The only rest came when the Japanese would drill bore holes for dynamite and clear the area for the blast. Some men were so weak that they could not clear the area, and a number were hit with flying rocks. More than one man huddled inside a tipped-over ore car in order to survive the blasts. By the end of a long, harsh day of labor, the long walk back to the barracks drained the last bit of energy from the men. Some would need help to climb the two steps into the barracks.

"Food was in the center of our thoughts at all times," said Private Humphrey:

> Some of us had pencils and paper and we'd write down imaginary recipes and talk endlessly about food. Unable to steal anything, food occupied most of our waking thoughts.
>
> We worked seven to thirteen days in a row before getting [a] day of rest. On our days off, we would go over our infested clothes, seam by seam, squashing lice and their eggs. Although desperate for sleep, the bugs and fleas kept us awake most nights.
>
> On a rest break one day, I found an eel that had washed aground on the shoreline. I took it back to the shack, cut it up, roasted it on the fire, and gobbled it down. My stomach ached from hunger. Within a month, my physical condition deteriorated to the worst in my captivity. By the time I left Tanagawa, I had dysentery, beriberi, pellagra, edema, and my weight had dropped to 112 pounds. Our eyes were gaunt and we all had bony hands and knees. It was pure misery.
>
> The weather was bitterly cold. After many complaints, the Japs let us make a stove out of a fifty-five-gallon drum. We put a post in the barrel, packed it with sawdust and when the post was withdrawn, there was a hole clear to the bottom of the barrel. We lit the sawdust at the bottom of the barrel and fire burned up thru the center, exiting into a stove pipe that reflected heat, making the room bearable.
>
> This camp was so bad I doubt anyone could have survived the entire war in that place. The men from the Philippines, already weak when they arrived, dropped like flies.[4]

The harsh conditions turned at least one desperate man into a traitor. On a cleaning detail in the Japanese offices, a prisoner spotted a letter from another prisoner, directed to the camp commandant. Quickly looking around and seeing no one watching, he read just a few lines then quickly stuffed it into his pocket. On return to the barracks, the senior NCO read, in astonishment, that a fellow POW, a Navy chief radioman, had offered to reveal the radio codes used on Guam in return for being given an inland farm and a Japanese lady for company.

"We were stunned," another prisoner said, "but we convened a court-martial wherein we found him guilty of treason. The sentence was death. The problem was how to kill him and not let the Japanese retaliate. We placed slips of paper in a hat with one piece marked with an *X*. The man who drew the *X* was never revealed but a few days later on a work detail, the traitor 'fell' over a four-foot ledge and his back was broken. The traitor did not die but was permanently paralyzed from the waist down. We agreed that this was sufficient punishment and he was allowed to live. However, no one ever spoke to him again."

On Sunday morning, 16 May 1943, the Guam prisoners at Tanagawa were loaded onto a train for Osaka. At 11:30 a.m. the train ground to a halt at the Umeda Railway Station and the prisoners stepped off into a pouring rain. "Thank God that they shipped us to Osaka and the Umeda Bunsho," said Private Humphrey. "I had become so weak that I could barely remember to breathe."[5] Wet and chilled from the rain, the weary Tanagawa detail approached Umeda Bunsho. "We had to wait under an overpass," said Humphrey, "until the group of POWs in the camp came out. When they did come out, they were marched up to us. These guys were in great shape compared to our awful-looking condition. I never did know where they were taken."

The Japanese made the departing Umeda prisoners, mostly British and Australian, exchange clothes with the arriving men. The departing men, now dressed in noticeably worse clothing, were placed on another train and taken down to Tanagawa. The newly arrived Guam survivors of Tanagawa were given their first full meal in months as the welcoming inmates shared their hoarded food and cigarettes, anxious to bring them back not merely to health but to life. The bathhouse water had significantly cooled, but a bath, their first in five months, was a joy to the shivering, rain-soaked survivors of Tanagawa.

CHAPTER 18

Chikko

The Osaka Main Camp

WE SECURE OUR FRIENDS NOT BY ACCEPTING FAVORS BUT BY DOING
THEM.

—*Thucydides, The History of the Peloponnesian War*

A fter the Eighty Eightballs were dispatched from the stadium prison
(Minato-Ku) in Osaka to Hirohata, BMC Philip Earl Saunders remained,
still accepted by the Japanese as "the number one soldier." Within days, the
remaining men were transferred to a new prison, designated the Osaka Main Camp,
or Hoincho (aka Chikko).[1] Technically, the buildings housing the actual Osaka
Command Headquarters of the Japanese were two blocks away from Chikko.

The new camp, consisting of eight barracks-style buildings and quarters for the
Japanese, was located a block from the waterfront in south-central Osaka. Within
days, the camp would fill with prisoners, including a large contingent of survivors
from the *Lisbon Maru*,[2] who arrived in October. When the British and Australians
arrived, along with a few merchant seamen and Americans, Saunders continued to
keep his men in control of the kitchen.

"Our barracks," said PhM3 Al Mosher, "were occupied primarily with Navy and
Marines personnel from Guam. Other barracks were occupied by American Army ranks
from the Philippine Islands, British merchant marine officers, and seamen, including a
few Norwegians. There were quite a few Indians who I believe were crewmen of British
ships along with a number of prisoners of war from the Dutch East Indies."

Unfortunately, Saunders continued his obsequious toadying to the Japanese and
continued to favor his friends with the choice details and jobs as camp cooks. More
than one man noted his selfishness. On more than one occasion, Saunders sent very
sick men from the camp hospital out on heavy labor details then filled their empty
beds with his friends. As he was designated the camp leader by the Japanese, no prisoner, officer or enlisted, would dare protest. His fellow Navy chief petty officers shared
in his largesse, most often at the expense of the Army men from the Philippines who
later arrived from the hell camp of Tanagawa. Saunders' lack of leadership and his
reluctance to delegate responsibilities to anyone other than his friends was manifested
in numerous problems. Individual hygiene was neglected, the barracks were never
cleaned, and clothing was rarely washed. Small groups and divisive cliques formed,

most of them by service branch. Saunders and his friends were held in contempt by all but a few. The distrust often exploded into fights among the men.

By the beginning of 1943, the camp contained more than seven hundred prisoners. The majority of men were now Australians and British, who also chafed at Saunders' leadership. Work details, not unlike the details in many other camps in Osaka, were primarily stevedore work along the docks and nearby freight yards. However, numerous details were sent to work in cement plants, in asphalt plants, and at the Seiko steel mill. By the late spring of 1943, more than two hundred men had perished from disease, malnutrition, pneumonia, dysentery, scurvy, beriberi, and "accidents" deliberately caused by Japanese foremen. With no effective leadership, the selfishness of Saunders and his compatriots simply added to the misery.

"We continued doing the same backbreaking labor," said Al Mosher, "unloading ships, barges, rail cars, and working in warehouses that occupied that area of the city. Normally, the Japanese guards would take us to a work detail where we would be turned over to civilian supervisors who assigned us various jobs. These assignments were advantageous as we were fed a noon meal by the company for which we were working for that particular day. The Japanese had a simple policy: If you worked, you received a little more food."

Time dragged on as starvation took its deadly toll. Communication was limited to only those men on the same work detail or in an adjoining sleeping space. Extra friendships were avoided, as few could trust others outside their immediate circle. Betrayal to the Japanese for a morsel of food was not unusual. Of particular note, Saunders frequently squelched any complaints by threatening men, saying, "Do what I want or I'll report you to the guards." As in Zentsuji earlier in the war, it was not a meaningless threat.

The British forced Saunders to add some of their men to the kitchen detail and, as it later developed, consistently favored their own interests over those of their "colonial" brethren, the Australians. Attempts by the British leadership and Saunders to enforce saluting and kowtowing were thwarted by the abundant derision of the lower ranks of Americans and Australians.

Individual and mass punishments at Chikko were no different than at most camps. For self-protection, the men tended to associate only with their own work details. "Most of the time," said Mosher, "I worked with the same small group of six to eight men. We tried to keep a low profile to avoid any punishment by the Japanese guards or civilian supervisors. As a small group, we were able to bargain with the civilian *honchos* that if we finished an assigned amount of labor, we could take the rest of the day off. We could then rest until it was time to return to the camp."

Many men were not victims of severe brutality and were often unaware of what happened to other men at the various work sites. All, however, knew the penalties when caught at any offense. "I did know that if you were caught stealing food," said Mosher, "they would rough you up pretty badly. The Japanese guards would make offenders stand at attention outside the guard house, regardless of the weather, and the passing guards would assault them, frequently striking the men with their sticks."

Work details, scattered over the south end of Osaka, rarely deviated from day to day. Mosher noted that it was not until the later part of 1944 that he noticed a significant change. Work on board ships in the harbor dramatically decreased, and most details worked only on the barges in the city canals and empty waterfront. Beginning in the spring of 1945, more planes were spotted flying high overhead. "Sometimes," said Mosher,

> we could see only their contrails. Since we were working in an area where the harbor master was located, we knew when planes were expected because signal flags were flown from the mast above his building. In a short while, the sirens would sound and then the planes would come into view high in the sky.
>
> About the middle of March 1945, those of us out on work parties witnessed a B-29 bombing raid on Kobe, across the bay. The raid started in the morning and seemed to last at least two hours or possibly longer. The bombs used were incendiary, causing many fires and lots of smoke. There seemed to be an endless stream of bombers. Since this was our first indication that the war was coming to the Japanese mainland, we were pleased to watch as Kobe went up in flames.
>
> On the first day of June we experience a similar raid. The raid seemed to last approximately three hours. A wide swath of the city was incinerated as far as one could see. Fortunately we were out on work parties so could have a good view of the bombing. Unfortunately our camp was burned to the ground. We were quartered in an abandoned camp a couple of blocks away that had been occupied by British soldiers from Hong Kong. That night an observation plane flew over and there was near panic.[3]
>
> A day or two later we were taken by motor launch to another abandoned camp which was located among bombed out factories and steel mills. This camp was also near the waterfront. We were there only a few days when we experienced another bombing raid. This time we were kept in the barracks and could not see the target or the damage. Whatever the target was, it must have been close by because we could hear the bombs whistling overhead and hear their impacts and explosions. I don't know what the name of this camp was, but it was clearly unsafe for us to stay there any longer.[4]

The camp burned down that night. In the second week of May 1945, some one hundred survivors were sent up to Notogawa on the eastern shore of Lake Biwa to build a dike to reclaim land from the sea.

CHAPTER 19

Osaka-Umeda

Wartime Experiences

EXPERTO CREDE. (TRUST ONE WHO HAS EXPERIENCE.)

—Latin proverb

Pfc. Herb Humphrey and the ragtag band of Tanagawa survivors stood in ranks before the entrance to Umeda Camp. A ten-foot-high wall of corrugated tin panels, topped with sharpened bamboo and barbed wire, surrounded the camp. The camp's hinged gate, also of tin panels, blocked any view from the street. After repetitive *bangos* (head counts), the custody of the men was transferred to Umeda, the gates were opened, and the men entered the camp. Guards streamed out of the gate and formed the men into four ranks. A cacophony of verbal assaults and slaps added to the misery of the cold, pouring rain. Within a short time, the men were sent into the crowded barracks as the Japanese guards had no further desire to stand in the rain.

For the remainder of the day, the new arrivals from Tanagawa were crowded into the cold barracks, waiting for the repeated *bangos*. Amid complaints and refusals to cooperate, the new arrivals were squeezed into the racks of sleeping platforms; their spot would remain the same until Umeda was destroyed in an incendiary raid. Shivering in their wet clothes, they received a bowl of rice, much smaller than they had seen at Tanagawa. To the new arrivals, it did not augur well.

The existing occupants of Umeda, the old-timers, looked upon the new arrivals with suspicion, thinking that, because of inexperience, they might disrupt the methods used to loot food while on labor details. A grim, selfish attitude prevailed in the camp. No one shared the fruits of their thievery with others. Efforts to make theft a cooperative effort fell upon deaf ears. Stolen food was never shared outside of one's work detail, and unless it was closely guarded, it frequently was stolen. Animosity was frequently high, and the only glue that kept the men together was the universal hatred of the Japanese.

The Japanese looked on the men from the Philippines with even more contempt than the men from Guam, who had fortuitously learned to speak Japanese at Zentsuji. In the Philippines, most had never learned Japanese, other than the numbers for counting. The Japanese derisively called the Army men "Phils." Rather quickly all the internees called themselves "Phils," thus negating the desired effect.

The preferred labor detail was the Umeda rail yard receiving area, always called "the docks" by the prisoners.[1] From the gate, a five-block boulevard led directly to the waterfront piers. Fanning out from the boulevard were block-long, raised concrete platforms covered by eighteen-foot-high tin-roofed sheds. Midway down the boulevard, one bay contained a canvas-enclosed area that served as a "shack" for storage of prisoner clothes, tools, and food. At the shack, the men were parceled out to the various work details. Here they also gathered for lunch and a final assembly at the end of the day before returning to Umeda.

Freight was loaded and unloaded onto freight cars and sundry vehicles. The loot of war, ordinary supplies, and foodstuffs transited the port of Osaka. For the old-timers, each pile represented a possible source of food. At the docks, every imaginable kind of freight was handled and, when possible, looted by the prisoners.

Like the other men already in Osaka, Private Humphrey soon became adept at stealing food whenever possible. Nothing edible escaped his notice. Prized for food value were copra (dried coconut), fresh or dried tangerines, pressed soybean cakes, seaweed, dried squid, sugar, raw yams, whale blubber, raw or dried fish, sweetened condensed milk, dried egg, saccharin pills, raw rice, and persimmons.

Some of the details handled only coal, sulfur, graphite, lime, and scrap iron—just hard work with no food to steal. Working on such details meant subsisting on what the Japanese provided. Humphrey, being over six feet tall, was chosen more often for the better details in the Umeda railroad yards. One evening, another prisoner returned with a white powder he had stolen from a boxcar. Without testing it, he added it his ration of rice. He did not offer to share his loot. He began eating and shortly keeled over dead—it was poison. His lack of generosity was appreciated.

Within two months a movement was started within the prisoner ranks to find a way to cooperate in the theft of food. Although the old-timers initially opposed the proposal, a gradual realization emerged among them that more food could be obtained through cooperation. The Japanese, for unknown reasons, had adapted the Scottish ballad "Auld Lang Syne" as a children's song, complete with Japanese lyrics. The Japanese assumed that the prisoners knew of the Japanese children's song and simply sang English verses. Whenever the prisoners sang the song, the Japanese cheerfully joined, distracted from their oversight efforts as they tried to outdo the prisoners in volume. Within a short while, massive looting was conducted to the wistful lyrics penned by Robert Burns.

On 1 August 1943, the Japanese transferred forty officers to Zentsuji.[2] A few officers, including Lt. (jg) Charles Littleton Slane, USN,[3] were to remain. However, the Japanese were still intent on humiliating officers and refused all requests by selecting only enlisted men to be in charge of the camp. The departure of the officers lowered dissension in the camp because a majority of them were more intent on securing their own comfort than in caring for the enlisted men. Some were even known to be stealing from the stores of the enlisted ranks.

Dissatisfaction with the assigned leadership continued to cause problems until the Japanese allowed the men to select their own leadership. All the previous leadership was replaced, including Lieutenant Slane. While deeply admired by the prisoners for his actions on their behalf, Slane was simply ineffective because the Japanese were determined to thwart his efforts. Elected as camp leader was AG1 Zemo Tarnowski, USN,[4] along with a small number of assistants, including the popular Sgt. Cloyd C. McMurry of Guam.[5]

Immediately secret meetings were conducted and a "School of Thievery and Destruction" was begun. Experienced and successful men began to teach everyone the techniques of sabotage and thievery, including diversion methods to be used against the Japanese. Men learned the necessity and coordination of lookouts, methods and tools for picking locks, how to break and restore security seals, and techniques for smuggling items safely back to camp.

Typical were the actions of Pfc. Tom Nixon, a Marine from the Sumay Marine Detachment. Having completed training as a military policeman, he was slated to transfer to the Insular Patrol in January 1942. One of his numerous skills was the ability to make keys from flattened nails. With the help of fellow prisoners, he would lay a nail on a railroad track while his buddies rolled the train back and forth, flattening the nail to the desired thickness. Using makeshift items as a file, he would shape key after key for his fellow prisoners, earning him the nickname "Keys."

One of the most daunting tasks was to open the railway freight car locks without destroying a paper seal placed by the Japanese. The seal was a small bill of lading made of rice paper, carefully folded to approximately one-quarter inch, tied onto the lock, and marked with a rubber stamp, or "chop." Using discarded bills for practice, Nixon was able to master the untying of the paper and, when the thievery was completed, retying the knot so the "chop" appeared undisturbed. When a Japanese guard approached, the call would go out for "Keys." Nixon would rush to the car, secure the lock, and accurately retie the paper in seconds. The seal would meet the approval of any passing guard.

Most important, Tarnowski convinced the Japanese foremen to allow the men to add to the soup pot at the docks any floor scrapings of food they could find. In short order, almost every day the watery and thin soup was converted into a thick, nutritious meal from stolen foodstuffs. Details were rotated regularly to the docks, and the overall camp health dramatically improved.

A systematic plan was developed to co-opt every guard and civilian supervisor by the sharing of loot. Some reacted by beating the "presenter," but all eventually succumbed to the proficient bribery of the prisoners. Still, men caught stealing were subjected to punishment, or if the Japanese were unable to determine a guilty individual, mass punishment was exacted upon the entire camp. Tarnowski suggested, and all accepted, that if mass punishment was threatened, one man, selected by prior lottery by drawing a short straw, would step forth and accept blame. It was an elegant solution, and the master thieves who brought back the most looted food were usually able to avoid beatings. Even the camp commandant, Sergeant Kinari,[6] was co-opted enough to play along with the solution, apologizing after a beating was administered. He could not risk losing face to superiors nor risk being cut off from the looted food that fed his family.

By the spring of 1944, the prisoners were running a large *yami* (black market operation) at the docks, openly patronized by civilians and the local police. The prisoners were getting better trades than at the local *yami,* and unlike at other markets, the prisoners would accept payment in yen. CPhM Adolph W. Meyers, USN, took some of the *yami* profits and, accompanied by a Japanese guard, was allowed to scour the local pharmacies and purchase medicine and herbal remedies to treat the sick within the camp. Although any black market activity was punishable by death for the Japanese, the authorities choose to turn a blind eye to the prisoners' *yami*. Among the patrons for the obviously stolen merchandise were not just the railroad employees and local laborers but also the local police and military guards.

At most of the various work sites, similar *yamis* were established. Prisoners' markets became overstuffed with foodstuff and items used for exchange. The men were often generous beyond measure, giving huge stocks of rice, food, and clothing to Japanese civilians who were obviously suffering from starvation and other depravation. For a worthless pair of shoes offered by one very elderly lady, the men gave her ten kilos of rice, three suits, clothing, and shoes for herself and her children. Tears were in the eyes of all. It was not unusual to hear, "Nai! Nai kome kyo wa, oba san. Ashita tabun. Mo ikai do!" (No! No rice today, lady. Maybe tomorrow. Next!) At the *bunsho* punishments almost ceased.[7]

Japanese laborers became resentful of the favored treatment accorded the *gaijin* (non-Japanese) prisoners, especially their larger food rations. On the afternoon of 13 March 1944, a riot ensued when a number of Japanese attacked three Americans caught stealing sugar at the docks. Fellow prisoners rushed to help while other Japanese laborers, grabbing clubs and stevedore hooks, ran to join in the fray. The powerful Americans, towering over the Japanese but outnumbered twenty to one, managed to acquit themselves well by using their fists. The battle ended with the Japanese agreeing just to punish the three men who were caught. A few weeks later, the men were returned in reasonable health, although visibly affected from the beatings and starvation.

However, the Japanese workers had suffered many injuries and many were unable to work. The entire camp was placed on half rations for two days and restricted to the camp. With no work and ample foodstuffs squirreled away within the barracks, the work holiday became a reward to the men. On the third day the men were given a friendly greeting at the yards because the work had stacked up in their absence. Extra food was supplied by the Japanese officials, and numerous new laborers had replaced those who disliked the prisoners. The new men were quick to seek the favor of the Americans.

One year later bombing raids dramatically escalated across Japan. Pledging "blankets of fire" over Japanese cities, Gen. Curtis LeMay's bombers began raining incendiaries into Tokyo on the night of 10 March 1945. An estimated half a million Japanese residents of Tokyo would perish in the conflagration. In Osaka two nights later, 13 March 1945, the thunderous groan of B-29s could be heard coming from the east. Amid the blare of sirens, the men were hustled back into the barracks while the guards cowered in their foxholes. Searchlights and antiaircraft fire laced the sky as the first string of bombers flew over, disgorging tons of incendiaries. In what seemed an endless stream, more than three hundred bombers laid strings of fire across the city. Flames reached up thousands of feet into the air, tossing the later planes about as if they were floating pieces of paper. From their barracks' second-floor windows, the men had a ringside seat to the spectacle of Osaka being reduced to ashes. Unconcerned for their safety, they quietly cheered as the city disintegrated.

The following morning the prisoners from Umeda were assembled and moved in details of two hundred men to Tsuruga in the Hiroshima POW command area. From a smuggled newspaper, the men knew the war was getting closer as a battle raged on Iwo Jima.

CHAPTER 20

Thirty-Seven Months in Hell

JUSTICE WILL NOT COME TO ATHENS UNTIL THOSE WHO ARE NOT
INJURED ARE AS INDIGNANT AS THOSE WHO ARE.

—Thucydides

During the fiftieth anniversary of the liberation of Guam and Saipan at a ceremony in Arlington National Cemetery, Guam's congressman, Robert A. Underwood, said,

Fifty years ago to this day, June 25, 1944, was [to be] D-Day for the Liberation of Guam. However, due to the ferocity of the Battle for Saipan and the unexpected casualties, Guam's liberation was postponed until July 21.

In the intervening weeks, the people of Guam endured forced marches to concentration camps in Maimai, Malojloj, and Manengon. We experienced atrocities at the hand of a desperate enemy, such as beheadings, and the massacres of whole groups of our people in places like Fena, Faha and Tinta. And [any] display of loyalty to America was answered with a sword or a bullet.

This flurry of cruelty was the final chapter of two and a half years of an horrendous occupation, the only enemy occupation of Americans and United States territory during World War II.[1]

For the people of Guam (renamed Omiya Jima by the Japanese), the new masters exhibited no leniency in behavior or relaxation of farm productivity. Daily levies for labor were not to be ignored. The village and district commissioners were assigned supervisory positions as *sonchos* (leaders) and became the surrogates for the Japanese. Made a *soncho* in Barrigada, Ben Reyes, a native trained as a lawyer in the United States, remarked, "As *soncho*, I was responsible for the delivery of weekly and monthly quotas of food provisions. These goods included eggs, pigs, chickens, and an assortment of vegetables. I was also required to recruit workers for public works projects, primarily workers for the airstrip at Jalaguac."[2]

Failure to comply in any manner resulted in a *binta* (beating) for the *soncho*. For the farmers, quotas were rigidly enforced and compensation rarely given. All arable

155

land had to be cultivated, and the natives were forced to labor from sunrise to sundown. The primary crops became rice and vegetables. From Saipan, five men were brought to fish for the Japanese; this was an easy assignment because two days of fishing a week in an ocean teeming with fish would meet all the needs of the military. Any natives who nurtured a private garden did so only after all mandated labor for the day was completed.

At Orote Peninsula, Jalaguac (north of Agana), and Finaguagoc (near Mount Machanao), construction of three major airfields began in earnest using hand labor to cut away and level the jungle. Coral was mined and crushed, again by hand, to cover the runways. Except for the extensive use of laborers, and the continuing and often brutal search for the missing American, RM1 George Tweed, life on Guam settled into a routine of tedium. Most of the Japanese soldiers were quartered in or around Agana and generally kept to themselves. Food, candy, and even soap were regularly available until the massive return of Japanese troops in late 1943.[3]

Not all Guamanians accepted the sacrifices required to hide Tweed, the American sailor. Businessman and politician B. J. Bordallo agreed to help the Japanese in 1942 to find the missing man after a severe beating. "What I could not understand was while many of our people were being brutalized on account of him, Tweed was moving from place to place, attending parties and generally enjoying himself," Bordallo said. "Knowing that people were being killed or maimed, if Tweed had really been a hero, he would have come out and turned himself in so that the wholesale brutalization of our people would cease."[4] Fortunately Tweed chose to believe Mrs. Agueda Johnston, the wife of an American POW, who told the sailor he had become a symbol of America. Despite later requests to surrender, even as the beatings became pandemic, Tweed never considered surrender again. By the end of 1943, the search for Tweed became a daily ritual for nearly two hundred Japanese soldiers.

Throughout early 1942, the battles in the Pacific were a continuing string of victories for Japan as its tentacles of control spread east to Wake Island, south to the Netherlands East Indies, east to Guadalcanal in the Solomon Islands, and west into Siam (Thailand) and Burma (Myanmar). In Agana's movie theater, propaganda films featuring the heroic actions and victories of the Japanese were the staple of entertainment.

Japanese losses to the Allied forces were never acknowledged, but the people knew the tide was turning. Half a dozen radios were operating across the island and rumors abounded. The Japanese portrayed their defeats as "strategic deployments," adding fuel to the speculations. With a map in hand, anyone could ascertain the slow retreat of the Imperial Japanese Navy and Army as battles drew closer and closer to Japan. By October 1943 the American submarines were finally equipped with reliable torpedoes and began attacks on cargo and troop ships rather than seeking the major warships.[5] The critical lack of supplies, especially food, immediately created severe hardships for the people of Guam. The increasing levy of food by the Japanese reduced many Guamanians to starvation levels not unlike those experienced by the POWs interned in Japan.

Counting on continued Russian neutrality toward Japan, the Imperial Japanese Army secretly withdrew a million troops from Manchuria for redeployment. From mid-1943 a steady increase in troops, construction battalions, and farm machinery poured back into Guam and the Marianas. More than 50,000 retreating soldiers from the southern Pacific passed through Guam, and by the day of invasion, about 10,000 remained on Guam to battle the powerful landing forces. As the battle lines drew nearer Japan, the Japanese began a determined effort to make the Marianas an impregnable bastion for protecting the motherland.

Chamorros were pressed into service digging caves and building tank traps, machine-gun emplacements along the shores, dummy cannon (palm trees cut down in the plaza and painted black), and roadblocks. The completed airstrips at Orote and Jalaguac were reinforced with defensive emplacements, and greater efforts were made to complete the strip in the northeast near Agui.

The first Allied attacks came on 23 February 1944,[6] when nine U.S. Navy fighters swooped down and strafed the Orote airfield, destroying four Zeroes. Japanese suspicion of the natives intensified. Any open talk about the "Americans coming" lead to certain execution.[7] In the village of Tai, three young men were executed for espionage in June 1944. Japanese officers, dressed in impeccably white uniforms and gloves, forced the three youngsters to kneel in front of open graves. One by one they were beheaded in front of three hundred Chamorro laborers. Warned not to faint under threat of a similar death, the natives stood silent, choking back tears. As in Manila after the invasion by American forces, the Japanese military made the conscious decision that the natives were their enemy and would be treated as such. The wholesale murder of locals became the norm. Even young men seeking food for their families would be captured, tortured, and murdered.

Near Yigo the mutilated bodies of more than fifty men were discovered after the liberation of the island by American soldiers. They had been used to carry supplies inland for the Japanese. To prevent disclosure of their hiding place, the Japanese simply murdered all the laborers. Near Chaquina thirty beheaded bodies were found stacked in a truck. Numerous other finds were noted by the Americans as they swept the island. The concentration camp at Manengon housed more than 10,000 Chamorro slaves and was surrounded by Japanese machine-gun emplacements.[8]

As American bombardment of the island began in June 1944, the Japanese turned savagely against the locals. In turn numerous Chamorros attacked and killed small groups of two to six Japanese soldiers whenever possible. The Japanese sought out natives of American descent for elimination. One U.S. Navy retiree, Juan Pengelinan,[9] was enticed to go to the island's Japanese headquarters under the pretext that he was to be paid for farm produce he supplied to the Japanese army. He was seized, beaten, hog tied, and transported to Tai, where he was beheaded.

Particularly brutal was the fate of Father Jesus Baza Dueñas, age thirty, who was educated in the Philippines. Two sycophant priests were brought from Japan to serve the Catholic civilians. Politically aligned with the Japanese cause, they preached the glories of Japanese supremacy. One Japanese priest, Monsignor Fukahori, warned Dueñas to avoid verbally supporting the Americans. Dueñas replied, "I answer to God and the Japanese are not God."

A constant thorn in the side of the Japanese, Dueñas was arrested on 8 July 1944 along with his nephew, Eddie, and taken to a jail in Inarajan. The pretext for his arrest was that he had been heard to sing "God Bless America" and had reported to others that Saipan had fallen. On the night of their arrest both were beaten unmercifully. In the morning Dueñas was hog-tied and repeatedly subjected to the water treatment. Water was forced into his stomach through a hose, and when his stomach was fully bloated, the Japanese torturers leaped up and stomped on his prone body, causing incredible pain. Both Dueñas men were transported to the Kempeitai in Agana.[10] Taken to Tai, they were beheaded.

As the American aerial attacks intensified, the Japanese continued an orgy of murder, rape, and slaughter, determined to kill as many natives as possible. Natives, caught in groups of a few or hundreds, were forced into caves, bomb holes, open fields, and roadways, where they were machine gunned, bayoneted, or blown to death by grenades. Unarmed, they could mount little resistance against the Japanese savagery.

Shortly after the execution of Father Dueñas, thirty men and women from Agat and Sumay were forced into a cave in Fena. At the mouth of the cave, Japanese soldiers set up machine guns, and fired streams of bullets into the cave. When the firing ceased, soldiers rushed in a frenzy into the cave, bayoneting all those who remained alive. A few survived by hiding under the bodies of the slain.

In Merizo, six days prior to the American invasion, forty-six men and women, under the assurance they would be safer, were led into two caves and similarly massacred by hand grenades, rifle fire, and bayonet. Sixteen managed to survive. Those attempting to leave the cave were summarily beheaded.[11] Typical was the reaction of Japanese to American pilots shot down over Guam. For pilots who could not guide their crippled planes back to the sea for rescue, bailing out or crashing meant almost certain death. An American Hellcat crash-landed near civilian farmers at Finaguagoc. Three Chamorro men rushed to rescue the pilot, dragging him unconscious from the wreckage. The pilot, wearing a tag bearing the name Hamilton, was grabbed by nearby Japanese soldiers, taken to their field office, and immediately shot to death. The following morning, the three men who rescued the pilot were seized, tortured for three days, then beheaded.[12] Others of American descent or suspected of harboring ill will against the Japanese began to be rounded up and executed. The mere action of looking up at American planes would be sufficient for beatings or death.

On the late afternoon of 11 July 1944, during the preinvasion bombardment, George Tweed attracted the attention of a passing destroyer with his signal mirror.

Hiding in a sheltered outcropping of rocks near Uruno Point, Tweed grabbed his semaphore flags and began relaying detailed information about Japanese gun emplacements along the shoreline. Tweed's secret hiding place below the ranch of Antonio Artero gave him a clear view from the Orote Peninsula to the northern point of the island. He identified gun sites from Adelup Point, overlooking the invasion landing sites in Agana Bay, to Machanao on the northern end of the island. As evening drew close, the destroyer sent a boat close to shore, rescuing Tweed from his island prison. The elimination of these gun sites by subsequent precise bombardment saved hundreds, if not thousands, of lives during the invasion.

The long-awaited invasion began 21 July 1944 as Gen. Roy Geiger's III Amphibious Corps of 54,900 men stormed the beaches at Asan (west of Agana) and Agat (south of the Orote Peninsula). In nine days of fierce fighting, the southern half of the island was secured and construction battalions (Seabees) converted Guam into a massive staging area for future invasions. By 9 August, the last major Japanese units were annihilated, leaving a few stragglers to harass the Americans until months after the end of the war. Of the 10,000 Japanese defenders, fewer than 100 were captured alive. The Americans suffered almost 7,000 casualties, including 1,300 dead.

Concurrently American forces secured nearby Tinian and Biak in New Guinea. On the other side of the world, Allied forces broke through the Falaise Gap, swept through France and, with French general Leclerc's 4th Armored Division, entered Paris on 25 August. The ring was slowly closing around the Axis powers.

Throughout the occupation, some of those with Japanese heritage sought to exploit their newfound privileges. RM Bob Epperson recalled his experiences while he recuperated on Guam after the war:

> Most of us had an unusual bond of friendship with the natives of Guam. In the first month after we were captured in 1941, the Ada family came almost every day to visit us in the cathedral. They brought us soap, razor blades, toothbrushes and so forth, but they could not bring food. Every time they arrived, the Japanese guards beat them savagely, yet they always came, time and time again.
>
> On the way home after liberation, I spent two weeks recovering in the Guam Hospital. There I learned of the death of Elvira Ada, a young Chamorro lady that I had dated before the war. She was from a wonderful family and a lovely girl. A local Japanese man, who worked as a projectionist in the theater, wanted to take her out but she always refused. He threatened her, often saying that "when the Japanese invade, you will be sorry."
>
> One evening he threatened her while I was there, so I grabbed him, beat him to a pulp, and threw him over the fence. After the invasion in 1941, she continued to refuse to go out with him. One day he simply beat her to death.[13]

S1 Eddie Howard, the crewman from the USS *Penguin*, returned to Guam to discover his wife had been hacked to death as the Japanese fled into the jungle. Devastated and confused, he left the island, leaving his son, Chris Perez Howard, to be raised by his wife's relatives.

For many months after the American return to Guam, local natives scoured the hills seeking out and killing the Japanese holdouts. Such was the anger of the natives that no mercy was ever shown.

CHAPTER 21

Rokuroshi

With the fall of Okinawa in mid-June 1945, the Japanese military began to move captured officers deep into the mountains on the main island of Honshu. The war was fast approaching as Allied fighter planes and bombers now roamed almost unmolested. Selected solely by nationality, the officers were notified of a pending movement about 15 May. From a clandestine radio, the prisoners had learned of the fall of Iwo Jima at the end of March, and by the end of May, they knew Okinawa was essentially in Allied hands. Rumors swept through Zentsuji that even the Japanese civilians were hoping for an end to the war.

At 3:45 p.m. on 23 June 1945, 335 officers and a few enlisted men, including PhM1 Truman Keck, who served as Dr. Van Peenen's aide, were marched to the Zentsuji train station.[1] The Japanese refused to allow the remaining enlisted men to assist the departing officers or carry their parcels. As such, many articles were simply abandoned along the march. At the station, the officers were crammed into the few passenger cars—arms and legs fighting for space among the sparse parcels that represented each man's only possessions. All of the enlisted men returned to the Zentsuji camp. Arriving in Takamatsu at nightfall, the *tenkos* resumed, and long after dark, the men were jammed into the hold of a ferry. Crossing to Honshu Island,[2] the men were loaded on board another train to Okayama, where they would spend a sleepless night jammed together in the railroad station house. The squeal of air-raid sirens sounded through the night.

"At Okayama," said Lt. Dean Morgan, "two things came as a surprise. First, we all noticed that the civilians appeared really apathetic, as if they no longer cared about us. I got the feeling they felt they were just as bad off as we were as prisoners. Second—and this was truly unexpected—the Japs gave us a *bento* box that was like manna from heaven. I cannot begin to tell you how our spirits rose. We knew the Japanese were being clobbered and somehow the war would end soon. We just didn't know when or how."

As the warming sun rose the next morning, a second *bento* was given to each man. Morale began to soar as the men speculated that the new camp might be a prelude to better treatment or an exchange as the Japanese must have realized the war was lost. Could these deliveries of food indicate the men would be "fattened up" prior to a surrender? Spirits soared as the men were loaded on board another train. Curtains were drawn and the prisoners were instructed not to look outside. Slowly, the train pulled out of the station, was shunted to the main line, and headed east, passing through Himeji, Kobe, Osaka, Kyoto, Hikone, and Tsuruga to the final destination of Fukui, on the western coast of Honshu.

Disregarding the warnings of the guards, men surreptitiously lifted the curtains. All were aware of the B-29 raids, but none were prepared to see the absolute devastation of the cities. In stunned silence, the men saw that the once-thriving and bustling port cities of Kobe and Osaka had been reduced to flattened landscapes and gray piles of ash, with only a few smokestacks and burned-out shells of concrete buildings sprinkled across the horizon. What few people remained could be seen scurrying through scenes of devastation—living in tiny hovels fabricated from scant pieces of wreckage. "To add to this scene of horror," said Capt. Mortimer Marks, "the stench of human carrion penetrated the cars." With mixed emotions the men spoke in whispers, many feeling sorrow for the innocent Japanese swept away in the carnage of war. In all directions, the industrial heart of Japan, its steel mills and shipyards, were now reduced to flattened rubble.

Pausing in Osaka for a train connection, the men were removed from the train and were seated in a circle beneath a bridge. "Although it was past midnight, a large, shabbily clothed crowd gathered around us," said Marks. Unlike past encounters when Japanese civilians threw rocks and spit at the prisoners, "they simply stood there—silently staring at us. There was no expression of hostility nor any act of aggression. Everyone [had] probably lost a member of their family, a friend, or had their home destroyed."

Boarding another train, the men rumbled northward along the east side of Lake Biwa and arrived at Fukui, on the western coast of Japan, slightly north of the parallel for Tokyo. Again, the men were transferred to another train, described by one man as a "Wild Toonerville Trolley." For ninety minutes, he said, "we rode this strangest and wildest of streetcar rides. We traveled at top speed for 23 miles, up and down mountain precipices with drops of hundreds of feet."[3] At Ono, at the foot of a mountain, the men scrambled off the train and began a nine-kilometer walk up the mountain to Rokuroshi. Under a light overcast, the full moon cast a shadowy light. Few would appreciate the beauty of the surrounding landscape.

For the next four hours, the men struggled upward over a deeply rutted trail, covered with loose stones. For those with beriberi and, in particular, Lt. Fred Garrett,[4] who had had a leg amputated in prison, the steep march was a nightmare of pain and exhaustion. Captain Lineberry struggled to carry his heavy briefcase, hanging in a temporary sling from his bone-thin shoulders. He was determined to keep it with him for it was filled with notes, sketches of camp life, letters from dying men before they perished, handmade birthday and Christmas cards from fellow prisoners, and a complete list of those who had died. The weight was simply overwhelming to the malnourished doctor. Facing total exhaustion, Lineberry reluctantly let the strap slide off his shoulder, dropping his precious "bag of memories" alongside the dark trail. The records of the Zentsuji prisoners disappeared into the night. A steady stream of similar discards, the detritus of prison life, littered the mountain trail.

"As physical men, none of us was worth saving," wrote Dr. Van Peenen. "Tuberculosis and dangerous heart murmurs were in our ranks. We were fetid with dysentery and skeletal in appearance, and as POWs, we had the contempt of the Japanese. It was even logical to believe that machine-gunning in a mountain retreat was the most sensible means of extermination."

In a light rain, shortly after 4:00 a.m. on 25 June 1945, the men gave a spontaneous cheer as the march turned into the gates of Rokuroshi, formerly a mountain training camp for the Japanese army. After 275 miles, their ordeal was over. The estimated altitude of the camp was three thousand feet, making any labor extremely wearying for the already malnourished men.[5] Prior to the arrival of the American officers, thirty enlisted men and civilian internees had opened the camp sometime in early May.[6] "Upon our arrival," said Marks, "we were met by several enlisted men who had prepared hot water, a watery soup, and a handful of rice."

The new camp, isolated high in the Japanese Alps, was located in a barren, rock-strewn, windswept plain between two high mountain ridges. The prison compound was about 90 meters by 120 meters and was surrounded by a corral-type fence of three bars. After two days of rest to organize the camp, Colonel Unruh demanded of the Japanese that the prisoners be authorized to clear the land to create vegetable gardens. Despite reduced rations, all men, including the officers, were made to clear the rocks, till the soil, plant seeds, water, and fertilize the gardens. When the American officers went on strike demanding more food, the Japanese reduced the rations even further, although in reality there simply may not have been enough food supplied to the camp to adequately feed the number of prisoners. The "no work, no food" edict ended the strike within a day.

In conversations with the guards and prison staff, the men learned that they could expect snowfalls of ten feet or more should they remain at Rokuroshi for the coming winter. The camp's flimsy barracks, made mostly of clapboard and sliding paper doors, was absolutely inadequate for winter survival. Few prisoners believed they could survive another winter in any camp, but particularly in Rokuroshi. The strenuous labor and reduced rations also quickly became apparent as every man lost at least four to five kilograms of weight within the first two weeks. The continuing starvation diet took its final toll for one prisoner on 4 August 1945, when Lt. Jim Millette, a U.S. Army officer, died. In addition, two officers attempted an escape; they were captured, beaten, and sent to Osaka the next day.[7]

Harsh as the conditions were in Rokuroshi, a number of the more onerous rules and regulations were soon relaxed. Men were allowed to gather in groups of any size, smoking was permitted outdoors, and harassment within the barracks was minimal.

Still, mass punishments were freely administered, and men were frequently given the "sun treatment," in which they were stripped of clothes and forced to stand at rigid attention for hours in the sun.

Beginning in July 1944, the food rations of the officers were reduced below starvation levels. Only sporadically were meals that constituted a reasonable semblance to being adequate served. No longer were any officers able to depend upon the few morsels of stolen food shared by a few enlisted men. At Rokuroshi there were no labor details sent outside the camp; hence, there was no food to steal. Although the men saw the destruction of the cities on their trip to Rokuroshi, few remained optimistic. Harassment by the guards continued, religious ceremonies vanished for most, and no mail was permitted. Labor in the gardens drained their energy, and only occasionally were the men allowed to bathe in the one tub used by the Japanese staff. Bucket baths with cold water did nothing to stop the sagging morale.

High in the mountains with no clandestine radio or access to newspapers and magazines, speculation on Allied successes clearly favored the notion that Okinawa had fallen. But the lack of information exacerbated the isolation of Rokuroshi, and with absolutely no outside contact, it deepened the sense of weariness and depression among the emaciated men. No news of the war managed to enter the camp. Although American bombers could be seen occasionally passing overhead, no prisoner knew what progress the Allies had made since the invasion of Okinawa. As the starvation increased, the only thoughts in the prisoners' minds were of food. Their only blessing was that each morning, they found themselves still alive.

CHAPTER 22

Pathways to Hell

> TO CONQUER THE COMMAND OF THE AIR MEANS VICTORY; TO BE
> BEATEN IN THE AIR MEANS DEFEAT.
>
> —*Giulio Douhet,* The Command of the Air, *1921*

By the end of 1942, Japan had suffered two major setbacks. Not only had its navy been crippled at Midway and its army forced to retreat from Guadalcanal, but a more calamitous situation was developing regarding the food and material supplies needed in the homeland.

Much has been written of the ineffective American torpedoes designed before the start of World War II. Designed with a magnetic switch to explode beneath enemy ships, the torpedoes repeatedly failed, some even circling back to sink Allied submarines. Due to restricted prewar funding, these torpedoes had never been tested in an underwater firing. Adding to the frustration of submariners were the immense distances of the Pacific, which required weeks of travel to come within range of Japanese supply lines. A new torpedo—greatly improved and tested—began deliveries in late 1942.

The Japanese loss of Guadalcanal and the four carriers at Midway masked an even deeper loss: that of experienced naval aviators. Until these battles, Japanese naval aviators were trained over a two-year period, most having almost one thousand hours of experience before engaging enemy planes. The American and British military sent experienced pilots home as instructors whenever possible. Japanese pilots were retained with existing units, and new pilots were added at a perilously slow rate. The best and most experienced pilots were moved to frontline units as a matter of policy. The Battle of Midway and the air battles in the New Guinea and Guadalcanal campaigns decimated the ranks of experienced Japanese aviators. Those who did survive, like the legendary pilots Sakai, Sugita, Saito, Muto, and Okumiya, went on accumulating impressive numbers of kills against Allied planes, but the number of trained pilots continued to shrink.

In air battles throughout the Solomon Islands, the attrition of Japanese planes blocked any chance for effective counterattacks. Allied losses, albeit small in comparison to Japanese losses, were quickly replaced as American airplane manufacturing began to exceed American losses in large multiples. New high-performance fighter planes, such as the Hellcats, Bell P-39s, Curtiss P-40s, P-38 Lightnings, and B-26 Marauder attack bombers, began arriving in steady streams. General MacArthur's thrust across New Guinea, coupled with Admiral Nimitz's thrust through the Gilberts to the Marianas, trapped almost half a million Japanese soldiers in pockets—unable to be resupplied and left to starve.

+ + + + + + + + +

The U.S. Navy had completely broken the Japanese merchant marine code in 1943 (although this was kept secret until 1979) and could almost plot the exact course, position, and, in most cases, the cargo of every merchant ship. Inexplicably, the Japanese required that every afternoon, each ship was to report its current position and its estimated position at noon for the next day. To avoid suspicion that the codes had been broken, orders were to "sink them all," to destroy all ships, even those we knew carried prisoners of war. New submarine crews, trained at "Convoy College" in Honolulu, simply waited in submarine wolf packs for Japanese ships to arrive. By the end of 1942, the submarines were decimating the Japanese merchant marine. More important, new American submarines were launched at a rate of one each week, adding fifty-two new submarines alone to the U.S. Pacific Fleet in 1943. By the end of that year, food supplies in Japan had reached desperately low levels and were not to recover until well after the war ended.[1]

For the Japanese the shortage of shipping was the result of three problems, none of which were considered in prewar planning. First, there was a deliberate decision to build warships rather than transport vessels. The chronic shortage of merchant ships was simply ignored by the military as the militarists could not make the profits afforded by warships.

Second, huge numbers of Japanese troops were unexpectedly required to control and pacify the conquered lands. In the Philippines alone, the extensive guerrilla warfare tied up an additional 150,000 soldiers. These men had to be constantly provided with food, munitions, clothing, and matériel. French Indochina was drained of rice, and most crops in the Philippines were seized whenever possible. Philippine guerrillas destroyed thousands of acres of rice to forestall Japanese seizures. The harsh winter of 1942–43, coupled with a spring drought in Korea, further reduced Japan's basic supply of rice.

And third, the spring of 1943 saw the introduction of effective torpedoes, more than double the number of available submarines, and a new doctrine of submarine warfare for the United States. Warships, when sighted, were desired targets, but the primary goal was to sink merchant ships heading to Japan. The prewar shortage of merchant ships would prove a catastrophic blunder for the Japanese. By the end of the summer of 1943, Japan began to experience widespread food shortages and frontline troops could no longer be resupplied.

In POW camps scattered across Japan, the winter of 1943–44 was a nightmare of cold and hunger. Freezing storms poured out of Manchuria, one after another, slashing down and across Japan, bringing misery to the malnourished slaves. Food rations to the prisoners were again reduced below subsistence levels. Extra rations, supplied by the International Committee of the Red Cross, were never adequate to supplement the shortages. Food and clothing packages, already delivered infrequently, were often looted of half their weight or considered part of the already reduced rations by the prison camp officials.

Tons of supplies, shipped to Japan as part of the prisoner exchange programs, were never delivered. Sufficient supplies were delivered to Japanese officials to give every Allied prisoner the equivalent of one Red Cross box per month. A typical ten-pound box contained an assortment of coffee, powdered milk, candy, canned fruit, cigarettes, and soap. The Japanese removed cans of beef, chocolate bars, and cigarettes from many of the delivered boxes. Lucky were those who saw more than one box during their entire period of confinement. At almost every POW camp, when freedom came in August 1945, nearby Japanese military warehouses were found to be filled with Red Cross boxes. In Osaka even the residence of Swiss Red Cross representative Max Pestalozzi was discovered to be filled with looted boxes.

The prisoners were very aware that large quantities of Red Cross boxes were being withheld by the Japanese. Japanese newspapers clearly stated that large quantities of food and clothing had arrived on board the *Asama Maru* in July 1942 as part of the diplomatic exchange. Coupled with a later exchange of strictly British diplomats and missionaries, these Red Cross boxes were ample to stave off starvation. Neutral nations were commissioned to deliver additional quantities of supplies for the prisoners.

For the men in Hirohata, the first sign of the Red Cross boxes came on 18 November 1943, when three heavily loaded trucks delivered 486 boxes (each containing four ten-pound individual boxes). The sick-call prisoners joyously unloaded and stacked the boxes in barracks number two. Morale jumped "sky high" in anticipation of a relief from the gnawing hunger. One hundred boxes were immediately removed and morale plummeted until the men were told the boxes were to be given to four hundred Dutch prisoners in the nearby Harima POW camp.

The camp's interpreter informed the prisoners that they would also receive a comfort box in a few days. For almost a year, the men had never been given "enough food to maintain health," and the inadequately clothed men had been reduced to skin and bones. Upon return from work on 18 November, each man received a ten-pound box of food. EM2 Ed Hale would later write, "Ten pounds of food! . . . Never before or since have I had the thrill from anything that I had from opening that box. A sticker on the outside read, 'American Red Cross. Food Package for Prisoner of War.' We thank Thee God; we are not forgotten."

Opening the boxes, staring at the food, the smell of real chocolate wafting into their emaciated faces—it made grown men cry. Savoring the taste of a chocolate bar, Hale's description was echoed by everyone: "The effect was almost like an explosion in my stomach. I could feel the warmth spread through me like ink through a blotter as the powerful sensation of food took hold. In three minutes, I felt warm. . . . Gone was the chill, the horrible weakness [and hunger] that no one can imagine until he experiences it."[2] Cans of sardines, cocoa, freeze-dried coffee, corned beef, evaporated milk, and a package of cigarettes completed the food package. Small CCC boxes (comfort kits) were divided one for five men. Inside were toilet articles (toothpaste powder, soap), sewing kits, note paper, and pencils.

On Christmas Eve 1943 in Hirohata, sixteen ten-pound boxes from the Canadian Red Cross were delivered and quickly divided among the men. The box contents—cheese, butter, raisins, and powdered milk—were carefully divided, down to the single raisin and quarter teaspoon of powdered milk. While the amount of food was meager, the spirits of the men soared. On Christmas morning, following a short prayer service, each man added to his rice the tiny morsels saved from a day earlier. None doubted that the United States and its Allies would never forget them again.

At Zentsuji the first Red Cross boxes arrived on 9 November 1943. The following afternoon the work details returned to camp to discover the Japanese had removed every box. Almost two weeks later, the men were supplied with small comfort boxes filled only with toilet necessities.

———·—·—·—·—·—·—·———

From the initial B-29 raids against Japan proper, starting in June 1944, the pace of raids was desultory and of limited effectiveness. High-altitude bombing, unexpected winds, and extreme ranges combined to minimize their impact.[3] Air raids became a part of life in Japan, accepted as a nuisance but not terribly feared. In late 1944 the air bases on the newly secured islands of Saipan and Guam began receiving a steady flow of the new Super Fortress bombers. On 4 March 1945, the last daylight raid for months to come sent 159 bombers over Tokyo in an attempt to destroy the Musashino Airfield and airplane factory. For the next five days, Japan relaxed as only a few reconnaissance planes cruised overhead.

On the night of 9 March 1945, the familiar air-raid sirens began their plaintive wail as the people of Tokyo calmly moved into backyard shelters, barely adequate for safety from the high-explosive bombs. Japanese fighters soared upward to meet the expected waves of B-29s, which would silently stream over at 30,000 feet. On this bitterly cold night, the crews of the B-29s were even more fearful as they descended down below 30,000 feet and into the range of antiaircraft fire and ordinary fighter planes. A few minutes after the stroke of midnight, the first bombers crossed Tokyo at 2,500 feet, each plane spreading clusters of incendiaries that ignited a swath 350 feet wide by 2,000 feet long. For four hours, the bombers streamed overhead, each adding to the conflagration that spread across ten square miles of Tokyo.[4]

On the ground flames roiled up thousands of feet, and the fierce winds, fed by the ever-growing firestorm, blew down buildings and tossed cars into the air. Fireballs hundreds of feet in diameter rolled down the crowded streets and alleys, bursting across firebreaks. The heat tossed the bombers around like tenpins in a bowling alley, causing them to rise and drop thousands of feet in seconds and throwing some into inverted positions. The crisp air of a bitterly cold night became an outdoor incinerator as an estimated 100,000 residents perished and one million were left homeless. Submarines standing by at rescue stations, hundred of miles to sea, saw the glow of the fires rise like a setting sun on the horizon. Hell had finally come to Japan.

Over the next two days, Nagoya would see 285 planes create a similar firestorm. On the night of the thirteenth and fourteenth, Osaka and five secondary targets would be the recipients of another 274 bombers carrying the deadly incendiaries.

In the early hours of 17 March, Kobe received its baptism of fire. A few minutes past midnight, 307 planes began to level a major portion of the city. The raids abated when Bomber Command ran out of incendiaries, but a month later, they resumed in full fury. By 7 April P-51 Mustang fighters from newly captured Iwo Jima were strafing and bombing the southern areas of Honshu.[5] For the next few months, the major cities of Japan began to disappear as raid after raid burned them to the ground. Almost every day, the men from Guam would learn of another city obliterated. On 21 June the capture of Okinawa, which was just over an hour's flight from Japan, opened all of Japan to the endless attacks of fighters and attack bombers. Added to the land-based fighters, carrier planes began a continuous sweep over Japan, blasting Japanese fighters out of the air, strafing airports, trains, trucks, suspected ammunition dumps, and every military facility they could find. A few small Japanese ships could occasionally make the crossing from Korea or China, but the supplies to Japan became a mere trickle by summer. Days would pass without a single ship visible in the Sea of Japan; those that arrived were riddled with bullet holes. By mid-July up to two thousand fighter and light attack bombers were sweeping over Japan daily. U.S. Fleet battleships and cruisers sailed unobstructed as they bombarded coastal installations and factories.

* * * * * * * * * *

By the end of 1944, the inevitable defeat of Japan became obvious because of the Allies' strategy of bypassing Japanese strongholds, stranding millions of Japanese combat soldiers. The capture of the Philippines effectively isolated Japan from its oil- and mineral-rich conquests in French Indochina, Borneo, and the Netherlands East Indies. Unfortunately for the prisoners of war, food rations were uniformly reduced to starvation levels. The sea between Formosa and the Philippines became fertile hunting grounds for packs of Allied submarines, now equipped with radar, night-vision periscopes, and full knowledge of Japanese merchant ship schedules.

The Japanese fleet was essentially destroyed in two final battles, the Battle of the Philippine Sea in June 1944 (also called the Great Marianas Turkey Shoot) and the Battle of Leyte Gulf in October 1944. The fall of Iwo Jima (March 1945) and Okinawa (May 1945) made Japan vulnerable to ground-based fighters. The only effective weapons available to Japan to attack the Allied naval fleets were a few submarines and the suicide bombers, the kamikazes.

The southern pincers, under command of General MacArthur, had swept up to the Philippines in the fall of 1944, landing on the beaches of Lingayen Gulf on 9 January 1945. The flow of food, oil, ore, and rubber to Japan from its southern conquests ceased. During the battle for Okinawa, Japan could muster only enough fuel to send its few remaining warships on a catastrophic one-way sortie against the American invasion forces. None would ever complete the voyage, and few survivors returned.[6]

The prisoners in most POW camps were very aware of the daily destruction of Japan as the war's end drew near. The invasion of France, on D day, 6 June 1944, was known by the prisoners within a day. Prisoners recognized the loss of Japanese possessions by reading Japanese papers claiming the "glorious final attacks" by the emperor's soldiers in various battles, each disaster drawing closer to Japan. As in most camps, not all men could be trusted, and in Hirohata, a secret radio, its existence known by a handful of men, kept Sgt. Earl Ercanbrack and Sgt. George Shane aware of the war's progress. OSS operatives in Japan had located most of the major POW camps,[7] and whenever possible the prison areas were carefully avoided in the bombing raids.

The capture of Okinawa in May 1945 allowed land-based fighter planes to begin crisscrossing Japan, blasting every logistical target. Allied ships roamed the coastline unmolested, bombarding coastal facilities at will. With more than two thousand of the remaining airplanes hoarded for the kamikaze—and with more than one million troops secretly withdrawn from Manchuria, China, and Korea—Japan readied itself for the final defense of the homeland.[8] All schools were shuttered. The training of every civilian, including children, was commenced. The military leadership, regardless of hardship faced, was prepared to sacrifice every living Japanese rather than surrender. Throughout Japan, the last able-bodied men were mobilized, and all children and women were trained to use sharpened bamboo sticks as weapons. Prisoners, passing the local school on the way to the mill at Hirohata, could see the children practicing with the sticks.

Yayoe Tadokoro Smythe, at the time a young Japanese girl living in Hitachi, some two hundred miles north of Tokyo, recalled the desperate search for food and the final preparations for the expected invasion. "Everyone was hungry," she said. "Seeking refuge with relatives in the country or simply fleeing the incendiary raids upon the cities, the desperately hungry people simply looted the open fields and family gardens along the roads. As people passed my grandmother's home, they would pull the rice shoots from the ground. My cousin would beg them to 'wait until the rice could be harvested and there will be food for all!' but they took the sprouts anyway."

"Starvation was everywhere," said Yayoe. She remembered seeing Australian and American prisoners of war being used to glean the rice paddies for loose grains. "We were told at school," she continued, "that the enemy would soon come to attack our homeland. We were trained to attack individual soldiers using sharpened bamboo poles. Our teachers told us that 'It is expected that twenty of you may die to kill one enemy.'"[9]

Every POW understood that even the children were conditioned to view the prisoners as the hated enemy. No prisoner doubted the Japanese would kill them all when the homeland was invaded. Guards made it clear to individual prisoners that their orders were to eventually murder all the men. Guards openly bragged that they had received an "order to kill" the prisoners when the Allied forces invaded the mainland of Japan.[10] In almost every camp, the prisoners squirreled away makeshift knives and spears in anticipation. In the camps that enslaved men in the mines, massive amounts of dynamite and sundry makeshift weapons were secreted in the tunnels by other prisoners, equally determined to fight back and employ guerrilla tactics against the Japanese. In Hirohata, Ercanbrack organized plans to rush the guards if a massacre seemed imminent.[11] He was determined that his men would not be led to slaughter like sheep but would fight for their freedom.

General MacArthur, knowing the desperation of the Japanese, especially after the massacre of the American prisoners on Palawan,[12] understood that the Japanese planned to murder all the remaining prisoners when Japan was invaded. He created rescue teams that would be dropped into known prison camps to coordinate their defense and eventual rescue. Fortunately the Japanese surrendered before the massacres were to occur, and the emperor issued orders not to harm the prisoners.

CHAPTER 23

The End Nears

LET THEM HATE, SO LONG AS THEY FEAR.

—*Accius*

As the war progressed, every Japanese port saw fewer and fewer ships. Whereas fifteen to twenty ships arrived every week in 1942, by the spring of 1943, the arrivals had dropped to one or two a week. Allied torpedoes, now highly effective, had begun to take a toll. The shortage of food in Japan was not limited to the prisoners. The local civilians, working alongside the prisoners, suffered even more as the military was not responsible for their sustenance. Working in the same labor details, the civilians could be seen withering down to skeletal frames.

The summer of 1944 brought the war directly to Japan. Massive B-29 air raids over Japan began from Tinian by 16 June 1944. By the end of July 1944, all the Marianas were effectively cleared and runways were established for more B-29 bomber groups. The contrails of B-29 bombers, mere specks passing six miles in the sky, began on 15 June 1944, coinciding with the invasion of Saipan. Attacking from China, the first B-29s raided Yawata, a steel plant on the southernmost tip of Kyushu.[1] It proved inconsequential—the nearest bombs fell more than half a mile from the plant. Until this raid, the high-flying bombers, cruising at more than 30,000 feet, had never encountered the jet stream. As the planes began their final turn to align for bombing, they were swept aside by winds of more than a hundred miles an hour. Future raids required alignment when twenty to thirty miles away from the targeted cities in order to counter the expected jet stream.

At Zentsuji during the winter of 1944–45, a unique bond developed between some of the Guam officers and enlisted men when it became apparent that the officers were being starved to death. For the remaining enlisted men, work details provided opportunities to steal extra food, but the reduced rations of the officers were clearly causing a disparity in physical condition. The emaciated condition of the officers became a matter of concern among the Guam enlisted ranks.

Most officers, particularly the British, Dutch, and Americans (especially Army officers), still maintained an imperious rule over the lower ranks. However, the Guam officers, exemplified by Lt. Cdr. H. J. Van Peenen, Maj. Donald Spicer, and Capt. Charles S. Todd, insisted upon a more relaxed atmosphere. As Todd said, "We're all Americans here and as prisoners, are equal to each other." As a direct result, the Guam enlisted ranks would frequently "visit" their officers in their quarters, much to the consternation and disdain of the other officers, particularly fellow Americans. Some would shout, "Get those —— enlisted men out of officer country!" On the frequent visits, food was slipped to the favored officers. The physical improvement in the favored officers was sufficient to be noticeable.

Japanese diplomats considered seeking an armistice through tenuous contacts with the Russians, a plan to "freeze the battlefield" and retain most of the conquered territory. The officer-prisoners would be used as a bargaining chip in any negotiation. The exodus of officers began from Zentsuji with the Americans on 23 June 1945, and two days later the balance of the officers departed, leaving 109 enlisted men in the camp.[2] The remaining prisoners were moved into the west barracks, closest to the gate, and the size of the camp was reduced by a new fence, effectively blocking off the buildings that had housed the departed officers.

On 26 April 1945 the Japanese at Zentsuji had the prisoners dig a large trench within the prison compound. The trench, about eight feet wide, five feet deep, and one hundred feet long, remained open to the sky, and no attempt was made to provide protection from bombardment.[3] A mood of sullenness swept the camp as its purpose became obvious. When Japan was invaded, as previously mentioned, the Japanese had planned to execute all the prisoners.

Prisoners continued to provide work details at the rail yards and the port of Takamatsu. The few ships that managed to arrive showed the effects of strafing, torpedoes, and bombs: bullet holes throughout the ship, and any superstructures, if extant, were now burned and twisted piles of steel.

On the night of 3–4 July, 116 B-29s roared over Takamatsu, dropping a heavy load of incendiaries, now mixed with specialized 500-pound canisters that contained 20-pound bombs. At three thousand feet, the canisters exploded, tossing the small fragmentation bombs over a huge area in a manner similar to howitzer shells. The combination was deadly, and Takamatsu was reduced to a smoking rubble. The same night, another 106 B-29s visited the same destruction on Himeji, the last bomb dropping just short of the Hirohata POW camp.

Two days after the Takamatsu air raid, all seemed normal as the prisoners from Zentsuji returned to work details and the train passed through the countryside. Exiting the train and walking to the opposite side of the station, they were stunned to see that Takamatsu was no more—the city, especially the coast-side buildings, were piles of ash. Amid a flurry of confusion, the guards hustled the prisoners back onto the train and returned them to Zentsuji. The story of what the men had seen quickly spread, the prisoners and guards equally stunned at the total destruction of Takamatsu.

In the wake of the massive air raid on Takamatsu, the work details became cleanup details: removing rubble, loading twisted steel on board trains, and unloading the rare supply train that arrived in the rail yards of Sakaide, the nearby canals, or the port of Takamatsu. As the reality of the disaster spread among the Japanese guards, their mood became sullen. The prisoners, still subject to retaliation, adopted a code of silence regarding the air raids whenever in the presence of the Japanese. Those who ignored this caveat suffered swift and brutal beatings from the Japanese. Although American fighters roamed the sky, none ever attacked the prison area of Zentsuji.

The nature of Allied bombing, primarily using incendiaries, rarely disrupted the operation of the Japanese rail system throughout the war. At Sakaide the yards continued in use, but as happened with the barge traffic in the adjoining canal, the quantity of material diminished rapidly. Days passed when no labor details would leave Zentsuji for the Sakaide yards. The air offensive against Japan sought to turn every city and village into piles of ashes. To supply the military with arms and maté-riel, small plants were scattered everywhere, but mainly in the cities. The solution was simple—burn everything to the ground.

On 18 July 1944,[4] twelve Italian sailors were brought into Hirohata #2 and placed in a separate building at the rear of the Japanese commandant's office. No one knew who they were and conjecture abounded. Through one of the guards, the men learned that almost a year earlier, when Italy surrendered, 135 Italian crewmen on board an Italian freighter docked in Kobe had refused to continue their service to the Axis and scuttled their ship. They were immediately imprisoned in the same camp the Americans first occupied in Hirohata. A dozen of the Italian sailors later attempted to escape, were caught, and had now been brought to Hirohata #2.[5]

"When we found out they were Italian," said PhM3 Leroy Bowman,

> Tony Iannarelli figured out how we could communicate. Tony was with a singing group we called "The Bathhouse Gang" and one night, he pretended to sing an Italian song but really was telling the Italians on other side that we knew who they were.
>
> The Italians responded with shouts of "Bravo!" and loud applause. Tony continued talking back and forth as he pretended to sing songs in Italian. I doubt the Japs ever figured someone in camp could speak Italian and had a good singing voice!

One of the Italians was selected, stripped naked, hog-tied, and placed in the camp brig. The local Italian consul, when visiting the internees, was asked by the Japanese how long the man should be punished. The consul replied, "Kill him. Make him an example to the other [Italian] prisoners." The Kempeitai proceeded to beat the prisoner unmercifully.[6] "For the next three days and nights," said S1 Ed Settles, "the Japs beat him with whips, poured salt into his wounds, and beat him some more. His screams of agony rarely stopped and could be heard everywhere. This went on non-stop, day and night for three days, until he finally died." After Germany surrendered in May 1945, the surviving Italian sailors were released and simply told, "Go away!" In Kobe there was a large international community, mostly Russians and French, that sheltered others in a similar situation.

At Hirohata, as in all other camps, the Japanese guards and civilian *honchos* had been instructed not to talk to prisoners about the progress of the war. Even so, rumors abounded in every camp of the war's progress, and speculation that the war would end before Japan was blasted by Allied forces continued. "At the steel mill," said Pfc. Garth Dunn, "we would steal any newspaper and bring it back to camp for translation. We all knew what to expect." As with the civilians in Kobe, the prisoners knew the Allies would win, but no one was certain of their own fate. How the war would end became an endless subject of speculation.

By 17 June 1944, less than two days after the first B-29 raids on Japan, word reached Hirohata, Osaka, and Zentsuji that southern Kyushu had been bombed. SM1 Reg Reed, like many others, expressed mixed feelings about the news. Hoping for a peace treaty so he could be exchanged, he wrote, "16 June 1944: Bad news has come to us. The war has resumed in full fury with a (rumored) bombing by U.S. planes of southern Japan last night! I'm sorry to hear of it for I had hoped that, without further bloodshed, this war could be brought to an end."[7] Unknown to the prisoners, the OSS operatives in Japan had been quite successful in locating almost one hundred of the camps before the first air raids.

Reconnaissance missions started 1 November 1944 when a B-29, aptly named *Tokyo Rose*, loitered over Tokyo at 32,000 feet, taking more than seven thousand detailed pictures. On 24 November 1944, 111 planes conducted a daylight raid on Tokyo aircraft factories—the first raid from the Marianas. The targets, in order of precedence, were aircraft factories, manufacturing industries (coke, steel, oil), and Japanese shipping. By March, an adequate number of planes had arrived on Tinian and Guam to permit massive area bombing of urban centers.

After one air raid, the guard nicknamed "Bull" ordered two men stripped. He proceeded to lash their faces until they were very swollen. He then gave them the water torture and beat them unmercifully. The two-hour ordeal simply deepened the prisoners' hatred of the guards.

Another prisoner, Steve Raymond, remembered his feelings when first learning of the bombings:

> It was a day in which each of us feels the other out and hatred pulses just under the surface, both brown and white. It was a day, the first of what may be scores of days, when we pray for American bombers. They will get some of us but they will get Japs too. We want to see these coolies run—we want to see the fear in their eyes, the fear which is transferred from the weird whistling and whining of falling bombs to feet and hands and brain, the scream of death which sounds like it

is following you for a direct hit. We want to hear these people howl with anguish and fear and pain and frustration when their homes are destroyed and their families wiped out and their legs blown off. We want this revenge for what they have done to us. We want this even when we know they will retaliate.

This hate is part of the shield we carry against the misery, hunger and hopelessness of our captivity. We may wash this out of our systems sometime after this is over but today it is as necessary as air and water and food.[8]

The first sighting of a B-29 by the men at Hirohata came on 20 January 1945 when a recon B-29 soared overhead at six miles high, a black speck leading a thin, white contrail from the horizon. "For a long time," said EM2 Ed Hale, "one bright spot of almost every day was the sight of a single B-29 passing overhead, generally between 11:15 and 11:45 in the morning, his vapor trail as pretty as a painting. We gave him a few nicknames: 'Foto Fred' and 'Movietone Mike.' The guards would beat us if we looked up and were seen to smile. But we surely smiled inside."[9]

At Hirohata, as well as other POW camps across Japan, the frequent threat of air raids caused the Japanese to rush the prisoners out of the factories and back to the prison camps. The sound of the siren signaled, more often than not, B-29s continuing on to other targets, their long, white contrails laying streaks to the horizon. Within a few weeks, the Japanese began to ignore the bombers, safe in their belief that their emperor god would protect their homes and factories.

"By the end of 1944 in Hirohata," said Sgt. George Shane, "very few ships came into port, and those that did were badly shot up with .50-caliber machine-gun bullet holes. Few had food but we could steal money from the staterooms; then we would bribe the civilians to get us food. The guards, particularly the military, were always hard to bribe as you couldn't always trust them. You could be beaten just for asking."

At the Osaka-Umeda Camp, Pfc. Herb Humphrey saw the first B-29s fly overhead: "In late 1944, we started hearing and seeing the big planes coming over Osaka. Sometimes they would come one at a time, always very high, and all we could see were the white contrails." Japanese fighters, forewarned by lookouts on other islands, climbed to meet the attacks. Humphrey continued:

Sometimes we would see a streak fly down through a formation of them. Probably a Jap trying a suicide crash into a B-29. Quite frequently, only one plane appeared. He was obviously taking pictures, but sometimes, he would drop a bomb. When they dropped one, usually a large one, you could hear it whistle all the way down. There is no mistaking the sound of a falling bomb. It wasn't so bad in the daytime but at night, when you couldn't see anything because of the blackout, I was very nervous. You never knew where a lone bomb was going to land. It seemed like an eternity until it exploded. Sometimes it was close and sometimes it wasn't, but no matter where it landed, it never failed to make me break out in a cold sweat. After it hit and exploded, everyone in our barracks was relieved and happy knowing the Japanese were getting blasted and we hadn't been hit.

At Umeda the men could see the sky from the third-floor windows. "We began to see more and more American planes," said Humphrey. "Several times we were able to count forty to fifty planes in formation heading north or west. Flying in formation they looked so big and beautiful. The night the B-29 bombers bombed Osaka [13 March 1945] was quite a show." Humphrey continued:

> A plane flew over and dropped a flare about four blocks to the rear of our POW compound. It was almost over the top of a big Japanese hospital. The flare lit up the whole sky and area. About four blocks in front of our barracks was the big Umeda railroad station. From the southeast, what seemed like an endless stream of low flying planes started dropping incendiary bombs. We could see them come, in wave after wave. They were bigger than anything I had ever seen before. That night, they burned a strip thru the center of Osaka. It was at least three miles wide and twelve miles long. The largest fire I have ever seen or probably ever will see. I have no idea how many people were killed. We saw a good part of the area later and there was nothing left standing except rock walls, chimneys, or gutted cement buildings.[10]
>
> It was not too long after this fire bombing that we left Umeda Bunsho in Osaka. By this time, we had become so proficient in stealing food that I was in much better shape than when we arrived. I probably weighed about 160 pounds and was in good shape.

In fewer than five days, Humphrey and the men of Umeda were transferred by train to Tsuruga on the west-central coast of Honshu Island.

At the Osaka Main Camp, a British doctor, Charles E. Jackson, arrived in the spring of 1943 and was placed in charge. He became known for his dedication, medical ingenuity, and successful operations with razors and no anesthesia. His dedication, despite frequent bashings by the guards for his temerity in asking for medicines for his men, caused a cessation of the almost daily deaths. Except for injuries and a few cases of heart failure caused by beriberi, deaths became almost unknown.

At Chikko, the Osaka Main Camp, Pfc. Bud Budzynski recalled, the "second bombing of Osaka burned down the headquarters camp. The Japs put us up in another two story warehouse near the steel mill. During the next raid by the B-29s, a bunch of us climbed up into the attic and were able to see a lot of the action. One by one the bombers flew over, dropping their incendiaries and occasional high explosives over the city and docks. We were cheering and clapping like hell!"[11]

"A few days after the first big raid on Osaka," said PM3 Al Mosher,

> we could see the B-29s hitting Kobe during the night. Lots of flames, bomb explosions, and an endless stream of bombers. It felt pretty good to see Kobe going up in flames.
>
> The second raid on 1 June burned us out. They had to get us out of the area as nothing was left. I was moved, along with six buddies, up to a port camp called Toyama.[12] Some men, however, remained in the Osaka area, put into another warehouse by the port area. The Japs put us into an old cannery that was a pigsty, the barracks being a real mess. Along with the few guys from Guam were lots of Americans up from the Philippines. I believe we had about 300 men working in that camp. The Jap ships would come in from the Sea of Japan and steam up the river to the port. The food became scarcer and the work harder than ever.
>
> Towards the end of the war, we did not go out to the ships as in the past. Most times, we were handling barges that would tie up to the piers. Lots of coal barges but few ships. There were daily air raids, sirens, planes passing overhead and finally, planes almost every day and everywhere.

As the raids blasted Osaka and camps were burned to the ground, the Japanese began moving groups of men farther north. In groups of fifty to one hundred, most Chikko prisoners were moved to the shores of Lake Biwa, to Toyama Bay on the west coast, or into the mining camps north and northeast of Osaka. At the same time, men were shifted back and forth between the camps in Osaka to accommodate levies for slave labor. No camp roster remained accurate for more than a few days.

Umeda Camp in Osaka was evacuated on 14 March 1945, its wooden barracks a pile of ashes from an incendiary raid. The majority of the prisoners were sent some 120 miles north to Tsuruga, a small port city on the eastern edge of Wakasa Bay. A smaller number were sent ninety miles northeast to Maibara Bunsho, in the city of Shiga. Already present at Tsuruga was a large contingent of men, the last evacuees from Tanagawa. Thoroughly cowed by their experiences at Tanagawa, the men were extremely reluctant to steal from the Japanese. As in Osaka, the men continued to labor along the docks. With the arrival of the experienced "thieves of Umeda," food rations rose dramatically. It helped to have the former Japanese commander of Umeda arrive at Tsuruga to take command.

Thoroughly co-opted by the inmates at Umeda, the commander quickly fell into a pattern of receiving his share of stolen loot. Unfortunately, the men from the Philippines were not adept at thievery and, when caught, were severely punished. After numerous such incidents, the commander called all the men into ranks and said, "You men from Tanagawa bad. You bad stealru. If I catch you, I will beat you, No stealru! Let men from Umeda stealru for you. They no get caught."

* * * * * * * * * *

Work details in Hirohata continued in the mill and its related piers. Air raids continued to increase until the daily wail of sirens was considered normal. An air of nonchalance replaced the panic of earlier raids. The air-raid siren at the plant, called "Bleating Bertha" by the men, became a signal to relax, for it signaled that the men would soon be taken back to the camp.

Contrails of Japanese fighters could be seen as they tried to attack the high-flying bombers, and antiaircraft batteries surrounding the factory fired uselessly. Slowly, the number of Japanese planes decreased as the number of American bombers and fighters increased—almost exponentially. By the summer of 1945, the bombers rarely were molested, and few prisoners expected the war would last until winter.

Japanese guards, aware of the disasters of Tokyo, Osaka, Nagoya, and Kobe, frequently acknowledged the inevitable victory of the Allies. "More than one guard," said Pfc. Harris Chuck, "told me they realized Japan would have to accept an armistice or surrender very soon. If the war did not end soon, and the homeland was invaded, they said they had orders to kill all of the prisoners." As mentioned earlier, the same information was understood by prisoners throughout the Japanese Empire. "Sergeant Ercanbrack," said RM1 Bob Epperson, "immediately took measures for a defense against such an action. Discussions were held to decide what to do in case the slaughter started. We collected and hid clubs and knives. Squads were formed with specific assignments to attack the guard posts, seize weapons, and set up a defense." The plans would later prove useful when the surrender was announced.

Not all of the Japanese staff were savage in their treatment of the prisoners. Almost every camp had at least one Japanese guard or employee who treated the men humanely. At Hirohata the kindest was Tahara-san. "Our camp interpreter," said Epperson, "was born in America but had returned to Japan just before the war. Tahara, sympathetic to our conditions, did what he could to save us from some of the worst beatings. Toward the end of the war, the Japanese had become more suspicious of Tahara and planned to remove him from the camp. He warned us in late 1944 that orders had been received to murder all the prisoners should the mainland be invaded. The assumption was made that soldiers could not be spared to guard prisoners." Ercanbrack noted that Tahara would often warn of forthcoming searches and, when possible, what items were sought.

In Zentsuji a similar experience was noted by Capt. Mortimer Marks. The camp interpreter, a Mr. Tashima, was from the San Joaquin Valley of California and was able to assist many men in smuggling medicines and needed articles into the camp. Having lived in the United States, he was not trusted by the regular Japanese guards. At Umeda Camp in Osaka, the camp interpreter, a Mr. Hayashi, was considered by all as a decent man who went out of his way to help the prisoners on uncounted occasions.

The devastation of Japan's cities by the incendiary raids required the massive reassignment of the POW population. As factories, piers, and mills were destroyed, prisoner slaves were shifted to new camps on an almost daily basis. Often, entire camps were destroyed and the prisoners shifted to makeshift buildings or moved hundreds of miles away to ports or mines. The Japanese, now separated from supplies of raw materials, began opening abandoned coal and copper mines to secure their minimal needs. Levies for "white slaves" continued to siphon men from POW camps in the Osaka and Kobe areas. At Hirohata the first draft of 134 men departed for Nagoya on 23 May 1945 to clear bomb debris. A draft of 30 men on 16 June and a smaller draft a month later left only 302 men remaining in Hirohata.

The huge steel plant in Hirohata was never effectively bombed, but work details were reduced as the supplies of coke and ore slowed to a trickle. The destruction of nearby Himeji, on the night of 3–4 July 1945, was visible to the men in the barracks as incendiaries and high-explosive bombs cascaded down, the last bombs dropping within half a mile of the camp.[13] The following morning, as the men entered the mill area, local civilians threw stones at the prisoners until stopped by the guards. The mood of the civilian *honchos* was foul, and many civilians were wearing a white arm band to symbolize mourning for dead family members. The prisoners expected to be—and were—beaten for the slightest infraction.

From the barges and freight cars, men were still able to steal small amounts of food. The camp, under firm military control, was receiving more food than were the Japanese civilians. "Guards like Spider," noted Private Chuck, "even helped us to hide food and to sneak it off ships—as long as he got his share."

By the late spring of 1945, fighter planes were roaming at will over southern Japan. Prisoners stood in amazement at the speed of the low-flying fighters as they strafed and used the new aerial rockets. Frequently, they would wag their wings as if they recognized that the men were POWs. "Toward the end," said Ed Settles, "we saw our planes come over regularly. In one attack, one of our planes shot his rockets at a Jap barge carrying men out to an ammunition dump that was little more than a big rock in the middle of the sea. I'd never seen a rocket before. It was a loud swooshing sound and when it hit the barge, men and body parts flew all over."

With most of Japan already experiencing a severe food shortage—in fact, a famine—the Japanese guards increased the tempo of harassment. Fear of mob retaliation against the internees was a major concern of the internees, as were illness and disease as a consequence of malnutrition. The daily trek from Futatabi to Kobe for food and supplies became nightmarish. The men would slave like workhorses, hauling the handcart (without bearings or springs) up into the valley from Kobe, "struggling and sweating under loads of wood . . . half-starved, while the Jap guards and some of the people laughed and jeered."[14] Still guards and civilians were susceptible to bribes, or a portion of the take, whenever additional food or supplies could be smuggled into the camp. The gut-wrenching pangs of hunger conditioned men to steal whenever possible, mostly from the Japanese but also from each other. The occasional Red Cross box would ameliorate the pain for a few days, but the steady diet of watery rice and stewed onions pushed the men into starvation-induced lethargy.

Jim Thomas said,

> Because no fence surrounded the camp, crafty packers with makeshift backpacks slipped out after evening *tenko* and hoofed it down the trail to rendezvous points on the outskirts of Kobe for pickups. All transactions were cash on the barrel head. Money for food was collected in advance by the capitalist who'd arranged the exchange. He'd place his orders and prepay for the next pickup. Suppliers charged extra for the risks involved and the entrepreneur would raise his price for the same reason. The hungry customer took this double markup as a matter of course. Packers were paid in food, so everyone got something, including the guards, who got payola.
>
> Three or four of these illicit businessmen controlled the entire operation. Competition kept prices in line. Many yen came from the Swiss consul. Extra yen came from bartering clothing at the pickup point. An overcoat brought fifteen hundred yen one week, but inflation might increase its worth to eighteen hundred yen a week later. Shoes ran from five hundred to eight hundred yen, depending on size and condition. IOUs were taken under strict usury agreements. . . .
>
> As questionable as it may seem, black marketing kept the camp alive. I bought rice occasionally and supplemented my diet from Red Cross items. Nevertheless, my belly shrank and my weight dropped to 130 pounds. I rattled when I walked.
>
> Friction arose when the men from Guam watched in helpless hunger as the wives of the locals brought food on weekly visits. I realized it was hard for the locals to share their food fairly. I received an occasional gift of salted fish from Blyth, who was a vegetarian. When the next shipment of Red Cross packages arrived, the locals' share was reduced because of what their families had brought. Hot arguments ensued, but the Guamanians held fast. My sympathies were with the locals, because their families had sacrificed their own meager rations to bring food to the camp. It would have been nice for the husbands in turn to share their packages with their families. Hunger can destroy good manners.[15]

CHAPTER 24

The End Comes

In Zentsuji, Hirohata, Kobe, and Osaka, camp guards and civilian *honchos* had become increasingly hostile as the bombing progressed. The Japanese who survived the devastating incendiary raids in March had their miseries compounded by the Siberian winds that brought slashing, freezing rain almost every day that month. The defenseless prisoners were logical targets for retaliation.

On 6 August 1945, the ground trembled early in the morning at Hirohata. Looking westward, the men clearly saw a massive cloud rise and dissipate at high altitude. Most assumed it was an explosion at an ammunition dump. By midafternoon, a fine ash began to settle over the camp. That evening, the high-altitude dust created a distinctive glittering or twinkling effect in the sunset. Over the next few days, the fine dust continued to settle over the camp. The guards, learning of the devastation caused by the bomb, repeatedly warned, "If you see a lone plane, hide quickly—kills everything in sight!"[1]

The following morning, PhM1 Tony Iannarelli was informed at the mill by Mr. Tehara, the plant manager, that America had destroyed Hiroshima and killed thousands of people with a single bomb. That night the guard, Matsumoto, said he expected an invasion very soon but "you won't ever live to see them. We have our orders. We are going to have to kill all of you and fight the enemy to the death!"[2]

"We knew the Japs had armed all the local population with sharpened bamboo sticks for the final battles," said S1 Ed Settles. Every prisoner was aware of the order to kill them and feared the Japanese would fight until the last soldier and every civilian was dead. Fortunately, the atom bombs solved that problem. "The next day," said Settles, "we walked the two miles to work as usual. Kowa-san was reading a paper and said, 'They dropped this bomb and leveled Hiroshima—it weighed only four kilo!' A bit later, Ed Hale told us what it meant when they called it an atom bomb."[3] Sgt. George Shane also thought it was an ammunition explosion. "The next day," said Shane, "a great number of Dutch, Australian, and a few American POWs were sent over by the Japs to help clean up. None of my group was involved, but a lot of those guys died later from the radiation."

Without the POW officers present at Zentsuji, work details continued, but by the end of July, the pace of work in the train yards had diminished to a point where, most days, no work was required. Gardening, however, was still required to produce food. "We knew something was up," recalled Sgt. Tom Honan about the late morning of 15 August, "when they called us together at the freight yards and placed us in the shed. Someone had come up the road with a radio and all the other Japs gathered around where, we later learned, they heard the emperor say the war was over. One of them walked over to us and said, 'Tomodachi,' the Japanese word for friends. We waited there for a number of hours until they sent out extra guards to escort us back to camp." Other details had very similar experiences and were also told to stop working. Few understood immediately that it was the emperor who had announced the end of hostilities. The emperor never used the word "surrender." All work details were returned to Zentsuji camp.

For the next two days, the Japanese furiously burned records. The guards and staff skulked off into the night like schoolyard bullies who knew they were no longer in charge. A few days later, a Japanese lieutenant arrived with a contingent of teenage soldiers. He told the assembled prisoners that a "peace had been negotiated" and that they would soon be returning home. All were to "remain in camp under the control and protection of the Japanese guards."

A naval warrant officer stood up and said, "Bullshit!" He strode up to the lieutenant and demanded they immediately surrender all their weapons.[4] The Japanese complied without argument. As the former guards and staff had fled, the prisoners took over security of the camp.

⁕⁓⁓⁓⁓⁓⁓⁓⁕

When news of the second bomb on Nagasaki spread, the tension between the guards and prisoners reached a zenith. It was not enough just to harass the prisoners now. The Japanese guards did everything possible to make their lives even more miserable. The men, forced to dress in winter clothing with the top buttons closed, were marched at double time to and from work details. Those dropping back were subject to more beatings.

On 15 August PhM1 Tony Iannarelli recalled the men were working "like dogs at the mill." The Japanese *honcho* came out to say that the emperor had broadcast "an end of hostilities" and that all sides were to lay down their arms. Work was immediately stopped, and the men marched back to the rendezvous point then back to camp. The following morning the camp followed the usual routines, *tenko*, and breakfast. As they prepared to leave for work, the commandant announced that the mill was "closed for ten days, all men are to rest!" Sergeant Ercanbrack and Radioman Barnum reacted cautiously. Only they knew that the war was officially over and that Japan had surrendered unconditionally. The best-kept secret of Hirohata was that Ercanbrack had a hidden radio and knew the progress of the war and the details of the surrender.

The regular guards had disappeared during the night. The Japanese began to burn all records, and the guards were replaced by civilian counterparts. No work details were dispatched for the next week. On 22 August a Japanese soldier admitted to the prisoners that Japan had surrendered. Later that evening, the air-raid sirens wailed, creating a sudden sense of dread as everyone knew about the orders to kill all the prisoners. Fortunately the all clear sounded within minutes, and the camp relaxed.

The following morning Ercanbrack walked boldly into the office of the Japanese commandant and demanded that he relinquish control of the camp to him. Lieutenant Takenada bowed as he agreed. Ercanbrack rounded up his squad leaders and posted his own men at all guard posts, particularly at the entrance. Within minutes *PW* was painted on the roof of the main barrack. Ercanbrack ordered the Japanese to open the storerooms, and he began to prepare extra rations of food for the starving prisoners. The camp was now under American control, although the Japanese flag remained flying. The Japanese were disarmed, and their weapons were used by the prisoners to mount a guard against any other Japanese intruders. A few men went into Himeji, boarded the trains, and began to disarm transiting Japanese soldiers. A large number of Japanese swords were counted among the seized weaponry, the best being spirited away as souvenirs.

For the men of Hirohata, the war was over. For Cpl. Thomas M. Hammel, still carrying his strange toolbox and obviously still insane, the news from Ercanbrack was greeted with a sly smile. He walked up to Ercanbrack, handed him his treasured toolbox, and said, "Here—I don't need this anymore." Ercanbrack looked at him quizzically, and Hammel continued. "I didn't think I could keep up this insanity act another week!" he said. With a broad grin, he walked away while the entire camp stared in open-mouth awe.

"My God," said Pfc. Harris Chuck, "he pulled it off!" For a few moments, Hammel was the biggest celebrity in camp as he regaled everyone with his experiences.

High in the mountains of western Honshu, without a radio or any newspapers, Rokuroshi was effectively isolated from the war. Frequent flights of B-29s were seen heading north, but no bombings were heard until the evening of 19–20 July. At last, overhead were seen a string of 127 B-29s, their running lights glowing as they streamed toward Fukui.[5] For the next three nights the glow of fires (85 percent of Fukui had been destroyed) could be seen in the southwestern sky. With minor cities like Fukui now targeted for destruction, no prisoner doubted the ultimate victory of the Allies. Yet the hostility of a few guards was a constant reminder of the Japanese plans to kill all the POWs when Japan was invaded. Weak from hunger and unarmed, Colonel Unruh still made plans to seize control of the camp should word ever arrive of an invasion.

The news of the atom bombs never penetrated Rokuroshi, although guards did make comments about the "use of an inhumane bomb." On 17 August a Colonel Fitzpatrick, who was in charge of the work details, was informed that the prisoners would no longer be required to work in the gardens. No mention of surrender was made, but the next morning, the military guards disappeared. A scraggly group of

Japanese Reserves appeared to take charge of the camp—but still no announcement of the surrender was made. Japanese commandant Lieutenant Habe left that morning with orders to go to Osaka. "I just knew then that they had surrendered," said 2nd Lt. Ned Gallagher, "but no one seemed to believe the war was really over. For three days, I kept telling everyone, 'It's over! It's over!' yet no one would believe me."

On Wednesday afternoon, 22 August, Lieutenant Habe returned from Osaka and proceeded directly to Unruh's room. "With this big switch in samurai protocol," said Captain Marks, "we knew it was the official sign we were waiting for." Unruh stepped out of his room and announced, "The war is over." No wild celebration ensued, simply a collective sigh of relief from the assembled prisoners. Slowly, the reality set in as the men slapped one another's backs, proud and happy that "we've made it!" Quickly *PW*, in large letters, was painted on the roof. After a celebration dinner, the men conducted prayers and sang their respective national anthems. An accordion appeared, and songs echoed off the mountain sides. No one slept that night.

For the next few days, food was trucked into the camp from local villages, food rations increased, and ample cigarettes were supplied. The wood-rail fence was dismantled and used as firewood as the extra food was cooked and campfires glowed throughout the camp. Men gathered around the campfires, ate extra food, and chatted through the nights—breaking only to sleep. Day and night the activity of eating and swapping stories kept the camp at a feverish pitch as the men awaited rescue. But with no outside contact, the days passed slowly. On 29 August Habe, the Japanese commander, requested that Colonel Unruh and Captain Lineberry, along with two other men, join him and a Red Cross representative for a meeting in Kyoto.

Late on the evening of 2 September, the men returned, along with a truck full of American food acquired at Tsuruga. The American occupation army had not located their camp as a result of a clerical error that indicated Rokuroshi was simply another burned out camp in Osaka.[6] Although asleep when the officers returned, all the prisoners rose to learn that Japan had officially surrendered that very day. Only then were the newly free men to learn that Japan had accepted the unconditional surrender terms on 15 August. Rokuroshi now became an Allied base. Colonel Unruh secured permission and, within moments, an American flag was raised over Rokuroshi.[7] "Indeed," said Lieutenant Gallagher, "the war was over."

The following morning, 3 September 1945, the first B-29s circled the camp, dropped low into the canyon, and disgorged parachutes laden with drums of food and clothing. Crammed inside were newspapers and magazines that revealed for the first time the awesome power of the bombs that had ended the war. In the early afternoon, a delegation from a nearby school arrived bearing a large quantity of food. "Colonel Unruh," said Captain Marks, "had us line up before several tables laden with watermelons and vegetables." The school's headmaster said, "During the war the pupils worked hard in their gardens but now that the war is over, they want to express their joy and their kindly attitudes toward you by a gift of fruit, melons, and tomatoes from their war gardens." Local villagers prepared sweetened rice cakes that added to the evening meal.

The secret radio gave the men at Futatabi valid information on the war's progress. News of the Hiroshima bombing on 6 August was known the following morning. Jim Thomas noted, "The Japanese newspaper on the seventh carried a vague story about a new firebomb that was dropped by parachute. They told the people there was nothing to fear if everyone lay prone on the ground, wore extra garments, and shielded their eyes."

The same night Fred Oppenborn, listening to the San Francisco station, reported that the atomic bomb had an explosive power of 20,000 tons of TNT. "The report was incredible—a Buck Rogers nightmare," said Jim Thomas, learning along with the Japanese the magnitude of destruction. On 10 August the secret radio provided news of the Nagasaki bombing just minutes before the Japanese learned of it over their radio stations.

The incredible destruction of the new weapons shook Japan to its core. Rumors abounded—from surrender to total annihilation of the Japanese race in a forthcoming invasion. None doubted the ultimate destruction of Japan. For the men of Futatabi, they also feared Kobe was next on the target list for the new bombs. "Our radio fed the rumor mill," said Jim Thomas, "as we spread pieces of information from the shortwave."

"On the night of the tenth," Thomas continued, "we were sitting on the porch having an armchair session and analyzing rumors. . . . Looking over my shoulder, I noticed Fred Oppenborn sitting in his corner with an unusually happy look on his face and a cigar in his mouth." Oppenborn had promised to smoke his treasured cigar when the war ended. He strode over to Thomas, bent over, and whispered in his ear, "The war is over. Japan is ready to quit. Suzuki, the new premier, has agreed to unconditional surrender providing the Allies don't compromise the prerogatives of the emperor. If the Allies agree on that point, the war will be over. The radio says it would be best to have the emperor stay in power and help with the peace process. It's going to take five more days before we'll know for sure. But it looks certain that Japan is ready to throw in the towel. We'll have to keep it quiet because of our radio, so don't say a word outside of this room."

The suspense was excruciating to those who knew Japan was ready to surrender. One lone bomber appeared over Futatabi on the night of 14 August. Earlier that evening the men heard Japanese radio announcing that the emperor was to speak to the nation at noon the following day. The hidden radio spoke of expected treachery on the part of the Japanese. By the time the last of the 752 B-29s returned to the Marianas the morning of the fifteenth, President Harry S. Truman had announced the unconditional surrender of Japan. Thomas and his friends now knew the end was here.

The morning brought only silence as no planes were visible in the skies. At noon the camp was still and quiet. On the night of 14 August, as a single B-29 came directly over camp and as the antiaircraft shrapnel started falling, the men headed for the tunnel. "Our 'secret' radio warned us of Japanese treachery," Jim Thomas remembered. "We waited breathlessly. The local radio and press announced the emperor was to speak to the people at noon the next day. Everyone in camp knew the speech was coming, but only we six knew the contents of the message. There were no U.S. air raids that day, so the people could listen without distraction."

The prisoners saw the camp guards gather around the office radio, face north toward the emperor, and bow as the emperor spoke. Alone in their shock, the guards and staff remained motionless as the emperor announced the end. They were now "enduring the unendurable and suffering what is insufferable."

"We, too, were stunned," Jim Thomas said. "Everyone, including the guards, stood transfixed. The import of that statement was just too great. We had waited too long, had yearned, hoped, and prayed too hard to absorb the significance of victory so suddenly. Then, in a moment, with a sudden surge of emotion, everyone went stark raving mad with joy. We jumped, screamed, and yahooed with ecstasy. Working off four years of frustration, the inmates smashed furniture and threw it out the windows. Grown men began to cry. Everyone hugged everyone else. Screams of rapture filled the canyon. 'Sensō aware. The war is over.'"[8]

Freedom was an aphrodisiac to the starved men. The younger men poured out of the camp and entered what remained of Kobe. The vastness of the destruction was unexpected. In their wanderings, they connected with the military prisoners at nearby camps, exchanging tales not of horror but of what they hoped would greet them upon their return home.

CHAPTER 25

Operation RAMP

The Return of Allied Military Personnel

IT'S NOT WHETHER YOU GET KNOCKED DOWN. IT'S WHETHER YOU
GET BACK UP AGAIN.

—*Vince Lombardi*

The announcement the war had ended did not come quickly from the Japanese. The ignominy of surrender was considered to be unbearable to the Japanese soldier. The malicious superiority of the Japanese military and their faith in the unconquerable spirit of Japan, Nihon Nippon, was destroyed in the hellish whirlwinds that consumed Hiroshima and Nagasaki.

The atom bomb was the ultimate secret until its actual use. The suddenness of the Japanese surrender on 15 August 1945 caught many in the military by complete surprise. The night before accepting the surrender, the Japanese sent a radio message to every POW camp, ordering all records to be burned and authorizing the guards to flee and change identities so as to avoid prosecution for their brutality. Within minutes records were destroyed by fire, and, fully aware of their cowardly brutality, guards fled from every POW camp across Japan. In final savage acts, dozens of American B-29 crewmen were dragged from prisons and murdered in an attempt to cover up prior atrocities.[1]

On 15 August Japanese officials were instructed to notify all camps of the surrender, paint *PW* on the rooftops, and supply each camp with a radio pre-tuned to a station set up by General MacArthur. Few prison camp commandants obeyed this directive in the first week. Allied plans had been made for the surrender, but few expected it for many months, if not years. Navy ships were scattered in attacking task forces, circling the mainland and bombarding coastal factories. Carriers, geared for continuous flight operations, were suddenly cast in the role of observers, seeking to find the prison camps designated by the Japanese.

Unfortunately the Japanese were never forthcoming with an entire list of camps, even after General MacArthur landed on 30 August at Atsugi Airfield. MacArthur, now the Supreme Commander of Allied Personnel (SCAP), made the rescue of POWs the absolute first priority in all commands. The Japanese admitted to only seventy-three camps until confronted by MacArthur with his evidence of at least twenty more—evidence supplied by an extensive spy network throughout Japan operated by the OSS. Eventually 158 prisoner and internee camps were found within Japan and liberated.[2] Not a single camp that used only Chinese captives as slaves was listed by the Japanese. It was not until early October that hidden slave camps housing Chinese civilians were found in the Sendai area.

The surrender of Japan precipitated what can be described as a ballet of Navy and Army Air Corps movements. Admiral Nimitz gave orders to immediately strip all ships and facilities of extra food, medicines, and clothing for airdrops to POW camps. Naval forces, configured for shore bombardment and congregating for another invasion—especially hospital ships and carriers—had to be repositioned for rescue operations, with an emphasis on rescuing men from the known camps in the Tokyo, Osaka, and Kobe areas. POWs were told to remain in their camps until contacted by rescue teams, a frustration ameliorated only by the flood of food and supplies into located camps.

Ships poured into Apra Harbor on Guam and the San Jose Harbor on Tinian, disgorging endless tons of supplies. K rations and canned foods, especially canned peaches and Spam, were loaded into fifty-five-gallon drums and rigged with parachutes for aerial delivery to the POW camps. American fighter planes crisscrossed Japan, China, Formosa, and Korea, searching for camps. F4U Corsairs, TBFs, and Bearcats skimmed treetops and swept into ancient valleys of Japan—all hunting for signs of the POWs. Camp roofs were marked with large *PW* signs, made from paint, rags, or scraps of wood—any material the men could find. Fighter pilots, anxious to help their fellow soldiers held captive, dropped notes, cartons of cigarettes, and some food when they located a camp. "We see you. Rescue on the way. Welcome home! USS Wasp" was scrawled on a note dropped into the Omori prison camp.

Another pilot dropped a similar note and a large ham to the civilians interned at Futatabi. A Navy pilot in an F4U Corsair fighter made a low pass up the ridge to the Futatabi camp, leveled off, and tossed out a canned ham attached to a parachute. Tearing loose from the chute, the ham hurtled directly toward Jim Thomas. "I had a split second to step backwards and hit the dirt," said Thomas; the ham hit a dirt bank a few feet away and disintegrated into a gelatinous mist of ham and fat.[3] For the pilots, just days from aerial combat, the sight of the prisoners waving and jumping at their passing was addictive. Hundreds fought for the privilege of finding the camps.

Massive airdrops of food, clothing, and medicines were delayed until supplies could be assembled and proper methods of delivery determined. Severe rains and winds delayed the start another three days. Empty fifty-five-gallon drums were welded together, palletized, and rigged with chutes in hopes that this would be sufficient for the task.

On 28 August the first B-29s dropped tons of supplies to camps in the Tokyo, Osaka, Nagoya, and Kobe areas. Unfortunately, airdrops from high altitudes were scattered by the winds, landing miles from the targeted camps. Other chutes were torn away in the fall, the drums hurtling down like bombs. Manned by volunteer crews, the

B-29s swooped over camps, day after day, dropping more than four thousand tons to the estimated 63,500 surviving prisoners—an average of 125 pounds per man.

The relief missions were not without danger as eight planes were lost along with seventy-seven crew members. One B-29, flying a relief run into northern Korea, was attacked by Soviet fighters and forced to land.[4] During the initial flights, at least six POWs were killed on the ground when food supplies—parachutes torn away—fell like bombs. Working around the clock, the airmen on Saipan reloaded the B-29s for the second day of supply drops. Every man was anxious to be part of Operation RAMP—the Return of Allied Military Personnel. The danger of "chute-less" airdrops became apparent. On the second day, supplies were dropped outside the camps to prevent further injuries.

The first food drop on Hirohata was on 28 August. Not all the planes destined for Hirohata were able to find the camp through the overcast, dropping their loads instead into a nearby camp filled with Dutch prisoners from Java. Zentsuji received its first supply the following day. Weather blocked Futatabi for another day. Rokuroshi would not see its first relief supplies cascade down until 3 September, when four B-29s disgorged fifty chutes. More than nine hundred sorties were flown before the last food drop on 21 September.[5]

As Operation RAMP spread across southern Japan, rescued POWs flooded into Yokohama by rail, bus, and truck. Greeted by military bands blaring popular prewar songs and the modern sounds of swing, the men were quickly processed and, by the end of each day, transferred to warships or hospital ships in Tokyo Bay and Yokohama Bay. Within days, a similar operation was set up in Nagasaki Bay for arriving prisoners from the western sectors.

Fourteen days after the surrender of Japan, on the morning of 29 August, Colonel Murata, Japanese commandant over all the Osaka district, strode into the Hirohata camp. Accompanied by an American colonel and the Swiss Red Cross representative, he met with the camp staff. The sullen prisoners, refusing to clear the yard, watched in silence. Ten minutes later Murata told the assembled prisoners that the war was over and the documents would be signed in a few days. Only the presence of the American officer and the Red Cross official prevented the prisoners from murdering Murata at that instant. None of the Guam men had forgotten his humiliation of them at the train station in Osaka the day they left for Hirohata.

In numerous camps all over Japan, prisoners simply walked away, determined to get to Tokyo or Yokohama as quickly as possible—ignoring the orders of General MacArthur to remain until rescued by RAMP teams. Typical were the actions a few days after the surrender by a Guam Marine, Pfc. Herbert Humphrey, held prisoner at Tsuruga, a port city seventy-five miles north of Osaka on the western coast of Honshu.

"About six of us decided to go to where the Americans were," said Humphrey. "We figured they had be in Tokyo." They left the camp, went to the Tsuruga train station, and boarded the first passing train. "We made the people in the last seats get up and move forward so we could sit down. The following afternoon the train arrived in Tokyo. Tokyo was a mess, buildings down, and destruction as far as one could see. We searched all over but could not find the Americans. At a police station we were told the Americans were landing at Yokohama, some fifteen or twenty miles away. We boarded the electric train for Yokohama." In Yokohama, the men encountered an American guard at the station. They had never before seen a carbine or the new type helmet or fatigue uniform he was wearing. Even more interesting was his small truck, the Jeep.

Humphrey was welcomed by the Americans. He was questioned briefly then taken to the processing center in the Yokohama dock area. The men were deloused with DDT, stripped of all clothing, and advised to take a bath. "I remember real hot water and shampoo for the hair," said Humphrey. "It felt so wonderful. We were given new clothes, shoes, and socks. I did not keep a thing from my prison days, not even a spoon or piece of clothing. I was so happy to get out—there was nothing else I wanted."

At Hirohata a few men, led by the "Fox" (Y3 Fred Wells),[6] left Himeji by train for Tokyo rather than wait for the rescue details that arrived on 4 September. Others found their new freedom equally intoxicating. One Marine, Pfc. Frank Nichols, vividly recalled his first day of complete freedom on 3 September:

> A buddy of mine, [Cpl.] Clint Crichton,[7] and I decided we weren't going to wait around. We had a local civilian make us an armband that said, in Japanese, that we were the occupying forces. When we entered downtown Hirohata, we commandeered a bicycle from a Jap civilian and headed out of town towards Kobe. We stopped a truck coming in, forced him to turn around and made him take us to the Kobe train station.
>
> In Kobe, the train to Yokohama was filled with Japanese soldiers. We made them clear out an entire car just for the two of us. When we arrived in Yokohama, we had no idea where to go or what to do. We ran into a jeep filled with four reporters from the *Stars and Stripes*, the newspaper for the overseas military. After a short time, I said, "I'm tired of answering questions. Can you take us where we're supposed to go?"
>
> Finally, we made it to an Army area where they took us in. We were deloused, given a hot shower, new clothes, and freedom at last.

The Japanese rightly assumed that the mistreated prisoners would seek revenge against their captors. Any large-scale revenge killings became impossible, however, as the culpable staff and guards had fled from every camp within two days of the surrender.

But a unique phenomenon occurred in almost every camp. A universal feeling prevailed—not forgiveness, but a sense of sorrow for the average Japanese. As one POW remarked, "We all felt a bit of sorrow for the average schmuck. They'd been led to believe all this nonsense about Japanese superiority and that we were nothing more than animals. It was pitiful to see them now. Exhausted, powerless, hungry, and absolutely terrified of the future."

In Zentsuji during the war, when the POWs were transported in open stake-body trucks to work sites near the Sakaide train yards, they passed beneath an overpass. For the last year of the war, a Japanese woman was frequently seen rushing from her home to the overpass in order to rain dirt and small rocks down upon the defenseless men. "Probably a Jap mother who lost her son," remarked one of the POWs. With equanimity the men simply accepted the woman's hostile action and merely ducked whenever she appeared.

After Japan had surrendered but before the men left the prison camp, two prisoners, fluent in Japanese, paid a visit to the home of the infamous woman. Opening the door, she bowed deeply, expecting a severe retribution for her actions. Telling her to stand erect, they presented a large box of food and clothing. "We were not your enemy," they told her. Japan had been physically devastated, its people on the verge of starvation, and there was fear in the hearts of every native. Acts like this gave the prisoners a release from the hatred they felt in their bones—a hatred that had kept them alive since capture. In every camp the guards, civilian *honchos,* and local laborers who had aided the prisoners were sought out for a measure of reward.

For some, freedom meant the restoration of a simple pleasure, long denied but never forgotten. "I promised myself," said Sgt. Tom Honan, "that when the war was over, I'd take a bottle of sake and some canned chicken to the top of Osa Yama and have myself a picnic . . . and that's exactly what I did with a bunch of buddies."

When rescued the men of Zentsuji were transported to Takamatsu, where a ferry transported them across the Inland Sea to a train that carried them to Yokohama. After passing through Kobe and Osaka, the train paused at a small station. Peering out the window, a former prisoner noticed the familiar shape of Hosotani, the former commandant. Rushing out, he confronted Hosotani and demanded his sword. Hosotani bowed deeply and surrendered his sword.[8] With a broad grin on his face, the American reboarded the train to the cheers of his friends.

When the men from Zentsuji finally arrived in Guam, they discovered, to their utter delight, that Sgt. Red Newton was alive. Newton related the tale of his rescue on the day of the Japanese surrender on board the USS *Missouri,* 2 September. A number of Scottish soldiers in the Osaka area heard a rumor that some POWs were still being hidden at the Osaka Palace jail. Storming the jail, a British sergeant major found Newton. "Hi Yank!" he said. Taking a second look at Newton's condition, bloated and unable to move because of his severe beriberi, he turned to his mates and shouted, "Good bloody Christ! Get this man out of here!"[9] Newton, clinging to life, was rushed to the British medics, who were among the survivors of Chikko, the main camp in Osaka. He was later flown to the Guam hospital, where he rejoined his friends from Zentsuji. A few days later, Newton was flown directly to the states for further recuperation.

———————

At Hirohata, the Japanese and Koreans who aided the prisoners were rewarded for their efforts. When they appeared at the camps, the prisoners lavished them with excess food and clothing. A civilian *honcho* at the plant, who frequently made little gifts of food and cigarettes to the men, was heavily rewarded. With ample supplies of food and clothing from the B-29s, that particular civilian was given all the excess Japanese clothing, boxes of food, and discarded parachutes. He set up a table at the camp entrance and made a small fortune selling the supplies to the plant managers and villagers.

The plant doctor and dentist were also singled out for lavish supplies of cigarettes, food, and clothing for their innumerable kindnesses to the prisoners. Letters of commendation and appreciation were freely written for many civilians who also tried to comfort the prisoners during their long ordeal. "It was hoped," said one POW, "that these letters would serve as an introduction to the occupying forces and their kindness would be reciprocated. Perhaps the letters would help them to get jobs with the Americans."

However, certain guards and staff were deemed unworthy of any respect. As they waited for the rescue troops to arrive at Zentsuji, a number of men sought revenge upon the most sadistic guards and civilian *honchos*. A large number of men rode the train into Sakaide seeking the most vicious of the *honchos,* a man nicknamed "Harry the Horse" after a character in a Damon Runyon story. The *honcho* had never hesitated to use his stick to beat men mercilessly when he sensed a slowdown or spotted a man not working as efficiently as he desired. He had been a thorn in the side of every man at Sakaide, and they were relieved when he was sent for a short time to Takamatsu.

Compared to the men at Sakaide, the men at Takamatsu found more ways to "goof off" and avoid heavy labor. The Japanese sent "Harry the Horse" in to inspire the prisoners. His first act was to search the jackets of the men in the clothing shed. Here he found a pack of matches in the jacket of a prisoner. Using the possession of matches as an excuse (smoking was normal for all and matches were carried by many men), "Harry the Horse" selected the man for his sword play. He swung the sword at the man's neck, flipping it in the process. The man's ear was cut, causing a heavy flow of blood. Few doubted he would have equally enjoyed hitting the man with the sharp edge. Fortunately for the Japanese *honcho*, the men were not able to find him before they were sent home.

A few days before the final departure from Hirohata, Lorenzo, one of the Italian seaman, arrived at the gate seeking his old friend Tony Iannarelli. Both reveled in their freedom. Together, they went into Kobe to see the Italian consul. Iannarelli verbally lashed the consul, stating he witnessed the consul's orders to the Kempeitai to torture and murder one of the Italian seamen. In no uncertain terms, Iannarelli told the "pompous bastard" that a full report would be given to General MacArthur of his complicity in the torture and murder of the seaman.

As a diplomat the consul was immune from prosecution, but when it was discovered he had stolen and hoarded thousands of the Red Cross food packages for his personal use, he was quickly expelled from the Red Cross and the consular corps. He became an impoverished refugee and remained in Japan, an exile without a country.

At Hirohata Camp, at precisely 2:00 p.m. on Sunday, 2 September 1945, the very moment the documents of surrender were signed by the Japanese, the prisoners celebrated with an emotional and long-awaited ceremony. The flags of the United States and Great Britain, handmade with stars cut from a blue navy uniform and stripes from parachutes and the red drapery lining from the commandant's office, were carried by an honor guard to the newly erected flagpoles. The men, assembled in ranks, stood at rigid attention. The flags rose to a bugler's notes, and tears formed in the eyes of every man as he proudly rendered a military salute. All joined in singing the American and British national anthems.[10]

Two days after the formal surrender, an official rescue team appeared at the gates of Hirohata. In the late afternoon of 9 September, the men of Hirohata climbed on board trucks for the train station. As they departed the camp, the local civilians smiled and shouted their appreciation for the men's generosity in victory. Within moments they swarmed over the compound like ants, scavenging every morsel of food and shred of clothing.

As the stake-body trucks drove through the crowded streets of Himeji, another of the notorious guards was spotted riding by on a bicycle. Reaching over the side of the truck, a prisoner clobbered him on the head, knocking him to the ground. Jumping down from the truck, he proceeded to beat the former guard to a pulp. It was doubtful the guard would survive. No one said a word as the former prisoner climbed back on board. The convoy again restarted and continued to the train station. At the station the prisoners clambered on board the passenger train, spreading out in the clean, uncrowded cars. As the train departed, the Japanese camp commandant was seen waving good-bye to the train with a smile on his face.

After the processing at dockside, the men were taken on board the hospital ship *Benevolence*. By now, most men had gained at least thirty pounds of weight to their emaciated frames but all still appeared extremely thin. "For the first meal aboard the ship," said Pfc. Garth Dunn, "they gave us a choice and I loaded my plate with pork chops." Along with thousands of other liberated prisoners, Dunn was then transferred to the USS *Ozark* for the trip to Guam. As the lighters pulled along side, hands reached down to help the POWs up the ship's ladders to cheering crewmen, every one anxious to make these survivors feel that they were safe at last. Those too sick to walk were carried on board in the arms of the ship's crew or on stretchers. The open areas below deck were covered with cots, each with mattresses, sparkling white sheets, and soft pillows. With a shower, shave, and haircut, the POWs began to feel safe at last — home in the care of their fellow countrymen.

"But I also remember being sad," said Dunn,

> for I was used to being guarded all the time . . . being close to everyone and hungry and dirty and buggy. It was a big change. As bad as I was treated in those three and a half years, I did not hate the Japanese people. I suppose I should have, but the average Jap did not have it too good during the war either. He too was hungry and ragged most of the time.
>
> During the trip back aboard the ship we were treated to a movie nearly every night. The food was exceptional and all we could eat. At last we were able to do the things that most people take for granted— like going to the ship's store and buying candy bars, razors, or even a handkerchief. Imagine what it's like going three and a half years without a handkerchief.

Shipboard canteens (PXs) and mess halls remained open through the night with everything free to the POWs. Mess cooks, with one exception quickly corrected, prepared anything the ex-prisoners wanted to eat. Stacks of pancakes, bacon, eggs, steaks, ice cream, and fruit poured forth to satisfy dreams long held by starving men. Crews gathered around the POWs, listening with rapt attention to the stories of beatings, death, and starvation. Over and over, the POWs repeatedly thanked the crewmen for their efforts in rescuing them from certain death.

Guam was no longer the isolated tropical island of prewar days. "I could not recognize Guam," said Private Dunn. "The old Marine base was gone—covered over by an airfield. We could not look around much as there were Japanese soldiers still in the boondocks."

After a short period for physical examinations, thousands were placed on board the troop ship USS *Lamar*. The former POWs were told by the ship's captain that they could eat all the meals they wanted with only one condition: "Ex-POWs had to wash their own trays." Before the war, the prisoners had never seen the new-style metal trays with partitions for various foods. "Wash them? Heck, we simply flipped the trays overboard before returning for another meal." On the third day, the captain reversed the order because the ship had started to run out of trays.[11]

At Rokuroshi the newly freed men awaited the rescue squads. A group of officers, eager to regain the freedoms lost for over three years, ambled down the mountainside to Matsumura and took a bus to Ono, the small town where their train journey had ended almost three months earlier. They wanted to experience being "waited upon" in a restaurant. They brought their own rations as the local restaurants lacked even the barest of food to spare. "Being served in a restaurant was a remarkably joyous occasion," said Capt. Mortimer Marks. "The common, simple, everyday amenities that we had for so long taken for granted had vanished and were almost forgotten during our long, grueling, and restrictive life in captivity. I thank God for his great gift to man— the resilience to bounce back from despair to a normal life without scars."

On the afternoon of 7 September, a convoy of trucks slowly climbed up the mountainside to Rokuroshi. As the Americans strode into the camp, the men exploded with joy, surrounding the soldiers, all of whom appeared to be incredibly large and healthy next to their emaciated bodies. The never-before-seen Army women (WACs) were surrounded and hugged as pandemonium reigned. These were the first Americans they had seen since the war had ended three weeks earlier. Large tents were erected, chairs and tables were set up, and the process of filling out forms and performing cursory medical examinations began. The former prisoners, happy to sit next to any other Americans, gleefully cooperated in the seemingly endless details. The festive atmosphere continued through the day and all night as bonfires were built, copious quantities of food were prepared and eaten, and endless songs were sung. "I finally felt free for the first time since our ship went down," said 2nd Lt. Ned Gallagher, a survivor of the USS *Houston*, reflecting the innermost thoughts of every man in the camp.

The following morning, 8 September 1945, the men departed the camp in two shifts for Ono, where they boarded the same "Toonerville Trolley" for Fukui. Happy just to be alive, the men were greeted in Fukui by Japanese Red Cross women who had prepared a few treats and a meal of K rations. That evening the men from Rokuroshi, joined by men from several nearby POW camps, boarded a train for Yokohama. A day and a half later, the train pulled into the Yokohama station.

Greeting the train was a U.S. Army band, blaring "California, Here I Come," "Roll Out the Barrel," and the Marine Corps Hymn. Exiting the train, the men marched past ranks of the 1st Calvary Division standing to present arms in their honor. Dropping their new duffel bags on cots, the men were led into a field kitchen to gorge on mountains of flapjacks smothered in syrup and cream. They all received hot showers and another new issue of clothes. Each man was given a large card with the letter *J* printed on its face to pin on their shirt, designating their status as former POWs. Within a few hours, every single former POW was taken on board a nearby U.S. Navy ship, where they were greeted as heroes and immediately fed another home-cooked American meal. The magic *J* card meant that all galleys were to be made accessible to them, twenty-four hours a day.

Before dusk the Navy officers were taken on board the USS *Iowa* and the Marine officers to the USS *Wisconsin*. Again, the officers of Rokuroshi were fed and assigned cabins with real beds and sparkling white sheets. The crewmen of the ships plied them with questions and listened to their stories with rapt attention.

CHAPTER 26

Operation Magic Carpet

Home Again

HOME, THE SPOT OF EARTH SUPREMELY BLEST,
A DEARER SWEETER SPOT THAN ALL THE REST.

—Robert Montgomery, English poet

Jim Thomas, along with all the other civilians from Futatabi, decided to stretch and look around. "There on the platform," said Thomas,

> was the most beautiful sight we'd seen in forty-six months—a chic, neatly uniformed, vivacious, blonde WAC exuding all-American charm. A welcome sight to our hungry eyes. . . . Was she real? Mustering my nerve, I stepped forward.
>
> "Are you a real American girl and can you speak English? May I touch you to see if I'm dreaming?"
>
> She held out her hand, "Yes, I am real and you may touch me." The crowd roared. Every man began firing questions at her. How was America? Were there women in the B-29s? What were they going to do with us? Had America changed during wartime? Was Deanna Durbin dead? What was the latest song? The train's whistle told us our time was up. Climbing aboard, we settled down with the realization of what we had missed most in our cloistered lives. I wanted to tell her what a thrill she had given us that night.

Through the night, the train raced the 350 miles to Yokohama. After a raucous welcome at the Yokohama rail station, the civilians were bussed to the Yokosuka Naval Base, where they were again greeted by bands and fed a copious amount of food. A few hours later, all were transferred to Atsugi Air Base for departure.[1]

That evening the Pan Am men were gathered together for the long trip home, compliments of Pan Am's honored connections to the U.S. Navy. "At 7:15 p.m.," said Thomas, "we climbed aboard a C-54 Skyliner, and, following the instructions of the pretty stewardess, fastened our seat belts and pinched ourselves to see if we were dreaming. With the four engines echoing defiance, we headed down the runway. At 7:32 p.m. on September 9, 1945, with Mount Fuji silhouetted in the distance, I said good bye and to hell with Japan."

Thomas would follow a circuitous route from Okinawa to Manila, Saipan, Majuro in the Marshall Islands, Johnson Island, and Hawaii on board B-24 bombers and Catalina flying boats. Courtesy of Pan Am, the trip from Honolulu to San Francisco was on board the Honolulu Clipper, the very plane that had carried Thomas to Guam in 1941. Clipper glory had returned.

With an advance on his back pay, Thomas flew to Salt Lake City, caught a bus to Malad, Idaho, and just before midnight stepped onto the porch of his beloved home. He gently knocked on the door. He could hear his mother's steps as she left her bed and slowly walked to the door. The porch light lit as the door opened. Behind the screen, Jim saw his mother appear from the dark. "Jim," she exclaimed, "my God it's good to see you. Are you hungry? Could I fix you something to eat? Steen, wake up. Jim's home."

A few years later, Thomas would meet a pilot from one of the planes that bombed Kobe that terrible night in March. The pilot invited Thomas to his home, where he met the pilot's sister, Barbara. It was love at first sight, and within six months, they were married. Jim settled down in the San Francisco Bay area, where he remained until his death in 2005.

For Pfc. Barney Barnett, the long boat trip home merely enforced his desire to partake of the American dream. "The only difference," said Barnett, "was that I promised myself I would never work one day extra at any job I did not like. The minute it felt wrong, I would quit." Home for only a few days, Barnett was chatting with friends in the small town he called home when two FBI men in dark suits appeared and asked him to come with them. Stepping into their car, Barnett was whisked away to a side street where the car pulled up to the curb and parked.

"You are never to say a word to anyone about what happened to you as a POW or what you knew on Guam before the war. If you do, we'll charge you with treason and you'll spend the rest of your life in prison. Is that understood?"

"Yes sir!" said Barnett.

When he returned to his friends, he could not tell them why he was no longer able to speak of his experiences. Their suspicions aroused, they began withdrawing from their old friend. The situation became intolerable, so Barnett left for Arizona, never to return. He enjoyed a long career in the trucking industry and, until his death in 2001, traveled extensively in his large mobile home across the back roads of America.

Pfc. Harris Chuck returned to active duty after a long recuperation. His career with the Marines spanned the Korean War and Vietnam War. In both wars he was honored for his bravery and leadership. With more than thirty years of service, Chuck retired as a division top sergeant. At more than eighty years of age, Chuck still had the physical appearance of a young man—lean, wiry, and with a booming voice that commanded respect when interviewed recently. Like so many others, he remained the quintessential Marine.

Pfc. Garth Dunn left the Marines when he returned to the United States. He enrolled at the University of Southern California and enjoyed a long career in business.

Sgt. George Shane returned, was debriefed, and recovered for one year in Oak Knoll in Oakland. "Others were told not to discuss the atrocities of the Japs," said Shane. "I was told never to talk about the days just before the Japanese invasion of Guam since we all knew they were coming. As a good Marine, I saluted, said, 'Yes Sir!' and stayed in the Marines until I retired after thirty years." Shane passed away in 2001.

PhM1 Tony Iannarelli remained in the Navy and returned to Japan a year later with his new wife, Jean. Tony, fluent in four languages, including Japanese, settled in with Jean for a few years in Japan. Jean recalled how Tony often said the Japanese will always believe they are superior to Westerners. While they quietly waited for a bus one morning, Tony heard a Japanese man speak loudly to the crowd, telling them to push ahead to ensure that the "stupid Americans" did not have seats on the bus. Getting on last, Tony stood in front of the seated man and told him, in florid Japanese terms, to get out of his seat and for all other men to immediately stand up and give their seats to the women standing on the bus. "And don't ever let me catch you doing this again!"[2]

Pfc. Ralph Baggett finally returned home after almost two months of hospitalization and a slow boat back to California. He could hardly wait to see his beloved Sybil again. "I told everyone that if she was waiting, I'd propose again and we'd get married as soon as possible. Well, she did, I did and we did." His back pay was almost six thousand dollars—a heady amount in 1945 that could easily purchase a beautiful home. He enjoyed a long and successful career with Textron/Bell Helicopter designing rotor blades. "We went from wood to aluminum covering 16,000th-inch honeycomb and carbon composites," he said.

In 2000 Baggett received a replacement Championship Watch from Drake University and was honored as the grand marshal for the 2001 competitions. "Once a Drake Champion, you will always be a Drake Champion," wrote the president of the university. At the dinner in his honor, the school again gave him another watch, only this time an original 1940 Championship Watch had been found on eBay and fully restored. Choking back tears, Ralph could only muttered a quiet "Thank you" to the thunderous applause of the audience. Ralph passed away in 2004. Sybil now wears his watch.

⸙⸙⸙⸙⸙⸙⸙

For the waiting wives, the arrival of a former prisoner was met with trepidation. They did not know how their loved ones had changed. One former prisoner's wife walked a train platform, waiting for her husband's arrival. In the dim light she noticed a seemingly exhausted soldier lying prone on the platform, his head resting on his small duffel bag: "I thought to myself, whatever is he doing there? As I moved on, the figure rose and called my name. Then I was clasped in his arms but his body felt so thin and brittle that I pulled myself away. I knew this fellow from somewhere, I thought, and looked into the gaunt face and sunken eyes. Could this be my husband? He took my hands in his and raised them to his cheek, a very endearing habit he had, and which I loved. Yes! It was him and we clung to each other again."[3]

One month after returning home, Dr. Van Peenen still faced the daunting task of contacting the relatives of those who had died on Guam and in the prison camps of Zentsuji and Rokuroshi. Unfortunately, the needed documents were in the briefcase he had discarded that fateful night in June as he made the exhausting climb up a mountainous trail to Rokuroshi. He had planned to enclose in his letters the final notes from dying men or the trinkets of life that were to be passed as remembrances to families. The briefcase was gone, its contents surely scattered by the winds.

Dispirited at the loss of the records, he tried for days—but failed miserably—to recreate a diary from his fading memories. A few days before the end of his recuperation leave, Van Peenen opened his mailbox to discover a simple penny postcard:

> Dear Doctor
> I have your briefcase. Where should I send it?
> Yours,
> Keck[4]

Afterword

Editor's note: Roger Mansell, like many researchers and historians, believed the Japanese naval code had been broken by U.S. Naval Intelligence by October 1940, which was true. But he, like others, was under the misconception that the code remained unchanged, which was not true. According to longtime National Security Agency cryptanalyst and historian Robert J. Hanyok, the continuing decryption of Japan's naval code was far more complex.

In November 1941, shortly before the Japanese attack on Pearl Harbor, the Imperial Japanese Navy changed the ciphers in its code so that only 7–9 percent of it was recovered by the Office of Naval Intelligence (ONI). By May 1942 probably closer to 30 percent, Hanyok estimates, was readable. Code recovery is a cumulative process, Hanyok explained; the more you get, the faster the rate of future recovery. Since the war had already started, there was much more Japanese code traffic to decipher. So by May 1942, ONI could decipher whole phrases, allowing them to learn that the Japanese navy planned to rendezvous at Midway Island. This allowed the U.S. Navy to assemble its forces and surprise the Japanese at Midway, giving the United States its first major victory in the Pacific war. But, Hanyok noted, the Japanese navy changed its code in the middle of the Battle of Midway, shutting out ONI completely at the height of the battle.[1]

In October and November 1941, President Roosevelt, who had served as undersecretary of the Navy in the 1920s, became increasingly concerned after receiving reports of considerable buildup by Japanese naval forces in the Pacific, and he queried General MacArthur about it. Joseph Della Malva, a Corregidor survivor who was a member of the Army Military Intelligence staff in Manila, said MacArthur "tamped down" the intelligence reports Della Malva's office was processing and instead reassured Washington that the Japanese would not attack U.S. installations in the Pacific until the spring of 1942, at the earliest.[2]

But from the minute the Japanese attack fleet sailed on 26 November 1941 (25 November on the U.S. East Coast) from Hitokappu Bay (north of Honshu in the Kurile Islands), according to historian Robert Stinnett, the powerful radio stations on Corregidor, Dutch Harbor, and Hawaii were providing radio transmission "fixes" from the Japanese ships. Stinnett asserts that the Japanese fleet was not maintaining radio silence. Thus many of the men on Guam were aware that the Japanese fleet was heading toward Hawaii.

Back in Washington, President Roosevelt was wrestling with the inscrutability of Japan's diplomats. When a group of Japanese diplomats departed from a meeting at the White House in mid-1941, the president is said to have remarked to an aide, "They hate us. Sooner or later they'll come after us."[3]

Perhaps the most illuminating information about Japan's intentions in 1941 was rediscovered by Takao Iguchi, a professor of law and international relations at International Christian University in Tokyo, who gained access to recently declassified documents in Japan's Foreign Ministry archives. The papers show that factions within the Japanese government prevented a warning to the United States from being delivered as written. The original version of a final memorandum dated 3 December 1941, four days before the attack on Pearl Harbor, stated that Japan was forced to terminate negotiations concerning the continuing expansion in Asia and that the United States "would be responsible for any and all of the consequences that may arise in the future."[4]

Professor Iguchi also noted that the war diary of Japan's General Staff (comparable to the U.S. Joint Chiefs of Staff) indicated an ongoing debate in Tokyo over whether to notify Washington of Japan's intent to cease negotiations and start a war, in compliance with the provisions of the Hague Conventions of 1907. Since military members were given equal status with civilians in Japan's cabinet and enjoyed direct access to the emperor, their views usually prevailed. The apparent compromise was to draft a revised final memorandum with much weaker wording on 5 December and send it to Washington. This memorandum was intercepted by U.S. intelligence (the Japanese diplomatic code was broken in 1939 and, unlike the naval code, remained the same throughout the war) and read by President Roosevelt, who interpreted it as a declaration of war. But his aides disagreed, saying the memo contained nothing new, and their collective "wisdom" dissuaded the president from ordering an increase in preparations and a standby alert for war to our military stationed in Asia and the Pacific.

On the day before Pearl Harbor was attacked, an entry in the General Staff's war diary reads, "Our deceptive diplomacy is steadily proceeding toward success." Japan's diplomats in Washington were deliberately not notified of their government's plans.

Professor Iguchi further found that the staff in Tokyo specified that the watered-down message be delivered to our State Department at 1:00 p.m. Washington time on 7 December, but records show it was received by Secretary of State Cordell Hull at 2:30 p.m., about one hour after most of the U.S. Asiatic Fleet had been sunk or left burning in Pearl Harbor and 2,403 Americans had been killed. Professor Iguchi maintains that the hour-and-a-half delay in delivery of the memorandum was also deliberate, because it contained purposely garbled wording difficult to translate.

So at long last Professor Iguchi's research, which received scant attention in the Japanese press, appears to lay to rest the theory of a calculated plan on the part of President Roosevelt to sit back and allow the attack on Pearl Harbor to take place. To the contrary, it would seem that President Roosevelt was more alert than his aides to the bellicose plans of Japan toward the United States.

As Mansell points out,

> The decision to permit Emperor Hirohito to remain as a symbol of power will always grate upon the former POWs and most of the men who fought the bloody battles of the Pacific. The decision to leave the emperor in place was not made by General MacArthur but by Gen. George C. Marshall with the concordance of President Roosevelt and President Truman. The decision was made as a direct result of extensive interviews and summaries of the diplomats and missionaries who returned aboard the MS *Gripsholm* in the summer of 1942. The report's conclusion stated: "Japan is unique in that its national religion and philosophy of life is closely bound together with ancestor worship and loyalty to the Emperor. . . . This fact must be thoroughly comprehended in order to bring about a lasting peace. Accordingly, it is urged that 'political changes should be brought about without affecting the status of the Emperor whose relationship to the people is that of a father—a symbol of patriarchal care.'"[5]

The late Saburo Sakai, legendary air ace for the Japanese during World War II with more than sixty-four planes to his credit, repeatedly spoke out after the war about the arrogant Japanese leadership. As a national hero, his remarks could rarely be attacked by the Japanese revisionists who sought to shift blame for the entire war solely to the Western powers. Repeatedly, Sakai attacked the emperor as being totally responsible. In an interview by Robert Guest for the *Electronic Telegraph*, Sakai even questioned the manliness of Emperor Hirohito: "Whose name was on those battle orders? Over three million died fighting for the emperor, but when the war was over he pretended it was not his responsibility. What kind of a man does that?"[6]

The sheer hatred and brutality by the Japanese against the prisoners of war remains incomprehensible to the Western mind. Today's Japan exhibits a similar irrationality. Japanese youths routinely and randomly attack and savagely beat homeless men on the streets of major cities. Until questioned by the police, the ordinary young boys are unable to understand the horrific nature and depravity of their attacks. A deputy chief of police in Kawasaki called it the "shameful tendency in Japan to target the weak."[7]

For those prisoners who lived through the endless days of slavery in Japan, the nightmares never ceased. For the lifetimes of many, a conscious effort was made to blot out the awful experience. Still, bits and pieces floated to a level of consciousness every day. Memories often became distorted, and friends would hear the apocryphal tales of horror, often a series of events unwittingly blended to create a singular story in hopes that someone could understand the nature of the Japanese savagery. Stories told by comrades became part of their existence and belief structure.

Distortions abound, including a gallery of images regarding Gen. Douglas MacArthur. Most telling were those who "knew for a fact" all the malicious stories of MacArthur's hiding out on Corregidor then fleeing to Australia with planeloads of furniture and possessions. Considered by the Republican Party in 1936 as a potential presidential candidate, he garnered the permanent enmity of President Roosevelt and his supporters. Sobriquets of "Dugout Doug" and "Bug Out Doug" were the pejoratives of his political enemies and rigorously believed by those who sought to find someone to blame for the loss of Bataan and Corregidor. As late as 2001, veteran writers claim to have "witnessed" MacArthur placing large crates of gold and furniture on board the two B-17s that carried him, his wife, son, nurse, and critical staff to Australia. Fully fueled, armed, and with a crew of eight, no B-17 could have gotten airborne with the alleged load. Yet former POWs still believe such claims as gospel.

True history is rarely revealed until years have passed and the raw emotions have faded. A thousand years from now, World War II will still be a subject for active historical study.

The unsung heroes of Guam made a conscious effort to survive. Not only did the quiet heroes of Guam make this decision, but they would become the group with the singular distinction of having the highest survival rate among POWs. Once captured almost 38 percent of all Allied military prisoners died, but of the 414 men captured on Guam, less than 3 percent perished in captivity.

ADDENDUM

What follows is the "welcoming speech" by Major General Mizuhara to POWs on their first day at Zentsuji Camp. A copy of the speech was delivered to each prisoner.

> I am Major Mizuhara, superintendent of the Zentsuji War Prisoners Camp. Receiving you American Marines here, I should like to give some instructions to you all.
>
> You were faithful to your country; you fought bravely; and you were taken captive, unfortunately. As a warrior belonging to the Imperial Army, I could not help expressing the profoundest sympathy and respect toward you. I hope you will consider how this Greater East Asia War happened. To preserve the peace of the Pacific had always been the guiding principle of Japan's foreign policy and the Japanese government conducted patiently and prudently for eight long months diplomatic negotiations with the United States, endeavoring toward a peaceful settlement, while America and Britain increased military preparations on all sides of the Japanese Empire to challenge us. The very existence of our nation being in danger, we took up resolutely with unity of will strong as iron under our Sovereign to eliminate the sources of evil in East Asia. The rise and fall of our Empire that has a glorious history of 3,000 years and the progress or decline of East Asia depend upon the present war. Firm and unshakable is our National resolve that we should crush our enemies, the United States of America and the British Empire.
>
> Heaven is always on the side of justice. Within three days after the War Declaration our Navy annihilated both the American Pacific Fleet and the British Far Eastern Fleet. Within one month, our army captured Hong Kong and the Philippine Islands; and now the greatest parts of British Malaya have already been occupied by our army. Singapore being on the verge of capitulation and the Dutch East Indies too, having been suffering several surprise attacks by our landing forces since the 11th of the month. In the Pacific arena there is left not a single battleship belonging to the allied powers. Above our land there has appeared not a single aircraft belonging to them since

the outbreak of the war, their air forces having been entirely crushed elsewhere. Who can doubt this is the most brilliant success that has been recorded in the world history of war?

About the significance of the present war, I hope you will reconsider deeply with clairvoyant calmness of mind that you must have acquired after the life and death struggle.

What I would like to explain [are] some principles as to how we shall treat you and how you should behave yourselves.

1. Though treating you strictly in accordance with the regulations of our army, we will make every effort to maintain your honor of being warriors and your persons shall be fully under fair protection.

2. You should behave yourselves strictly in accordance with the discipline of the Japanese Imperial Army. Otherwise you will be severely punished according to Martial Law.

3. As far as Japan is concerned, you must do away with the false superiority complex idea that you seem to have been entertaining towards the Asiatic people. You should obey me and the other officers of the Japanese Army.

4. Prejudice against labor and grumbling over food, clothing and housing are strictly prohibited. Because we are now launching death-defying attacks on the Anglo-American military preparations in East Asia, all the nation with a unity of will, strong as iron. There is not a single man or woman who is idling about in this country; everyone is working as hard as possible in order to attain the aim of the present campaign. Therefore you must regard it as natural that you should not be allowed to be loose and reckless in your living. You ought to work as hard as the people of this country do.

5. Don't be demoralized and do take good care of yourselves. As long as the war continues, your present mode of living will remain as it is. In order to endure this mode of living you should encourage each other in avoiding demoralization and taking good care of yourselves. Don't fail to hold the hope that peace will be recovered in the future and you will be allowed to return to your homes. I have ordered our medical officers to offer enough medical treatments to you in case you should be taken ill.

6. Among you officers and men of the American Marines you must attain discipline. Be obedient to your seniors; be graceful to your juniors. None of you must bring disgrace upon the American Navy's glory.

7. If you should have any troubles in your personal affairs don't refrain from telling our officers of them.

With the deepest sympathy with you as captives, I and our officers will be pleased to be consulted with and will make every effort to alleviate your pain. Trust me and our officers.

Closing my instructions, I advise you all to study the Japanese language. I wish you to master it in a degree that you will not feel much difficulty in understanding instructions and I hope you will be able to establish friendly relations between Japan and America when peace is restored in the future.[1]

NOTES

PROLOGUE

1. *New York Times*, 11 December 1941, 1.
2. International Military Tribunal for the Far East, Document 2701, Exhibit O, Box 218, RG 238, NARA. This "order" was actually a 1 August 1944 clarification of a longstanding policy of the Japanese military, directing all POW camp commandants that if the surrender of their position was imminent, they should take steps to execute all prisoners and "not to leave any traces." The question had arisen as to what steps a camp commandant could take on his own without waiting for orders from Tokyo. The 1 August 1944 reply was a response stipulating those circumstances. The directive had already been carried out on Wake Island in October 1943, when the commandant, fearing a U.S. Navy invasion, had executed all POWs. Again in December 1944 on Palawan Island, the commandant, fearing invasion by General MacArthur's forces, torched alive 157 Marines. Eleven survived.

CHAPTER 1. LAST DAYS OF PARADISE

1. Charles A. Lindbergh became the most famous man in the world when his solo flight crossed the Atlantic Ocean on 20 May 1927. His success spurred a furious expansion of aviation worldwide.
2. The first flight to Guam arrived on 13 October 1935, with R. O. D. Sullivan in command and Fred S. Noonan as navigator. Noonan disappeared on 2 July 1937 with Amelia Earhart, attempting to circumnavigate the world. The 1939 Pan Am Clipper fares from San Francisco to Manila were $799 one way and $1,438 round trip. Adjusted for modern prices, comparable fares would be $10,139 and $18,248, respectively. For comparison, before flights were discontinued, a round trip from London to New York on the Concorde was approximately $6,600.
3. The plane was called the China Clipper.
4. James O. Thomas, author interview, 12 November 1999. For convention, local days and dates will be used. When relating events that occurred in Washington, D.C., days and dates will reflect Washington time. Guam, being across the dateline, was one day later. Hence, Pearl Harbor was attacked 8 December Guam time.

5. Diaries and Memoirs of Charles Gregg, Hoover Institution Library and Archives, Stanford University, Stanford, CA (hereafter cited as Hoover Institution).

6. Charles Todd, USMC, author interview, September 2003: "In the July typhoon, the wind was so strong that a piece of corrugated roofing sliced through a palm tree so clearly that you could see the pattern of the corrugated ridges in the stump."

7. Thomas interview. The same comments were given in interviews with Capt. Glen Dean Morgan, USMC (Ret.), September 2003, and Gen. Charles Todd, USMC (Ret.), September 2003.

8. Barnett enjoyed life in the barracks: "It was an easy life. We had a large closet for our clothes and which had a light on at all times to keep down the mildew."

9. Carabao are water buffalo.

10. Gregg Diary, Diaries and Memoirs of Charles Gregg, Hoover Institution (hereafter cited as Gregg Diary).

11. The coral, locally called *cascajo*, has a coarse and crumbling consistency when crushed. However, when used to build a road, it again becomes an extremely hard and durable surface. It is slippery when wet and so traffic speeds on it are limited. Evelyn Nelson and Frederick Nelson, *Island of Guam* (Washington, DC: Ana Publishing, 1992).

12. The USS *Penguin* was a *Lapwing/Bird*–class of minesweeper, with a displacement of 840 tons and length of 187 feet 10 inches.

13. Two yard boats, YP-16 and YP-17 (yippies), served as transports within the harbor. Approximately sixty feet in length, each was operated with a crew of six Navy men and four native Reservists.

14. Chris Perez Howard, *Mariquita: A Tragedy of Guam* (Suva, Fiji: Institute of Pacific Studies, University of the South Pacific, 1986), 28. Edward Howard, father of Chris, married a local girl, Maria "Mariquita" Perez, and lived in a small home near the Piti Yard. Mariquita was murdered by Japanese soldiers during the liberation of Guam by American forces in 1945.

15. In the late 1930s, to say someone was "swell" was considered the best compliment one could give.

16. Edward E. Hale and Helen H. Gordon, *First Captured, Last Freed: Memoirs of a POW in World War II Guam and Japan* (Santa Barbara, CA: Grizzly Bear Press, 1995), 10.

17. The term "mansion" is a misnomer as the building, built in the 1920s, was a combination office and home for the ranking military officer, a Navy captain who served as the governor.

18. After the Spanish-American War, Germany acquired the Marianas (including Guam), the Carolines, Palau, and the Marshall Islands from Spain. Although Japan's seizure was protested, the League of Nations accepted Japan's control.

19. "Chamorro" is the accepted term for the natives of Guam.

20. According to Al Mosher, in 1940 Richland was an extremely small town—before the government decided to build atom bombs and created the nearby Hanford Atomic Energy facility: "If you counted the chickens, we probably had a little more than 250 people. It was the quintessential western farm town where we grew crops like cherries, apricots, strawberries, and large fields of alfalfa." PhM3 Alfred R. Mosher, author interview, 8 July 2000.

21. PhM3 Alfred R. Mosher, author interviews, 8 July 2000, 3 July 2001.

22. RM2 Harold Eugene Joslin, USN, author interview, 24 June 2002.

23. Sgt. George Shane, USMC, author interview, 3 February 2000.

24. Charles S. Todd served primarily as the military aide to the governor. He retired as a brigadier general.

25. At that time, the Drake Relays was considered the top competitive event next to the Olympics. The Drake Relays Championship Watch was almost as prestigious as an Olympic Gold Medal.

26. Cpl. Albert J. Robinson, 4th Marines. He was eventually taken prisoner on Corregidor and survived the war. He was rescued at Sendai POW Camp 7 at Hanaoka.

27. PhM1 John F. Ploke, USN.

28. Twelve of the twenty-eight patrolmen lived in a two-story house on the south side of the plaza. The sleeping quarters were on the second floor with mess facilities and a lounge below. Two Chamorros served as a cook and housekeeper for the Marines. The rest of the men lived in the outstations. Each outstation was a small, two-story house with an assigned Navy corpsman and native household help. The men would come into Agana only for pay and provisions. The smaller towns served by the Insular Patrol were Piti, Sumay, Agat, Umatac, Merizo, Inarajan, Talofofo, Yona, Barrigada, Dededo, Yigo, and Machanao.

29. Anthony N. Iannarelli Sr. and John G. Iannarelli, *The Eighty Thieves* (San Diego: Patriot Press, 1991), 8.

30. PhM3 Peter H. Marshall, USN, U.S. Naval Hospital, author interview, 8 September 2002.

31. Pvt. Ralph Baggett, USMC, author interview, 3 October 2000.

32. Gregg memoir, 1984 summary, Diaries and Memoirs of Charles Gregg, Hoover Institution.

33. Sgt. George Shane, USMC, author interview, 14 September 2000.

34. Joslin interview.

35. Rear Adm. Edwin T. Layton and Capt. Roger Pineau with John Costello, *And I Was There* (New York: William Morrow, 1985), 255. The order came directly from Admiral Hart, Commander of the Asiatic Fleet. The Guam military was under Hart's command. This was Friday, 5 December, in Hawaii. On Guam, across the International Dateline, it was Saturday, 6 December. Almost every man from Guam confirmed this statement.

36. *New York Times*, 6 December 1941, 1.
37. The Japanese attack began at 7:10 a.m., or 3:10 a.m. on Guam.

CHAPTER 2. JAPAN ATTACKS

1. Baggett interviews, February and 3 October 2000. Only eighty-six rifles were on the island.
2. Transcript, Diaries and Memoirs of Charles Gregg, Hoover Institution. The SATREL was a report to the departing station regarding the weather at the next destination. On this morning, Gregg would send a satisfactory report. The station manager and pilots on Wake Island would review the SATREL, and, if they agreed, the flight would depart.
3. "Banzai" literally means "ten thousand years of life" but is shouted in unison three times as a substitute for "hurrah" or "cheers." The shout always preceded attacks. When dying, it was used as a salute to the emperor.
4. Robert Stinnett, *Day of Deceit: The Truth about FDR and Pearl Harbor* (New York: Free Press, 2000), 61. Adm. Thomas Hart was one of a select few privy to the decrypts of the Japanese naval codes. Hart also commanded the secret intercept operation on Corregidor known as CAST, which served as the exchange link to the British in Hong Kong (Stonecutter's Island) and Singapore (Navy Dockyard) as well as the Dutch station in Java (Bandoeng). Hart never informed his counterparts on Hawaii of the Japanese attack plans.
5. Capt. George McMillin, postwar report, U.S. Navy Historical Museum; Capt. Glen Dean Morgan, USMC, Sumay barracks, author interview, 20 April 2000. What McMillin never placed in writing was that he called MacNulty a week prior to the outbreak of war to say that the Marine barracks at Sumay were to surrender without a fight. Noted in the Charles Gregg transcript "Diary and Recollections," Diaries and Memoirs of Charles Gregg, Hoover Institution. Gregg participated in a meeting with all the commanders about 1 December to determine behavior and survival plans in what all considered to be an inevitable attack.
6. Donald T. Giles, *Captive of the Rising Sun: The POW Memoirs of Rear Admiral Donald T. Giles* (Annapolis: Naval Institute Press, 1994), 28; Todd interview.
7. Giles, *Captive of the Rising Sun*, 29; Joslin interview.
8. Lyle W. Eads, *Survival Amidst the Ashes* (New York: Carleton Press, 1978), 36, asserts that the Japanese nationals were not rounded up until Tuesday afternoon. This is not very likely as they were bombed on Monday afternoon while in the jail. In an interview with the author, Todd confirmed that Japanese nationals were rounded up before noon on first day. These "nationals" were Japanese citizens who resided in Guam mostly for business reasons. Many Japanese families had lived there for generations but remained loyal to the emperor of Japan. Few considered themselves as Guamanians or Americans.

9. Transcript, Diaries and Memoirs of Charles Gregg, Hoover Institution. The Pan Am Clipper, a B-314, departed Wake for the 1,500-mile flight to Guam with a small complement of passengers, mail, and two hundred aircraft tires destined for Gen. Claire Chennault's American Volunteer Group, the Flying Tigers, fighting alongside the Chinese against Japan. Notified within ten minutes, Captain Hamilton dumped three thousand pounds of fuel and returned to Wake. The plane had actually been recalled before the Guam messages were received. Box 168, Pan Am Archives, University of Miami.

10. Forty-one Pan Am employees were stranded on Wake. Overloaded with civilians, they fled back to Hawaii, leaving Waldo Raugust and forty natives of Guam. Ten of Pan Am's native Guam men would die in the defense of Wake, and two more would die as prisoners of the Japanese.

11. Beardsley [first name unknown], unpublished memoir, 13, Roger Mansell Collection, Hoover Institution.

12. Affidavit of Lt. Reginald W. Reed, USN (formerly S1), USS *Penguin*, 30 July 1948, War Claims Commission, states the message was delivered by WT1 Jack Leninger, Piti Navy Yard. Robert Epperson, in a letter to the author dated 25 November 2000, states a commissioned officer delivered the actual letter. Most likely, Leninger merely operated the boat because Giles (*Captive of the Rising Sun,* 28) had dispatched a messenger to the *Penguin* with orders only to "take appropriate action." Military custom dictates an officer would deliver such messages; hence Epperson is certainly more credible.

13. Howard, *Mariquita,* 51; Reginald Reed, unpublished memoir, 35-C1-1, U.S. Army Military History Center, Carlisle, PA (hereafter cited as Reed memoir).

14. Hale and Gordon, *First Captured, Last Freed,* 13.

15. Japanese Monograph 48, Central Pacific Operations Record, vol. 1, December 1941–August 1945; and Japanese Monograph 139, July 1949, U.S. Army Center for Military History, Fort McNair, Washington, DC; Remaining Business Liquidation Division, 2nd Demobilization Bureau. Planes were from the 17th Air Group, Saipan. Japanese sources state nine planes were from the 17th Air Unit, attached to the 4th Naval Base Force and detached to Saipan. The 17th also had an unspecified number of Betty-type bombers. Additional planes, bringing the total to eighteen, were brought from Truk by the special aircraft carrier *Seikawa Maru* before 7 December. The *Seikawa Maru* was a freighter that was converted to a "Jeep"-type carrier. The men who were interviewed from the USS *Penguin* all stated that larger planes (most likely the Betty bombers) bombed from a higher altitude as the Petes (Mitsubishi floatplanes) strafed the ship.

16. John Ploke, PhM1, POW Diary, 1, Roger Mansell Collection, Hoover Institution (hereafter cited as Ploke Diary).

17. Japanese Petes were Mitsubishi F1M biwing, reconnaissance, single-engine, single-float fighters carrying two forward 7.7-mm machine guns, two 120-pound bombs and a rear-facing gunner with the same 7.7-mm gun.

18. Ens. Robert G. White, USNR, was engaged to marry Marian (Taitano) Johnston, daughter of the movie theater owner William G. Johnston. Mr. Johnston died in Kobe from starvation in 1943.

19. S1 Ed Settles, author interview, 22 February 2000. Both Settles and Epperson noted that there were "high-flying bombers, probably 'Bettys,' high overhead." These could be the source of the bombs.

20. Haviland's lower left arm was hanging by a thread and Seaman First Class Ratzman was severely wounded in the abdomen by a bomb fragment. EM3 Rex Elwood Wilson was severely wounded in the groin area. With the exception of two or three men, every crew member had been wounded.

21. Two days later Haviland learned that six of the men who had gone ashore were killed in the invasion.

22. The officer was Lt. Arnold John Carlson, U.S. Navy Supply.

23. Epperson, a member of the *Penguin* crew, to author, 25 November 2000. Giles, *Captive of the Rising Sun,* 34, wrote from secondhand knowledge that the officer in charge of supplies had stated that "the stateroom [ship's store] has been ordered closed until further notice. I have orders to destroy everything when the Japs invade. You fellows will have to do the best you can."

24. "Boonies" is military slang for unoccupied hills or areas away from camp.

25. Mosher interview, 8 July 2000.

26. As the governor's aide, part of Todd's duty was to command the Insular Patrol.

27. Todd interview, 10 July 2000.

28. Giles, *Captive of the Rising Sun,* 65. On 17 January 1942, Domei, the Japanese news agency, broadcast an interview with Captain McMillin. He stated, "I want to tell President Roosevelt we of the American forces fought valiantly and defended our posts until the last." He further stated that he was transported to Japan and his treatment was "satisfactory." This was the first Japanese acknowledgment that the men and women on Guam were prisoners of war. *Los Angeles Herald-Express,* 19 February 1942, 1, O'Guinn Collection, Hoover Institution. The Japanese sent a list of 1,200 civilians and all 2,210 Navy and Marine POWs from China, Wake Island, and Guam before 18 February 1942. The Department of the Navy released the list for publication on 19 February. It was not until 23 March 1942 that the Swiss Red Cross representative presented a highly inaccurate list to the State Department.

29. Pfc. Garth G. Dunn, USMC, Insular Patrol, author interview, 8 March 2000. Japanese postwar interviews did not acknowledge a single loss during the invasion, a contention readily dismissed by every man interviewed. McMillin submitted a written postwar report describing the actions during the defense of Guam. He not only denied any planes being shot down but also insisted that only nine planes attacked Guam. Even here, the Japanese assert twenty-seven Petes and Betty bombers attacked, a scenario confirmed by numerous personnel.

30. The USS *Robert L. Barnes* was an immobilized tanker commanded by Lt. J. L. Nestor, USN. Its galley was used to train new Navy mess stewards and recruits for the Guam Insular Guard.

31. Letter from Ploke's daughter, Irene Sgambelluri, to Stanley L. Snow, 14 January 2002, Roger Mansell Collection, Hoover Institution.

32. Sgt. Thomas Honan, USMC.

33. Pfc. Leonard Stanley Kozlowsky, USMC.

34. Cpl. Harry E. Anderson, USMC, died in the first air raid, at the Sumay barracks. The bomb exploded ten feet from the radio shack from which he was attempting to send messages. He died a few days later without regaining consciousness. Giles, *Captive of the Rising Sun,* 30; Barnett and Nichols interviews.

35. Babbs is Pfc. James W. Babb, USMC. His leg was amputated.

36. Pfc. Carroll D. Barnett, USMC, author interview, 1 February 2000. Wounded by the same bomb was Corporal Legato and Sergeant Moore. Mortimer Marks, "Zentsuji: Before, During and After World War II" (Asheville, NC: n.p., 2000), 21 (hereafter cited as Marks memoir); MacNulty's refusal to accept command was tantamount to desertion, but charges were never made. The service was happy to be rid of him after the war.

37. McMillin states that under orders from MacNulty, the Marines took up a position in the butts of the Marine rifle range. In fact, MacNulty hid alone in the butts while Major Spicer directed the Marines to scatter into the jungle. MacNulty waved away other men, fearing they would draw attention to his location. ("Butts" were the pits at the end of the rifle range from which targets were raised and lowered. The floor was normally eight feet below the surface with a protective mound of dirt sloping away from the rear. Except for a direct hit, the butts afforded good protection from all bombs.)

38. Tony Palomo, *An Island in Agony* (n.p.: self-published, 1984), 4. Killed were Larry Lujan Pangelinan and Teddy Flores Cruz.

39. Driving MacNulty's station wagon, Pfc. John D. Rucker, USMC, carried the wounded into Agana from Sumay. The Japanese consistently tried to strafe him from the air. Pfc. Harbert Nixon, USMC, author interview, 9 September 2001.

40. Morgan interview, 9 April 2001. When asked if MacNulty was a disgrace to his uniform, Morgan said, "MacNulty? That SOB was not only a disgrace to the Marines but to the entire human race."

41. James O. Thomas, "Trapped with the Enemy" (Mountain View, CA: n.p.). The U.S. government honored Pan Am's claim for reimbursement after the war.

42. Ibid., 61–63.

43. Dorn Hall Elementary School, named after a previous governor, was also used by the Navy chaplains for Sunday services.

44. Iannarelli and Iannarelli, *Eighty Thieves,* 18, claim never more than nine planes, but most men interviewed claim eighteen plus the appearance of some Japanese Betty bombers high over the USS *Penguin,* Piti, and Sumay.

CHAPTER 3. THE JAPANESE INVASION

1. McMillin's postwar report is highly inaccurate regarding the total number of defenders present. He implied that "hundreds" of military defenders were present at the plaza. However, in numerous author interviews, the men on scene confirm the number as being fewer than one hundred.

2. Giles, *Captive of the Rising Sun,* 47, states the name was Hiromu Hayashi. Although Naval Assault Force is frequently called the "Japanese Marines," it bore no resemblance to the U.S. Marines. The force was a highly specialized attack unit of the Imperial Japanese Army.

3. Japanese Monograph 48, 3.

4. Palomo, *Island in Agony,* 23.

5. The two sailors were BM1 Felix Colavecchio and WT1 Eudy Early, both of the USS *Robert L. Barnes.*

6. Robert Epperson, author interview, 29 August 2000; Robert Epperson to author, 10 July 2000.

7. Hale and Gordon, *First Captured, Last Freed,* 18, 22. Killed at Recreation Beach were USS *Penguin* crew members SM3 R. W. Ernst, RM1 R. G. Fraser, SM3 S. G. Hurd, BM1 F. J. O'Neill, Cox. L. T. Pennault, and GM1 J. Schweighart. These men were last seen by CWO Hale as the initial attack began. In their book Iannarelli and Iannarelli state that an ambulance was detailed to pick up the six bodies after the surrender. All had been repeatedly bayoneted in the throat and back, with heads bashed in, but none were beheaded.

8. Harris Chuck, author interviews, 7 February 2000, 27 June 2001.

9. Both Bomar and Burt were killed in action.

10. Chuck interview, 27 June 2001.

11. The Plaza de España was also referred to as Susana Plaza.

12. Eads, *Survival Amidst the Ashes,* 41.

13. Hale and Gordon, *First Captured, Last Freed,* 30. The weapons were 70-mm pack howitzers.

14. Report: Bright, Graham P., Lt., USN, Office of the Provost Marshal General, RG 389, NARA.

15. Report: Smoot, Malvern, CMM, USN; and Report: Klugel, John, Office of the Provost Marshal General, RG 389, NARA.

16. Report: Eads, Lyle, Y1, USN; and Blaha, Joseph, CY, USN, Office of the Provost Marshal General, RG 389, NARA.

17. EM1 Ralph H. Gwinnup, USN, USS *Penguin.*

18. Pfc. Robert M. Hinkle, USMC.

19. Palomo, *Island in Agony,* 28. Most likely, the two men were native members of the Insular Force and included Angel Flores.

20. Giles, *Captive of the Rising Sun,* 46. Sensing a pending slaughter, Giles crawled and ran to the Chevrolet parked in front of the Government House, opened the

door, and sounded three long blasts from the car horn. He believed the American military would read this as a signal to cease fire and put their weapons down. Giles' postwar report states the time as "about 0545."

21. McMillin, postwar report. For unknown reasons he never mentioned the actions of the Marine Insular Patrol. CPhM John Ploke, who also acted as the island's mortician, noted in his diary that he counted more than two hundred Japanese dead.

22. One scenario of the firing was that Pfc. Bill Bomar, USMC, and Pfc. Hal Burt, USMC, were also spotted by a Japanese patrol. Confusion exists as to the exact disposition of these men. A few men claim only one man, outside the view of the plaza, was beheaded. Both the Epperson and Meletis depositions, taken at the time of liberation, state Bomar and Burt were taken to the plaza and beheaded. Meletis states that the Japanese officer was Lieutenant Nayama. No further corroboration can be found in the provost marshal's records. A second scenario is proffered by Palomo, *Island in Agony,* 27, wherein NS1 Pedro Cruz, USN, again starts to fire at the Japanese. The return fire killed Ramon Camacho, a civilian volunteer assisting the machine gunner.

23. Chuck interview, 27 June 2001. Chuck emphatically states, "Using a bullhorn, an interpreter for a Japanese officer called across the plaza, "You are surrendered. You must surrender. Send over your governor."

24. The *New York Times,* 10 December 1941, 1, notes, "Tokyo Radio declares Guam has been occupied and that Japanese forces were firmly established there." No further reference was made in the paper to the Guam military for more than a month. In a postwar summary for the U.S. Army Military History Center, the Japanese declared the seizure of Guam was "bloodless."

25. Chuck interview, 27 June 2001. Pfc. John Kauffman, USMC, voluntarily joined the defense of the plaza. He had been in the hospital the morning of the first attack. He was slain by Japanese corporal Ichido, according to the affidavit of Paul Meletis. In another interview, Private First Class Nichols, USMC, stated that Kauffman, upon being shoved, turned to the Japanese soldiers and said something in protest, although both Shane and Chuck vehemently dispute this version.

26. Pfc. Richard Ballinger, USMC.

27. Pfc. Paul Meletis, affidavit regarding Hirohata and Nagoya Camp #9, 3 October 1945, Box 64, RG 153, NARA.

28. Baggett interview, 9 July 2003: "I was still in Agat when bombing started. I woke from a sound sleep and came out in my skivvies. Within a few minutes, Burt pulled up in a truck. He was holding a native man on the seat next to him, his guts laying out on the floor. 'Where's the corpsman?' Ploke and Burt took the victim to Agana. As they left, I called out to Burt, 'Y'all come back so we can make it out of this together.' I never saw him again. His remains were eventually brought to Fort Worth for burial. Along with my new wife, Sybil, I looked up his mother and we became close to the family."

29. Jan K. Herman, *Prison Diary of Adolph Wessel Meyers, CPhM*, article in *U.S. Navy Medicine* 70 (September–October 1979); and Meyers Diary, U.S. Naval Historical Museum, Washington, DC (hereafter cited as Meyers Diary).
30. Mosher interview, 8 July 2000. Mosher stated that a service was conducted as the men were buried along the beach. The bodies were recovered after the war, and most were moved to the Punchbowl Cemetery in Hawaii.
31. Thomas interview.
32. The bugler was FM1 Dewey Danielson, USMC.
33. Marks memoir, 26–29; Palomo, *Island in Agony*, 57. Chief Yeoman Luther Fariss remained with the officers.
34. Barnett interviews, 1 February 2000, 4 May 2001. Stationed at the Sumay barracks, Barnett was captured late in the day—after the surrender of most of the Marines in Agana shortly after noon.
35. Only Pfc. Arnaud De Saulniers, USMC, is identified as being one of the fellow Marines.
36. Sgt. John H. Lyles and Pfc. John H. Jones, both USMC.
37. S1 Walter Magelssen, USS *Penguin*, was wounded in the leg before the ship sunk. All knew him by his nickname, "Maggie."
38. Numerous members of the native Insular Guard were beaten and whipped in an effort to find those suspected men, guns, and equipment. Rear Adm. Sadatoshi Tomieka, chief of Operational Section, Imperial General Headquarters, states (Japanese Monograph 48) that Japan believed there were 300 Marines and 1,500 native soldiers.
39. Letter from Ploke's daughter, Irene Sgambelluri, to Stanley Snowe, 14 January 2002.
40. Morgan interview, 20 August 2000.
41. In the front of Max's car were Max Brodofsky, Charles Gregg, and Dick Arvidson. In back were Grant Wells, Bob Vaughn, George Conklin, and Jim Thomas. In the second car were Fred Oppenborn, E. Penning, Al Hammelhof, and George Blackett.
42. Thomas interview.
43. Gregg mistakenly used the name Anderson in his written diary. A Marine corporal, Harry Anderson, was killed inside the Marine radio shack at Sumay during the first bombing.
44. A number of men still hid out across the island. The actual count at this time was thirteen U.S. military, four members of the Native Force, and an unknown number of civilians.

CHAPTER 4. THE JAPANESE OCCUPY GUAM

1. Morgan interview, 20 August 2000.
2. Robert W. O'Brien, BMC, USN, USS *Penguin.*
3. Epperson interview, 9 April 2001.
4. Mount Tenyo, elevation 1,098 feet, was approximately five miles southwest of Agana.
5. Joslin interview. The radio, discarded along the road from the mountain, was found by the Japanese. Tweed became an evader and was finally rescued during the liberation of Guam.
6. The eight men of Radio Libugon were RM2 Harold Eugene Joslin, CRM Donald W. Barnum, RM1 Merkle Smith, RM2 Stuart Faulkner, RM2 Rexford Parr, RM2 Edward Dullard, and RM2 Donn McCune.
7. Settles interview.
8. Giles, *Captive of the Rising Sun,* 63–68. According to Giles, the Navy (not the Marine Corps) decided, in an act of absurdity, that since the men were listed as missing in action, they were not available for duty. As such, they would no longer be paid and stateside dependent allotments were immediately suspended. Fortunately, protests by those dependents to congressmen forced the military to reverse the decision some two months later.
9. Thomas interview; Gregg Diary.
10. Iannarelli and Iannarelli, *Eighty Thieves,* 21.
11. Hale memoirs, Hale Collection, Hoover Institution, 32 (hereafter cited as Hale memoirs).
12. Homer Lea, *The Valor of Ignorance* (1906; reprint, New York: Harper & Brothers, 1942). As early as 1906, the military strategist Lea posited that Japan would wage a war of aggression for economic superiority and, if it acted wisely, its victory over the Allies could be complete. Key to Japan's success would be an attack upon Pearl Harbor. The text was required reading for all Japanese officers.
13. Beriberi is a debilitating disease resulting from a lack of thiamine in the diet.
14. Palomo, *Island in Agony,* 61–62.
15. Ibid., 121. "Omiya Jima" is translated as "Great Shrine Island." Agana became Akashi, the "Red City."
16. Gregg Diary.
17. Only one, RM1 George Tweed, USN, was to survive the war. Over the next two and a half years, the Japanese maintained a large patrol with the sole mission to capture Tweed.

CHAPTER 5. VOYAGE INTO PRISON

1. Stephen Howarth, *The Fighting Ships of the Rising Sun: The Drama of the Imperial Japanese Navy, 1895–1945* (New York: Atheneum, 1983), 281.

2. Capt. Edward N. Bewley, 76th Aviation Ordnance, 19th Bomb Group, letter of 7 January 1942, Hoover Institution. A native of Los Altos, California, he was later captured on Mindinao. He died 7 September 1944 on the *Shinyo Maru*, which was torpedoed by an American submarine.

3. Howard, *Mariquita,* 60; numerous author interviews.

4. Hale memoirs, 36.

5. U.S. Naval Historical Center, Washington, DC: The *Argentina Maru,* a 12,755-ton troop transport, was built as a civilian passenger liner at Nagasaki, Japan. Completed in 1939, it was requisitioned in mid-1941 and served as a transport during the first year of the Pacific war. (The USNHC is in error stating the ship was returning from South America. The *Argentina Maru* sailed from Yokosuka to Kwajalein after 5 December 1941 carrying the Japanese Special Landing Forces for Wake Island, per Shigeyoshi Ozeki in his book *Wake in Sight*). The *Argentina Maru* is included in the postwar UN report as being part of the Wake invasion force. From December 1942 to November 1943, it was converted into an aircraft carrier and renamed the *Kaiyo.* Conversion was completed November 1943, and the ship served during the rest of the Pacific War as an escort carrier, aircraft transport, and training carrier. It was seriously damaged by British Royal Navy planes in Beppu Bay, Kyushu, on 24 July 1945. It never again entered combat.

6. Iannarelli and Iannarelli, *Eighty Thieves,* 22.

7. Morgan interview.

8. Chief Nurse Marion B. Olds and Nurses Leona Jackson, Doris M. Yetter (misidentified by McMillin as Margaret, per interview with Audry Mauser), Lorraine Christiansen (Halliday), and Virginia J. Fogarty (Mann). Nurse Jackson eventually became director of the Navy Nurse Corps.

9. Deemed too pregnant for travel when the USS *Henderson* departed in November, the wife of John Anthony Hellmers, chief commissary steward in the Agana Administrative Group, gave birth to her daughter a few days before war started.

10. While held captive in Agana, the prisoners saw Japanese movies of the celebrations of their conquests of Hong Kong and Manila. Despite the obvious Japanese victories, it was impossible for the men to disbelieve the prewar assurances that America was more powerful than any other nation. However, Homer Lea's premise posited in his 1906 book had come true. Japan had, as Lea foresaw, started a war of aggression for economic superiority. Lea was ignored by the American military. Few Americans realized that by 1941 the Japanese had a massive superiority over the decimated American military. In the War Department and the corridors of the White House, analysts realized that, had Japan chosen to invade

the western United States, they could easily have swept past Denver before being stopped. Hawaii, destined to become a staging area for victory over Japan, would have lain prostrate had the Japanese had the foresight to invade rather than hit and run.

11. Gregg Diary, 16. Eight men were crowded into a room six by nine feet (two paces by three paces). One section marked "Capacity 84" was jammed with 210 men.

12. Hale memoirs, 37.

13. Thomas interview.

14. Gregg Diary, 17. Gregg's is one of the rare contemporaneous civilian journals. Hence, his time references appear to be most accurate.

15. The unidentified ship or barge had a completely open hold, approximately ten feet in depth.

CHAPTER 6. THOSE LEFT BEHIND

1. Giles, *Captive of the Rising Sun,* 126. Joseph H. Blaha, chief yeoman, Administrative Staff, and Frank Perry. A civilian employed in the cable station, Blaha had severe leg and chest injuries from bullet and bayonet wounds. His leg was shortened as a result. Perry suffered permanent nerve loss in one leg, a result of a bullet wound in his back. As a civilian, Perry should have been sent to join the other civilians in Kobe but was interned in Zentsuji. As usual, no reason was given.

2. Sidney R. Wallace, captured in the Gilbert Islands (Kiribati) and held in Zentsuji POW camp in Shikoku. Sidney R. Wallace, "Diary of a New Zealand Coast Watcher," edited by Patricia Wallace Mayer, Hoover Institution. The two men arrived in Zentsuji on 8 September 1942.

3. Palomo, *Island in Agony,* 31.

4. Ibid.

5. Ibid., 34.

6. "Comfort women" was a term applied to women forced to become prostitutes serving the Japanese soldiers. While a number were native Japanese, most were enslaved women from China, Korea, and the Philippines. Thousands of comfort women were used by Japanese forces throughout their empire. Abusive treatment was normal, and many died servicing the troops. In the latter stages of the war, many were simply murdered as Japanese troops were forced to retreat. Sixty years later, the Japanese government still refused to acknowledge these abuses, although a meager compensation and limited "regrets" have been offered to some of the surviving women.

7. Palomo, *Island in Agony,* 125.

8. The official symbols were the Hinomuru (Rising Sun flag) and the Kimigayo (national anthem of the Japanese Empire). Both were banned after the war but were reinstated by the Japanese Diet in August 1999.

9. Such edicts were from an inherent bigotry and racism in what had slowly become an almost all white military at the behest of President Woodrow Wilson. In the Navy, the only place for African Americans was service as messmen or stewards. No African Americans served in the Marines. In the Army, African Americans, if any, were used as laborers or truck drivers. The Jim Crow laws of the former Confederacy, sanctioned by the Supreme Court's *Plessy v. Ferguson* decision permitting separate but equal treatment of African Americans, gave sanction to similar restrictions within the military.

10. O'Brien's honeymoon was on board the supply ship, the USS *Gold Star*. Referred to by the military as the *Goldie Maru*, the Guam supply and transport ship made monthly voyages to Manila, China, and Japan for supplies, coal, fresh provisions, and mail. Many men traveled on board for their annual leave. It was near Australia when the war began and saw no combat.

11. Edward Hale, *Who's Who in Chamorro History*, vol. 1 (Agana, Guam: Political Status Education Coordinating Commission, 1995). Perez, retired in 1935, had served as a clerk to every governor, including the first one, Capt. Richard P. Learny, USN. He rose to the highest native position available, chief clerk, now called secretary of Guam, or lieutenant governor.

12. Palomo, *Island in Agony*, 105.

13. Military secret police, equivalent to the infamous Gestapo of Hitler's Nazi regime, only many times worse and feared by Japanese and Allied military alike.

14. Palomo, *Island in Agony*, 109–13.

15. Now covered over by Anderson Air Force Base.

16. Urunau is also covered by Anderson Air Force Base. The cave in which Tweed hid for the last few days is visible at Uruno Point, on the west side of the base.

17. Apla was renamed Apara Maru by the Japanese. Jalaguac became Harada Maru.

18. A single strip airfield on the Orote Peninsula (Orote Field) and another field, two and a half miles northeast of Agana (Harman Field), were completed. Both are now abandoned.

CHAPTER 7. ZENTSUJI

1. Leona Jackson, RN, *U.S. Navy Medicine*, September–October 1998, 16–18.

2. Gregg Diary, 17–19.

3. Camp Zentsuji, located on the northwest corner of the island of Shikoku, was considered by the Japanese a showplace for visiting Red Cross officials. The POWs from Guam were the first large group of prisoners brought to Japan.

4. Giles, *Captive of the Rising Sun*, 72, states that upon arrival in Zentsuji, the prisoners were "herded toward the camp a few miles away, at the eastern edge of town." Upon departure in 1945, Giles (184) states that the distance was one mile.

5. Gregg Diary, 17–19. Typical of personal diaries, Gregg did not note the experience of others. No additional food other than that served on the docks was given to

the military prisoners until the next morning. Only the high-ranking civilians and officers were in rooms with tatami mats. Enlisted men received only four blankets.

6. Joseph R. Brown, *We Stole to Live* (Cape Girardeau, MO: Missourian Litho & Printing, 1982), 29. Brown states it was "a seven-foot-high wooden fence. About four feet inside the fence was another fence of strands of barbed wire nailed to wooden posts; it was about four feet high." Mortimer Marks states that "twelve-foot wooden walls surrounded our compound." The prison complex was part of a larger Japanese army base. Only after Private Baggett, USMC, was caught stealing sugar from a building outside the fence were sharpened bamboo spikes affixed to the top of the wood plank walls to "prevent escapes."

7. Iannarelli and Iannarelli, *Eighty Thieves,* state that there were twelve men, including one American, two Dutch, four English, and a few New Zealanders and Australians. Giles (*Captive of the Rising Sun,* 73) states that the following were present: Lt. Cdr. Orel Pierson, master of the SS *President Harrison*; RM1 Arthur Griffith, USN, American Consulate, Tsingtao; and H. C. R. Fulford-Williams, a civilian administrator on Butaritari on the Makin Atoll, Gilbert Islands. (Giles erroneously places Butaritari in the Marshall Islands and assigns the title of governor to Williams. Giles also erroneously states the twelve men arrived the next day. In fact, nine were present upon arrival; all others arrived the second day.)

8. Oliver A. Gillespie, *The Pacific* (Wellington, NZ: War History Branch, Department of Internal Affairs, 1952), 233; Peter McQuarrie, *Conflict in Kiribata: A History of the Second World War* (Wellington, NZ: War History Branch, Department of Internal Affairs, 1952), 57–61; Kevin Menzies, letters to the author. The seven Coast Watchers from New Zealand were as follows: captured on Bikati, Pvt. Michael Menzies, NZEF, his brother, Pvt. Jack Menzies, NZEF, and John M. Jones, a civilian radio operator; captured on Little Makin, Pvt. Basil "Pat" Were, Pvt. L. E. H. Muller, and Cpl. M. P. McQuinn; from Abiang, Cpl. Syd Wallace. H. C. R. Fulford-Williams, the administrator, was captured in the village of Butaritari. The Coast Watchers and Fulford-Williams were held in a tin shed at On Chong's Wharf on Butaritari until transferred on board a Japanese minesweeper to Juliet Island on 27 December 1941. From Juliet Island, the men were sent to Yokohama in the hold of the *Yamagiri Maru*. Pvt. Kevin Menzies, NZEF, son of Michael Menzies, stated in a letter to the author, 9 June 2000: "My father was captured [as a soldier/Coast Watcher in the Gilbert Islands] on the islet of Bikati, the northern tip of the Makin Atoll on 10 December 1941 and [later] began his incarceration in the University of Life at Zentsuji. He and his comrades, among them his brother Jack, were among the first Allied prisoners in Japan, arriving in Yokohama on 7 January 1942. The American Marine from Tsingtao [Griffiths] joined them on 10 Jan. 1942. When he would talk about his experiences (not often), he would tell us how he was in Zentsuji when in the middle of the night he was [wakened] by the Marines from Guam entering the camp. From then on,

Dad built up strong bonds with these men which never left him. He told me, not long before his death, that often he lay awake at night and pictured their faces."

9. A Japanese pillow is a cloth cylinder filled with sand or rice husks.

10. Hale, *Who's Who*, 43. Note that this description coincides with Gregg's. As is typical of controversial memories, Ralph Baggett and others vividly recall that the sleeping platforms were in place in all the buildings. Hale's book is constructed from notes and partially written memoirs by his niece, and this account may be confused with later camps in Osaka and Hirohata, where he was assigned. Officers Mortimer Marks and Glen Dean Morgan confirmed the existence of the platform upon arrival in their building. The officers were housed separately.

11. In numerous interviews, a wide disparity was noted regarding the available heating equipment. For example, Lt. Milton Marks, in contemporaneous notes, saw a potbellied stove but remarked it was removed the next day.

12. Colonel K. Sugiyama was overall commander of the Zentsuji army training base. The POW camp was located within the outside perimeter of the training base. On 12 April 1942, Captain V. Hosotani became the POW camp commander, replacing Colonel T. Kondo and Colonel S. Kanabu, who briefly exercised command.

13. Jackson, *U.S. Navy Medicine*, 15–18.

14. Chief Nurse Marion B. Olds, USN.

15. Dunn interview, 8 March 2000.

16. Thomas, "Trapped with the Enemy." This was Friday, 16 January 1942.

17. The total time of captivity from the surrender on Guam until liberation was three years, eight months, and four days.

18. *Tenkos* is the Japanese word for "roll call" or "muster."

19. Thomas and Gregg describe this first morning in contemporaneous journals. Giles, *Captive of the Rising Sun*, 83, asserts no food was served this day. However, he also states that he did not begin taking notes until February 1942.

20. Iannarelli and Iannarelli, *Eighty Thieves*, 34.

21. Assignments were as follows: BMC Robert Lane, supervise enlisted men and coordinate with Japanese; BMC R. W. O'Brien, assigned to the galley; BMC Homer Townsend, assigned to the buildings and grounds, with sanitation being the priority; and BMC P. E. Saunders and BMC W. H. Fisher, assigned command of the work parties and camp details. Among others favored with choice assignments were BM G. B. Wells (Piti), C. Y. Luther Ferris (Administrative Group), and Frank Linn (Administrative Group).

22. Giles, *Captive of the Rising Sun*, 88: "Concrete tub that measures approximately eight by ten by three feet deep." The size stated is close to the average descriptions by Nichols, Gregg, and Thomas.

23. A *fundoshi* is a G-string garment used as underwear. The string on one end is tied around the waist, the cloth hangs down behind, then it is drawn between the legs and over the string in front. The remainder hangs over the string in front.

24. Iannarelli and Iannarelli, *Eighty Thieves,* 38.

25. In 1971 the author participated in an experiment designed by Addressograph-Multigraph Corporation to determine how people evaluate others. Twenty-five men worked, studied, and lived together for a five-day period. Upon conclusion, all were asked to evaluate all others, answering fifty opinion questions using a scale of 1 to 10. For example, "Is the man honest?" (1 being "never" and 10 being "always"). Second, each man was asked to answer the same questions as they believed each of the others would evaluate him. The correlation was over 98 percent. The unmistakable conclusion was "People think of you exactly the way you think they think about you." For prisoners to believe they could mask their feelings of hatred was naïve.

26. Gregg's diary claims that the Japanese issued each person an orange and a pack of ten cigarettes at this time. As he makes no reference to the guards retrieving the aforementioned items (noted by almost all of those interviewed), it may be concluded that he was unaware of the propaganda incident.

27. Lt. Cdr. H. J. Van Peenen (MC), USN.

28. Japanese staff: Major General Mizuhara, commandant of prisons (rarely seen after first week); Colonel Sugiyama, camp commandant, later replaced by Captain Yuhei Hosotani as acting camp commander; three staff, consisting of Lieutenant Nakajima (aka Sake Pete), Lieutenant Saito (aka Dr. Sade), and a supply officer (no name mentioned, but aka "Smiling Jack"); plus the civilian interpreter, Kobiashi, and a varying number of guards. A distinction must be made between military and civilian camps. Harsh as some civilian camps may have been, few civilian camps were as bad as the best military camps, either in facilities, food, or treatment. However, in some areas, particularly in the Philippines and Dutch East Indies, a number of the Japanese commandants of civilian internee camps deliberately withheld food in an effort to murder the internees. Nearly 23,000 Dutch men, women, and children died in internee camps.

29. Mrs. Ruby T. Hellmers and daughter Charlene. Martin's book, *Yanks Don't Cry,* used the fictional names of Marion and Ellen, respectively.

30. The five Navy nurses departed Zentsuji on 12 March 1942. The nurses were sent to the Eastern Lodge Hotel in Kobe and were later sent to board the *Asama Maru* to transfer to the *Gripsholm.* A State Department memo, 12 September 1942, references *Gripsholm* repatriates: OSS E109 Files, Box 75, RG 226, NARA.

31. Shane interview, 14 September 2000.

32. Reed memoir, 74-C4-8.

33. Giles, *Captive of the Rising Sun,* 82.

34. Baggett interview, 4 May 2001.

35. In the latter stages of the war when tobacco was in short supply, the Japanese created a supply called "hair tobacco." Rice stalks were ground into a hair-like condition and then soaked in a mixture of tobacco juice and opium. Smoked in

small clay pipes, the combination was extremely addictive, exacerbating the starving conditions for those willing to swap food for tobacco.

36. Ambassador Grew arranged for his personal library of more than two thousand books to be brought into the camp in March. On 25 June 1942, Grew left Japan on board the *Asama Maru*.

37. The newspapers were the *Osaka Mainichi* and *Japan Times & Advisor*. Both had enjoyed widespread circulation before the war since many foreigners lived in Japan. The lingua franca of the expatriates, businessmen, and diplomatic personnel was English. The subscription expired after one year, and the Japanese would not allow a renewal. However, prisoner work details would steal local newspapers, which then would be translated upon return to camp. Other news magazines available were the *Japan Weekly*, a weekly news magazine; *Contemporary Japan*, a monthly magazine; and *Sakura*, a monthly picture magazine similar to *Life*. By reading between the lines, one could ascertain a change in Japanese military fortunes.

38. 2nd Lt. Clinton C. Seymour, author interview, 31 October 2000.

39. The Meyers Diary is on display at the Navy Historical Museum in Washington, D.C.

40. Barnett interview, 24 October 2000.

41. Seymour interview, 24 October 2000.

42. Nichols interview.

43. Giles, *Captive of the Rising Sun,* 102, states that thirteen men arrived on 29 January 1942 (Thursday), including Cdr. Campbell Keene, and on 18 February 1942, four more men arrived from Wake (an ensign and three other men) in an emaciated and weakened condition, apparently delayed in an "interrogation camp" (Ofuna) as they were communications personnel. Men were transferred on board the *Nitta Maru*. Before arrival in Japan on the *Nitta Maru,* five enlisted men were taken from the hold and beheaded. In an contemporary diary, Wallace recorded that the men arrived as follows: 29 January 1942 (thirteen), 28 February 1942 (four), 30 April 1942 (six). No names or ranks were listed. Total Listing of the Casualties and Disposition of Wake Island Personnel, 1941–45, File 1L, United States Marine Corps Historical Archives, Washington, DC. This report is extremely erroneous as to dates and numbers of men involved. Duane Schultz, *Wake Island: The Heroic Gallant Fight* (New York: St. Martin's Press, 1978), 175, states eight officers and twelve other men were removed from the ship and initially taken to a POW camp in Yokohama. Included were officers Adjutant Putnam, Major Potter, Lieutenant Kliewer, and Commander Keene. The balance was taken to Woosung Prison near Shanghai. No source was cited. Bartlett Kerr, *Surrender and Survival: The Experience of American POWs in the Pacific, 1941–1945* (New York: William Morrow, 1985), lists no reference to men

removed. John F. Kinney, *Wake Island Pilot* (Washington, DC: Brassey's, 1995), lists no men removed.

44. The loss of two British ships, the HMS *Prince of Wales* and the HMS *Repulse* on 10 December 1941 shocked Great Britain. The ships had departed Singapore and headed north along the eastern coast of Malaya to attack the Japanese landing forces. Without air support, the ships were doomed. The Japanese bombers and torpedo planes destroyed the ships in a one-sided battle lasting less than two hours. The loss paved the way for the dominance of aircraft carriers in all further sea battles.

45. The heavy cruiser USS *Houston*, known as the "Galloping Ghost of the Java Coast," and the Australian cruiser HMS *Perth* were en route to the Sunda Strait between Java and Sumatra. Seeking to escape to Australia after a battle in the Java Sea, the ships were passing Banta Bay near midnight when they steamed into the middle of a Japanese invasion force. The *Perth* and *Houston* were sunk in the furious battle and the survivors taken prisoner. About one-third of the survivors perished while being used as slaves to build the infamous "River Kwai" railroad (actually the Noor River). Except for the few officers taken to Zentsuji, none of the survivors were heard of again until late in the war.

46. The military retreat of Japan's armies started 21 July 1942, when General MacArthur rushed troops to the Southwest Pacific Area Command to Port Moresby (Papua New Guinea) to attack the Japanese, advancing over the Own Stanley Mountains on the Kokoda Trail. The first attacks by the forces of Admiral Nimitz began with the seizure of Makin Island (Gilberts) by Maj. Ralph C. Smith's (USA) famed 27th Division, concurrent with the Marines' seizure of Tarawa.

47. Pvt. Luther Orr Jr., USMC.

48. Dunn interview, 8 March 2000.

49. *Benjo* is the Japanese word for "toilet" or "outhouse."

50. Giles, *Captive of the Rising Sun,* 84.

51. Baggett interview, 4 May 2001.

52. Vitamin A (retinol) is found in fish oils, butter, and green and yellow vegetables. Protein is found in eggs, beans, and meat.

53. Deep yellow and dark green vegetables such as carrots, sweet potatoes, winter squash, spinach, kale, and broccoli are also normal sources of vitamin A. Sweet potatoes (*camotes*) and carrots are exceptionally rich in vitamin A. Often unacknowledged, a starvation-induced depression was termed "give-up-itis" by the prisoners. For many men, the effects would last their entire lifetime.

54. Hale, *Who's Who,* 46.

55. Red Cross interview with Captain McMillin, 23 November 1945, by Captain Pence (USN); Mr. James Wallace Diary, Box 2130, RG 389, NARA.

56. Eads, *Survival Amidst the Ashes,* 65.

57. Joe Brown (author interview and notes, 4 May 2001) stated that only the Marine cooks Fld. ck. Paul Ritthater, Pfc. Jay Combs, and Sgt. Walter Damon ever worked in the kitchen, and only then for short periods.
58. Hale, *Who's Who*, 44.
59. Giles, *Captive of the Rising Sun*, 79.
60. Dunn interviews, 8 March 2000, 24 October 2000.
61. Nichols interview.

CHAPTER 8. CIVILIANS IN KOBE

1. Thomas interview.
2. Private residence owned by Butterfield and Swire, a coastal steamship company that traveled ports from Japan to Singapore. Also known as the Blue House.
3. The house was one of hundreds of seamen's missions established by the British government in ports around the world. Ostensibly they were to serve stranded British mariners who missed ship departures or were stranded for any reason.
4. Thomas interview.
5. James O. Thomas, "Kogane Maru" (Mountain View, CA: n.p.), 101.
6. Gregg Diary, 13 June 1942.
7. Giles, *Captive of the Rising Sun*, 96–97: "Nurse Leona Jackson [upon her return] spent half a day with my family in Annapolis, providing them with details on camp life and on my health and well being." Giles states that nurses and [erroneously] Hellmers, with her daughter, departed in late March and [correctly] Griffith departed in May. Giles erroneously infers that Ambassador Grew was in this group. Grew was not interned in Zentsuji. He was detained in Tokyo and was transferred directly to the *Gripsholm* on 17 June 1942.
8. These were businessmen, families, and missionaries who had had legitimate reasons for being in Japanese-controlled areas.
9. Doris Sterner, *In and Out of Harm's Way* (Seattle: Peanut Butter Publishing, 1997), 131.
10. Among the guards, few were memorable. Guards were known by nicknames such as "Ozone" and the "Skull" (Matsuda-san). Others were simply referred to by name: Sakamoto-san and Hamaoka-san. Petty regulations controlled how clothes were to be stored, window shades drawn, and pieces of coal used for heat, and there were patently ridiculous rules regarding where and when men could move about within the compound.
11. The *Tatsuda Maru* was a separate exchange negotiated by the British and did not include any military personnel.
12. Mr. Champond was the Swiss consul at that time.
13. Gregg Diary.
14. The *Lisbon Maru*, after departing Hong Kong with 1,816 British POWs, was sunk by the American submarine *Grouper*. The Japanese shot and murdered men

trying to escape the slowly sinking ship: 846 men died and some 500 of the survivors were sent to Osaka and Kobe. More than 200 of these men died the first winter in Japan from starvation and dysentery. The seamen's mission became known as "Kobe House" to the new prisoners.

15. The first islands invaded in the Gilbert Island chain were Butaritari (Makin Atoll) and Betia (Tarawa Atoll). In three days of fighting, Maj. Gen. R. C. Smith, USA, captured Butaritari, announcing with a cryptic communication, "Makin taken." The news electrified America. A day later, Betio would fall to the Marines under Maj. Gen. H. M. Smith, USMC.

16. The internees were allowed to forage for firewood in the nearby hills, but one-third had to be given to the local police.

17. The Battle of the Philippine Sea became known in naval aviation lore as the "Great Marianas Turkey Shoot." During the invasion of Saipan on 20 June 1944, Task Force 58 sent 950 planes against a total of 550 Japanese land- and carrier-based planes. The Americans shot down 340 Japanese aircraft, losing only twenty-nine men in the conflict. Fifty more Japanese planes were destroyed on the ground. Two Japanese carriers, the *Taiho* and *Shikoku,* were sunk by submarines shortly after their planes were launched. One American battleship, the *South Dakota,* was damaged by a bomb.

18. Gregg Diary, 126.

19. Thomas, "Kogane Maru," 170.

CHAPTER 9. LIFE IN ZENTSUJI

1. Associated Press wire story, 17 January 1942.

2. These shortwave broadcasts generally began at 2:00 a.m., Pacific time.

3. Giles, *Captive of the Rising Sun,* 66.

4. Swiss minister Camille Gorgé notified Ambassador Grew on 9 December 1941 that Switzerland would immediately take charge of American interests. Complicating diplomacy, the Japanese selected Spain (a fascist government) to represent their interests in the United States.

5. P. Scott Corbett, *Quiet Passages: The Exchange of Civilians between the United States and Japan during the Second World War* (Kent, OH: Kent State University Press, 1987), 178–79. By the end of 1942, the Swiss became acceptable in most areas of Japanese occupation. The United States gave the Swiss a blank check to provide for the prisoners' and internees' needs wherever permitted. Other than Red Cross boxes, little assistance was given to the military captives. David C. Lowman, *Magic: The Untold Story of U.S. Intelligence and the Evacuation of Japanese Residents from the West Coast during World War II* (Provo, UT: Aetna Press, 2001), 91–95. Lowman was a former special assistant to the director of National Security Agency.

6. Giles, *Captive of the Rising Sun,* 89, states "in February"; Hale, *Who's Who,* 49, said he was informed in mid-February that half the men would work every day except Sunday.

7. After the first few months, pay to the officers increased, but the amount remains questionable. Reports of up to one hundred yen are recorded. One hundred sen equals one yen; one yen was considered equal to one American dollar.

8. Eads, *Survival Amidst the Ashes,* 70. In the normal confusion of postwar memories, Eads states the first party was 180 men. Normally the Japanese created work parties of 80 men. In interviews by the author, Nichols and Dunn agreed that the 150 figure is the most accurate.

9. An oversized hoe that would serve as both pickax and shovel. The laborer would pull the dirt toward himself, lift, and toss the dirt behind himself in one motion.

10. Iannarelli and Iannarelli, *Eighty Thieves,* 49.

11. Brown, *We Stole to Live,* 51. Other than being required to work in all temperatures, the labor on the mountain was not considered difficult. During rain or snow, the men were excused from work. During extreme freezing temperatures the workday was shortened. The guards on the mountain rarely beat on the prisoners.

12. The emperor was, in the minds of the Japanese, a direct descendant of the sun goddess. Homage was rendered by bowing toward the rising sun.

13. Shane interview, 14 September 2000.

14. Giles, *Captive of the Rising Sun,* 93. The shirt-like garment is a *hakama,* the light-weight coat is a *haori.*

15. Lt. (jg) Thomas Magee III, USNR, served in Guam as the island's communications intelligence officer (COMINT) and was fluent in Japanese. The Japanese never learned of his role in the interception of coded messages by their naval and Merchant Marine fleets, the primary purpose of the Libugon station. He was careful never to be seen reading a Japanese newspaper by the prison staff. Newspapers were prized, not just for news, but as extra toilet paper.

16. Shane interview, 14 September 2000.

17. Referring to actor John Wayne hitting the "bad guy" with a swinging, roundhouse punch to the jaw.

18. Barnett interview, 24 October 2000.

19. PhM1 Truman W. Keck, USN.

20. Shane interview, 14 September 2000.

21. Mrs. H. J. Van Peenen, "Touchstone from Zentsuji," *Retired Officer Magazine,* December 1986.

22. Lt. Cdr. H. J. Van Peenen, letter to Red Cross, 16 December 1945, Box 2130, RG 389, NARA.

23. Morgan interview. The Guamian wife of Chief O'Brien was a native of Japan. She was permitted to move to Japan after the surrender on Guam. She worked her

way to Zentsuji, where she secretly coordinated the purchase and smuggling of drugs and medical supplies into the camp.

24. Brown, *We Stole to Live,* 103.
25. Ibid., 111. Also GM3 David Allen, USN, who was keeper of the chickens and served as lookout.
26. PhM1 Abner Rowe, USN.
27. Iannarelli and Iannarelli, *Eighty Thieves,* 47.
28. Baggett interview, 4 May 2001. Baggett had won the famed Drake Relays championship in the spring of 1941, setting a record that would stand until 1958.

CHAPTER 10. LABOR AT ZENTSUJI
1. Brown, *We Stole to Live,* 70.
2. Pfc. Herbert Humphrey, USMC, author interview, 23 October 2000.
3. Pfc. Lawrence Budzynski, USMC, author interview, 22 October 2000.
4. RM1 Arthur Griffiths, USN.
5. Bruce Lee, *Marching Orders: The Untold Story of World War II* (New York: Crown, 1995), 104; Howarth, *Fighting Ships,* 307.
6. Baggett interview, 3 October 2000.
7. Comic strip character with "dashing looks."
8. Marks memoir, 104–12; Baggett interview, 3 October 2000.
9. Brown, author interview, stated "Red" Newton, also sent to a civilian prison, reported similar treatment and sightings of albino cockroaches.
10. Pfc. Howard Ross, USMC, author interview, May 4, 2001.
11. Brown, *We Stole to Live,* 66.
12. Ibid., 58, interview with Pfc. Martin Peak, USMC.
13. Ibid., 87, interview with Artis Jones.

CHAPTER 11. TRANSFER TO OSAKA
1. Giles, *Captive of the Rising Sun,* 105, states that men moved to Osaka on 8 June 1942 (Monday). Reed's contemporaneous diary noted the date of movement as 8 June, with the arrival at 7:00 a.m. on 9 June with 150 men. His memoir includes a complete listing of names, confirmed in the Ploke Diary.
2. In an article written by Cpl. Robert J. Lee, USMC, Lee erroneously states a train was taken to Osaka from the port of entry on Honshu. No support to this statement was given by the numerous POWs interviewed.
3. Formally known as Osaka Camp, Branch #1. Later used and designated as Ichioka Hospital. SCAP (Supreme Command, Allied Powers—General MacArthur's headquarters), also designated it "Undoro Mae."
4. Hale, *Who's Who,* 60.
5. Brown, *We Stole to Live,* 42, Hinkle interview.
6. 1 kilogram, 220 pounds, was the standard weight for sacks of grain. Grains were placed in tightly woven straw sacks called *kabasu.*

7. Lt (jg) Henry Williams, MC, USN, was rescued at Hirohata; Lt. (jg) James Eppley, MC, USNR, was rescued at Ohashi in Sendai.

8. James B. Darden III, *Guests of the Emperor: The Story of Dick Darden* (Clinton, NC: Greenhouse Press, 1990), 207.

9. Shane interview, 28 July 2001.

10. Mosher interview, 8 July 2000.

11. RM2 M. A. Windham, captured on Wake Island.

12. Epperson interview, 29 August 2000.

13. Settles interview.

14. Iannarelli and Iannarelli, *Eighty Thieves,* 78.

15. Reed memoir, 78-C5-4. The camp commandant at this time was Umeda.

CHAPTER 12. THE DOOLITTLE RAID

1. Giles, *Captive of the Rising Sun,* 98.

2. "Diet" is the Japanese name for their parliament.

3. Robert A. Fearey, "Might the Pacific War Have Been Avoided?" *Japan Journal,* 1992.

4. Dunn interview, 8 March 2000.

5. Article in *U.S. Navy Medicine,* July 1998.

6. Gregg to Mari and David, 30 August 1985, CSUZ86056-A, Diaries and Memoirs of Charles Gregg, Hoover Institution.

7. Thomas, "Trapped with the Enemy," 57.

8. Hale, *Who's Who,* 59.

9. Ibid.

10. Mosher interview, 8 July 2000.

11. U.S. Army Air Forces, *Mission Accomplished: Interrogation of Japanese Industrial, Military and Civil Leaders of World War II* (Washington, DC: Government Printing Office, 1946), interview with Captain Y. Watanabe, CIC of Second Fleet, Imperial Japanese Navy, at Midway, 15 October 1945.

12. Newspapers normally available in camp were the *Osaka Mainichi* and the *Tokyo Nichi-Nichi-Shimbun.* Magazines included the *Japan Times Weekly,* a weekly newsmagazine, *Contemporary Japan* (monthly), and *Sakura* (monthly), a picture magazine similar to *Life.* By reading between the lines, one could ascertain the change in Japanese military fortunes.

13. This was to be the rationalization for executing hundreds of aviators and crewmen shot down over Japanese territory, especially over Japan proper. So bitter were the Japanese that even after the emperor announced unconditional surrender in August 1945, many fliers were dragged from their prison cells and executed.

14. Eight crewmen of one plane were captured in China by the Japanese after they were betrayed. All were tried and convicted in Shanghai of committing "a cruel and unjust act against Japan." Three crewmen, tied to a low cross in a kneeling

position, were executed by a firing squad. The remaining five, their death sentences commuted to life imprisonment by War Minister Tojo, were isolated in a Shanghai jail. Of these one was deliberately starved to death by the Japanese.

15. Of the 1,732 B-29 crewmen lost over Japanese territory, 362 were returned. By comparison, no other nation, including Nazi Germany, tried or executed any aviators for actions committed during their missions. The Japanese followed a pattern of bombing cities and innocent civilians in every theater of the Pacific war. Kenneth Werrell, *Blankets of Fire* (Washington, DC: Smithsonian Institution Press, 1996), 238.

16. During the Doolittle raid, a bomb severely damaged the carrier *Ryuhu* in a dry dock in Yokusuka while it was undergoing conversion from the former submarine depot ship *Taigei*.

17. Box 218, RG 238, NARA. The directive was not a military order but a clarification by the vice minister of war in response to a query from the commanding general of POW camps, headquartered on Taiwan. The clarification was circulated to all POW camp commandants throughout Japanese-occupied territory, intercepted by British intelligence, and broadcast on the BBC Far East shortwave radio network in hopes that some POWs with clandestine radios would hear it and take precautions. Some did. See Linda Goetz Holmes, *Unjust Enrichment: American POWs under the Rising Sun* (Old Saybrook, CT: Konecky & Konecky, 2008), chap. 12, for a full discussion of this directive and the one that preceded it.

CHAPTER 13. HIROHATA #1

1. Located at Nitta Mura (Nitta village) in central Osaka.

2. Anthony Iannarelli, affidavit, Box 2130, RG 289, NARA.

3. Hale, *Who's Who,* 73.

4. Sgt. Earl B. Ercanbrack, affidavit, 10 September 1945, Box 2130, RG 359, NARA: two Australians and seventy-eight Americans.

5. Reed memoir, 86-C6-2.

6. The spelling of these company names varies, but phonetic alternates are Kumigumi and Tomi Shima. WT1 Jack Leininger, affidavit, Box 2130, RG 389, NARA (hereafter cited as Leininger affidavit).

7. Reed memoir, 140-C11-6; Raymond memoir calls the yard company Tabata as the primary detail site for loading slag and rail cars. He offers two spelling versions: Okove and Okoue for the second company.

8. PhM3 Leroy Bowman, author interviews, 10 April and 20 April 2000.

9. The Ercanbrack affidavit stated that the Japanese medic, Tsujino, met with an accident after liberation: "[I do not know] if he survived, but I doubt if he did." In File 3, Box 1321, RG 331 is a list of Japanese staff at Osaka prisons. In fact, the medic was beaten to death, but this author pledged not to reveal the name of the POW who killed him.

10. Iannarelli and Iannarelli, *Eighty Thieves,* 88; Hale, *Who's Who,* 100; File 3, Box 1321, RG 331, NARA.
11. PhM3 Richard Salisbury, USN.
12. Joe "Fingers" Brown, *Zentsuji in Kansas* (Marble Hill, MO: Stewart Publishing, 1986), 40.
13. Leininger affidavit.
14. Shane interview, 3 October 2000.
15. Chuck interview, 27 June 2001; Iannarelli and Iannarelli, *Eighty Thieves,* 81.
16. Reed memoir, 150-C12-6.
17. Iannarelli and Iannarelli, *Eighty Thieves,* 62.
18. Ibid., 137–39.
19. Reed memoir, 94-C70.
20. Ibid.
21. Settles interview.
22. F1 Arthur Dahlstedt, USN.
23. Bowman interview, 10 April 2000.
24. Leininger affidavit. Leininger states, "ETO beat me with a baseball bat across the back of my legs and my back. He hit me approximately eight times with it as hard as he could swing the bat, but this being in the nude in the winter time, there was snow on the ground." Also, Shane interview, 3 February 2000.
25. Iannarelli and Iannarelli, *Eighty Thieves,* 109–11.
26. Bowman interview, 10 April 2000.
27. Red Cross complaint statistics, File 1, SCAP Legal Section, RG 331, NARA. The Red Cross official was Max Pestalozzi, who headed the Swiss Red Cross delegation following the death of Pavaracini in December 1943. After the surrender, it was discovered that Pestalozzi had hoarded, for his own use, more than a hundred boxes of Red Cross food designated for POWs. Called "spineless" by his staff, he had arranged delivery of one hundred other boxes to numerous friends in the Japanese military. As a diplomat, he was simply dismissed from service.
28. Ercanbrack affidavit regarding the Red Cross distribution to Hirohata: one box each, November 1942; one-fifth box each, December 1942; one box each, November 1943; thirty-two boxes for 487 men, 25 December 1943; three boxes each, November 1944 (issued piecemeal from November 1944 to May 1945). Red Cross boxes were delivered to Japan in quantities that would allow one five-pound box per month per prisoner.

CHAPTER 14. THE FIRST CHRISTMAS IN JAPAN

1. Pilot Officer Peter N. Kenny, RAF.
2. Marks memoir, 143–44. The singing was organized by Major Spicer, and members included Wood, Bateman, Hoffman, Vandergrift, Gallagher, Loft, Page, and Hilton.

CHAPTER 15. THE MEN OF BATAAN AND CORREGIDOR ARRIVE

1. The attack on Pearl Harbor occurred on 8 December local time.
2. *The Papers of Dwight David Eisenhower* (Baltimore: Johns Hopkins University Press, 1970), 1:22, 35–37. MacArthur was specifically instructed to inform his troops that "streams of planes" and "armadas of ships" were headed to him. There is no doubt that he was deliberately misinformed. The troops under MacArthur's command simply assumed "Mac" lied to deceive them.
3. Tojo became prime minister in October 1941, having previously served as war minister and, in that capacity, supervised the plans for the attack on Pearl Harbor.
4. An excellent overview of the Japanese behavior toward conquered nations is found in the seminal works of Iris Chang, *The Rape of Nanking: The Forgotten Holocaust of World War II* (New York: Penguin, 1998); David Bergamini, *Japan's Imperial Conspiracy,* vol. 1, *How Emperor Hirohito Led Japan into War against the West* (New York: William Morrow, 1971); and Sterling Seagrave and Peggy Seagrave, *The Yamato Dynasty: The Secret History of Japan's Imperial Family* (New York: Broadway Books, 1999). An additional factor is that the Japanese suffered 10,000 casualties taking Bataan, and some admit that they took it out on the Americans. POWs of other nationalities have remarked that the Japanese were especially harsh on the Americans.
5. Holmes, *Unjust Enrichment,* 23–25. Japanese commanders were instructed not to send a "POW of mixed blood whose appearance might be mistaken for Orientals."
6. Memoir of Donald Versaw, edited by Kinue Tokudome. Originally written in Japanese for the March 2004 issue of *Ronza.*

CHAPTER 16. HIROHATA #2

1. 1st Lt. Kohkichi Asakawa, list of Japanese staff, Osaka prisons, File 3, Box 1321, Legal Section, SCAP, RG 331, NARA.
2. Van Waterford, *Prisoners of the Japanese in World War II* (Jefferson, NC: McFarland, 1994), 199, designates the camp as POW 87. Confusion existed before the surrender regarding Hirohata 2, The first official notice of the camp came from the International Red Cross Committee via cable on 24 March 1943, seven months before the occupancy (Box 2130, RG 389, NARA). The report stated that Hirohata 2 is near Himeji, a city with a population of 200,000: "Camp is 8k away, opened 10 Dec. 1942 [actual opening 15 September 1943] and described as follows: 'Total area 1530 square meter [.378 acre], building area 930 square meters [.2298 acre]. Six barracks of wooden frame with mud and plaster. Ventilation good, heating still available from 5 to 7 p.m. Taps, bath with water pumped from well. Six latrine[s]. [Actually two with 36 total holes.] Canteen in this camp is well supplied and food for prisoners here is more abundant than in other camps. Kitchen has 6 cauldrons and food is cooked by one Navy cook and three assistants. . . . Prisoners have hikes in country on Sundays. . . . Two slight

work accidents and no deaths.'" Further confusion of camp designations is made by additional notations by CINCPAC communications on 1 February 1945 and 15 June 1945 wherein the names of Harima, Himeji, "O" Camp, and Osaka Divisional Camps 26 and 27 were interchanged in usage and coordinates. The Red Cross report of 21 February 1944 listed seven camps in the Osaka vicinity: Chikku, Sakurajima, Amagasaki, Kobe, Kawasaki, Hirohata, and Harima. C. A. Kengelbacher, the Red Cross representative, stated most prisoners were from the ill-fated *Lisbon Maru*; 150 of the 2,650 who had landed in January 1943 had already died. He further stated he believed other camps in Osaka were hidden from his three-day visit.

3. Gregory Michno, *Death on the Hellships: Prisoners at Sea in the Pacific War* (Annapolis: Naval Institute Press, 2001), 313; James Rand, *Bataan Diary* (n.p.: self-published, 1984), 34, states he was on the *Yasama Maru*.

4. Epperson interview, 19 August 2000.

5. File 3, Box 1321, RG 331. These three men were omitted from the prison camp staff lists provided by the Japanese 15 August 1945.

6. Chuck interview, 7 February 2000.

7. Iannarelli and Iannarelli, *Eighty Thieves*, 124, attribute death to an infected boil. (Chuck, in an author interview, stated Ercanbrack donated a pint of blood in a futile effort to save Bustamente.) The medical term for "give-up-itis" is inanition.

8. Ercanbrack affidavit. The death rate for Hirohata was 2.9 percent. Of the 487 men, 14 died in camp and 2 in the Kobe hospital. One of the 14, Pvt. Walter Westbrook, died from a job-site accident.

9. Reed memoir, 150-C12-6; Iannarelli, and Iannarelli, *Eighty Thieves*, 146–47; one other man, Neville Lindley, lost his ability to remember anything for more than a few seconds.

10. S3 Frederick Wells, USN.

11. Iannarelli and Iannarelli, *Eighty Thieves*, 93.

12. Bowman interview, 14 April 2000.

13. Pvt. Russell Dalrymple, USMC; Pfc. John Rucker, USMC.

14. Hale, *Who's Who*, 67.

15. Nichols interview, 18 February 2000.

16. Hale, *Who's Who*, 115.

17. When the editor took these photos to a photo shop in New York City, the staff, handing back the prints, asked, "Are these photos from Nazi concentration camps?" The editor answered, "No, they are from Japanese prison camps." "What?" The astounded staff people said, "The Japanese did this too?"

CHAPTER 17. TANAGAWA

1. *Bunsho*, in this context, means "labor camp." Tanagawa was Osaka Branch #14 and designated as near the Wakayama Railway Station. The Japanese company employing the POWs was Sumitomo Metal. Box 1321, RG 331, NARA: the first camp commandants were 2nd Lt. Toshitiro Have (22 November 1942–8 December 1942) and 1st Lt. Kosaku Hazama (1 January 1943–19 August 1943). Evidence of the camp was deliberately obliterated by the Japanese after the surrender.

2. Sterling Warren, author interview, 10 July 2003: "After we left Tanagawa, we stopped at Umeda (Osaka) on the way to Zentsuji. I asked another POW if he had seen my close friend and fellow Academy classmate, Fred Yeager [West Point, class of 1940]. The man stared at me and said, 'I'm Yeager.' We were so bedraggled we couldn't recognize each other."

3. Michno, *Death on the Hellships,* 312. The hellship *Nagato Maru* departed Manila on 7 November 1942, carrying 1,600 POWs. Twenty men perished during the voyage to Moji, the ship arriving 23 November 1942.

4. Twenty-seven officers and forty-seven enlisted men died in this camp before 1 June 1943, seventy-four out of two hundred prisoners. An unknown number were sent to the Ichioka "hospital" in order to reduce the camp death toll.

5. They departed 16 May 1943, according to the Meyers Diary; Stephen Marek, *Laughter in Hell* (Caldwell, ID: Caxton, 1954), 19.

CHAPTER 18. CHIKKO

1. Box 1321, RG 331, NARA. Much confusion was generated by the initial summary of camps developed by the OSS and State Department when listing camps before the Japanese surrendered. In the report, the stadium was called "hoin-cho" and no camp was called "Chikko." Likewise, the location of Rokuroshi was shown as being inside the burned out areas of Hiroshima, with the result that no search was done for almost two weeks. The headquarters camp was known by most prisoners as Chikko. The confusion was further exacerbated as the list submitted by the Japanese did not include any camps that had burned down, were evacuated, or were (as the Japanese knew) scenes of extreme prisoner abuse, such as the Ofuna interrogation camp.

2. The *Lisbon Maru*, with 1,816 on board, departed from Hong Kong on 27 September 1942 and was torpedoed three days later, 30 September, by the USS *Grouper*. The prisoners were forced into the holds, which were then secured. The Japanese intended for them to drown. After two days, as the ship slid under the water, the men staged a breakout, and 974 survived by swimming to shore near the Sing Pan Islands. Most of the survivors eventually arrived in Japan on the *Shinsei Maru*. It is known that 429 were sent to Chikko and almost 500 sent to Kobe.

3. On 13 March 1945, 301 B-29s bombed Osaka, bombing only two blocks away from the POW camps and one block from the waterfront. Kobe was bombed on 17 March 1945 for the first time. Osaka was bombed again on 2 June by 458 B-29s, on 8 June by 409 planes, and on 16 June by 444 B-29s. For all practical purposes, the city became nonfunctional. Robert Haney, *Caged Dragon: An American POW in WWII Japan* (Ann Arbor, MI: Sabre Press, 1991), 132.
4. Mosher interview, 3 July 2001.

CHAPTER 19. OSAKA-UMEDA

1. Marek, *Laughter in Hell,* 34. Umeda Bunsho supplied workers to sixteen work sites. In addition to the docks, the major locations were Katamachi, Saskurajima, Ajigawa, Minotomachi, and Imania. Only the docks were worked every day.
2. Affidavit of Capt. Samuel Goldblith, USA, Box 2130, RG 389, NARA.
3. Lieutenant Slane was a Naval Intelligence officer captured on Guam.
4. In September 1946, Tarnowski, captured on Corregidor, was retroactively appointed warrant officer at 10:00 a.m.—as of 1942. By 11:00 he had advanced to ensign and lieutenant (jg), as of 1943 and 1945 respectively. He retired with the rank of commander in 1965.
5. Marek, *Laughter in Hell,* 62. McMurry was with the USMC. He was killed when he stepped from behind one train into the path of an electric train passing the Umeda docks.
6. Prisoners nicknamed him "Canary" and "Songbird" for his squeaky voice.
7. Marek, *Laughter in Hell,* 146.

CHAPTER 20. THIRTY-SEVEN MONTHS IN HELL

1. Underwood neglected to mention a few Aleutian Islands in the Alaska territory.
2. Palomo, *Island in Agony,* 123–24. Jalaguac was a few miles north of the U.S. Navy Air Base and the northern field became Andersen Air Force Base. The base on Orote was Agana Airport and is now abandoned.
3. Joseph Ada and his three sons were forced, under guard, to make their high-quality coconut oil soap exclusively for the Japanese. In spite of the danger of being caught and punished, Ada always managed to sneak some soap to his friends and family.
4. Palomo, *Island in Agony,* 161.
5. Lee, *Marching Orders,* 182, cites SRS (Secret Radio Summary) 1156. From a decryption of the Japanese Purple (diplomatic) code messages, 22 December 1943, analysts pieced together various intercepts that revealed the necessity for rice imports to continue the war. This confirmed the value of submarine efforts to intercept and sink ships coming from the conquered areas. Japan's rice surpluses could sustain them for only one year without the imports. The rice crop of Korea, accounting for 10 percent of Japan's needs, had failed because of a drought. Baron

Oshima, Japan's ambassador to Germany, confirmed the problems by stating, "Unfortunately, present ship losses offset production, but we are firmly confident that by next March, at the latest, we can overcome this *crisis* [emphasis added] and that ship construction will begin to exceed ship losses."

6. Philip Crowl, *Campaign in the Marianas* (self-published, 1994), 26. These were fighters from Adm. Marc Mitscher's Task Force 58. Over the next month, numerous photographic missions were flown from Eniwetok to determine Japanese strengths and strongholds.

7. Palomo, *Island in Agony*, 162, Pedro Dumanal told a bus driver that the Americans would be returning soon. For this remark, Dumanal was caught and murdered, and seven of his family members were executed.

8. Such actions were very ordinary for Japanese soldiers. Killing natives amounted to no more than an act of washing one's hands. In a diary of a Japanese soldier killed at Bagunbayan, Luzon, he casually wrote of his company, "12 Feb. we killed 100 men and returned at midnight." The next day he wrote, "For security reasons, all inhabitants of the town [presumably Anilao] and all their possessions were confiscated." More than four hundred died in this massacre. Further, he wrote that, under orders to "punish" the natives, the company killed thousands more. On 17 March 1945, he casually noted, "Caught and killed 4 natives (three children and their mother)." Box 2700, RG 486, NARA.

9. Palomo, *Island in Agony*, 175. Pangelinan hid Tweed in the latter part of 1942.

10 Ibid., 179–82.

11. Ibid., 183–84.

12. Ibid., 185–86.

13. Epperson interview, 19 August 2000.

CHAPTER 21. ROKUROSHI

1. Conflicting numbers exist, but Unruh states that 334 officers were present when liberated (Marks memoir, 182, states that 370 men departed Zentsuji) on 23 June 1945 (Colonel Miller says 24 June [341]). All were American officers except for two warrant officers and one Army major. The actual number departing was 335, and 1 officer died at Rokuroshi. Fifty Australian officers were moved earlier to the Sendai Command 7B Detachment, a mine near Odate near the northern tip of Honshu (Gavan Daws, *Prisoners of the Japanese* [New York: William Morrow, 1995], 328). Forty-five of these Australians were later rescued at Hakodate #4. The British officers were rescued at Mitsushima. (Van Peenen states that only 10 died at Zentsuji and Rokuroshi. During the last fifteen months, the camp had 760 men, of whom 640 were officers of various nations.)

2. Most likely the port city of Nagasaki.

3. Van Peenen, "Touchstone from Zentsuji."

4. Lt. Fred Garrett, USAAF.

5. Unruh affidavit. The camp was located on the slopes of Mount Haku (Haku-yama), now part of the Hakusan National Park. Having smuggled along a map under his shirt, 2nd Lt. Russ Swearingen, USA, noted their location was twenty-five miles east of Fukui.

6. The Unruh affidavit stated, "The thirty POWs, either enlisted men or civilians from Wake or Guam, several Dutch and British, were in the camp 30 to 60 days [earlier]." The Spicer affidavit lists the total camp population at 365, including 266 Army, 60 Navy, 19 Marines, 10 civilians, 5 British, and 5 Australian. No breakdown of rank was noted.

7. Unruh affidavit; 2nd Lt. Samuel Dillard and 2nd Lt. Travis Smith (both USA) were transferred to Osaka Headquarters Camp for escape attempt.

CHAPTER 22. PATHWAYS TO HELL

1. Lee, *Marching Orders,* 121, 182; SRS Summary 1156 (see chap. 20, n. 5).

2. Hale, *Who's Who,* 87. See also Holmes, *Unjust Enrichment,* chap. 11, "Double-Crossed Relief," for a detailed explanation of how the Japanese government thwarted its agreement with the Swiss Bank to distribute relief funds donated by the U.S., UK, and Dutch treasuries.

3. The hypothesis of high-level winds was first proposed by Japanese meteorologist Wasaburo Ooishi in the early 1920s. The Japanese, relying on these jet streams, sent balloons over the Pacific in hopes of creating fires of disruption along our West Coast. A number did cause damage, but a tight seal of security prevented the Japanese from ever determining their effectiveness. The subject was ignored until high-altitude bombers encountered these jet streams over Europe on some B-17 raids. The jet streams were not considered a problem after the first few missions. The pilots merely changed turning points to take advantage of the speed to effect a faster escape or shorter time to target.

4. Unlike the mix of phosphorus and napalm bombs used against Dresden, Germany, the incendiaries used in Japan were all made using the newly developed napalm, a jellied gasoline that sprayed flame over a large area. Each plane carried from eighteen to twenty-eight 400-pound clusters, each cluster containing thirty-eight incendiary bombs. In use the bombs hit every fifty feet.

5. Thomas, "Trapped with the Enemy," 182–87. Thomas and other prisoners left the compound during the raid as the guards had fled. From the top of a nearby hill, they witnessed the ramming of the B-29s directly overhead at less than two thousand feet. Two men parachuted and survived. Both were captured and executed within a few days. One man, Robert Nelson, was brought into the camp temporarily. As he departed, he gave a joyous wave and flashed the "OK" sign with his hand. The prisoners received permission to locate and bury the bodies

from the plane. Within two weeks, all the remains were recovered and buried in carefully marked and mapped graves. Dog tags and other personal items were stored and turned over to rescue personnel at the end of the war.

6. Samuel Eliot Morison, *Victory in the Pacific: 1945* (New York: Little, Brown, 1960), 14:24. The first air raids over Japan proper, as part of the offensive against Iwo Jima, were carrier planes from the USS *Enterprise* and USS *Saratoga*.

7. The OSS is the Office of Strategic Services.

8. As a direct result of this troop withdrawal by the Japanese, the USSR, after declaring war against Japan on 8 August 1945, was able to sweep through Manchuria and the northern part of Korea with almost no resistance.

9. Yayoe Smythe, author interview, 10 September 2008.

10. Shortly after surrender, on 20 August 1945, all camp commanders were ordered to destroy all records of "orders to kill." Actual copies of the directive were found on Taiwan and are now at Box 2100, RG 331, NARA. For a detailed explanation of the origin and recovery of this directive, see Holmes, *Unjust Enrichment,* chap. 12.

11. File 2015, Box 2911, RG 238, NARA, designated as Document 2710, marked Exhibit O in Document 2687. In Box 2012, RG 238, is a prior request (31 July 1944) asking for suggestions of methods to dispose of all prisoners and internees.

12. On 14 December 1944, the Japanese murdered some 157 Marines on Palawan Island because the commandant assumed General MacArthur was about to invade the island (he wasn't). The men were herded into an air-raid shelter, then gasoline was poured into the entrance and ignited. Eleven men escaped and survived to tell the story.

CHAPTER 23. THE END NEARS

1. Werrell, *Blankets of Fire,* 254.

2. The fifty Australian officers were moved to Sendai Branch 7B, a mine near Odate near the northwestern tip of Honshu, and were later moved to Hokkaido, where they were rescued. Most British were rescued at Mitsushima.

3. Letter from Kevin Menzies, citing his father's notes, July 2001, and confirmed by C. D. Barnett, 9 August 2001.

4. Reed memoir, 141-C11-7. Italy surrendered 8 September 1943, but no date is known for the capture of the Italian sailors at Kobe.

5. Hale, *Who's Who,* 123.

6. Bowman interview, 27 June 2000; Iannarelli and Iannarelli, *Eighty Thieves,* 130; and Leininger affidavit. The Italian consul's actions were reported to General MacArthur's headquarters by Anthony Iannarelli after the surrender of the Japanese.

7. Reed memoir, 136-C11-2.

8. Stephen Raymond, unpublished draft memoir, October 2002.

9. Hale to mother, 13 September 1945, Hale Collection, Hoover Institution.

10. The raid consisted of 274 planes, all but five bombing Osaka. At least one plane was lost in the raid, crashing in the northern edge of Osaka. All men on board perished.

11. John Kidd, author interview, 25 July 2000. The camp population was 604 men at that time. The date of the raid was 1 June 1945; Twentieth Air Force History states 10 of the 458 bombers were lost, along with 27 P51 escort fighters, almost all lost to poor navigation and weather. Two more major raids, on 7 and 26 June, with 409 and 510 B-29s, respectively, made Osaka uninhabitable.

12. Toyama is a small port about 270 miles northeast of Osaka on the south end of Toyama Bay. In July, B-29s dropped mines into a nearby river that floated into the harbor, destroying numerous Japanese ships. Fortunately, the prisoners were working at the piers. The actual camp for Mosher was Nagoya POW Branch Camp 10, Fushiki (Nomachi), located near the city of Toyama.

13. Iannarelli and Iannarelli, *Eighty Thieves,* 168–69; Twentieth Air Force History.

14. Gregg Diary, 134.

15. Thomas interview.

CHAPTER 24. THE END COMES

1. Stephen Kammerich, author interview, 25 February 2001.

2. Iannarelli and Iannarelli, *Eighty Thieves,* 170.

3. Settles interview.

4. Reed memoir, 153-C12-9. Either WO A. P. Daul or WO R. C. Hahn, USN.

5. Eric Hammel, *Air War Pacific Chronology* (Pacifica, CA: Pacifica Press, 1988); Mission 277 delivered a mixed load of incendiaries and high explosives.

6. Box 1321, RG 331, NARA. The list prepared for MacArthur by the intelligence services placed Rokuroshi at the site of the Tsumori Detachment 18-D in Osaka. A second listing placed it in Hiroshima.

7. Giles, *Captive of the Rising Sun,* 156–57. Cdr. Wilson Harrington, USN, had hidden the full-sized flag inside his rice pillow. It had passed through numerous hands before being given to him by a British soldier. Raising the flag were Maj. Donald Spicer, USMC, Lt. Cmdr. W. Jackson Galbraith, USN, and Capt. Jack K. Boyer, USA.

8. Thomas interview.

CHAPTER 25. OPERATION RAMP

1. Exhibit J, Document 2687, Orders from Chief of Prisoner of War Camps, Tokyo, 15 August 1945, War Crimes Record Group, Box 2011, RG 238, NARA: "Personnel who mistreated prisoners of war and internees or who are held in extremely bad sentiment by them are permitted to take care of it by immediately transferring or by fleeing without trace. Moreover, documents which would be

unfavorable to us in the hands of the enemy are to be treated in the same way as secret documents and destroyed when finished with."

2. The Japanese supplied a list purported to include all prisoner camps in Japan. No list supplied by the Japanese included Rokuroshi or the Shanghai prison holding the remaining Doolittle fliers. Of particular note, camps that had been evacuated or recorded major atrocities, for example, Sado Island, were never listed in any Japanese report. John D. DeBergh, Capt., U.S. Infantry, investigative report, Box 12, RG 407, NARA (hereafter cited as DeBergh report), records details regarding the discovery of just one of the Chinese slave camps near Hanaoka. In just a few months, 337 of the 987 prisoners had perished from abuse and starvation.

3. Thomas interview.

4. Werrell, *Blankets of Fire*, 222. The crew, but not the plane, was recovered. Less than two years later, the USSR produced identical planes for its long-range missions.

5. In the Ohashi camp area, the local Japanese Kempeitai painted PW on a series of buildings and simply looted all the dropped supplies. DeBergh report.

6. Dunn interview, 8 March 2000.

7. Cpl. Clint Crichton, USMC.

8. Hosotani was tried as a war criminal, convicted, and sentenced to twenty years. He was released after the peace treaty was signed in 1952. The camp doctor, Saito, also known as Dr. Sade, was tried, convicted, and hanged.

9. Joe "Fingers" Brown interview of Newton, May 1995.

10. The U.S. flag was made by Sgt. Elwin Bigelow, USMC, 4th Marines, and is now on display at the Marine Corps Recruiting Center in San Diego. The flag was retained by Lt. Col. Franklin Fliniau, USMC, and presented to the Marine Corps Museum in San Diego.

11. Dunn interview, 24 October 2000.

CHAPTER 26. OPERATION MAGIC CARPET

1. Operation "Magic Carpet," USMC History, Appendix A: 9,061 left for United States from Nagasaki (685 on stretchers) and 2,575 left from Wakayama, a port thirty miles south of Osaka. The balance of men were flown directly to Guam, mostly from Atsugi Airfield near Tokyo.

2. Anthony Iannarelli, author interview, 20 October 2000.

3. Letter from Irene Jones Beckwith, FEPOW News, Peverell, England, 1985.

4. Van Peenen, "Touchstone from Zentsuji."

AFTERWORD

1. Message from Robert J. Hanyok to the editor, 13 November 2011.

2. Joseph Della Malva, interview with the editor, 25 February 2000.

3. P. Scott Corbett, *Quiet Passages* (Kent, OH: Kent State University Press, 1987), 6.

4. Cited in the *New York Times*, 9 December 1999, in a story written by correspondent Howard W. French.

5. In File 383.7, p. 7, U.S. Army Military History Center, Carlisle, PA.

6. Robert Guest, *Electronic Telegraph*, 15 August 1995.

7. Norimitsu Onishi, article in the *New York Times*, 11 December 2003.

ADDENDUM

1. Thomas, "Trapped with the Enemy."

BIBLIOGRAPHY

ARCHIVES

Hoover Institution Library and Archives. Stanford University, Stanford, CA.
    Diaries and Memoirs of Charles Gregg
    Hale Collection
    O'Guinn Collection
    Roger Mansell Collection
Modern Military Records, National Archives and Records Administration, College
    Park, MD
    RG 153, Office of the Judge Advocate General
    RG 154, War Finance Corporation
    RG 155, Wage and Hour Division
    RG 156, Office of the Chief of Ordnance
    RG 157, Maritime Labor Board
    RG 226, Office of Strategic Services (OSS)
    RG 238, National Archives Collection of World War II War Crimes
    Records (International Military Tribunal of the Far East)
    RG 289, Naval Intelligence Command
    RG 331, Allied Operational and Occupation Headquarters, World War II
    RG 359, Office of Service and Technology Policy
    RG 389, Office of the Provost Marshal General
    RG 407, Office of the Adjutant General
    RG 486, Trade and Development Program
U.S. Army Center for Military History, Fort McNair, Washington, DC
    Central Pacific Operational Record, vol. 1
U.S. Army Military History Center, Carlisle, PA
    File 383.7, Box 35-C1-1 and Box 78-C5-4
U.S. Marine Corps Historical Archives, Arlington, VA
    File 1 L, Appendix A, USMC History
U.S. Naval Historical Museum, Washington, DC
    McMillin Report
    U.S. Navy Medicine, vol. 70
    Meyers Diary

BOOKS

Bergamini, David. *Japan's Imperial Conspiracy.* Vol. 1. New York: William Morrow, 1971.

Brown, Joe, comp. *Zentsuji in Kansas: Stories from the POW Reunions.* Marble Hill, MO: Stewart Publishing, 1986.

Brown, Joseph R. *We Stole to Live.* Cape Girardeau, MO: Missourian Litho & Printing, 1982.

Chang, Iris. *The Rape of Nanking: The Forgotten Holocaust of World War II.* New York: Penguin, 1998.

Corbett, P. Scott. *Quiet Passages: The Exchange of Civilians between the United States and Japan during the Second World War.* Kent, OH: Kent State University Press, 1987.

Crowl, Philip. *Campaign in the Marianas.* Kent, OH: Self-published, 1994.

Darden, James B., III. *Guests of the Emperor: The Story of Dick Darden.* Clinton, NC: Greenhouse Press, 1990.

Daws, Gavan. *Prisoners of the Japanese.* New York: William Morrow, 1995.

Eads, Lyle W. *Survival amidst the Ashes.* New York: Carleton Press, 1978.

Giles, Donald T. *Captive of the Rising Sun: The POW Memoirs of Rear Admiral Donald T. Giles.* Annapolis: Naval Institute Press, 1994.

Hale, Edward. *Who's Who in Chamorro History.* Vol. 1. Agana, Guam: Political Status Education Coordinating Commission, 1995.

Hale, Edward E., and Helen H. Gordon. *First Captured, Last Freed: Memoirs of a POW in World War II, Guam and Japan.* Santa Barbara, CA: Grizzly Bear Press, 1995.

Haney, Robert. *Caged Dragons: An American POW in WWII Japan.* Ann Arbor, MI: Sabre Press, 1991.

Holmes, Linda Goetz. *Unjust Enrichment: American POWs under the Rising Sun.* Old Saybrook, CT: Konecky & Konecky, 2008.

Howard, Chris Perez. *Mariquita: A Tragedy of Guam.* Suva, Fiji: Institute of Pacific Studies, University of the South Pacific,1986.

Howarth, Stephen. *The Fighting Ships of the Rising Sun: The Drama of the Imperial Japanese Navy, 1895–1945.* New York: Atheneum, 1983.

Iannarelli, Anthony, Sr., and John G. Iannarelli. *The Eighty Thieves: American POWs in World War II Japan.* San Diego: Patriot Press, 1991.

Kerr, E. Bartlett. *Surrender and Survival: The Experience of American POWs in the Pacific, 1941–1945.* New York: William Morrow, 1985.

Kinney, John, with James M. McCaffrey. *Wake Island Pilot: A World War II Memoir.* Washington, DC: Brassey's, 1995.

Layton, Rear Adm. Edwin T., and Capt. Roger Pineau, with John Costello. *And I Was There.* New York: William Morrow, 1985.

Lea, Homer. *The Valor of Ignorance.* 1906. Reprint, New York: Harper & Brothers, 1942.

Lee, Bruce. *Marching Orders: The Untold Story of World War II.* New York: Crown, 1995.

Lowman, David. *Magic: The Untold Story of U.S. Intelligence and the Evacuation of Japanese Residents from the West Coast during World War II.* Provo, UT: Aetna Press, 2001.

Marek, Stephen. *Laughter in Hell.* Caldwell, ID: Caxton, 1954.

McQuarrie, Peter. *Conflict in Kuribata: A History of the Second World War.* Wellington, NZ: War History Branch, Department of Internal Affairs, 1952.

Michno, Gregory. *Death on the Hellships: Prisoners at Sea in the Pacific War.* Annapolis: Naval Institute Press, 2001.

Morison, Samuel Eliot. *Victory in the Pacific: 1945.* Vol. 14. 1960. Reprint, n.p.: Book Sales, 2001.

Nelson, Evelyn, and Frederick Nelson. *Island of Guam: Description and History from a 1934 Perspective.* Washington, DC: Ana Publishing, 1992.

Palomo, Tony. *An Island in Agony.* N.p.: Self-published, 1984.

Rand, James. *Bataan Diary.* N.p.: Self-published, 1984.

Schultz, Duane. *Wake Island: The Heroic Gallant Fight.* New York: St. Martin's Press, 1978.

Seagrave, Sterling, and Peggy Seagrave. *The Yamato Dynasty: The Secret History of Japan's Imperial Family.* New York: Broadway Books, 1999.

Stinnett, Robert. *Day of Deceit: The Truth about FDR and Pearl Harbor.* New York: Free Press, 2000.

U.S. Army Air Forces. *Mission Accomplished: Interrogations of Japanese Industrial, Military, and Civil Leaders of World War II.* Washington, DC: Government Printing Office, 1946.

Waterford, Van. *Prisoners of the Japanese in World War II.* Jefferson, NC: McFarland, 1994.

Werrell, Kenneth. *Blankets of Fire.* Washington, DC: Smithsonian Institution Press, 1996.

NEWSPAPERS AND PERIODICALS

Contemporary Japan
Japan Times & Advisor
Japan Weekly
Los Angeles Herald-Express
New York Times
Retired Officers Magazine
Sakura
U.S. Navy Medicine

MEMOIRS AND DIARIES

Gregg, Charles. Diaries and Memoirs. Hoover Institution Library and Archives. Stanford University, Stanford, CA.

O'Guinn Collection. Hoover Institution Library and Archives. Stanford University, Stanford, CA.

Reed, Reginald. Diary. 1972. Roger Mansell Collection. Hoover Institution Library and Archives. Stanford University, Stanford, CA.

UNPUBLISHED MANUSCRIPTS

Beardsley [first name unknown]. Memoir. Roger Mansell Collection. Hoover Institution Library and Archives. Stanford University, Stanford, CA.

Marks, Mortimer. "Zentsuji Before, During and After World War II." Asheville, NC: n.p., 2000.

Thomas, James O. "Kogane Maru." Mountain View, CA: n.p.

———."Trapped with the Enemy: Four Years a Civilian POW in Japan." Mountain View, CA: n.p., 2000.

Wallace, Sidney R. "Diary of a New Zealand Coast Watcher." Edited by Patricia Wallace Mayer. Hoover Institution Library and Archives. Stanford University, Stanford, CA.

INDEX

Wisconsin, 197
Wood, Edwin A., 18

Y
Yablonsky, Adolphe, 56
Yamamoto, Admiral, 108–9
Yamamoto, Masaji, 123
Yawata, 172
Yetter, Doris, 76
Yokohama, 190, 192, 196

Z
Zentsuji, 59, 61–63, 65–69, 72, 82, 84,
    86, 89, 93, 97, 102, 106, 145, 151,
    163, 168, 172–75, 180, 182–83,
    190–93, 201

ABOUT THE AUTHOR

Roger Mansell (1935–2010) was born in Brooklyn, New York, and grew up in Long Island. After attending Brown University, Roger was commissioned in the U.S. Army Artillery and was stationed in Korea and then at Fort Bliss, Texas. Having completed his military service, in 1962 he moved to California and began a successful business career. It would be the deep impression made upon him by an employee who, as a child, had been a prisoner under the Japanese during World War II that set him on a course to discover more. Later, when he met a veteran who had been taken prisoner by the Japanese on Guam, he realized that many of the ex-POWs, now elderly, had never told anyone about their experiences in what was a crucially important part of the history of the Pacific War. Upon his retirement, he founded the Center for Research, Allied POWs Under the Japanese, and for more than two decades he dedicated himself to this research, which he posted at www.mansell.com. The Web site is an important resource for POW research about those held by the Japanese in World War II. He also created databases for every camp in the Japanese Empire, funding his research out of his own pocket. Shortly before his death in 2010, he donated his archive to the Hoover Institution's library. His personal Web site, maintained by his family, is www .rogermansell.com.

Linda Goetz Holmes was the first Pacific War historian appointed to the Nazi War Crimes and Japanese Imperial Records Interagency Working Group (IWG), established by executive order of President Clinton following passage by Congress of the Nazi War Crimes and Japanese Imperial Records Act of 2000. The IWG, tasked with getting government and military agencies to declassify World War II documents, presented its final report to Congress in 2007.

Ms. Holmes is the author of three books about Allied POWs in Japanese custody during World War II: *4000 Bowls of Rice: A Prisoner of War Comes Home*, *Unjust Enrichment: American POWs under the Rising Sun*, and *Guests of the Emperor: The Secret History of Japan's Mukden POW Camp*. Her work and research have been cited in legal and court documents, as well as by fellow historians, researchers, and columnists across the globe.

A former editor at the CBS Television Network, Ms. Holmes is a graduate of Wellesley College. She is a member of the Overseas Press Club of America and past president of the nation's oldest press club, the Society of the Silurians. She lives in Shelter Island, NY.

The Naval Institute Press is the book-publishing arm of the U.S. Naval Institute, a private, nonprofit, membership society for sea service professionals and others who share an interest in naval and maritime affairs. Established in 1873 at the U.S. Naval Academy in Annapolis, Maryland, where its offices remain today, the Naval Institute has members worldwide.

Members of the Naval Institute support the education programs of the society and receive the influential monthly magazine *Proceedings* or the colorful bimonthly magazine *Naval History* and discounts on fine nautical prints and on ship and aircraft photos. They also have access to the transcripts of the Institute's Oral History Program and get discounted admission to any of the Institute-sponsored seminars offered around the country.

The Naval Institute's book-publishing program, begun in 1898 with basic guides to naval practices, has broadened its scope to include books of more general interest. Now the Naval Institute Press publishes about seventy titles each year, ranging from how-to books on boating and navigation to battle histories, biographies, ship and aircraft guides, and novels. Institute members receive significant discounts on the Press's more than eight hundred books in print.

Full-time students are eligible for special half-price membership rates. Life memberships are also available.

For a free catalog describing Naval Institute Press books currently available, and for further information about joining the U.S. Naval Institute, please write to:

Member Services
U.S. Naval Institute
291 Wood Road
Annapolis, MD 21402-5034
Telephone: (800) 233-8764
Fax: (410) 571-1703
Web address: www.usni.org